Microsoft®

Inside the Microsoft® Build Engine: Using MSBuild and Team Foundation Build

Sayed Ibrahim Hashimi

William Bartholomew

PUBLISHED BY
Microsoft Press
A Division of Microsoft Corporation
One Microsoft Way
Redmond, Washington 98052-6399

Library of Congress Control Number: 2008940523

Printed and bound in the United States of America.

1 2 3 4 5 6 7 8 9 QWT 4 3 2 1 0 9

Distributed in Canada by H.B. Fenn and Company Ltd.

A CIP catalogue record for this book is available from the British Library.

Microsoft Press books are available through booksellers and distributors worldwide. For further information about international editions, contact your local Microsoft Corporation office or contact Microsoft Press International directly at fax (425) 936-7329. Visit our Web site at www.microsoft.com/mspress. Send comments to mspinput@microsoft.com.

Acquisitions Editor: Ben Ryan
Developmental Editor: Devon Musgrave
Project Editor: Rosemary Caperton
Editorial Production: S4Carlisle Publishing Services
Technical Reviewer: Brian Kretzler and Martin Danner;
Technical Review services provided by Content Master, a member of CM Group, Ltd.
Cover: Tom Draper Design

Body Part No. X15-25186

I would like to dedicate this book to my parents, Sayed A. Hashimi and Sohayla Hashimi. They have sacrificed more than I could imagine in order to give us (their 4 sons) the opportunity to succeed. Without their sacrifices, guidance, and inspiration I am sure that I would not have written my second book; in fact I have no idea where I would be now. Thank You.

—Sayed Hashimi

I'd like to dedicate the book to my family - Rosanna, Roy, Carey, and Kate and to my partner Vanessa.

—William Bartholomew

Contents at a Glance

Table of Contents

Part V Team Foundation Build

Appendixes

Foreword

Automated build systems are the workhorses of the software development team. They tirelessly do what they are told. They get. They clean. They build. They rebuild. They copy. They deploy. They test. And they don't judge those who break the build. Without emotion, they just do what they are told. We can't live without them.

The problem is that an automated build system such as this can be more difficult to construct than the underlying application the team really cares about. Why is this? From my experience, it's caused by several factors. MSBuild is not widely understood and is quite complex. There are no IDEs that support a visual "drag and drop" editing and debugging experience. Most teams don't have a dedicated "build master" to learn this new language and wrangle all of those angle brackets. As a result, scripts are located on the Web and spliced together to make something that works without the editor really understanding what's going on. This is unacceptable.

When Microsoft first introduced MSBuild with .NET 2.0, it was without a bang. This stealthy feature surfaced only when you tried to open a Visual Studio 2003 project in Visual Studio 2005 and you were forced to upgrade your project—primarily because of the conversion of the project file to an MSBuild format. The curious would poke around by opening their .CSPROJ files in Notepad and taking a look. The truly curious would take it a step further and start learning this new language, in order to make their desktop builds more interesting. My interest in MSBuild came from a Team Foundation Build perspective. Knowing that Team Foundation Build is a critical piece of the Visual Studio Team System puzzle, I spent a considerable amount of energy learning its inner workings. Fortunately, the majority of functionality in Team Build is provided by MSBuild so, as a side benefit, I was able to learn this new dark art. And it rocks!

What's been missing until now is a solid reference and tutorial on MSBuild. *Inside the Microsoft Build Engine* fills that void. No longer will build engineers or build stuckees be forced to search for understanding and examples. From the very first chapter you will learn the key elements: tasks, targets, and properties. This provides a quick start into using MSBuild and sends you down the road of productivity.

Continuing on, you will drill down to learn all of the other capabilities, tricks, and time-saving features of MSBuild, enabling you to automate the really difficult builds. The final chapters reveal a nice surprise, which is a discussion of Team Foundation Build, and how MSBuild uniquely works within it.

I'm sure you will enjoy this read. Each chapter contains scripts, screenshots, and troubleshooting advice, and not just commentary. In fact, the commentary section is almost finished—just give me one more thought. I'd just like to make a prediction. I predict that this book will become stained by coffee, crumbs, and greasy fingers and otherwise mistreated due its close proximity to the keyboard and general overuse.

Richard Hundhausen
VSTS MVP, RD

Author of *Working with Microsoft Visual Studio 2005 Team System* (Microsoft Press, 2005)
www.accentient.com

Acknowledgements

Sayed Ibrahim Hashimi

Writing a book is a massive effort, not only on the part of the authors but for everyone involved. One of the big reasons that this book is in print is the MSBuild team, specifically Dan Moseley, so I would especially like to thank him. Dan helped get the book started and has continued to help throughout the course of the book. Dan and a few other members of the MSBuild team, namely Chris Mann, Jay Shrestha, and Cliff Hudson have spent countless hours poring over my chapters and my emails. Thanks for all your help; it has helped tremendously.

I would like to thank my coauthor William Bartholomew, the Team Build expert! With his added content the book really has risen to the next level. As more organizations adopt Team Build, they will have a guide to assist them.

I would also like to thank Richard Hundhausen for writing the foreword, and for his feedback on the book. There were two technical reviewers involved whose insight was astonishing: Brian Kretzler and Martin Danner. Technical reviewers are not given enough credit, they read each chapter multiple times looking for errors and pointing out improvements. Several of the chapters have been significantly rewritten based on tech review feedback. Without their edits and feedback, this book would not be nearly what it is now.

I am also grateful to several people involved from Microsoft Press who helped complete this book: Ben Ryan, product planner and acquisitions editor; Devon Musgrave, development editor; and Rosemary Caperton, project editor. Throughout the course of the book it seemed that Rosemary delivered an endless chain of emails in an effort to keep us on schedule. I thank her for those emails, and I hope we didn't slip that far off schedule. Also I would like to thank Jean Ives for her attention to details while copyediting and DeAnn Montoya, project editor at S4Carlisle, for her efforts.

Without the assistance of each of these individuals this book could not have been completed. I sincerely thank all of them for helping to create this book.

William Bartholomew

A large number of people have contributed to this book coming together, I would especially like to thank my coauthor Sayed Ibrahim Hashimi for his organization, planning, and MSBuild expertise and also Grant Holliday (now working for Microsoft) for introducing me to Sayed and this project. I thank Ben Ryan, Devon Musgrave, Rosemary Caperton, and the production team from Microsoft Press for their assistance, guidance, and patience.

I'd also like to thank Martin Danner and Richard Hundhausen for their insights and comments while reviewing the drafts. Finally, I'd like to thank the numerous individuals who have worked on Team Foundation Build and Visual Studio Team System for their advice, clarifications, and corrections; specifically I'd like to thank Buck Hodges, Jim Lamb, Aaron Hallberg, Brian Harry, and Charles Sterling.

Introduction

As software complexity continues to increase, more emphasis is being placed on proper build practices. Previously (before .NET 2.0) the build process for .NET applications was mostly a black box. Now this process has been completely externalized in the Microsoft Build Engine, MSBuild. MSBuild allows you to take control over every aspect of the build process. Since the release of MSBuild, there has been a need for a definitive reference. *Inside the Microsoft Build Engine* is that definitive reference! We have been working for over a year on this book, and the MSBuild team has been involved right from the beginning.

MSBuild files are just XML files. Starting with Visual Studio 2005 managed projects use the MSBuild file format. Because of this you are able to fine-tune, or even completely change, how your projects are built. Using MSBuild you can customize your build process by adding steps such as code generation, unit testing, or code analysis. You can also use MSBuild to assist in automating the build and deployment process, as well as implementing continuous integration.

In this book we start with the fundamentals of MSBuild, like properties and items, and work up to advanced topics such as custom tasks and batching. Throughout these chapters you will be guided with expert insight and powerful examples. You will learn how MSBuild evaluates properties, items and conditions as well as how targets are executed. Chapters 8 and 9 are dedicated to applying the MSBuild concepts learned. Chapter 9 focuses on topics relating to Web development.

This book contains 12 chapters, nine of which are devoted to MSBuild. The remaining three chapters are focused on Team Foundation Build 2008 (Team Build). Team Build 2008 is the latest version of the build automation component of Visual Studio Team System. It takes MSBuild to the next level by allowing it to scale to the team, product, or enterprise level. This is achieved by tight integration with the other components of Visual Studio Team System, including version control, testing, work item tracking, and reporting.

Team Build was one of the most enhanced components in Visual Studio Team System 2008 and addressed a number of limitations in earlier versions resulting in an extremely powerful platform for automating build processes. This version includes functionality such as allowing builds to be queued on build machines, retention policies to automatically remove unneeded builds, and an improved and easier-to-use API for integrating Team Build into your own applications or external processes.

The latter part of this book explores the functionality that ships with Team Build 2008 and how it can be configured, customized, and extended to automate the end-to-end build process. This includes how to customize the build process to implement common requirements such as generating API documentation, zipping build outputs and source code, and versioning assemblies. Finally, we'll look at some of the Team Build functionality in Visual Studio Team System 2010 (code named "Rosario").

Who Is This Book For?

This book is written for everyone who uses MSBuild or Team Build. If you are using Visual Studio to write managed applications then you are already using MSBuild. *Inside the Microsoft Build Engine* is for all .NET developers and build masters. If you are interested in learning more about how your applications are being built and how you can customize this process then you need this book. If you are currently using or are interested in using Team Build then this book is for you.

This book will help the needs of enterprise teams as well as individuals. Readers should be familiar with creating .NET applications. The reader is not required to be familiar with the build process, as this book will start from the basics and build on that. Because one of the most effective methods for learning is through examples, this book contains many examples.

Organization of This Book

Inside the Microsoft Build Engine is divided into five parts:
Part I, "Overview," describes all the fundamentals of creating and extending MSBuild project files. Chapter 1, "MSBuild Quick Start," is a brief chapter to get you started quickly with MSBuild. If you are already familiar with MSBuild then you can skip this chapter; its content will be covered in more detail within chapters 2 and 3. Chapter 2, "MSBuild Deep Dive, Part 1," discusses such things as static properties, static items, targets, tasks, and msbuild.exe usage. Chapter 3, "MSBuild Deep Dive, Part 2," extends on Chapter 2 with dynamic properties, dynamic items, how properties and items are evaluated, importing external files, and extending the build process.

Part II, "Customizing MSBuild," covers the two ways that MSBuild can be extended: custom tasks and custom loggers. Chapter 4, "Custom Tasks," covers all that you need to know to create your own custom MSBuild tasks. Chapter 5, "Custom Loggers," details how to create custom loggers and how to attach them to your build process.

Part III, "Advanced MSBuild Topics," discusses advanced MSBuild concepts. Chapter 6, "Batching and Incremental Builds," covers two very important topics, MSBuild batching and supporting incremental building. Batching is the process of categorizing items and processing them in batches. Incremental building enables MSBuild to detect when a target is up-to-date and can be skipped. Incremental building can drastically reduce build times for most developer builds. Chapter 7, "External Tools," provides some guidelines for integrating external tools into the build process. It also shows how NUnit and FXCop can be integrated in the build process in a reusable fashion.

Part IV, "MSBuild Cookbook," consists of two chapters that are devoted to real-world examples. Chapter 8, "Practical Applications, Part 1," contains several examples, including: setting the assembly version, customizing the build process in build labs, handling errors, and replacing values in configuration files. Chapter 9, "Practical Applications, Part 2," covers more examples, most of which are targeted toward developers who are building Web applications using .NET. It includes Web Deployment Projects, starting and stopping services, zipping output files, compressing Javascript file, and encrypting the web.config file.

Part V, "Team Foundation Build," is devoted to Team Build. Chapter 10, "Team Build Quick Start," covers the installation, configuration, and usage of Team Build. Chapter 11, "Team Build Deep Dive," covers how to get the most out of Team Build by customizing and extending the default build process and how to integrate with Team Build using the Team Build API. It also covers things to be aware of when upgrading from Team Build 2005. Finally, Chapter 12, "Team Build Cookbook," covers a number of common build requirements such as generating API documentation, zipping binaries and source, sharing customizations, and more.

System Requirements

The following list contains the minimum hardware and software requirements to run the code samples provided with the book.

- .NET 3.5 Framework
- Visual Studio 2008 Express Edition or greater
- 50 MB of available space on the installation drive

For Team Build chapters:

- Visual Studio 2008 Professional with Team Foundation Client 2008
- Some functionality (such as Code Analysis) requires Visual Studio Team System 2008 for Software Developers
- Some functionality (such as Web and Load Tests) requires Visual Studio Team System 2008 for Testers
- Access to a server running Team Foundation Server 2008
- Access to a build machine running Team Foundation Build 2008 (Chapter 10 walks you through installing this)
- A trial Virtual PC with Visual Studio Team System 2008 Team Suite, Team Foundation Server, and Team Foundation Build is available from *http://www.microsoft.com/downloads/details.aspx?FamilyID=c7a809d8-8c9f-439f-8147-948bc6957812*

Technology Updates

As material for the book is updated, you can find additional information at the Microsoft Press Technology Updates Web page. You can find updates regarding Visual Studio 2008 and other technologies at

http://www.microsoft.com/mspress/updates/

The Companion Web Site

This book features a companion Web site that is available to you. All the code samples for the book can be downloaded from this Web site. The address of the site is *http://www.microsoft.com/mspress/companion/9780735626287.*

Support for This Book

Every effort has been made to ensure the correctness of this book and its companion Web site. As corrections or changes are collected they will be added to a Microsoft Knowledge Base article.

Microsoft Press provides support for books and companion content at the following Web site:

http://www.microsoft.com/learning/support/books/.

Part I

Overview

In this part:

Chapter 1

MSBuild Quick Start

When you are learning a new subject, it's exciting to just dive right in and get your hands dirty. The purpose of this chapter is to enable you to do just that. I'll describe all the key elements you need to know to get started using MSBuild. If you're already familiar with MSBuild, feel free to skip this chapter—all of the material presented here will be covered in later areas in the book as well.

The topics covered in this chapter include the structure of an MSBuild file, properties, targets, items, and invoking MSBuild. Let's get started.

Project File Details

An MSBuild file—typically called an "MSBuild project file"—is just an XML file. These XML files are described by two XML Schema Definition (XSD) documents that are created by Microsoft: Microsoft.Build.Commontypes.xsd and Microsoft.Build.Core.xsd. These files are located in the %WINDIR%\Microsoft.NET\Framework\vNNNN\MSBuild folder, where vNNNN is the version folder for the Microsoft .NET Framework 2.0 or 3.5. (In this book, I'll assume you are using .NET Framework 3.5, unless specified otherwise.) As a side note, a new version of MSBuild was not shipped with .NET 3.0. Microsoft.Build.Commontypes.xsd describes the elements commonly found in Visual Studio-generated project files, and Microsoft.Build. Commontypes.xsd describes all the fixed elements in an MSBuild project file. The simplest MSBuild file would contain the following:

```
<Project xmlns="http://schemas.microsoft.com/developer/msbuild/2003">
</Project>
```

This is the XML fragment that will identify this as an MSBuild file. Inside the Project element is where all your content will be placed. Specifically, we will be declaring properties, items, targets, and a few other items directly under the Project element. When building software applications, you will always need to know two pieces of information: what is being built and what are the build parameters being used. Typically, files are being built, and these would be contained in MSBuild items. Build parameters, like Configuration or OutputPath, are contained in MSBuild properties. We'll now discuss how to declare properties and following that we'll discuss items.

Properties and Targets

MSBuild properties are simply key-value pairs. The key for the property is the name that you will use to refer to the property. The value is its value. When you declare static properties, they are always contained in a *PropertyGroup* element, which occurs directly within the *Project* element. We will discuss dynamic properties, those declared and generated dynamically inside targets, in the next chapter. The following snippet is a simple example of declaring static properties:

```
<Project xmlns="http://schemas.microsoft.com/developer/msbuild/2003">
  <PropertyGroup>
    <AppServer>\\sayedApp</AppServer>
    <WebServer>\\sayedWeb</WebServer>
  </PropertyGroup>
</Project>
```

As previously stated, the *PropertyGroup* element, inside the *Project* element, will contain all of our properties. The name of the properties is the XML tag name of the element, and the value of the property is the value inside the element. In this example, we have declared two properties: AppServer and WebServer with values \\sayedApp and \\sayedWeb, respectively. You can create as many *PropertyGroup* elements under the Project tag as you want. The previous fragment could have been defined like this:

```
<Project xmlns="http://schemas.microsoft.com/developer/msbuild/2003">
  <PropertyGroup>
    <AppServer>\\sayedApp</AppServer>
  </PropertyGroup>
  <PropertyGroup>
    <WebServer>\\sayedWeb</WebServer>
  </PropertyGroup>
</Project>
```

The MSBuild engine will process all elements sequentially within each *PropertyGroup* in the same manner. If you take a look at a project created by Visual Studio, you'll notice that many properties are declared. These properties have values that will be used throughout the build process for that project. Here is a region from a sample project that I created:

```
<Project DefaultTargets="Build"
    xmlns="http://schemas.microsoft.com/developer/msbuild/2003">
  <PropertyGroup>
    <Configuration Condition=" '$(Configuration)' == '' ">Debug</Configuration>
    <Platform Condition=" '$(Platform)' == '' ">AnyCPU</Platform>
    <ProductVersion>8.0.50727</ProductVersion>
    <SchemaVersion>2.0</SchemaVersion>
    <ProjectGuid>{A71540FD-9949-4AC4-9927-A66B84F97769}</ProjectGuid>
    <OutputType>WinExe</OutputType>
    <AppDesignerFolder>Properties</AppDesignerFolder>
    <RootNamespace>WindowsApplication1</RootNamespace>
    <AssemblyName>WindowsApplication1</AssemblyName>
  </PropertyGroup>
```

```
  <PropertyGroup Condition=" '$(Configuration)|$(Platform)' == 'Debug|AnyCPU' ">
    <DebugSymbols>true</DebugSymbols>
    <DebugType>full</DebugType>
    <Optimize>false</Optimize>
    <OutputPath>bin\Debug\</OutputPath>
    <DefineConstants>DEBUG;TRACE</DefineConstants>
    <ErrorReport>prompt</ErrorReport>
    <WarningLevel>4</WarningLevel>
  </PropertyGroup>
 ....
</Project>
```

You can see that values for the output type, the name of the assembly, and many others are defined in properties. Defining properties is great but we also need to be able to utilize them, which is performed inside targets. We will move on to discuss Target declarations.

MSBuild has two execution elements: tasks and targets. A task is the smallest unit of work in an MSBuild file, and a target is a sequential set of tasks. A task must always be contained within a target. Here's a sample that shows you the simplest MSBuild file that contains a target:

```
<Project xmlns="http://schemas.microsoft.com/developer/msbuild/2003">
  <Target Name="HelloWorld">
  </Target>
</Project>
```

In this sample, we have created a new target named HelloWorld, but it doesn't perform any work at this point because it is empty. When MSBuild is installed, you are given many tasks out of the box such as; Copy, Move, Exec, ResGen, Csc, etc. You can find a list of these tasks at the MSBuild Task Reference (*http://msdn2.microsoft.com/en-us/library/7z253716.aspx*). We will now use the Message task. The message task is used to send a message to the logger(s) that are listening to the build process. In many cases this means a message is sent to the console that is executing the build process. When you invoke a task in an MSBuild file, you can pass its input parameters by inserting XML attributes with values. These attributes will vary from task to task depending on what inputs the task is expecting. From the documentation of the Message task (*http://msdn2.microsoft.com/en-us/library/6yy0yx8d.aspx*) you can see that it accepts a string parameter named Text. The following snippet shows you how to use the Message task to send the classic message "Hello World!"

```
<Project xmlns="http://schemas.microsoft.com/developer/msbuild/2003">
  <Target Name="HelloWorld">
    <Message Text="Hello world!" />
  </Target>
</Project>
```

Now we will verify that this works as expected. To do this, place the previous snippet into a file named HelloWorld.proj. Now open a Visual Studio command prompt, found in the Visual Studio Tools folder in the Start menu for Visual Studio. When you open this prompt, the path to msbuild.exe is already on the path. Msbuild.exe is the command you will be invoking to start MSBuild. The basic usage for the command is as follows:

```
msbuild [INPUT_FILE] /t:[TARGETS_TO_EXECUTE]
```

So the command in our case would be

```
msbuild HelloWorld.proj /t:HelloWorld
```

This command says, execute the HelloWorld target, which is contained in the HelloWorld.proj file. The result of this invocation is shown in Figure 1-1.

```
C:\Data\MSBuildExamples\QuickStart>msbuild HelloWorld.proj /t:HelloWorld /nologo

Build started 5/16/2008 7:18:34 PM.
Project "C:\Data\MSBuildExamples\QuickStart\HelloWorld.proj" on node 0 (HelloWo
rld target(s)).
  Hello world!
Done Building Project "C:\Data\MSBuildExamples\QuickStart\HelloWorld.proj" (Hel
loWorld target(s)).


Build succeeded.
    0 Warning(s)
    0 Error(s)
```

FIGURE 1-1 Result of HelloWorld target

We can see that the HelloWorld target is executed and that the message "Hello World!" is displayed on the console. The Message task also accepts another parameter, Importance. The possible values for this parameter are high, normal, or low. The Importance value may affect how the loggers interpret the purpose of the message. If you want the message logged no matter the verbosity, use the `high` importance level. We're discussing properties, so let's take a look at how we can specify the text using a property. I've extended the HelloWorld.proj file to include a few new items. The contents are shown here:

```
<Project xmlns="http://schemas.microsoft.com/developer/msbuild/2003">
  <Target Name="HelloWorld">
    <Message Text="Hello world!" />
  </Target>

  <PropertyGroup>
    <HelloMessage>Hello from property</HelloMessage>
  </PropertyGroup>
  <Target Name="HelloProperty">
    <Message Text="$(HelloMessage)" />
  </Target>
</Project>
```

I have added a new property, HelloMessage, with the value "Hello from property", as well as a new target, HelloProperty. The HelloProperty target passes the value of the property using the $(*PropertyName*) syntax. This is the syntax you use to evaluate a property. We can see this in action by executing the command `msbuild HelloWorld.proj /t:HelloProperty`. The result is shown in Figure 1-2.

```
C:\Data\MSBuildExamples\QuickStart>msbuild HelloWorld.proj /t:HelloProperty /nol
ogo
Build started 5/16/2008 7:23:29 PM.
Project "C:\Data\MSBuildExamples\QuickStart\HelloWorld.proj" on node 0 (HelloPr
operty target(s)).
  Hello from property
Done Building Project "C:\Data\MSBuildExamples\QuickStart\HelloWorld.proj" (Hel
loProperty target(s)).


Build succeeded.
    0 Warning(s)
    0 Error(s)
```

FIGURE 1-2 Result of HelloProperty target

As you can see, the value of the property was successfully passed to the Message task. Now that we have discussed targets and basic property usage, let's move on to discuss how we can declare properties whose values are derived from other properties.

To see how to declare a property by using the value of an existing property, take a look at the project file, NestedProperties.proj:

```
<Project xmlns="http://schemas.microsoft.com/developer/msbuild/2003">
  <PropertyGroup>
    <Configuration Condition=" '$(Configuration)' == '' ">Debug</Configuration>
    <Platform Condition=" '$(Platform)' == '' ">AnyCPU</Platform>
    <DropLocation>
      \\sayedData\MSBuildExamples\Drops\$(Configuration)\$(Platform)\
    </DropLocation>
  </PropertyGroup>
  <Target Name="PrepareFilesForDrop">
    <Message Text="DropLocation : $(DropLocation)" />
  </Target>
</Project>
```

We can see here that three properties have been declared. On both the Configuration and Platform properties, a `Condition` attribute appears. We'll discuss these attributes later in this chapter. The remaining property, DropLocation, is defined using the values of the two previously declared items. The DropLocation property has three components: a constant value and two values that are derived from the Configuration and Platform properties. When the MSBuild engine sees the $(*PropertyName*) notation, it will replace that with the value of the specified property. So the evaluated value for DropLocation would be \\sayedData\MSBuildExamples\Drops\Debug\AnyCPU\. You can verify that by executing the PrepareFilesForDrop target by using MSBuild. The reference for properties can be found at *http://msdn2.microsoft.com/en-us/library/ms171458(VS.80).aspx.*

When you use MSBuild, a handful of properties are available to you out of the box that cannot be modified. These are known as reserved properties. Table 1-1 contains all the reserved properties.

TABLE 1-1 Reserved Properties

Name	Description
MSBuildProjectDirectory	The full path to the directory where the project file is located.
MSBuildProjectDirectoryNoRoot	The full path to the directory where the project file is located, excluding the root.
MSBuildProjectFile	The name of the project file, including the extension.
MSBuildProjectExtension	The extension of the project file including the '.'.
MSBuildProjectFullPath	The full path to the project file.
MSBuildProjectName	The name of the project file, without the extension.

TABLE 1-1 Reserved Properties

Name	Description
MSBuildToolsPath* (MSBuildBinPath)	The full path to the location where the MSBuild binaries are located. For MSBuild 2.0 this property is named MSBuildBinPath and is deprecated in MSBuild 3.5.
MSBuildProjectDefaultTargets	Contains the list of the default targets.
MSBuildExtensionsPath	The full path to where MSBuild extensions are located. This is typically under the Program Files folder.
MSBuildExtensionsPath32*	The full path to where MSBuild 32 bit extensions are located. This is typically under the Program Files folder. For 32 bit machines this value will be the same as MSBuildExtensionsPath.
MSBuildNodeCount*	The number of nodes (processes) that are being used to build the project. If the /m switch is not used, then this value will be 1.
MSBuildStartupDirectory*	The full path to folder where the MSBuild process is invoked.
MSBuildToolsPath*	The full path to the MSBuild tools being used to build the project.
MSBuildToolsVersion*	The version of the tools being used to build the project. Possible values include 2.0 and 3.5.

* Denotes parameters new with .NET 3.5.

You would use these properties just as you would properties that you have declared in your own project file. To see an example of this, look at any Visual Studio-generated project file. When you create a new C# project, you will find the import statement `<Import Project="$(MSBuildToolsPath)\Microsoft.CSharp.targets" />` located toward the bottom. This import statement uses the MSBuildToolsPath reserved property to resolve the full path to the Microsoft.CSharp.targets file and insert its content at this location. This is the file that drives the build process for C# projects. We will discuss its content throughout the remainder of this book. In Chapter 3, "MSBuild Fundamentals, Part 2," we discuss specifically how the Import statement is processed.

Items

Building applications usually means dealing with many files. Because of this, you use a specific construct when referencing files in MSBuild: items. Items are usually file-based references, but they can be used for other purposes as well. If you create a project using Visual Studio you may notice that you see many *ItemGroup* elements as well as *PropertyGroup* elements. The *ItemGroup* element contains all the statically defined items. Static item definitions are those declared inside the *Project* element. Dynamic items, which we discuss in the next chapter, are those defined inside a target. When you define a property you are declaring a key-value pair, which is a one-to-one relationship. When you declare items, one item can contain a list of many values. In terms of code, a property is analogous to a variable and an item to an array. Take a look at how an item is declared in the following snippet taken from the ItemsSimple.proj file:

```
<Project xmlns="http://schemas.microsoft.com/developer/msbuild/2003">
  <ItemGroup>
    <SolutionFile Include="..\MSBuildExamples.sln" />
  </ItemGroup>
  <Target Name="PrintSolutionInfo">
    <Message Text="SolutionFile: @(SolutionFile)" />
  </Target>
</Project>
```

In this file there is an *ItemGroup* that has a subelement, *SolutionFile*. *ItemGroup* is the element type that all statically declared items must be placed within. The name of the subelement, *SolutionFile* in this case, is actually the item type of the item that is created. The *SolutionFile* element has an attribute, Include. This determines what values the item contains. Relating it back to an array, *SolutionFile* is the name of the variable that references the array, and the *Include* attribute is used to populate the array's values. The *Include* attribute can contain the following types of values (or any combination of): one distinct value, a list of values delimited with semicolons, or a value using wildcards. In this sample, its *Include* attribute contains one value. When you need to evaluate the contents of an item, you would use the @(*ItemName*) syntax. This is similar to the $(*PropertyName*) syntax for properties. To see this in action, take a look at the PrintSolutionInfo target. This target passes the value of the item into the Message task to be printed to the console. You can see the result of executing this target in Figure 1-3.

```
C:\Data\MSBuildExamples\QuickStart>msbuild ItemsSimple.proj /t:PrintSolutionInfo
 /nologo
Build started 5/16/2008 7:24:30 PM.
Project "C:\Data\MSBuildExamples\QuickStart\ItemsSimple.proj" on node 0 (PrintS
olutionInfo target(s)).
  SolutionFile: ..\MSBuildExamples.sln
Done Building Project "C:\Data\MSBuildExamples\QuickStart\ItemsSimple.proj" (Pr
intSolutionInfo target(s)).


Build succeeded.
    0 Warning(s)
    0 Error(s)
```

FIGURE 1-3 PrintSolutionInfo result

In this case, the item *SolutionFile* contains a single value, so it doesn't seem very different from a property because the single value was simply passed to the Message task. Let's take a look at an item with more than one value. This is an extended version of the ItemsSimple.proj file shown earlier:

```
<Project xmlns="http://schemas.microsoft.com/developer/msbuild/2003">
  <ItemGroup>
    <SolutionFile Include="..\MSBuildExamples.sln" />
  </ItemGroup>
  <Target Name="PrintSolutionInfo">
    <Message Text="SolutionFile: @(SolutionFile)" />
  </Target>

  <ItemGroup>
    <Compile
     Include="Form1.cs;Form1.Designer.cs;Program.cs;Properties\AssemblyInfo.cs" />
  </ItemGroup>
```

```
  <Target Name="PrintCompileInfo">
    <Message Text="Compile: @(Compile)" />
  </Target>
</Project>
```

In the modified version I have created a new item, Compile, which includes four values that are separated by semicolons. The PrintCompileInfo target passes these values to the Message task. When you invoke the PrintCompileInfo target on the MSBuild file just shown, the result will be `Compile: Form1.cs;Form1.Designer.cs;Program.cs;Properties\AssemblyInfo.cs`. It may look like the Message task simply took the value in the Include attribute and passed it to the Message task, but this is not the case. The Message task has a single input parameter, Text, as discussed earlier. This parameter is a string property. Because an item is a multivalued object, it cannot be passed directly into the Text property. It first has to be converted into a string. MSBuild does this for you by separating each value with a semicolon. In Chapter 2, "MSBuild Deep Dive, Part 1," I will discuss how you can customize this conversion process.

An item definition doesn't have to be defined entirely by a single element. It can span multiple elements. For example, the Compile item shown earlier could have been declared like this:

```
<ItemGroup>
  <Compile Include="Form1.cs" />
  <Compile Include="Form1.Designer.cs" />
  <Compile Include="Program.cs" />
  <Compile Include="Properties\AssemblyInfo.cs" />
</ItemGroup>
```

In this version, each file is placed into the Compile item individually. These Compile elements could also have been contained in their own *ItemGroup* as well; as shown in the next snippet.

```
<ItemGroup>
  <Compile Include="Form1.cs" />
</ItemGroup>
<ItemGroup>
  <Compile Include="Form1.Designer.cs" />
</ItemGroup>
<ItemGroup>
  <Compile Include="Program.cs" />
</ItemGroup>
<ItemGroup>
  <Compile Include="Properties\AssemblyInfo.cs" />
</ItemGroup>
```

The end result of these declarations would all be the same. You should note that an item is an ordered list, so the order in which values are added to the item is preserved and may in some context affect behavior based on usage. When a property declaration appears after a previous one, the previous value is overwritten. Items act differently from this in that the value of the item is simply appended to instead of being overwritten. We've now discussed two of the three ways to create items. Let's look at using wildcards to create items.

Typically items refer to existing files. If this is the case, you can use wildcards to automatically include files that meet the constraints of the wildcards. You can use three wildcard elements with MSBuild: ?, *, and **. The ? descriptor is used to denote that exactly one character can take its place. For example, the include declaration of `b?t.cs` could include values such as bat.cs, bot.cs, bet.cs, b1t.cs, and so on. The * descriptor can be replaced with zero or more characters (not including slashes), so the declaration `b*t.cs` could include values such as bat.cs, bot.cs, best.cs, bt.cs, etc. The ** descriptor tells MSBuild to search directories recursively for the pattern. In effect, "*" matches any characters except for "/" while "**" matches any characters, including "/". For example, `Include="src\**\*.cs"` would include all files under the src folder (including subfolders) with the .cs extension.

Item Metadata

Another difference between properties and items is that items can have metadata associated with them. When you create an item, each of its elements is a full-fledged .NET object, which can have a set of values (metadata) associated with it. The metadata that is available on every item, known as well-known metadata, is summarized in Table 1-2.

TABLE 1-2 Well-Known Metadata

Name	Description
Identity	The value that was specified in the Include attribute of the item after it was evaluated.
FullPath	Full path of the file.
Rootdir	The root directory to which the file belongs.
Filename	The name of the file, not including the extension.
Extension	The extension of the file, including the '.'.
RelativeDir	The path to the file relative to the current working directory.
Directory	Directory of the item, without the root directory.
RecursiveDir	This is the part of the directory path that is replaced by the first ** of the Include declaration. If no ** is present, then this value is empty.
ModifiedTime	The last time the file was modified.
CreatedTime	The time the file was created.
AccessedTime	The last time the file was accessed.

To access metadata values, you have to use this syntax:

```
@(ItemType->'%(MetadataName)')
```

ItemType is the name of the item, and MetadataName is the name of the metadata that you are accessing. This is the most basic syntax. To examine what types of values the well-known metadata returns, take a look at the file, WellKnownMetadata.proj, shown here:

```
<Project xmlns="http://schemas.microsoft.com/developer/msbuild/2003">
  <ItemGroup>
    <src Include="src\one.txt" />
  </ItemGroup>
  <Target Name="PrintWellKnownMetadata">

    <Message Text="===== Well known metadata ====="/>
    <!-- %40 = @ -->
    <!-- %25 = % -->
    <Message Text="%40(src->'%25(FullPath)'): @(src->'%(FullPath)')"/>
    <Message Text="%40(src->'%25(Rootdir)'): @(src->'%(Rootdir)')"/>
    <Message Text="%40(src->'%25(Filename)'): @(src->'%(Filename)')"/>
    <Message Text="%40(src->'%25(Extension)'): @(src->'%(Extension)')"/>
    <Message Text="%40(src->'%25(RelativeDir)'): @(src->'%(RelativeDir)')"/>
    <Message Text="%40(src->'%25(Directory)'): @(src->'%(Directory)')"/>
    <Message Text="%40(src->'%25(RecursiveDir)'): @(src->'%(RecursiveDir)')"/>
    <Message Text="%40(src->'%25(Identity)'): @(src->'%(Identity)')"/>
    <Message Text="%40(src->'%25(ModifiedTime)'): @(src->'%(ModifiedTime)')"/>
    <Message Text="%40(src->'%25(CreatedTime)'): @(src->'%(CreatedTime)')"/>
    <Message Text="%40(src->'%25(AccessedTime)'): @(src->'%(AccessedTime)')"/>

  </Target>
</Project>
```

Note In order to use reserved characters such as the % and @ you have to escape them. This is accomplished by the syntax %HV where HV is the hex value of the character. This is demonstrated here with %25 and %40.

This MSBuild file prints the values for the well-known metadata for the src item. The result of executing the PrintWellKnownMetadata target is shown in Figure 1-4.

```
C:\Data\MSBuildExamples\QuickStart>msbuild WellKnownMetadata.proj /t:PrintWellKn
ownMetadata /nologo
Build started 5/16/2008 7:25:24 PM.
Project "C:\Data\MSBuildExamples\QuickStart\WellKnownMetadata.proj" on node 0 (
PrintWellKnownMetadata target(s)).
  ===== Well known metadata =====
  @(src->'%(FullPath)'): C:\Data\MSBuildExamples\QuickStart\src\one.txt
  @(src->'%(Rootdir)'): C:\
  @(src->'%(Filename)'): one
  @(src->'%(Extension)'): .txt
  @(src->'%(RelativeDir)'): src\
  @(src->'%(Directory)'): Data\MSBuildExamples\QuickStart\src\
  @(src->'%(RecursiveDir)'):
  @(src->'%(Identity)'): src\one.txt
  @(src->'%(ModifiedTime)'): 2008-02-25 00:05:28.1718750
  @(src->'%(CreatedTime)'): 2008-05-03 09:33:20.1093750
  @(src->'%(AccessedTime)'): 2008-05-03 09:33:20.1093750
Done Building Project "C:\Data\MSBuildExamples\QuickStart\WellKnownMetadata.pro
j" (PrintWellKnownMetadata target(s)).


Build succeeded.
    0 Warning(s)
    0 Error(s)
```

FIGURE 1-4 PrintWellKnownMetadata result

The figure gives you a better understanding of the well-known metadata's usage. Keep in mind that this demonstrates the usage of metadata in the case where the item contains only a single value.

To see how things change when an item contains more than one value, let's examine MetadataExample01.proj:

```
<Project xmlns="http://schemas.microsoft.com/developer/msbuild/2003">
  <ItemGroup>
    <Compile Include="*.cs" />
  </ItemGroup>

  <Target Name="PrintCompileInfo">
    <Message Text="Compile fullpath: @(Compile->'%(Fullpath)')" />
  </Target>
</Project>
```

In this project file we simply evaluate the FullPath metadata on the Compile item. From the examples with this text, the directory containing this example contains four files: Class1.cs, Class2.cs, Class3.c, and Class4.cs. These are the files that will be contained in the Compile item. Take a look at the result of the PrintCompileInfo target in Figure 1-5.

```
C:\Data\MSBuildExamples\QuickStart\Simple Metadata Example>msbuild MetadataExamp
le01.proj /t:PrintCompileInfo /nologo
Build started 5/16/2008 7:26:38 PM.
Project "C:\Data\MSBuildExamples\QuickStart\Simple Metadata Example\MetadataExa
mple01.proj" on node 0 (PrintCompileInfo target(s)).
  Compile fullpath: C:\Data\MSBuildExamples\QuickStart\Simple Metadata Example\
  Class1.cs;C:\Data\MSBuildExamples\QuickStart\Simple Metadata Example\Class2.c
  s;C:\Data\MSBuildExamples\QuickStart\Simple Metadata Example\Class3.cs;C:\Dat
  a\MSBuildExamples\QuickStart\Simple Metadata Example\Class4.cs
Done Building Project "C:\Data\MSBuildExamples\QuickStart\Simple Metadata Examp
le\MetadataExample01.proj" (PrintCompileInfo target(s)).


Build succeeded.
    0 Warning(s)
    0 Error(s)
```

FIGURE 1-5 PrintCompileInfo result

You have to look carefully at this output to decipher the result. What is happening here is that a single string is created by combining the full path of each file, separated by a semicolon. The `@(ItemType->'...%()...')` syntax is an "Item Transformation." We will cover transformations in greater detail in Chapter 2. In the next section, we'll discuss conditions. Before we do that, take a minute to look at the project file for a simple Windows application that was generated by Visual Studio. You should recognize many things.

```
<Project DefaultTargets="Build"
xmlns="http://schemas.microsoft.com/developer/msbuild/2003">
  <PropertyGroup>
    <Configuration Condition=" '$(Configuration)' == '' ">Debug</Configuration>
    <Platform Condition=" '$(Platform)' == '' ">AnyCPU</Platform>
    <ProductVersion>8.0.50727</ProductVersion>
    <SchemaVersion>2.0</SchemaVersion>
    <ProjectGuid>{0F34CE5D-2AB0-49A9-8254-B21D1D2EFFA1}</ProjectGuid>
    <OutputType>WinExe</OutputType>
    <AppDesignerFolder>Properties</AppDesignerFolder>
```

```
    <RootNamespace>WindowsApplication1</RootNamespace>
    <AssemblyName>WindowsApplication1</AssemblyName>
  </PropertyGroup>
  <PropertyGroup Condition=" '$(Configuration)|$(Platform)' == 'Debug|AnyCPU' ">
    <DebugSymbols>true</DebugSymbols>
    <DebugType>full</DebugType>
    <Optimize>false</Optimize>
    <OutputPath>bin\Debug\</OutputPath>
    <DefineConstants>DEBUG;TRACE</DefineConstants>
    <ErrorReport>prompt</ErrorReport>
    <WarningLevel>4</WarningLevel>
  </PropertyGroup>
  <PropertyGroup Condition=" '$(Configuration)|$(Platform)' == 'Release|AnyCPU' ">
    <DebugType>pdbonly</DebugType>
    <Optimize>true</Optimize>
    <OutputPath>bin\Release\</OutputPath>
    <DefineConstants>TRACE</DefineConstants>
    <ErrorReport>prompt</ErrorReport>
    <WarningLevel>4</WarningLevel>
  </PropertyGroup>
  <ItemGroup>
    <Reference Include="System" />
    <Reference Include="System.Data" />
    <Reference Include="System.Deployment" />
    <Reference Include="System.Drawing" />
    <Reference Include="System.Windows.Forms" />
    <Reference Include="System.Xml" />
  </ItemGroup>
  <ItemGroup>
    <Compile Include="Form1.cs">
      <SubType>Form</SubType>
    </Compile>
    <Compile Include="Form1.Designer.cs">
      <DependentUpon>Form1.cs</DependentUpon>
    </Compile>
    <Compile Include="Program.cs" />
    <Compile Include="Properties\AssemblyInfo.cs" />
    <EmbeddedResource Include="Properties\Resources.resx">
      <Generator>ResXFileCodeGenerator</Generator>
      <LastGenOutput>Resources.Designer.cs</LastGenOutput>
      <SubType>Designer</SubType>
    </EmbeddedResource>
    <Compile Include="Properties\Resources.Designer.cs">
      <AutoGen>True</AutoGen>
      <DependentUpon>Resources.resx</DependentUpon>
    </Compile>
    <None Include="Properties\Settings.settings">
      <Generator>SettingsSingleFileGenerator</Generator>
      <LastGenOutput>Settings.Designer.cs</LastGenOutput>
    </None>
    <Compile Include="Properties\Settings.Designer.cs">
      <AutoGen>True</AutoGen>
      <DependentUpon>Settings.settings</DependentUpon>
      <DesignTimeSharedInput>True</DesignTimeSharedInput>
    </Compile>
  </ItemGroup>
```

```
  <Import Project="$(MSBuildToolsPath)\Microsoft.CSharp.targets" />
  <!-- To modify your build process, add your task
inside one of the targets below and uncomment it.
       Other similar extension points exist,
see Microsoft.Common.targets.
  <Target Name="BeforeBuild">
  </Target>
  <Target Name="AfterBuild">
  </Target>
  -->
</Project>
```

Simple Conditions

When you are building, you often have to make decisions based on conditions. MSBuild allows almost every XML element to contain a conditional statement within it. The statement would be declared in the *Condition* attribute. If this attribute evaluates to false, then the element and its entire child elements are ignored. In the sample Visual Studio project that was shown at the end of the previous section, you will find the statement `<Configuration Condition=" '$(Configuration)' == '' ">Debug</Configuration>`. In this declaration the condition is checking to see if the property is empty. If so, then it will be defined; otherwise the statement will be skipped. This is a method to provide a default overridable value for a property. Table 1-3 describes a few common types of conditional operators.

TABLE 1-3 Simple Conditional Operators

Symbol	Description
==	Checks for equality; returns true if both have the same value.
!=	Checks for inequality; returns true if both do not have the same value.
Exists	Checks for the existence of a file. Returns true if the provided file exists.
!Exists	Checks for the nonexistence of a file. Return true only if the file provided is not found.

Since you can add a conditional attribute to any MSBuild element (excluding the Otherwise element), this means that we can decide to include entries in items as necessary. For example, when building ASP.NET applications, in some scenarios you might want to include files that will assist debugging. Take a look at the MSBuild file, ConditionExample01.proj:

```
<Project xmlns="http://schemas.microsoft.com/developer/msbuild/2003">
  <PropertyGroup>
    <Configuration>Release</Configuration>
  </PropertyGroup>
  <ItemGroup>
    <Content Include="script.js"/>
    <Content Include="script.debug.js" Condition="$(Configuration)=='Debug'" />
  </ItemGroup>

  <Target Name="PrintContent">
    <Message Text="Configuration: $(Configuration)" />
    <Message Text="Content: @(Content)" />
  </Target>
</Project>
```

If we execute the command `msbuild ConditionExample01.proj /t:PrintContent`, the result would be what is shown in Figure 1-6.

```
C:\Data\MSBuildExamples\QuickStart>msbuild ConditionExample01.proj /t:PrintConte
nt /nologo
Build started 5/16/2008 7:34:07 PM.
Project "C:\Data\MSBuildExamples\QuickStart\ConditionExample01.proj" on node 0
(PrintContent target(s)).
  Configuration: Release
  Content: script.js
Done Building Project "C:\Data\MSBuildExamples\QuickStart\ConditionExample01.pr
oj" (PrintContent target(s)).


Build succeeded.
    0 Warning(s)
    0 Error(s)
```

FIGURE 1-6 PrintContent target result

As you can see, because the Configuration value was not set to Debug, the script.debug.js file was not included in the Content item. Now we will examine the usage of the *Exists* function. To do this, take a look at the target _CheckForCompileOutputs, taken from the Microsoft.Common.targets file, a file that is included with MSBuild that contains most of the rules for building VB and C# projects:

```
<Target
    Name="_CheckForCompileOutputs">

    <!--Record the main compile outputs.-->
    <ItemGroup>
        <FileWrites
          Include="@(IntermediateAssembly)"
          Condition="Exists('@(IntermediateAssembly)')" />
    </ItemGroup>

    <!-- Record the .xml if one was produced. -->
    <PropertyGroup>
        <_DocumentationFileProduced
          Condition="!Exists('@(DocFileItem)')">false</_DocumentationFileProduced>
    </PropertyGroup>

    <ItemGroup>
        <FileWrites
          Include="@(DocFileItem)"
          Condition="'$(_DocumentationFileProduced)'=='true'" />
    </ItemGroup>

    <!-- Record the .pdb if one was produced. -->
    <PropertyGroup>
        <_DebugSymbolsProduced
           Condition="!Exists('@(_DebugSymbolsIntermediatePath)')">false
        </_DebugSymbolsProduced>
    </PropertyGroup>

    <ItemGroup>
        <FileWrites
          Include="@(_DebugSymbolsIntermediatePath)"
          Condition="'$(_DebugSymbolsProduced)'=='true'" />
    </ItemGroup>
</Target>
```

> **Note** This is using new syntax available in .NET 3.5. *ItemGroup* and *PropertyGroup* elements inside of targets are new. If you are using .NET 2.0 you will have to use the CreateItem and CreateProperty tasks instead.

From the FileWrites item definition the condition is defined as Exists(@(IntermediateAssembly)). This will determine whether the file referenced by the IntermediateAssembly item exists on disk. If it doesn't, then the CreateItem task is skipped. This was a brief overview of conditional statements, but it should be enough to get you started. Let's move on to learn a bit more about targets.

Default/Initial Targets

When you create an MSBuild file, you will typically create it such that a target, or a set of targets, will be executed most of the time. In this scenario, these targets can be specified as default targets. These targets will be executed if a target is not specifically chosen to be executed. Without the declaration of a default target, the first defined target in the logical project file, after all imports have been resolved, is treated as the default target. A logical project file is the project file with all Import statements processed. Using default target(s) is how Visual Studio builds your managed project. If you take a look at Visual Studio-generated project files, you will notice that the Build target is specified as the default target:

```
<Project DefaultTargets="Build"
xmlns="http://schemas.microsoft.com/developer/msbuild/2003">
...
</Project>
```

As mentioned previously, you can have either one or many targets be your default target(s). If the declaration contains more than one, the target names need to be separated by a semicolon. When you use a command such as `msbuild ProjectFile.proj`, because you have not specified a target to execute, the default target(s) will be executed. It's important to note that the list of DefaultTargets will be preserved, not modified, through an Import, provided that a project previously processed hasn't had a DefaultTargets list. This is one difference between DefaultTargets and InitialTargets. Values for InitialTargets are aggregated for all imports because each file may have its own initialization checks.

These targets listed in InitialTargets will always be executed even if the project file is imported by other project files. Similar to default targets, the initial targets list is declared as an attribute on the *Project* element with the name InitialTargets. If you take a look at the Microsoft.Common.targets file you will notice that the target _CheckForInvalidConfigurationAndPlatform is declared as the initial target. This target will perform a couple sanity checks before allowing the build to continue. I would strongly encourage the use of default targets. InitialTargets should be used to verify initial conditions before the build starts and raises an error or warning if applicable. Next, we will discuss the command line usage of the msbuild.exe command.

MSBuild.exe Command Line Usage

In this section, we'll discuss the most important options when invoking msbuild.exe. When you invoke the msbuild.exe executable, you can pass many parameters to customize the process. We'll first take a look at the options that are available with .NET 2.0, and then we'll discuss what differences exist for .NET 3.5. Table 1-4 summarizes the parameters you can pass to msbuild.exe. Many commands include a short version that can be used; these versions are listed in the table within parentheses.

TABLE 1-4 MSBuild.exe Parameters

Switch	Description
/help (/?)	Displays the usage information for msbuild.exe.
/nologo	Suppresses the copyright and startup banner.
/version (/ver)	Displays version information.
@file	Used to pick up response file(s) for parameters.
/noautoresponse (/noautoresp)	Used to suppress automatically including msbuild.rsp as a response file.
/target (/t)	Used to specify what target(s) should be built. If specifying more than one target, they should each be separated by a semicolon.
/property:<n>=<v> (/p)	Used to specify properties. If providing more than one property, they should each be separated by a semicolon. Property values should be specified in the format: name=value These values would supersede any static property definitions.
/verbosity (/v)	Sets the verbosity of the build. The options are quiet (q), minimal (m), normal (n), detailed (d), and diagnostic (diag). This is passed to each logger and the logger is able to make its own decision about how to interpret it.
/validate (/val)	Used to ensure that the project file is in the correct format before the build is started.
/logger (/l)	Attaches the specified logger to the build. This switch can be provided multiple times to attach any number of loggers. Also you can pass parameters to the loggers in this switch.
/consoleloggerparameters (/clp)	Used to pass parameters to the console logger.
/noconsolelogger (/noconlog)	Used to suppress the usage of the console logger, which is otherwise always attached.
/filelogger* (/fl)	Attaches a file logger to the build.
/fileloggerparameters* (/flp)	Passes parameters to the file logger. If you want to attach multiple FileLoggers you do so by specifying additional parameters in the switches /flp1, /flp2, /flp3, etc.
/distributedFileLogger* (/dl)	Used to attach a distributed logger. This is an advanced switch that you will most likely not use, and could have been excluded all together.

TABLE 1-4 MSBuild.exe Parameters

Switch	Description
/maxcpucount * (/m)	Sets the maximum number of processes that should be used by msbuild.exe to build the project.
/ignoreprojectextensions* (/ignore)	Instructs MSBuild to ignore the extensions passed.
/toolsversion* (/tv)	Specifies the version of the .NET tools that should be used to build the project.
/nodeReuse* (/nr)	Used to specify whether nodes should be reused or not. Typically there should be no need to specify this; the default value is optimal.

* Denotes parameters new with .NET 3.5.

In Table 1-4, the most commonly used parameters are target, property, and logger. If you are using .NET 3.5, you might also be using the FileLogger switch. To give you an example, I will use an MSBuild file that we discussed earlier, the ConditionExample01.proj file. Take a look at the following command that will attach the file logger to the build process: `msbuild ConditionExample01.proj /l:FileLogger,Microsoft.Build.Engine`. If you are using .NET 3.5, you can use the much simpler `msbuild ConditionExample01.proj /fl`. Because we didn't specify the name of the log file to be written to, the default, msbuild.log, will be used. Using this same project file, let's see how to override the Configuration value. From that file, the Configuration value would be set to Release, but we can override it from the command line with the following statement: `msbuild ConditionExample01.proj /p:Configuration=Debug /t:PrintContent`. In this command we are using the /p (property) switch to provide a property value to the build engine, and we are specifying to execute the PrintContent target. The result is shown in Figure 1-7.

```
C:\Data\MSBuildExamples\QuickStart>msbuild ConditionExample01.proj /t:PrintConte
nt /p:Configuration=Debug /nologo
Build started 5/16/2008 7:31:47 PM.
Project "C:\Data\MSBuildExamples\QuickStart\ConditionExample01.proj" on node 0
(PrintContent target(s)).
  Configuration: Debug
  Content: script.js;script.debug.js
Done Building Project "C:\Data\MSBuildExamples\QuickStart\ConditionExample01.pr
oj" (PrintContent target(s)).

Build succeeded.
    0 Warning(s)
    0 Error(s)
```

FIGURE 1-7 Specifying a property from the command line

The messages on the console show that the value for Configuration was indeed Debug, and as expected, the debug JavaScript file was included in the Content item. Now that you know the basic usage of the msbuild.exe command, we'll move on to the last topic, extending the build process.

Extending the Build Process

With versions of Visual Studio prior to 2005, the build was mostly a black box. The process by which Visual Studio built your applications was internal to the Visual Studio product itself. The only way you could customize the process was to use execute commands for pre- and post-build events. With this you were able to embed a series of commands to be executed. You were not able to change how Visual Studio built your applications. With the advent of MSBuild, Visual Studio has externalized the build process and you now have complete control over it. Since MSBuild is delivered with the .NET Framework, Visual Studio is not required to build applications. Because of this we can create build servers that do not need to have MSBuild installed. We'll examine this by showing how to augment the build process. Throughout the rest of this book we will describe how to extend the build process in more detail.

The pre- and post-build events mentioned earlier are still available, but you now have other options. The three main ways to add a pre- or post-build action are:

- Pre- and post-build event
- Override BeforeBuild/AfterBuild target
- Extend the BuildDependsOn list

The pre- and post-build event is the same as described previously. This is a good approach for backward compatibility and ease of use. Configuring this using the Visual Studio IDE doesn't require knowledge of MSBuild. Figure 1-8 shows the Build Events tab on the ProjectProperties page.

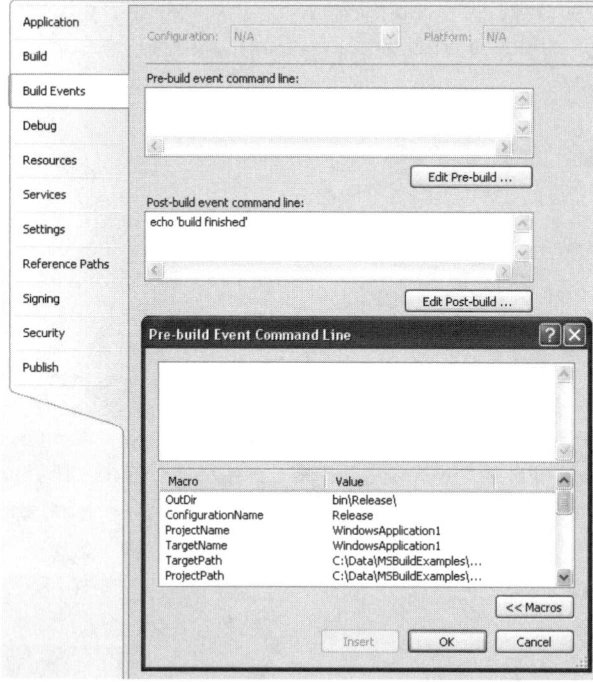

FIGURE 1-8 Build Events tab

Here you can see the two locations for the pre- and post-build toward the center of the image. The dialog that is displayed is the pre-build event command editor. This helps you construct the command. You create this command to be executed for you at the appropriate time using the Exec (*http://msdn2.microsoft.com/en-us/library/x8zx72cd.aspx*) task. Typically these events are used to copy/move files around before or after the build.

Using the pre- and post-build event works fairly well if you want to execute a set of commands. If you need more control over what is occurring, you will want to manually modify the project file itself. When you create a new project using Visual Studio, the project file generated is an MSBuild file, which is an XML file. You can use any editor you choose, but if you use Visual Studio you will have IntelliSense when you are editing it! With your solution loaded in Visual Studio, you can right-click the project, select Unload Project, right-click the project again, and select Edit. If you take a look at the project file you will notice this statement toward the bottom of the file.

```
<!-- To modify your build process, add your task inside one
     of the targets below and uncomment it.
     Other similar extension points exist, see Microsoft.Common.targets.
<Target Name="BeforeBuild">
</Target>
<Target Name="AfterBuild">
</Target>
-->
```

From this snippet we can see that there are predefined targets designed to handle these types of customizations. We can simply follow the directions from the project file, by defining the BeforeBuild or AfterBuild target. You will want to make sure that these definitions are after the *Import* element for the Microsoft.*.targets file, where * represents the language of the project you are editing. For example, you could insert the following AfterBuild target:

```
<Target Name="AfterBuild">
  <Message Text="Build has completed!" />
</Target>
```

When the build has finished, this target will be executed and the message '`Build has completed!`' will be passed to the loggers. We will cover the third option in Chapter 3, "MSBuild Deep Dive, Part 2."

In this chapter we have covered many features of MSBuild, including properties, items, targets, and tasks. Now you should have all that you need to get started customizing your build process. From this point on, the remainder of the book will work on filling in the details that were left out here so that you can become an MSBuild expert!

Chapter 2

MSBuild Deep Dive, Part 1

In the previous chapter, we gave a brief overview of all the key elements in MSBuild. In this chapter and the next, we'll examine most of those ideas in more detail. We'll examine properties, items, targets, tasks, transformations, and much more. After you have completed this chapter you will have a solid grasp of how to create and modify MSBuild files to suit your needs. After the next chapter we'll explore ways to extend MSBuild as well as some advanced topics.

What is MSBuild? MSBuild is a general-purpose build system created by Microsoft and is used to build all managed .NET projects. MSBuild is shipped with the .NET Framework. What this means is that you do **not** need to have Visual Studio installed in order to build your applications. This is very beneficial because you don't need to purchase licenses of Visual Studio for dedicated build machines. Another benefit is that MSBuild will be installed on many machines. If .NET 2.0 or above is available on a machine, so is MSBuild. The following terms have been used to identify an MSBuild file: MSBuild file, MSBuild project file, MSBuild targets file, etc.

An MSBuild file is just an XML file. You can use any editor you choose to create and edit MSBuild files. The preferred editor is Visual Studio, because it provides IntelliSense on the MSBuild files as you are editing them. This IntelliSense will greatly decrease the amount of time required to write an MSBuild file. The IntelliSense is driven by a few XML schema documents (XSD). These XSD files, which are all in the Visual Studios XML directory, are Microsoft.Build.xsd, Microsoft.Build.Core.xsd and Microsoft.Build.Commontypes.xsd. The Microsoft.Build.xsd file imports the other two files, and provides an extension point for task developers to include their own files. The Microsoft.Build.Core.xsd file describes all the fundamental elements that an MSBuild file can contain.

Microsoft.Build.Commonttypes.xsd defines all known elements; this is mainly used to describe the elements that Visual Studio generated project files can contain. Now that we have discussed what it takes to edit an MSBuild file, let's discuss properties in detail. If you are not familiar with invoking msbuild.exe from the command line, take a look back at Chapter 1; this is not covered again here.

Properties

MSBuild has two main constructs for representing data: properties and items. A property is a key-value pair. Each property can have exactly one value. An item differs from a property in that it can have many values. In programming terms, a property is similar to a scalar variable, and an item similar to an array variable. Properties are declared inside the *Project* element in a *PropertyGroup* element. We'll now take a look at how properties are declared. The following file, Properties01.proj, demonstrates declaration and usage of a property.

```
<Project xmlns="http://schemas.microsoft.com/developer/msbuild/2003">

  <PropertyGroup>
    <Configuration>Debug</Configuration>
  </PropertyGroup>

  <Target Name="PrintConfig">
    <Message Text="Config: $(Configuration)" />
  </Target>

</Project>
```

As stated previously, we needed a *PropertyGroup* element, and the Configuration property was defined inside of that. By doing this we have created a new property named Configuration and given it the value *Debug*. When you create properties using the PropertyGroup you are not limited to defining only one property per group. On the contrary, you can define any number of properties inside a single *PropertyGroup* element. In the target PrintConfig, the Message task is invoked in order to print the value of the Configuration property. You can execute that target with the command `msbuild.exe Properties01.proj /t:PrintConfig`. The results of this command are shown in Figure 2-1.

```
C:\Data\MSBuildExamples\Fundamentals>msbuild Properties01.proj /t:PrintConfig /n
ologo
Build started 5/18/2008 12:29:33 PM.
Project "C:\Data\MSBuildExamples\Fundamentals\Properties01.proj" on node 0 (Pri
ntConfig target(s)).
  Config: Debug
Done Building Project "C:\Data\MSBuildExamples\Fundamentals\Properties01.proj"
(PrintConfig target(s)).


Build succeeded.
    0 Warning(s)
    0 Error(s)
```

FIGURE 2-1 PrintConfig target results

From the result in Figure 2-1, we can see that the correct value for the Configuration property was printed as expected. As properties are declared, their values are recorded in a top-to-bottom order. What this means is that if a property is defined, and then defined again, the last value will be the one that is applied. Take a look at a modified version of the previous example; this one is contained in the Properties02.proj file.

```
<Project xmlns="http://schemas.microsoft.com/developer/msbuild/2003">

  <PropertyGroup>
    <Configuration>Debug</Configuration>
  </PropertyGroup>

  <PropertyGroup>
    <Configuration>Release</Configuration>
  </PropertyGroup>
```

```
  <Target Name="PrintConfig">
    <Message Text="Config: $(Configuration)" />
  </Target>

</Project>
```

In this example, we have declared the Configuration property once again, after the existing declaration and to have the value *Release*. Because the new value is declared **after** the previous one, we would expect the new value to hold. If you execute the PrintConfig target on this file, you will see that this is indeed the case. Properties in MSBuild can be declared any number of times. This is not an erroneous condition, and there is no way to detect this. Now we will look at another version of the previous file, a slightly modified one. Take a look at the contents of the following Properties03.proj file.

```
<Project xmlns="http://schemas.microsoft.com/developer/msbuild/2003">

  <PropertyGroup>
    <Configuration>Debug</Configuration>
  </PropertyGroup>

  <PropertyGroup>
    <Configuration>Release</Configuration>
  </PropertyGroup>

  <Target Name="PrintConfig">
    <Message Text="Config: $(Configuration)"/>
  </Target>

  <PropertyGroup>
    <Configuration>CustomRelease</Configuration>
  </PropertyGroup>

</Project>
```

This example is a little different in the sense that there is a value for Configuration declared after the PrintConfig target. That value is *CustomRelease*. So if we execute the PrintConfig target, what should be the result, *Release* or *CustomRelease*? We can execute `msbuild.exe Properties02.proj /t:PrintConfig` to find out. The results of this command are shown in Figure 2-2.

```
C:\Data\MSBuildExamples\Fundamentals>msbuild Properties03.proj /t:PrintConfig /n
ologo
Build started 5/18/2008 12:51:31 PM.
Project "C:\Data\MSBuildExamples\Fundamentals\Properties03.proj" on node 0 (Pri
ntConfig target(s)).
  Config: CustomRelease
Done Building Project "C:\Data\MSBuildExamples\Fundamentals\Properties03.proj"
(PrintConfig target(s)).


Build succeeded.
    0 Warning(s)
    0 Error(s)
```

FIGURE 2-2 PrintConfig result for Properties03.proj

As can be seen from the results in Figure 2-2, the value for Configuration that was printed was *CustomRelease*! How is this possible? It was defined after the PrintConfig target! This is because MSBuild processes the entire file for properties and items **before** any targets are executed. You can imagine all the properties being in a dictionary, and as the project file is processed its values are placed in the dictionary. Property names are **not** case sensitive, so Configuration and CoNfiguratION would refer to the same property. After the entire file, including imported files, is processed, all the final values for statically declared properties and items have been resolved. Once all the properties and items have been resolved, targets are allowed to execute. We'll take a closer look at this process in our discussion on items later in this chapter.

Environment Variables

We have described the basic usage of properties. Now we'll discuss a few other related aspects. When you are building your applications, sometimes you might need to extract values from environment variables. This is a lot simpler than you might imagine using MSBuild. You can access values, just as you would properties, for environment variables. For example, take a look at the following project file, Properties04.proj.

```
<Project xmlns="http://schemas.microsoft.com/developer/msbuild/2003">

  <Target Name="PrintEnvVar">
    <Message Text="Temp: $(Temp)" />
    <Message Text="Windir: $(windir)" />
    <Message Text="VS80COMNTOOLS: $(VS80COMNTOOLS)" />
    <Message Text="VS90COMNTOOLS: $(VS90COMNTOOLS)" />
  </Target>

</Project>
```

In this example, we can see that no properties have been declared and no other files are imported. Inside the target, PrintEnvVar, we can see that we have made a few messages to print the values of some properties. These values are being pulled from the environment variables. When you use the `$(`*`PropertyName`*`)` syntax to retrieve a value, MSBuild will first look to see if there is a corresponding property. If there is, its value is returned. If there isn't, then it will look at the environment variables for a variable with the provided name. If such a variable exists, its value is returned. If you execute the command `msbuild.exe Properties04.proj /t:PrintEnvVar` you should see a result similar to that shown in Figure 2-3.

```
C:\Data\MSBuildExamples\Fundamentals>msbuild Properties04.proj /t:PrintEnvVar /n
ologo
Build started 5/19/2008 7:50:57 PM.
Project "C:\Data\MSBuildExamples\Fundamentals\Properties04.proj" on node 0 (Pri
ntEnvVar target(s)).
  Temp: C:\DOCUME~1\Ibrahim\LOCALS~1\Temp
  Windir: C:\WINDOWS
  VS80COMNTOOLS: C:\Program Files\Microsoft Visual Studio 9.0\Common7\Tools\
  VS90COMNTOOLS: C:\Program Files\Microsoft Visual Studio 9.0\Common7\Tools\
Done Building Project "C:\Data\MSBuildExamples\Fundamentals\Properties04.proj"
(PrintEnvVar target(s)).


Build succeeded.
    0 Warning(s)
    0 Error(s)
```

FIGURE 2-3 Environment variable usage

As demonstrated in Figure 2-3, the values for the appropriate environment variables were printed as expected. If you do not have Visual Studio installed on the machine running this file, then the last two values may result in an empty value for the variable. You can get the value for an environment variable by using the property notation. Assigning a value to a property that has the same name as an environment variable has no effect on the environment variable itself. The $(*PropertyName*) notation can get a value only from an environment variable; it will never assign values to environment variables. Let's move on to discuss reserved properties.

Reserved Properties

There are a fixed number of reserved properties. These are properties that are globally available to every MSBuild script and that can never be overwritten. These properties are provided to users by the MSBuild engine itself, and many of them are very useful. These are summarized in Table 2-1.

TABLE 2-1 Reserved Properties

Name	Description
MSBuildProjectDirectory	The full path to the directory where the project file is located.
MSBuildProjectDirectoryNoRoot	The full path to the directory where the project file is located, excluding the root.
MSBuildProjectFile	The name of the project file, including the extension.
MSBuildProjectExtension	The extension of the project file, including the '.'.
MSBuildProjectFullPath	The full path to the project file.
MSBuildProjectName	The name of the project file, without the extension.
MSBuildToolsPath* (MSBuildBinPath)	The full path to the location where the MSBuild binaries are located. For MSBuild 2.0 this property is named MSBuildBinPath and is deprecated in MSBuild 3.5.
MSBuildProjectDefaultTargets	Contains a list of the default targets.
MSBuildExtensionsPath	The full path to where MSBuild extensions are located. This is typically under the Program Files folder.
MSBuildExtensionsPath32*	The full path to where MSBuild 32 bit extensions are located. This is typically under the Program Files folder. For 32-bit machines this value will be the same as MSBuildExtensionsPath.
MSBuildNodeCount *	The number of nodes (processes) that are being used to build the project. If the /m switch is not used, then this value will be 1.
MSBuildStartupDirectory*	The full path to folder where the MSBuild process is invoked.

TABLE 2-1 Reserved Properties

Name	Description
MSBuildToolsPath*	The full path to the MSBuild tools being used to build the project.
MSBuildToolsVersion*	The version of the tools being used to build the project. Possible values include 2.0 and 3.5.

* denotes parameters new with .NET 3.5.

You would use these properties in the same way as you would any other properties. In order to understand what types of values these properties are set to, I have created the following sample file, ReservedProperties01.proj, to print out all these values.

```
<Project xmlns="http://schemas.microsoft.com/developer/msbuild/2003"
         ToolsVersion="3.5">
  <Target Name="PrintReservedProperties">
    <Message Text="MSBuildProjectDirectory: $(MSBuildProjectDirectory)" />
    <Message Text="MSBuildProjectDirectoryNoRoot: $(MSBuildProjectDirectoryNoRoot)" />
    <Message Text="MSBuildProjectFile: $(MSBuildProjectFile)" />
    <Message Text="MSBuildProjectExtension: $(MSBuildProjectExtension)" />
    <Message Text="MSBuildProjectFullPath: $(MSBuildProjectFullPath)" />
    <Message Text="MSBuildProjectName: $(MSBuildProjectName)" />
    <Message Text="MSBuildToolsPath: $(MSBuildToolsPath)" />
    <Message Text="MSBuildProjectDefaultTargets: $(MSBuildProjectDefaultTargets)" />
    <Message Text="MSBuildExtensionsPath: $(MSBuildExtensionsPath)" />
    <Message Text="MSBuildStartupDirectory: $(MSBuildStartupDirectory)" />
    <Message Text="MSBuildProjectDirectoryNoRoot: $(MSBuildProjectDirectoryNoRoot)" />
    <Message Text="MSBuildExtensionsPath32: $(MSBuildExtensionsPath32)" />
    <Message Text="MSBuildToolsVersion: $(MSBuildToolsVersion)" />
    <Message Text="MSBuildNodeCount: $(MSBuildNodeCount)" />
  </Target>


</Project>
```

If you execute this build file using the command `msbuild.exe ReservedProperties01.proj /t:PrintReservedProperties` you would see the results shown in Figure 2-4.

```
C:\Data\MSBuildExamples\Fundamentals>msbuild ReservedProperties01.proj /t:PrintR
eservedProperties /nologo
Build started 9/22/2008 1:39:26 AM.
Project "C:\Data\MSBuildExamples\Fundamentals\ReservedProperties01.proj" on nod
e 0 (PrintReservedProperties target(s)).
  MSBuildProjectDirectory: C:\Data\MSBuildExamples\Fundamentals
  MSBuildProjectDirectoryNoRoot: Data\MSBuildExamples\Fundamentals
  MSBuildProjectFile: ReservedProperties01.proj
  MSBuildProjectExtension: .proj
  MSBuildProjectFullPath: C:\Data\MSBuildExamples\Fundamentals\ReservedProperti
  es01.proj
  MSBuildProjectName: ReservedProperties01
  MSBuildToolsPath : C:\WINDOWS\Microsoft.NET\Framework\v2.0.50727
  MSBuildProjectDefaultTargets: PrintReservedProperties
  MSBuildExtensionsPath: C:\Program Files\MSBuild
  MSBuildStartupDirectory : C:\Data\MSBuildExamples\Fundamentals
  MSBuildProjectDirectoryNoRoot: Data\MSBuildExamples\Fundamentals
  MSBuildExtensionsPath32: C:\Program Files\MSBuild
  MSBuildToolsVersion: 2.0
  MSBuildNodeCount: 1
Done Building Project "C:\Data\MSBuildExamples\Fundamentals\ReservedProperties0
1.proj" (PrintReservedProperties target(s)).

Build succeeded.
    0 Warning(s)
    0 Error(s)
```

FIGURE 2-4 Reserved properties

All of these values are straightforward. You should note that the values relating to the MSBuild file are always qualified relative to the MSBuild file that is invoking the entire process. This becomes clear when you use the *Import* element to import additional MSBuild files. We will take a look at importing external files in the next chapter.

Command Line Properties

You can also provide properties through the command line. As stated in Chapter 1, "MSBuild Quick Start," we can use the /property, short version /p, to achieve this. We will see how this works now. When you use the /p switch you must specify the values in the format /p:<n>=<v> where <n> is the name of the property and <v> is its value. You can provide multiple values by separating the pairs by a semicolon. We will demonstrate a simple case by the following project file, Properties05.proj.

```
<Project xmlns="http://schemas.microsoft.com/developer/msbuild/2003">

  <Target Name="PrintInfo">
    <Message Text="AssemblyName: $(AssemblyName)" />
    <Message Text ="OutputPath: $(OutputPath)" />
  </Target>

</Project>
```

Because there are no values for AssemblyName or OutputPath it would be pointless to execute this MSBuild file. If we pass them in through the command line, you can see their values. If you specify a value for the AssemblyName and OutputPath with the command `msbuild.exe Properties05.proj /t:PrintInfo /p:AssemblyName=Sedo.Namhu .Common;OutputPath="deploy\Release\"` then the result would be what is shown in Figure 2-5.

```
C:\Data\MSBuildExamples\Fundamentals>msbuild Properties05.proj /t:PrintInfo /p:A
ssemblyName=Sedo.Namhu.Common;OutputPath="deploy\Release\" /nologo
Microsoft (R) Build Engine Version 3.5.21022.8
[Microsoft .NET Framework, Version 2.0.50727.1433]
Copyright (C) Microsoft Corporation 2007. All rights reserved.

Build started 9/22/2008 1:51:26 AM.
Project "C:\Data\MSBuildExamples\Fundamentals\Properties05.proj" on node 0 (Pri
ntInfo target(s)).
  AssemblyName: Sedo.Namhu.Common
  OutputPath: deploy\Release" /nologo
Done Building Project "C:\Data\MSBuildExamples\Fundamentals\Properties05.proj"
(PrintInfo target(s)).


Build succeeded.
    0 Warning(s)
    0 Error(s)
```

FIGURE 2-5 PrintInfo result for Properties05.proj

From Figure 2-5, we can see that the values for the properties that were provided at the command line were successfully passed through. Note in this example that we passed the OutputPath contained in quotes. In this case the quotes are optional, but if you are passing paths that contain spaces, then they are required. When you provide a value for a property through the command line it takes precedence over all other static property declarations. To demonstrate this, take a look at a different version of this file, Properties06.proj, with the values defined.

```
<Project xmlns="http://schemas.microsoft.com/developer/msbuild/2003">

  <PropertyGroup>
    <AssemblyName>assemblyName</AssemblyName>
  </PropertyGroup>

  <Target Name="PrintInfo">
    <Message Text="AssemblyName: $(AssemblyName)" />
    <Message Text ="OutputPath: $(OutputPath)" />
  </Target>

  <PropertyGroup>
    <OutputPath>outputPath</OutputPath>
  </PropertyGroup>

</Project>
```

In this file, we have specified a value for both AssemblyName and OutputPath. To show that the location of the property, with respect to targets, doesn't affect the result, I have placed one value at the beginning of the file and the other at the end. If you execute the command `msbuild.exe Properties06.proj /t:PrintInfo /p:AssemblyName=Sedo.Namhu.Common;OutputPath=deploy\Release\` the result would be the same as that shown in Figure2-4. Thus far we have covered pretty much everything you need to know about statically-created properties. Now we'll move on to discuss dynamic properties.

Dynamic Properties

When you create properties in your build scripts, most of the time static properties will be good enough. But there are many times when you need to either create new properties or to modify the values of existing properties. These types of properties can be called dynamic properties. Let's take a look at how we can create and use these properties.

In MSBuild 2.0 there was only one way to create dynamic properties, and that was using the CreateProperty task. In MSBuild 3.5 there is a much clearer approach, and we'll examine that technique here as well. Before we discuss how we can use the CreateProperty task, we have to discuss how to get a value from a task out to the MSBuild file calling it. When a task exposes a value to MSBuild this is known as an Output property. MSBuild files can extract output values from tasks using the *Output* element. The *Output* element must be placed inside the tags of the task to extract the value out. To demonstrate this, take a look at the following project file.

```
<Project xmlns="http://schemas.microsoft.com/developer/msbuild/2003">

  <Target Name="PrintProperty">
    <Message Text="AssemblyName: $(AssemblyName)" />
```

```
    <CreateProperty Value="Sedodream.Build.Tasks">
      <Output TaskParameter="Value" PropertyName="AssemblyName" />
    </CreateProperty>

    <Message Text="AssemblyName: $(AssemblyName)" />
  </Target>

</Project>
```

In this file, the PrintProperty target first prints the value for AssemblyName, which hasn't been defined so it should be empty. Then the CreateProperty task is used to define the AssemblyName property. Let's take a close look at this so we can fully understand the invocations. The statement `<CreateProperty Value="Sedodream.Build.Tasks">` invokes CreateProperty and initializes the property named Value to Sedodream.Build.Tasks. The inner statement, <Output TaskParameter="Value" PropertyName="AssemblyName" />, populates the `MSBuild` property AssemblyName with the value for the .NET property `Value`. The *Output* element must declare a TaskParameter, which is the name of the task's .NET property to output, and can either contain a value of PropertyName or ItemName depending on if it is supposed to output a property or item respectively. In this case, we are emitting a property so we use the value PropertyName. Looking back at the example shown previously, we would expect that after the CreateProperty task executes, the property AssemblyName will be set to *Sedodream.Build.Tasks*. The result of the PrintProperty target is shown in Figure 2-6.

```
C:\Data\MSBuildExamples\Fundamentals>msbuild Properties07.proj /t:PrintProperty
/nologo
Build started 4/21/2008 12:13:44 AM.
Project "C:\Data\MSBuildExamples\Fundamentals\Properties07.proj" on node 0 (Pri
ntProperty target(s)).
  AssemblyName:
  AssemblyName: Sedodream.Build.Tasks
Done Building Project "C:\Data\MSBuildExamples\Fundamentals\Properties07.proj"
(PrintProperty target(s)).

Build succeeded.
    0 Warning(s)
    0 Error(s)
```

FIGURE 2-6 PrintProperty results

From the results shown in Figure 2-6, we can see that the value for AssemblyName was set, as expected, by the CreateProperty task. In this example, we are creating a property that did not exist previously, but the CreateProperty task also can modify the value for existing properties. If you use the task to output a value to a property that already exists then it will be overwritten. This is true unless a property is reserved. Command line parameters cannot be overwritten by statically declared properties.

If you are using MSBuild 3.5 you can use the CreateProperty task, but there is a cleaner method. You can place PropertyGroup declarations directly inside of targets. With this new approach you can create static and dynamic properties in the same manner. The MSBuild 3.5 version of the previous example is shown as follows. This is contained in the Properties08.proj file.

```
<Project xmlns="http://schemas.microsoft.com/developer/msbuild/2003">

  <Target Name="PrintProperty">
    <Message Text="AssemblyName: $(AssemblyName)" />
```

```
    <PropertyGroup>
      <AssemblyName>Sedodream.Build.Tasks</AssemblyName>
    </PropertyGroup>

    <Message Text="AssemblyName: $(AssemblyName)" />
  </Target>

</Project>
```

The results of the preceding project file are identical to the example shown in Properties07.proj, but the syntax is much clearer. If you are using MCBuild 3.5, then using the PropertyGroup directly inside the target is the preferred approach. This syntax is not supported by MSBuild 2.0 so be sure not to use it in such files. Now that we have thoroughly covered properties, we'll move on to discuss items in detail.

Items

When software is being built, files and directories are used heavily. Because of the usage and importance of files and directories, MSBuild has a specific construct to support these. This construct is items. In the previous section we covered properties. As stated previously, in programming terms properties can be considered a regular scalar variable. This is because a property has a unique name and a single value. An item can be thought of as an array. This is because an item has a single name but can have multiple values. Properties use the PropertyGroup to declare properties; similarly, items use an *ItemGroup* element. Take a look at the following very simple example from Items01.proj.

```
<Project xmlns="http://schemas.microsoft.com/developer/msbuild/2003">

  <ItemGroup>
    <SrcFiles Include="src\one.txt" />
  </ItemGroup>

  <Target Name="Print">
    <Message Text="SrcFiles: @(SrcFiles)" />
  </Target>

</Project>
```

As stated previously, statically declared items will be inside an *ItemGroup* element. The value for the *Include* attribute determines what values get assigned to the item. Of the few types of values that can be assigned to the *Include* attribute, we'll start with the simplest. The simplest value for the Include is a text value. In the previous sample one item, SrcFiles, is declared. The SrcFiles item is set to include one file, which is located at src\one.txt. To get the value of an item you use the `@(ItemName)` syntax. In the Print target this is used on the SrcFiles item. The result of the `Print` target is shown in Figure 2-7.

```
C:\Data\MSBuildExamples\Fundamentals>msbuild Items01.proj /t:Print /nologo
Build started 5/30/2008 11:55:09 PM.
Project "C:\Data\MSBuildExamples\Fundamentals\Items01.proj" on node 0 (Print ta
rget(s)).
  SrcFiles: src\one.txt
Done Building Project "C:\Data\MSBuildExamples\Fundamentals\Items01.proj" (Prin
t target(s)).

Build succeeded.
    0 Warning(s)
    0 Error(s)
```

FIGURE 2-7 Print target result for Items01.proj

From the result shown in Figure 2-7, you can see that the file was assigned to the SrcFiles item as expected. From this example an item seems to behave exactly as a property; this is because we assigned only a single value to the item. The behavior changes when there are more values assigned to the item. The following example is a modified version of the previous example. This modified version is contained in the Items02.proj file.

```
<Project xmlns="http://schemas.microsoft.com/developer/msbuild/2003">

  <ItemGroup>
    <SrcFiles Include="src\one.txt" />
    <SrcFiles Include="src\two.txt" />
  </ItemGroup>

  <Target Name="Print">
    <Message Text="SrcFiles: @(SrcFiles)" />
  </Target>

</Project>
```

In this version, the SrcFiles item type is declared twice. When more than one item declaration is encountered the values are appended to each other, instead of overwritten like properties. Alternatively you could have declared the SrcFiles item on a single line by placing both values inside the *Include* attribute, separated by a semi-colon. So the previous sample would be equivalent to the following one. With respect to item declarations, ordering is significant and preserved.

```
<Project xmlns="http://schemas.microsoft.com/developer/msbuild/2003">

  <ItemGroup>
    <SrcFiles Include="src\one.txt;src\two.txt" />
  </ItemGroup>

  <Target Name="Print">
    <Message Text="SrcFiles: @(SrcFiles)" />
  </Target>

</Project>
```

If you execute the Print target on this file the result will be what is shown in Figure 2-8.

```
C:\Data\MSBuildExamples\Fundamentals>msbuild Items02.proj /t:Print /nologo
Build started 5/31/2008 12:39:11 AM.
Project "C:\Data\MSBuildExamples\Fundamentals\Items02.proj" on node 0 (Print ta
rget(s)).
  SrcFiles: src\one.txt;src\two.txt
Done Building Project "C:\Data\MSBuildExamples\Fundamentals\Items02.proj" (Prin
t target(s)).


Build succeeded.
    0 Warning(s)
    0 Error(s)
```

FIGURE 2-8 Print target results for Items02.proj

In this version, we have supplied two values into the SrcFiles item. If you look at the documentation for the Message task you will notice that the Text property is a string. Fundamentally there are two types of values in MSBuild: single-valued values and multi-valued values. Another name for these is *scalar values* and *vector values* respectively. Properties are scalar values, and items are vector values. What happens when we have a vector value where we need to pass to a task that is accepting only scalar values? MSBuild must first flatten the item before sending it to the task. The value that is passed to the Text property on the Message can be only a single-valued parameter, not a multi-valued one. For the SrcFiles item to be flattened before it is sent into the task, the @(*ItemName*) operator takes care of this for us. When using the @(*ItemName*) if there is only one value inside the item, that value is used. If there is more than one value contained by the item, then all values are combined, separated by a semicolon. This is the most basic example of an item transformation. We'll discuss this in more detail later in this chapter. For now, let's move on to see how items are more commonly used.

Copy Task

A very common scenario for builds is copying a set of files from one place to another. How can we achieve this with MSBuild? There are several ways we will demonstrate in this chapter. Before we discuss how to copy the files, we'll first take a close look at the Include statement of an item. I have created some sample files shown in the following tree, which we will use for the remainder of the chapter.

```
C:\Data\MSBuildExamples\Fundamentals
¦
¦ ...
¦
+---src
    ¦   one.txt
    ¦   two.txt
    ¦   three.txt
    ¦   four
    ¦
    +---sub
            sub_one.txt
            sub_two.txt
            sub_three.txt
            sub_four.txt
```

Previously, I said that three types of values can be contained in the Include declaration of an item. Those three are:

1. A single value
2. Multiple values separated by a ";"
3. Declared using wildcards

We have shown how 1 and 2 work, so now we'll discuss the remaining item—using wildcards to declare items. These wildcards always resolve values to items on disk. There are three wildcard declarations: *, **, and ?. You may already be familiar with these from usage in other tools, but we will quickly review them once again here. The * descriptor is used to declare that either zero or more characters can be used in its place. The ** descriptor is used to search directories recursively, and the ? is a placeholder for only one character. Effectively the "*" descriptor matches any characters except for "/" while "**" descriptor matches any characters, including "/". For example, if file.*proj used this declaration, the following values would meet the criteria: file.csproj, file.vbproj, file.vdproj, file.vcproj, file.proj, file.mproj, file.1proj, etc. In contrast, the file.?proj will allow only and exactly the character 1 to replace the ? character. Therefore, from the previous list of matching names, only file.mproj and file.1proj meet those criteria. We will examine the ** descriptor shortly in an example. Take a look at the snippet from the following Copy01.proj file.

```
<Project xmlns="http://schemas.microsoft.com/developer/msbuild/2003">

  <ItemGroup>
    <SrcFiles Include="src\*" />
  </ItemGroup>

  <Target Name="PrintFiles">
    <Message Text="SrcFiles: @(SrcFiles)" />
  </Target>

</Project>
```

In this example, we have used the * syntax to populate the SrcFiles item. Using this syntax we would expect all the files in the src\ folder to be placed into the item. In order to verify this, you can execute the PrintFiles target. If you were to do this, the result would be the statement '`SrcFiles: src\four.txt;src\one.txt;src\three.txt;src\two.txt`'—so we were able to successfully populate the item. Back to the ** wildcard: take a look at the following portion of the Copy02.proj file.

```
<Project xmlns="http://schemas.microsoft.com/developer/msbuild/2003">

  <ItemGroup>
    <SrcFiles Include="src\**\*.txt" />
  </ItemGroup>

  <Target Name="PrintFiles">
    <Message Text="SrcFiles: @(SrcFiles)" />
  </Target>
</Project>
```

In this version of the SrcFiles declaration, we used the **descriptor to denote that the src\ folder should be searched recursively for files matching the pattern *.txt. We could have stayed with the * pattern here as well, but I changed it for demonstration. We would expect all the files in the src\ and src\sub\ folder to be placed into the SrcFiles item. If you execute the PrintFiles target on this file, you would get the result shown in Figure 2-9.

```
C:\Data\MSBuildExamples\Fundamentals>msbuild Copy02.proj /t:PrintFiles /nologo
Build started 5/31/2008 1:50:22 PM.
Project "C:\Data\MSBuildExamples\Fundamentals\Copy02.proj" on node 0 (PrintFile
s target(s)).
  SrcFiles: src\four.txt;src\one.txt;src\sub\sub_four.txt;src\sub\sub_one.txt;s
  rc\sub\sub_three.txt;src\sub\sub_two.txt;src\three.txt;src\two.txt
Done Building Project "C:\Data\MSBuildExamples\Fundamentals\Copy02.proj" (Print
Files target(s)).


Build succeeded.
    0 Warning(s)
    0 Error(s)
```

FIGURE 2-9 PrintFiles result for Copy02.proj

As expected, the SrcFiles item does contain all the files in both of those folders. Now that we have discussed items declared using wildcards, we'll revert back to the copy files discussion.

In order to copy files from one location to another we can use the built-in Copy task. This task has a few different input parameters, which are summarized in Table 2-2.

TABLE 2-2 Copy Task Parameters

Name	Description
SourceFiles	Contains the files that should be copied.
DestinationFolder	Path to the folder where the files should be copied. If this parameter is specified, then the DestinationFiles parameter cannot be used.
DestinationFiles	Contains the locations where the files should be copied to. If this is used there must be a one-to-one correspondence between this list and the SourceFiles list. Also if this is used, the DestinationFolder parameter cannot be used.
CopiedFiles	Output parameter that contains the files that were successfully copied.
SkipUnchangedFiles	If true, then only changed files, based on their timestamp, will be copied. Otherwise all files will be copied.
OverwriteReadOnlyFiles*	If set to true, then read only files will be overwritten. Otherwise read-only files will not be overwritten.

* denotes new parameters with .NET 3.5

When you use the Copy task you will always use the SourceFiles property to define what files should be copied. As for the location where the files will be copied to, you have a choice of using **either** DestinationFolder **or** DestinationFiles. The only time you should use the DestinationFolder over the DestinationFiles is when you are copying files into the same destination directory. Take a look at the following complete version of the Copy01.proj; the text in **bold** is the added parts.

```
<Project xmlns="http://schemas.microsoft.com/developer/msbuild/2003">

  <ItemGroup>
    <SrcFiles Include="src\*" />
  </ItemGroup>

  <PropertyGroup>
    <Dest>dest\</Dest>
  </PropertyGroup>

  <Target Name="PrintFiles">
    <Message Text="SrcFiles: @(SrcFiles)" />
  </Target>
  <Target Name="CopyFiles">
    <Copy SourceFiles="@(SrcFiles)"
          DestinationFolder="$(Dest)" />
  </Target>
</Project>
```

This file now contains a CopyFiles target, which invokes the Copy task in order to copy the files in the src folder to the dest folder. Notice that the Dest property ends with a slash; when creating properties that point to directories, it is a best practice to to declare them ending in a trailing slash. Either a forward or backward slash will work equally well. In this example, the DestinationFolder property is used to specify the folder into which the files should be copied. If you execute the PrintFiles target the result will be what is shown in Figure 2-10.

```
C:\Data\MSBuildExamples\Fundamentals>msbuild Copy01.proj /t:CopyFiles /nologo
Build started 9/4/2008 12:07:53 AM.
Project "C:\Data\MSBuildExamples\Fundamentals\Copy01.proj" on node 0 (CopyFiles
 target(s)).
  Copying file from "src\four.txt" to "dest\four.txt".
  Copying file from "src\one.txt" to "dest\one.txt".
  Copying file from "src\three.txt" to "dest\three.txt".
  Copying file from "src\two.txt" to "dest\two.txt".
Done Building Project "C:\Data\MSBuildExamples\Fundamentals\Copy01.proj" (CopyF
iles target(s)).

Build succeeded.
    0 Warning(s)
    0 Error(s)
```

FIGURE 2-10 CopyFiles result for Copy01.proj

From the result shown in Figure 2-10, we can see that the files were copied successfully. We can now take a look at how we can copy files from more than one folder to another location. In order to achieve this we will use the DestinationFiles instead of DestinationFolder property. We could use DestinationFolder along with batching, an advanced technique discussed in Chapter 6, "Batching and Incremental Builds." For now we will use the DestinationFiles approach. The completed version of the Copy02.proj file is shown here:

```
<Project xmlns="http://schemas.microsoft.com/developer/msbuild/2003">

  <ItemGroup>
    <SrcFiles Include="src\**\*.txt" />
  </ItemGroup>

  <PropertyGroup>
    <Dest>$(MSBuildProjectDirectory)\dest\</Dest>
  </PropertyGroup>
```

```
  <Target Name="PrintFiles">
    <Message Text="SrcFiles: @(SrcFiles)" />
  </Target>
  <Target Name="CopyFiles">
    <Copy SourceFiles="@(SrcFiles)"
          DestinationFiles=
          "@(SrcFiles->'$(Dest)%(RecursiveDir)%(Filename)%(Extension)')" />
  </Target>
</Project>
```

In this sample, the portions in **bold** are the regions that have been added. This MSBuild file declares the SrcFiles item to include all the files in the src\ folder as well as all folders underneath it. In the CopyFiles target the DestinationFiles parameter is used to specify the location where the files are to be copied to. The value for the DestinationFiles is called an item transformation on the SrcFiles item. We'll take a closer look at these later in this chapter. Item transformations also depend on item metadata, which we will discuss in the next section. Until we cover those it is impossible to properly examine this example, so we will revisit this example later in this chapter. With that being said, we can at least execute the CopyFiles target to see if it does work as expected. The result of this invocation is captured in Figure 2-11.

```
C:\Data\MSBuildExamples\Fundamentals>msbuild Copy02.proj /t:CopyFiles /nologo
Build started 5/31/2008 5:02:35 PM.
Project "C:\Data\MSBuildExamples\Fundamentals\Copy02.proj" on node 0 (CopyFiles
 target(s)).
  Copying file from "src\four.txt" to "C:\Data\MSBuildExamples\Fundamentals\des
  t\four.txt".
  Copying file from "src\one.txt" to "C:\Data\MSBuildExamples\Fundamentals\dest
  \one.txt".
  Creating directory "C:\Data\MSBuildExamples\Fundamentals\dest\sub".
  Copying file from "src\sub\sub_four.txt" to "C:\Data\MSBuildExamples\Fundamen
  tals\dest\sub\sub_four.txt".
  Copying file from "src\sub\sub_one.txt" to "C:\Data\MSBuildExamples\Fundament
  als\dest\sub\sub_one.txt".
  Copying file from "src\sub\sub_three.txt" to "C:\Data\MSBuildExamples\Fundame
  ntals\dest\sub\sub_three.txt".
  Copying file from "src\sub\sub_two.txt" to "C:\Data\MSBuildExamples\Fundament
  als\dest\sub\sub_two.txt".
  Copying file from "src\three.txt" to "C:\Data\MSBuildExamples\Fundamentals\de
  st\three.txt".
  Copying file from "src\two.txt" to "C:\Data\MSBuildExamples\Fundamentals\dest
  \two.txt".
Done Building Project "C:\Data\MSBuildExamples\Fundamentals\Copy02.proj" (CopyF
iles target(s)).


Build succeeded.
    0 Warning(s)
    0 Error(s)
```

FIGURE 2-11 Result of CopyFiles task for Copy02.proj

From the result shown in Figure 2-11, we can see that the files from src\ and src\sub\ were successfully copied into the dest folder. Now we'll move on to discuss item metadata, which is another distinction between items and properties.

Well-Known Item Metadata

When you create items, each value in an item also has a set of metadata associated with it. This is another difference between items and properties. A property is a key-value pair, but each element in an item is much richer than a property. Each of these can have zero or more metadata values associated with them. These metadata are also key-value pairs. For files and directories you are given a set of metadata automatically, these are well-known metadata. These values are read-only and are summarized in Table 2-3.

TABLE 2-3 Well-Known Metadata

Name	Description
FullPath	Full path of the file.
RootDir	The root directory to which the file belongs, for example C:\.
Filename	The name of the file, not including the extension.
Extension	The extension of the file, including the '.'.
RelativeDir	The path to the file relative to the current working directory.
Directory	Directory of the item, without the root directory.
RecursiveDir	This is the directory path that replaces the first ** of the include declaration. If no ** is present, then this value is empty.
Identity	The value that was specified in the *Include* attribute of the item.
ModifiedTime	The last time the file was modified.
CreatedTime	The time the file was created.
AccessedTime	The last time the file was accessed.

We will now see how we can use these well-known metadata, and later we'll discuss custom metadata. In order to demonstrate using well-known metadata, take a look at the following simple project. This is taken from the file WellKnownMetadata.proj.

```
<Project xmlns="http://schemas.microsoft.com/developer/msbuild/2003">
  <ItemGroup>
    <src Include="src\one.txt" />
  </ItemGroup>
  <Target Name="PrintWellKnownMetadata">

    <Message Text="===== Well known metadata =====" />
    <!-- %40 = @ -->
    <!-- %25 = % -->
    <Message Text="%40(src->'%25(FullPath)'): @(src->'%(FullPath)')" />
    <Message Text="%40(src->'%25(Rootdir)'): @(src->'%(Rootdir)')" />
    <Message Text="%40(src->'%25(Filename)'): @(src->'%(Filename)')" />
    <Message Text="%40(src->'%25(Extension)'): @(src->'%(Extension)')" />
    <Message Text="%40(src->'%25(RelativeDir)'): @(src->'%(RelativeDir)')" />
    <Message Text="%40(src->'%25(Directory)'): @(src->'%(Directory)')" />
    <Message Text="%40(src->'%25(RecursiveDir)'): @(src->'%(RecursiveDir)')" />
    <Message Text="%40(src->'%25(Identity)'): @(src->'%(Identity)')" />
    <Message Text="%40(src->'%25(ModifiedTime)'): @(src->'%(ModifiedTime)')" />
    <Message Text="%40(src->'%25(CreatedTime)'): @(src->'%(CreatedTime)')" />
    <Message Text="%40(src->'%25(AccessedTime)'): @(src->'%(AccessedTime)')" />

  </Target>
</Project>
```

From the preceding project, one item is created, the src item. This item purposefully contains only a single file, one.txt. In order to extract a single metadata value from an item, you can use the `@(ItemType->'%(MetadataName)')` syntax, where ItemType is the name of the item and MetadataName is the name of the metadata to extract. We can see that in the PrintWellKnownMetadata target all the well-known values from Table 2-3 are printed. The `@(ItemType->'%( MetadataName)')` syntax is a simplified version of an item transformation, which we will discuss in the next section. If you execute the PrintWellKnownMetadata target on this file, the result will be what is shown in Figure 2-12.

```
C:\Data\MSBuildExamples\Fundamentals>msbuild WellKnownMetadata.proj /t:PrintWell
KnownMetadata /nologo
Build started 6/1/2008 12:44:05 AM.
Project "C:\Data\MSBuildExamples\Fundamentals\WellKnownMetadata.proj" on node 0
 (PrintWellKnownMetadata target(s)).
  ===== Well known metadata =====
  @(src->'%(FullPath)'): C:\Data\MSBuildExamples\Fundamentals\src\one.txt
  @(src->'%(Rootdir)'): C:\
  @(src->'%(Filename)'): one
  @(src->'%(Extension)'): .txt
  @(src->'%(RelativeDir)'): src\
  @(src->'%(Directory)'): Data\MSBuildExamples\Fundamentals\src\
  @(src->'%(RecursiveDir)'):
  @(src->'%(Identity)'): src\one.txt
  @(src->'%(ModifiedTime)'): 2008-02-25 00:05:28.1718750
  @(src->'%(CreatedTime)'): 2008-05-22 00:22:48.4687500
  @(src->'%(AccessedTime)'): 2008-05-22 00:22:48.4687500
Done Building Project "C:\Data\MSBuildExamples\Fundamentals\WellKnownMetadata.p
roj" (PrintWellKnownMetadata target(s)).


Build succeeded.
    0 Warning(s)
    0 Error(s)
```

FIGURE 2-12 Well-known metadata

The result in Figure 2-12 demonstrates most of the well-known metadata that are available to be used for files and directories. One metadata value that needs further explaination is the RecursiveDir. In order to see this value being populated you need to create an item with the ** wildcard declaration. To see this, we can examine a slightly modified version of the previous file, the following WellKnownMetadata02.proj file.

```
<Project xmlns="http://schemas.microsoft.com/developer/msbuild/2003">
  <ItemGroup>
    <src Include="src\**\sub_one.txt" />
  </ItemGroup>
  <Target Name="PrintWellKnownMetadata">

    <Message Text="===== Well known metadata =====" />
    <!-- %40 = @ -->
    <!-- %25 = % -->
    <Message Text="%40(src->'%25(FullPath)'): @(src->'%(FullPath)')" />
    <Message Text="%40(src->'%25(Rootdir)'): @(src->'%(Rootdir)')" />
    <Message Text="%40(src->'%25(Filename)'): @(src->'%(Filename)')" />
    <Message Text="%40(src->'%25(Extension)'): @(src->'%(Extension)')" />
    <Message Text="%40(src->'%25(RelativeDir)'): @(src->'%(RelativeDir)')" />
    <Message Text="%40(src->'%25(Directory)'): @(src->'%(Directory)')" />
    <Message Text="%40(src->'%25(RecursiveDir)'): @(src->'%(RecursiveDir)')" />
    <Message Text="%40(src->'%25(Identity)'): @(src->'%(Identity)')" />
    <Message Text="%40(src->'%25(ModifiedTime)'): @(src->'%(ModifiedTime)')" />
    <Message Text="%40(src->'%25(CreatedTime)'): @(src->'%(CreatedTime)')" />
    <Message Text="%40(src->'%25(AccessedTime)'): @(src->'%(AccessedTime)')" />

  </Target>
</Project>
```

The section that has changed from the previous version has been placed in bold. I have modified this to use the ** qualifier, but at the same time to allow only a single file to be in the item. If you were to execute this MSBuild file, you would see results very similar to the previous, but the main difference in the output is the line `@(src->'%(RecursiveDir)'): sub\`. As Table 2-3 states, the RecursiveDir will take the value that replaces the ** declaration. In this case, the value used was sub\, which is exactly what we would expect. The summary in Table 2-3 is not entirely correct for RecursiveDir, but it is more concise than the correct definition. The actual behavior of the RecursiveDir is to return the remaining portion of the path to the file from the item specification that starts with the **. Take a look at the same file, slightly modified again, as follows; this new file is saved as WellKnownMetadata03.proj.

```
<Project xmlns="http://schemas.microsoft.com/developer/msbuild/2003">
  <ItemGroup>
    <src Include="src\**\sub\sub_one.txt" />
  </ItemGroup>
  <Target Name="PrintWellKnownMetadata">

    <Message Text="===== Well known metadata =====" />
    <!-- %40 = @ -->
    <!-- %25 = % -->
    <Message Text="%40(src->'%25(FullPath)'): @(src->'%(FullPath)')" />
    <Message Text="%40(src->'%25(Rootdir)'): @(src->'%(Rootdir)')" />
    <Message Text="%40(src->'%25(Filename)'): @(src->'%(Filename)')" />
    <Message Text="%40(src->'%25(Extension)'): @(src->'%(Extension)')" />
    <Message Text="%40(src->'%25(RelativeDir)'): @(src->'%(RelativeDir)')" />
    <Message Text="%40(src->'%25(Directory)'): @(src->'%(Directory)')" />
    <Message Text="%40(src->'%25(RecursiveDir)'): @(src->'%(RecursiveDir)')" />
    <Message Text="%40(src->'%25(Identity)'): @(src->'%(Identity)')" />
    <Message Text="%40(src->'%25(ModifiedTime)'): @(src->'%(ModifiedTime)')" />
    <Message Text="%40(src->'%25(CreatedTime)'): @(src->'%(CreatedTime)')" />
    <Message Text="%40(src->'%25(AccessedTime)'): @(src->'%(AccessedTime)')" />

  </Target>
</Project>
```

The line that has been changed is bold, and the part to make note of is that part of the path is specified after the ** declaration on the src item. If you print the recursive dir value for this new item you will get the same result of '`@(src->'%(RecursiveDir)'): sub\`', so the result was the same even though we specified the subdirectory name after the **. This is because the RecursiveDir metadata doesn't examine what the item specification declared after the initial **. It looks at the item specification, finds the first occurrence of **, and returns the remaining section of the path from that specification. In fact, if you have multiple **s in a single item specification, it wouldn't affect the result of the RecursiveDir; it would still behave as I described, by finding the first occurrence of the ** and return the path following. Now that we have discussed well-known metadata in depth, we will move on to discuss custom metadata followed by item transformations.

Custom Metadata

When you declare items that point to files or directories you get a set of metadata for free—this is the well-known metadata that we discussed in the previous section. What if you have the need to associate some additional data with an item? You can do this; they are called custom metadata and they behave exactly the same as well-known metadata, with the exception that well-known metadata are read-only. When you declare an item you will associate the metadata with its declaration. In this section, we will describe how to create and use custom metadata in your build scripts.

Metadata behaves similarly to properties, in the sense that they are key-value pairs. So each piece of metadata, custom or not, has a name, which is the key, and a value. For statically-created items you will declare the metadata as a child of the item element itself. The metadata key is the element name, and the value of the metadata is the value of the XML element. For example, take a look at the following project file, Metadata01.proj.

```
<Project xmlns="http://schemas.microsoft.com/developer/msbuild/2003">

  <ItemGroup>
    <Server Include="Server1">
      <Type>2008</Type>
      <Name>SVR01</Name>
      <AdminContact>Sayed Ibrahim Hashimi</AdminContact>
    </Server>
    <Server Include="Server2">
      <Type>2003</Type>
      <Name>SVR02</Name>
      <AdminContact>Sayed Y. Hashimi</AdminContact>
    </Server>
    <Server Include="Server3">
      <Type>2008</Type>
      <Name>SVR03</Name>
      <AdminContact>Nicole Woodsmall</AdminContact>
    </Server>
    <Server Include="Server4">
      <Type>2003</Type>
      <Name>SVR04</Name>
      <AdminContact>Keith Tingle</AdminContact>
    </Server>
  </ItemGroup>

  <Target Name="PrintInfo" Outputs="%(Server.Identity )">
    <Message Text="Server: @(Server)" />
    <Message Text="Admin: @(Server->'%(AdminContact)')" />
  </Target>

</Project>
```

In this project file, we have declared an item, Server, which will have four metadata values associated with it. If you take a look at each item's declaration you will see that each has three XML child elements. These are Type, Name, and AdminContact. Each of these is custom metadata, and after the item is created you can access those values using the same syntax as you would with well-known metadata. You can have any number of metadata elements declared. Also you should note that if your item's declaration uses wildcards, then each item value created from the Include will have the attached metadata. You are not limited to text in declaring these values; you can use any MSBuild statements as a metadata value declaration. In the previous project file there is one target, PrintInfo, which, as it is named, prints the information for the Server item. This target uses another technique called batching, which in this case will cause the target to be executed once per each value in Server. We will thoroughly examine batching in Chapter 6. If you execute this target, the result will be what is shown in Figure 2-13.

```
C:\Data\MSBuildExamples\Fundamentals>msbuild Metadata01.proj /t:PrintInfo /nolog
o
Build started 6/6/2008 12:19:25 AM.
Project "C:\Data\MSBuildExamples\Fundamentals\Metadata01.proj" on node 0 (Print
Info target(s)).
  Server: Server1
  Admin: Sayed Ibrhaim Hashimi
PrintInfo:
  Server: Server2
  Admin: Sayed Y. Hashimi
PrintInfo:
  Server: Server3
  Admin: Nicole Woodsmall
PrintInfo:
  Server: Server4
  Admin: Keith Tingle
Done Building Project "C:\Data\MSBuildExamples\Fundamentals\Metadata01.proj" (P
rintInfo target(s)).

Build succeeded.
    0 Warning(s)
    0 Error(s)
```

FIGURE 2-13 PrintInfo target results on Metadata01.proj

The PrintInfo target extracts custom metadata values in the same way as well-known metadata values are extracted. The Figure 2-13 demonstrates that this does work exactly as expected. Well-known metadata are always read-only, whereas custom metadata are not. Therefore, if you provide a value for already existing metadata, that value will be overwritten.

Item Transformations

When you are using MSBuild there are many times that you would like to take an existing item, modify it a bit, and then pass it to a task. For example, if you are copying a set of files from one place to another, you would like to take an item that points to an existing set of files, change its location to point to the destination, and then give it to the Copy task for the DestinationFiles property. MSBuild has a mechanism for this behavior built in: this process is called item transformations and we will discuss it in detail in this section. A transformation can be expressed as A => A' where A is the original item and A' is the transformed item. The most important thing to remember is that A and A' will always have the same number of elements. This is because the transformation is processed on each element to generate the new item. A transformation can be visualized as that shown in Figure 2-14.

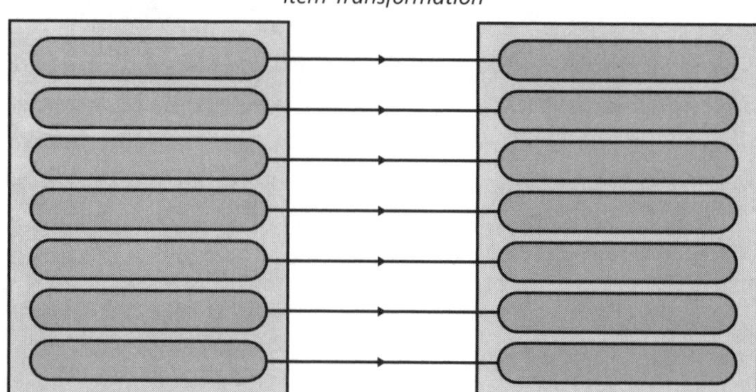

FIGURE 2-14 Item transformation visualization

As stated previously, the visualization in Figure 2-14 reemphasizes that an item transformation is a one-to-one translation.

Now that we have defined what an item transformation is, we will take a look at the transformation syntax and explain how it can be effectively used. Here is the syntax

```
@(ItemType->'TransformModifer[TransformModifer…]'[,Seperator]),
```

where ItemType is the name of the item being transformed, TransformModifier is a transform modifier, and Seperator is an optional parameter that will be used as the separator between values. The default value for the separator is ";". You can use the syntax `@(ItemType,[Seperator])` where you do not declare any modifiers but only override the separator. The three acceptable types of transform modifiers are summarized in Table 2-4.

TABLE 2-4 Transform Modifiers

Type	Description	Example
Text	Any plain text	C:\Test
Property	Property value extraction statement	$(Configuration)
Item Metadata	Item metadata extraction statement	%(FullPath)

As stated, there are only three possible types of transform modifiers and we will demonstrate all of them in this section. You should note that there is no restriction on what type/order modifiers are declared in the transformation. To start our discussion on transformations we will examine the following file, Transformation01.proj.

```
<Project xmlns="http://schemas.microsoft.com/developer/msbuild/2003"
         DefaultTargets="All">
  <ItemGroup>
    <SrcFiles Include="src\**\*" ></SrcFiles>
  </ItemGroup>
```

```
  <PropertyGroup>
    <DestFolder>copy\</DestFolder>
  </PropertyGroup>

  <!-- %40 = @ -->
  <!-- %25 = % -->
  <Target Name="PrintSrcFiles">
    <Message Text="%40(SrcFiles):"
             Importance="high" />
    <Message Text="@(SrcFiles)" />
  </Target>
  <Target Name="Demo01">
    <Message Text="%40(SrcFiles->'%25(Filename)'):"
             Importance="high" />
    <Message Text="@(SrcFiles->'%(Filename)')" />
  </Target>
  <Target Name="Demo02">
    <Message Text="%40(SrcFiles->'%25(Filename)%25(Extension)'):"
             Importance="high"/>
    <Message Text="@(SrcFiles->'%(Filename)%(Extension)')" />
  </Target>
  <Target Name="Demo03">
    <Message Text="%40(SrcFiles->'%25(Filename)%25(Extension).bak'):"
             Importance="high" />
    <Message Text="@(SrcFiles->'%(Filename)%(Extension).bak')" />
  </Target>

  <ItemGroup>
    <Transform01
      Include="@(SrcFiles->'$(DestFolder)%(RecursiveDir)%(Filename)%(Extension)')" />
  </ItemGroup>

  <Target Name="Demo04">
    <Message Text="%40(Transform01):"
             Importance="high" />
    <Message Text="@(Transform01)" />
    <Message Text="===== Copying files ====="
             Importance="high" />
    <Copy SourceFiles="@(SrcFiles)" DestinationFiles="@(Transform01)" />
  </Target>



  <Target Name="All"
          DependsOnTargets="PrintSrcFiles;Demo01;Demo02;Demo03;Demo04" />

</Project>
```

Note In order to use reserved characters such as the % and @ you have to escape. This is accomplished by the syntax %HV where HV is the hex value of the character. This is demonstrated here with %25 and %40.

At the top of the project file there is one item as well as one property declared. The item, SrcFiles, points to some files that will be used throughout the example. The property, DestFolder, contains a path to where some files should be copied. There is another item defined toward the bottom of the file, which we will discuss later. This file contains five relevant targets, one of which, PrintSrcFiles, prints out the list of files in the SrcFiles item for reference when executing the other targets. Each of these targets essentially contains one transformation that you should understand. The All target is declared simply to execute the other targets for demonstration here. In the following list we will describe these targets and the transformations' purpose.

Demo01

The transformation on the SrcFiles target is defined as @(SrcFiles->'%(Filename)'). This will transform the SrcFiles item list into a list containing the Filename metadata value. If you recall from Table 2-2, this is the file name, no path information and no extension.

Demo02

The transformation in this target, @(SrcFiles->'%(Filename)%(Extension)'), extends the previous transformation to add the extension, using the extension well-known metadata.

Demo03

The transformation in this target, @(SrcFiles->'%(Filename)%(Extension).bak'), demonstrates how we can use a combination of metadata values along with free text. This transformation adds .bak to the end of the name of the file.

Demo04

This target is a little different in the sense that it doesn't actually contain the transformation itself. This target uses the `Transform01` item, which is a transformed version of the `SrcFiles` item. The transformation to create this item is defined as @(SrcFiles->'$(DestFolder)%(RecursiveDir)%(Filename)%(Extension)'). In this transformation, we create a new item that uses the DestFolder path to create a list of file paths where the SrcFiles files should be copied to. Since the SrcFiles item can contain items in subfolders, it uses the RecursiveDir metadata value to re-create the appropriate directory structure in the DestFolder.

This file starts with a very simple example and then builds on it. These four transformations describe the three types of transform modifiers that are available. Now let's take a look at the result of executing all these targets, which is shown in Figure 2-15.

In the result shown in Figure 2-15, you can take a look at each transformation and make sure that it performs the transformation that you would expect. Also, for the Demo04 target, we can see that the files were successfully copied into the appropriate location.

```
C:\Data\MSBuildExamples\Fundamentals>msbuild Transformation01.proj /t:All /nolog
o
Build started 6/5/2008 12:37:10 AM.
Project "C:\Data\MSBuildExamples\Fundamentals\Transformation01.proj" on node 0
(All target(s)).
  @(SrcFiles):
  C:\Data\MSBuildExamples\Fundamentals\src\four.txt;C:\Data\MSBuildExamples\Fun
  damentals\src\one.txt;C:\Data\MSBuildExamples\Fundamentals\src\sub\sub_four.t
  xt;C:\Data\MSBuildExamples\Fundamentals\src\sub\sub_one.txt;C:\Data\MSBuildEx
  amples\Fundamentals\src\sub\sub_three.txt;C:\Data\MSBuildExamples\Fundamental
  s\src\sub\sub_two.txt;C:\Data\MSBuildExamples\Fundamentals\src\three.txt;C:\D
  ata\MSBuildExamples\Fundamentals\src\two.txt
Demo01:
  @(SrcFiles->'%(Filename)'):
  four;one;sub_four;sub_one;sub_three;sub_two;three;two
Demo02:
  @(SrcFiles->'%(Filename)%(Extension)'):
  four.txt;one.txt;sub_four.txt;sub_one.txt;sub_three.txt;sub_two.txt;three.txt
  ;two.txt
Demo03:
  @(SrcFiles->'%(Filename)%(Extension).bak'):
  four.txt.bak;one.txt.bak;sub_four.txt.bak;sub_one.txt.bak;sub_three.txt.bak;s
  ub_two.txt.bak;three.txt.bak;two.txt.bak
Demo04:
  @(Transform01):
  C:\Data\MSBuildExamples\Fundamentals\copy\four.txt;C:\Data\MSBuildExamples\Fu
  ndamentals\copy\one.txt;C:\Data\MSBuildExamples\Fundamentals\copy\sub\sub_fou
  r.txt;C:\Data\MSBuildExamples\Fundamentals\copy\sub\sub_one.txt;C:\Data\MSBui
  ldExamples\Fundamentals\copy\sub\sub_three.txt;C:\Data\MSBuildExamples\Fundam
  entals\copy\sub\sub_two.txt;C:\Data\MSBuildExamples\Fundamentals\copy\three.t
  xt;C:\Data\MSBuildExamples\Fundamentals\copy\two.txt
  ===== Copying files =====
  Copying file from "C:\Data\MSBuildExamples\Fundamentals\src\four.txt" to "C:\
  Data\MSBuildExamples\Fundamentals\copy\four.txt".
  Copying file from "C:\Data\MSBuildExamples\Fundamentals\src\one.txt" to "C:\D
  ata\MSBuildExamples\Fundamentals\copy\one.txt".
  Copying file from "C:\Data\MSBuildExamples\Fundamentals\src\sub\sub_four.txt"
   to "C:\Data\MSBuildExamples\Fundamentals\copy\sub\sub_four.txt".
  Copying file from "C:\Data\MSBuildExamples\Fundamentals\src\sub\sub_one.txt"
  to "C:\Data\MSBuildExamples\Fundamentals\copy\sub\sub_one.txt".
  Copying file from "C:\Data\MSBuildExamples\Fundamentals\src\sub\sub_three.txt
  " to "C:\Data\MSBuildExamples\Fundamentals\copy\sub\sub_three.txt".
  Copying file from "C:\Data\MSBuildExamples\Fundamentals\src\sub\sub_two.txt"
  to "C:\Data\MSBuildExamples\Fundamentals\copy\sub\sub_two.txt".
  Copying file from "C:\Data\MSBuildExamples\Fundamentals\src\three.txt" to "C:
  \Data\MSBuildExamples\Fundamentals\copy\three.txt".
  Copying file from "C:\Data\MSBuildExamples\Fundamentals\src\two.txt" to "C:\D
  ata\MSBuildExamples\Fundamentals\copy\two.txt".
Done Building Project "C:\Data\MSBuildExamples\Fundamentals\Transformation01.pr
oj" (All target(s)).


Build succeeded.
    0 Warning(s)
    0 Error(s)
```

FIGURE 2-15 Transformation01.proj result

We will now revisit a previous example, the one contained in the following Copy02.proj file.

```
<Project xmlns="http://schemas.microsoft.com/developer/msbuild/2003">

  <ItemGroup>
    <SrcFiles Include="src\**\*.txt" />
  </ItemGroup>

  <PropertyGroup>
    <Dest>$(MSBuildProjectDirectory)\dest\</Dest>
  </PropertyGroup>

  <Target Name="PrintFiles">
    <Message Text="SrcFiles: @(SrcFiles)" />
  </Target>
  <Target Name="CopyFiles">
    <Copy SourceFiles="@(SrcFiles)"
          DestinationFiles=
          "@(SrcFiles->'$(Dest)%(RecursiveDir)%(Filename)%(Extension)')" />
  </Target>
</Project>
```

We'll now fully describe the Copy statement in this build file. Let's dissect the DestinationFiles value. This value, @(SrcFiles->'$(Dest)%(RecursiveDir)%(Filename)%(Extension)'), is a transform. The components of the value are:

1. $(Dest)
2. %(RecursiveDir)
3. %(Filename)
4. %(Extension),

where $(Dest) is an evaluation of the `Dest` property and the others are evaluations for metadata values on the SrcFiles item. From this transformation there is only one static value, which is the value for $(Dest). Aside from that, all the values will be taken from the metadata for each item element. These metadata values were previously discussed in this chapter. The output of the CopyFiles target is shown in Figure 2-16.

```
C:\Data\MSBuildExamples\Fundamentals>msbuild Copy02.proj /t:CopyFiles /nologo
Build started 6/3/2008 12:28:16 AM.
Project "C:\Data\MSBuildExamples\Fundamentals\Copy02.proj" on node 0 (CopyFiles
 target(s)).
  Copying file from "src\four.txt" to "C:\Data\MSBuildExamples\Fundamentals\des
  t\four.txt".
  Copying file from "src\one.txt" to "C:\Data\MSBuildExamples\Fundamentals\dest
  \one.txt".
  Copying file from "src\sub\sub_four.txt" to "C:\Data\MSBuildExamples\Fundamen
  tals\dest\sub\sub_four.txt".
  Copying file from "src\sub\sub_one.txt" to "C:\Data\MSBuildExamples\Fundament
  als\dest\sub\sub_one.txt".
  Copying file from "src\sub\sub_three.txt" to "C:\Data\MSBuildExamples\Fundame
  ntals\dest\sub\sub_three.txt".
  Copying file from "src\sub\sub_two.txt" to "C:\Data\MSBuildExamples\Fundament
  als\dest\sub\sub_two.txt".
  Copying file from "src\three.txt" to "C:\Data\MSBuildExamples\Fundamentals\de
  st\three.txt".
  Copying file from "src\two.txt" to "C:\Data\MSBuildExamples\Fundamentals\dest
  \two.txt".
Done Building Project "C:\Data\MSBuildExamples\Fundamentals\Copy02.proj" (CopyF
iles target(s)).


Build succeeded.
    0 Warning(s)
    0 Error(s)
```

FIGURE 2-16 CopyFiles target result on Copy02.proj

From the output we can see that eight files were successfully copied to the destination as expected. We will examine the first copy message in more detail now to describe the transformation. In this example the original item was specified as *src\four.txt* and it was transformed into the file on the right-hand side. In the transformed specification, the $(Dest) value was assigned C:\Data\MSBuildExamples\Fundamentals\dest\; the %(RecursiveDir) did not return a value, so it was an empty string; the %(Filename) evaluated to the value "four"; and %(Extension) became .txt. If you take a look at the output for the files in the subdirectory, you can see that the %(RecursiveDir) metadata returned the path correctly. Now we have covered what you need to know about item transformations, which are used extensively throughout MSBuild files.

In this chapter, we have introduced a lot of material, including properties, items, metadata, and transformations. We will move on to the next chapter, in which we will continue this discussion and add the topics of dynamic properties and dynamic items. In the next chapter, you will learn how properties and items are evaluated, and how to import other MSBuild files and extend the build process.

Chapter 3
MSBuild Deep Dive, Part 2

In the previous chapter, we discussed a variety of topics, including static properties, static items, and transformations. In this chapter, we will extend that discussion and conclude with a foundation that is required to successfully use MSBuild. We will start by discussing dynamic properties and items. We will also see how properties and items are evaluated as well as how you can extend your own build process. Following this chapter, we will discuss custom tasks, custom loggers, and other advanced topics.

Dynamic Properties and Items

Many times when building software, static items and properties, those defined outside of targets, will do the job fine. For example, most of the time you know what files you are building and the possible values for Configuration. From that you can determine what files need to be built. Despite this, there are many instances where you will need to create properties and items as your build is occurring. For example, if you want to build your product and then copy the binaries from the output path to another location you will need to be able to discover those created files. Properties and items that are created as your build process is executing are called dynamic properties and dynamic items. In this section, we will examine how to use these dynamic values. MSBuild 3.5 introduced a new, simpler syntax for dynamic properties and items; we will first cover that syntax then discuss the older 2.0 syntax, which is still valid in MSBuild 3.5. Since the new syntax is preferred, more emphasis will be placed on its coverage.

Dynamic Properties and Items: MSBuild 3.5

MSBuild 3.5 introduced the ability to use the *PropertyGroup* and *ItemGroup* elements inside targets. With this enhancement we can declare dynamic properties and items just as we would normally declare them. You can see how dynamic properties are created in the following example taken from Dynamic01-35.proj.

```
<Project xmlns="http://schemas.microsoft.com/developer/msbuild/2003"
         DefaultTargets="All">

  <PropertyGroup>
    <Configuration>Debug</Configuration>
  </PropertyGroup>

  <Target Name="PrintConfig">
    <Message Text="Config: $(Configuration)" />
  </Target>
```

```
  <Target Name="PrintConfig2">
    <PropertyGroup>
      <Configuration>Release</Configuration>
    </PropertyGroup>

    <Message Text="Config: $(Configuration)" />
  </Target>

  <Target Name="All" DependsOnTargets="PrintConfig;PrintConfig2" />
</Project>
```

If you execute the All target, which simply executes the other targets, the result is that shown in Figure 3-1.

```
C:\Data\MSBuildExamples\Fundamentals>msbuild Dynamic01-35.proj /t:All /nologo
Build started 10/6/2008 12:18:10 AM.
Project "C:\Data\MSBuildExamples\Fundamentals\Dynamic01-35.proj" on node 0 (All
 target(s)).
  Config: Debug
PrintConfig2:
  Config: Release
Done Building Project "C:\Data\MSBuildExamples\Fundamentals\Dynamic01-35.proj"
(All target(s)).


Build succeeded.
    0 Warning(s)
    0 Error(s)
```

FIGURE 3-1 Dynamic property result

As you can see from the result shown in Figure 3-1, the value for the Configuration property was overridden dynamically inside the PrintConfig2 target. The usage of the PropertyGroup is not limited to modifying values for existing properties; you can create new properties as well.

To demonstrate that new properties can be created, the previous example has been modified. Take a look at the new file, Dynamic02.proj, which is shown next.

```
<Project xmlns="http://schemas.microsoft.com/developer/msbuild/2003"
         DefaultTargets="All">

  <PropertyGroup>
    <Configuration>Debug</Configuration>
  </PropertyGroup>

  <Target Name="PrintConfig">
    <Message Text="Config: $(Configuration)" />
  </Target>

  <Target Name="PrintConfig2">
    <PropertyGroup>
      <Configuration>Release</Configuration>
      <OutputPath>$(Configuration)\dest\</OutputPath>
    </PropertyGroup>

    <Message Text="Config: $(Configuration)" />
    <Message Text="OutputPath: $(OutputPath)" />
  </Target>

  <Target Name="All" DependsOnTargets="PrintConfig;PrintConfig2" />
</Project>
```

In this example, the changed areas have been highlighted. Inside the PrintConfig2 target a new property, OutputPath, is created using the *PropertyGroup* element. This new property will contain the value of the `Configuration` property followed by *dest*. After that, the newly created property, as well as the value of the Configuration property are printed out. Figure 3-2 shows the result of running this script.

```
C:\Data\MSBuildExamples\Fundamentals>msbuild Dynamic02.proj /t:All /nologo
Build started 6/6/2008 6:43:40 PM.
Project "C:\Data\MSBuildExamples\Fundamentals\Dynamic02.proj" on node 0 (All ta
rget(s)).
  Config: Debug
PrintConfig2:
  Config: Release
  OutputPath: Release\dest\
Done Building Project "C:\Data\MSBuildExamples\Fundamentals\Dynamic02.proj" (Al
l target(s)).


Build succeeded.
    0 Warning(s)
    0 Error(s)
```

FIGURE 3-2 Results for Dynamic02.proj

From the results shown in Figure 3-2, you can see that the OutputPath property was indeed created and initialized successfully. Now that we have discussed dynamic properties we can take a look at how dynamic items are created.

The problem with static items is that the value for static items is **always** evaluated **before** any target executes. Thus, if you need an item to contain any generated files you must create the item dynamically. To create dynamic items you can use the *ItemGroup* element inside of a target. Inside a target, the *ItemGroup* element even has some new features. You are able to remove values from an item and you can modify the metadata value for an item. Doing so was not possible using MSBuild 2.0. Consider the following sample, which is contained in the Metadata_01-35.proj file.

```
<Project xmlns="http://schemas.microsoft.com/developer/msbuild/2003">
  <ItemGroup>
    <Server Include="Server1">
      <Type>2008</Type>
      <Name>SVR01</Name>
      <AdminContact>Sayed Ibrahim Hashimi</AdminContact>
    </Server>
    <Server Include="Server2">
      <Type>2003</Type>
      <Name>SVR02</Name>
      <AdminContact>Sayed Y. Hashimi</AdminContact>
    </Server>
    <Server Include="Server3">
      <Type>2008</Type>
      <Name>SVR03</Name>
      <AdminContact>Nicole Woodsmall</AdminContact>
    </Server>
    <Server Include="Server4">
      <Type>2003</Type>
      <Name>SVR04</Name>
      <AdminContact>Keith Tingle</AdminContact>
    </Server>
  </ItemGroup>
```

```
  <Target Name="PrintInfo">
    <Message Text="%(Server.Identity) : %(Server.AdminContact)" />

    <!-- just for new line -->
    <Message Text=" " />
    <Message Text="Overriding AdmingContact" Importance="high" />
    <!-- Override the AdminContact if it is set to Keith Tingle -->
    <ItemGroup>
      <Server Condition="'%(Server.AdminContact)' == 'Keith Tingle'">
        <AdminContact>Sayed Ibrahim Hashimi</AdminContact>
      </Server>
    </ItemGroup>
    <Message Text="%(Server.Identity) : %(Server.AdminContact)" />

    <Message Text=" "/>
    <Message Text="Removing item" Importance="high" />
    <!-- Remove an item  -->
    <ItemGroup>
      <Server Remove="Server2" />
    </ItemGroup>
    <Message Text="%(Server.Identity) : %(Server.AdminContact)" />

    <!--<Message Text="Server: @(Server)" />
    <Message Text="Admin: @(Server->'%(AdminContact)')" />-->
  </Target>
</Project>
```

In this MSBuild file we have created an item type, Server, which contains a list of references to servers. Each item value contains some custom metadata that describes it, including AdminContact. Inside the PrintInfo target the ItemGroup declaration of the Server item is redefining the AdminContact metadata value, but only for items whose AdminContact is set to the value 'Keith Tingle'. If the condition was not placed on the Server item type, then it would affect all of the Server item values. Following that, you can see how an item value is removed. Now we can see if all this works by executing the PrintInfo target of this MSBuild file. The results are shown in Figure 3-3.

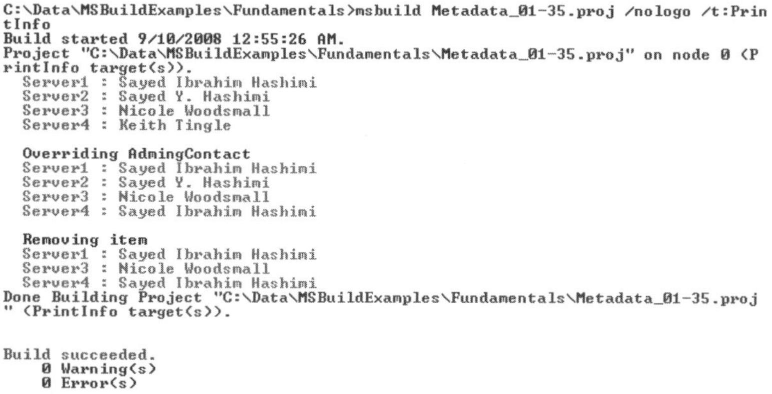

```
C:\Data\MSBuildExamples\Fundamentals>msbuild Metadata_01-35.proj /nologo /t:Prin
tInfo
Build started 9/10/2008 12:55:26 AM.
Project "C:\Data\MSBuildExamples\Fundamentals\Metadata_01-35.proj" on node 0 (P
rintInfo target(s)).
  Server1 : Sayed Ibrahim Hashimi
  Server2 : Sayed Y. Hashimi
  Server3 : Nicole Woodsmall
  Server4 : Keith Tingle

  Overriding AdmingContact
  Server1 : Sayed Ibrahim Hashimi
  Server2 : Sayed Y. Hashimi
  Server3 : Nicole Woodsmall
  Server4 : Sayed Ibrahim Hashimi

  Removing item
  Server1 : Sayed Ibrahim Hashimi
  Server3 : Nicole Woodsmall
  Server4 : Sayed Ibrahim Hashimi
Done Building Project "C:\Data\MSBuildExamples\Fundamentals\Metadata_01-35.proj
" (PrintInfo target(s)).

Build succeeded.
    0 Warning(s)
    0 Error(s)
```

FIGURE 3-3 Metadata_01-35.proj result

As you can see from the output, first the value for the AdminContact metadata was modified and then an item value was removed from the Server item type. If you are used to MSBuild 2.0, you should keep in mind that these new features are available when you are using MSBuild 3.5. Now that we have seen how dynamic items are created we will move on to a more realistic example.

Consider this typical scenario: After you build a project you would like to copy all the files in the output directory to another location. I will show you how this can be achieved using dynamic items. In the sample files, I have created a simple Windows application, WindowsApplication2. In the `.csproj` file for the project I have added this functionality. The following sample shows an abbreviated version of the WindowsApplication2.csproj file, which contains all the portions that were added.

```
<Project ToolsVersion="3.5"
  DefaultTargets="Build"
  xmlns="http://schemas.microsoft.com/developer/msbuild/2003">
      ...

  <Import Project="$(MSBuildToolsPath)\Microsoft.CSharp.targets" />

  <!-- Extend build to copy the files in output dir -->
  <PropertyGroup>
    <BuildDependsOn>
      $(BuildDependsOn);
      CopyOutputFiles
    </BuildDependsOn>
    <OutputCopyFolder>$(MSBuildProjectDirectory)\CustomOutput\</OutputCopyFolder>
  </PropertyGroup>
  <Target Name="CopyOutputFiles">
    <!-- Dynamically create the item because these files
         are created during build -->
    <ItemGroup>
      <OutputFiles Include="$(OutputPath)**\*" />
    </ItemGroup>
    <MakeDir Directories="$(OutputCopyFolder)" />
    <Copy SourceFiles="@(OutputFiles)"
          DestinationFiles=
  "@(OutputFiles->'$(OutputCopyFolder)%(RecursiveDir)%(FileName)%(Extension)')" />
  </Target>
</Project>
```

In this snippet, I first re-declare the BuildDependsOn property; this is the property that contains the list of targets that will be executed when the build target runs. I extend this value by using a reference to itself using the `$(BuildDependsOn)` declaration. So I take the current list of targets and add the `CopyOutputFiles` to the end of the list. We will talk more about this later in this chapter; the important part to understand now is that this target will be executed **after** the project has been built. Take a look at the usage of the ItemGroup inside the CopyOutputFiles target. The Include value on this picks up all the files in the OutputPath as well as subfolders. These files are placed into a new item named OutputFiles. Following this the additional output directory is created if it doesn't exist, and then the files are copied to this new location. The Copy task is passed a value of @(OutputFiles->'$(OutputCopyFolder)%(RecursiveDir)%(FileName)%(Extension)') for the DestinationFiles parameter. If you recall from the previous chapter, this is an Item Transformation. In this transformation we place all the files under the OutputCopyFolder directory in the same relative location to where they are in the OutputPath folder. We achieve this by using the RecursiveDir well-known metadata. We can see if this works by building the project. I will execute the Rebuild target to ensure that all artifacts from previous builds are removed. The result of this is shown in Figure 3-4.

```
C:\Data\MSBuildExamples\WindowsApplication2>msbuild WindowsApplication2.csproj /
t:Rebuild /fl /nologo
Build started 6/8/2008 1:25:37 PM.
Project "C:\Data\MSBuildExamples\WindowsApplication2\WindowsApplication2.csproj
" on node 0 (Rebuild target(s)).
  Deleting file "C:\Data\MSBuildExamples\WindowsApplication2\obj\Debug\WindowsA
  pplication2.Properties.Resources.resources".
  Deleting file "C:\Data\MSBuildExamples\WindowsApplication2\obj\Debug\WindowsA
  pplication2.csproj.GenerateResource.Cache".
  Deleting file "C:\Data\MSBuildExamples\WindowsApplication2\obj\Debug\WindowsA
  pplication2.exe".
  Deleting file "C:\Data\MSBuildExamples\WindowsApplication2\obj\Debug\WindowsA
  pplication2.pdb".
CustomAfterClean:
  Deleting file "C:\Data\MSBuildExamples\WindowsApplication2\CustomOutput\Windo
  wsApplication2.exe".
  Deleting file "C:\Data\MSBuildExamples\WindowsApplication2\CustomOutput\Windo
  wsApplication2.pdb".
  Removing directory "C:\Data\MSBuildExamples\WindowsApplication2\CustomOutput\
  ".
CoreResGen:
  Processing resource file "Properties\Resources.resx" into "obj\Debug\WindowsA
  pplication2.Properties.Resources.resources".
CopyFilesToOutputDirectory:
  Copying file from "obj\Debug\WindowsApplication2.exe" to "bin\Debug\WindowsAp
  plication2.exe".
  WindowsApplication2 -> C:\Data\MSBuildExamples\WindowsApplication2\bin\Debug\
  WindowsApplication2.exe
  Copying file from "obj\Debug\WindowsApplication2.pdb" to "bin\Debug\WindowsAp
  plication2.pdb".
CopyOutputFiles:
  Creating directory "C:\Data\MSBuildExamples\WindowsApplication2\CustomOutput\
  ".
  Copying file from "bin\Debug\WindowsApplication2.exe" to "C:\Data\MSBuildExam
  ples\WindowsApplication2\CustomOutput\WindowsApplication2.exe".
  Copying file from "bin\Debug\WindowsApplication2.pdb" to "C:\Data\MSBuildExam
  ples\WindowsApplication2\CustomOutput\WindowsApplication2.pdb".
Done Building Project "C:\Data\MSBuildExamples\WindowsApplication2\WindowsAppli
cation2.csproj" (Rebuild target(s)).


Build succeeded.
    0 Warning(s)
    0 Error(s)
```

FIGURE 3-4 Build of WindowsApplication2.csproj

In the log shown in Figure 3-4, you can see that the `CopyOutputFiles` was called after the build target executed and you can see that the files were copied into the folder specified. One other thing to note about this project file is that I extend the clean process to remove these files. The relevant elements added to the project file are shown in the following snippet.

```
<!-- Extend clean process to delete created files -->
<PropertyGroup>
  <CleanDependsOn>
    $(CleanDependsOn);
    CustomAfterClean
  </CleanDependsOn>
</PropertyGroup>
```

```
<Target Name="CustomAfterClean">
 <ItemGroup>
    <CopiedFilesToDelete Include="$(OutputCopyFolder)**\*" />
  </ItemGroup>
  <Delete Files="@(CopiedFilesToDelete)" />
  <RemoveDir Directories="$(OutputCopyFolder)" />
</Target>
```

If you extend the build process to create additional files you should **always** extend the clean process to remove these files. MSBuild will clean up all the files it generates, but you are responsible for cleaning yours. If you are implementing incremental building you should especially listen to this advice. This is because projects that are not properly cleaned may result is incorrect builds when building incrementally. We will talk more about incremental building in Chapter 6, "Batching and Incremental Builds." In this example, I am manually deleting the created files but sometimes there is a better way.

For C# or VB.NET projects there is a simple way to have your files automatically deleted for you. If you are creating files early in the build process, you can append files that should be deleted on clean by appending them to the FileWrites item. This is an item that the C# and VB.NET MSBuild files use to determine which files need to be deleted the next time the project is cleaned. The contents of this item are written into a file named $(MSBuildProjectFile).FileListAbsolute.txt in the intermediate output path folder. You can use this method only if you are appending the value to the FileWrites list before the Clean/IncrementalClean target is executed and the file resides under the output path folder. This is a great way to make sure that generated code files are deleted at the appropriate time. This is discussed in more detail in Chapter 8, "Practical Applications, Part 1."

Removing Items

Previously, it was mentioned that you can remove values from items using the *ItemGroup* element. In MSBuild 2.0, once a value was placed inside an item there was no way to remove it, so items were append-only. The remove function is included in MSBuild 3.5. This is facilitated by a new attribute, Remove, on the *ItemGroup* element. This is supported for both static and dynamic items. I will demonstrate this with dynamic items. The usage of this is shown in the following Dynamic05.proj file, which again is an MSBuild 3.5 specific construct.

```
<Project xmlns="http://schemas.microsoft.com/developer/msbuild/2003">

  <PropertyGroup>
    <SourceRoot>$(MSBuildProjectDirectory)\src\</SourceRoot>
  </PropertyGroup>
  <ItemGroup>
    <SrcFiles Include="$(SourceRoot)**\*" />
  </ItemGroup>

  <Target Name="Build">
    <Message Text="SrcFiles: @(SrcFiles)" />
    <Message Text="Removing from to item" />
```

```
    <ItemGroup>
      <SrcFiles Remove="$(SourceRoot)sub\*" />
    </ItemGroup>
    <Message Text="SrcFiles: @(SrcFiles)" />
  </Target>

</Project>
```

In this sample, the SrcFiles is initially created to include all files in and under the *src* folder. Then in the Build target all the files in the *src\sub* are removed from the SrcFiles item. You can see that this works as described by examining the results shown in Figure 3-5.

```
C:\Data\MSBuildExamples\Fundamentals>msbuild Dynamic05.proj /t:Build /nologo
Build started 6/8/2008 2:10:44 PM.
Project "C:\Data\MSBuildExamples\Fundamentals\Dynamic05.proj" on node 0 (Build
target(s)).
  SrcFiles: C:\Data\MSBuildExamples\Fundamentals\src\four.txt;C:\Data\MSBuildEx
  amples\Fundamentals\src\one.txt;C:\Data\MSBuildExamples\Fundamentals\src\sub\
  sub_four.txt;C:\Data\MSBuildExamples\Fundamentals\src\sub\sub_one.txt;C:\Data
  \MSBuildExamples\Fundamentals\src\sub\sub_three.txt;C:\Data\MSBuildExamples\F
  undamentals\src\sub\sub_two.txt;C:\Data\MSBuildExamples\Fundamentals\src\thre
  e.txt;C:\Data\MSBuildExamples\Fundamentals\src\two.txt
  Removing from to item
  SrcFiles: C:\Data\MSBuildExamples\Fundamentals\src\four.txt;C:\Data\MSBuildEx
  amples\Fundamentals\src\one.txt;C:\Data\MSBuildExamples\Fundamentals\src\thre
  e.txt;C:\Data\MSBuildExamples\Fundamentals\src\two.txt
Done Building Project "C:\Data\MSBuildExamples\Fundamentals\Dynamic05.proj" (Bu
ild target(s)).


Build succeeded.
    0 Warning(s)
    0 Error(s)
```

FIGURE 3-5 Demonstration of removing values from items

The results here are pretty straightforward; several files were removed from the SrcFiles after the *ItemGroup* element was processed by the MSBuild engine. We will now move on to cover how dynamic properties and items are handled in MSBuild 2.0, which are all still valid methods in MSBuild 3.5.

Dynamic Properties and Items: MSBuild 2.0

If you are using MSBuild 2.0, you will have to create dynamic values with either the CreateProperty or CreateItem task. In MSBuild 3.5 you can continue to use these, but the previously discussed options are preferred. The CreateProperty task has one key property, Value, that you will use to create the properties. In MSBuild 3.5 there is another property, ValueSetByTask, which is created for a very specific and uncommon use and will not be discussed here. You will use the Value property to pass a value into the task. You will also use the Value property to assign the value to a property using the *Output* element. Take a look at the following Dynamic01.proj file to see an example of this.

```
<Project xmlns="http://schemas.microsoft.com/developer/msbuild/2003"
         DefaultTargets="All">

  <PropertyGroup>
    <Configuration>Debug</Configuration>
  </PropertyGroup>
```

```
  <Target Name="PrintConfig">
    <Message Text="Config: $(Configuration)" />
  </Target>

  <Target Name="PrintConfig2">

    <CreateProperty Value="Release">
      <Output PropertyName="Configuration" TaskParameter="Value" />
    </CreateProperty>

    <Message Text="Config: $(Configuration)"/>
  </Target>

  <Target Name="All" DependsOnTargets="PrintConfig;PrintConfig2" />
</Project>
```

This sample builds on a previous example by inserting a new target, PrintConfig2. This target uses the CreateProperty to provide a new value for the Configuration property value. In this declaration, we provide the value Release to the task with the statement `<CreateProperty Value="Release">`. Then using the *Output* element we place this value into the Configuration property. Take a look at the result of this in Figure 3-6.

```
C:\Data\MSBuildExamples\Fundamentals>msbuild Dynamic01.proj /t:All /nologo
Build started 6/6/2008 11:22:59 AM.
Project "C:\Data\MSBuildExamples\Fundamentals\Dynamic01.proj" on node 0 (All ta
rget(s)).
  Config: Debug
PrintConfig2:
  Config: Release
Done Building Project "C:\Data\MSBuildExamples\Fundamentals\Dynamic01.proj" (Al
l target(s)).


Build succeeded.
    0 Warning(s)
    0 Error(s)
```

FIGURE 3-6 Dynamic properties demonstration

In the preceding build script, we declare the Configuration property to have the value Debug, and this is the value that was printed in the PrintConfig target. Inside the PrintConfig2 target the CreateProperty task is used to override the existing value with Release. We can see that this works as expected: The value for the Configuration property was successfully overwritten.

If you are using MSBuild 3.5, feel free to use the easier-to-use syntax, but remember that if you need to use your scripts for use with MSBuild 2.0, these features are not available. You can use MSBuild 3.5 scripts and target .NET 2.0. To build assemblies for a specific framework version, you can specify the property TargetFrameworkVersion to be either v2.0, v3.0, or v3.5. There is also an attribute on the project element, ToolsVersion. This determines which version of .NET tools is used to build the project. The valid values are 2.0, 3.0, and 3.5. If this is set to 2.0, then only 2.0 assemblies can be created.

When declaring new dynamic properties, or modifying existing properties, you use the CreateProperty task; similarly, you can use the CreateItem task to create dynamic items. This task can also append to existing items, as well as creating new items.

When you create new static items they are **always** evaluated **before** any target has executed. The implication of this is that they will never contain any files that were created by your build process; this obviously is a limitation. The solution is dynamic items. The CreateItem task has three properties, which are summarized in Table 3-1.

TABLE 3-1 CreateItem Properties

Name	Description
Include	Describes the values that should be included in the item. This uses the same syntax as when creating static items. This parameter is the only **required** value.
Exclude	Describes values that should be excluded from the Include attribute. This uses the same syntax as the Include attribute.
AdditionalMetadata	Facilitates the addition of custom metadata to the created item. You should provide the values in the format <n>=<v> where <n> is the name of the metadata and <v> is its value. If you are passing more than one value, simply separate them with a semicolon.

When you use the CreateItem task you need to specify a value for the Include property. This is the same property that you will use with the *Output* element to place the value into the include attribute of a new or existing item in the build script. Now let's move on to see how this works.

To demonstrate dynamic items we will start with a simple example, as in the following Dynamic03.proj file.

```
<Project xmlns="http://schemas.microsoft.com/developer/msbuild/2003">

  <PropertyGroup>
    <SourceRoot>$(MSBuildProjectDirectory)\src\</SourceRoot>
  </PropertyGroup>

  <Target Name="Build">
    <Message Text="SrcFiles: @(SrcFiles)" />
    <Message Text="Creating item"/>
    <CreateItem Include="$(SourceRoot)**\*">
      <Output ItemName="SrcFiles" TaskParameter="Include" />
    </CreateItem>
    <Message Text="SrcFiles: @(SrcFiles)" />

  </Target>

</Project>
```

This simple project file does not declare any static items. In the Build target we output the value for the SrcFiles item, which doesn't exist, and then we create it and output it again. To see if this works, we can execute the Build target. You can see the results of this target in the Figure 3-7.

```
C:\Data\MSBuildExamples\Fundamentals>msbuild Dynamic03.proj /t:Build /nologo
Build started 6/8/2008 1:12:26 PM.
Project "C:\Data\MSBuildExamples\Fundamentals\Dynamic03.proj" on node 0 (Build
target(s)).
  SrcFiles:
  Creating item
  SrcFiles: C:\Data\MSBuildExamples\Fundamentals\src\four.txt;C:\Data\MSBuildEx
  amples\Fundamentals\src\one.txt;C:\Data\MSBuildExamples\Fundamentals\src\thre
  e.txt;C:\Data\MSBuildExamples\Fundamentals\src\two.txt;C:\Data\MSBuildExample
  s\Fundamentals\src\sub\sub_four.txt;C:\Data\MSBuildExamples\Fundamentals\src\
  sub\sub_one.txt;C:\Data\MSBuildExamples\Fundamentals\src\sub\sub_three.txt;C:
  \Data\MSBuildExamples\Fundamentals\src\sub\sub_two.txt
Done Building Project "C:\Data\MSBuildExamples\Fundamentals\Dynamic03.proj" (Bu
ild target(s)).

Build succeeded.
    0 Warning(s)
    0 Error(s)
```

FIGURE 3-7 Build target on Dynamic03.proj

As expected, the SrcFiles item was initially empty, but then it was indeed populated using the CreateItem task. Now that we have discussed how to create new items, we will take a look at appending to existing items.

When you use the CreateItem task, or the built-in syntax for MSBuild 3.5, it creates a new item only if the item is not already defined. If the item is already defined, then the new values are simply appended to the existing item. To see this at work, take a look at the following Dynamic04.proj file.

```
<Project xmlns="http://schemas.microsoft.com/developer/msbuild/2003">

  <PropertyGroup>
    <SourceRoot>$(MSBuildProjectDirectory)\src\</SourceRoot>
  </PropertyGroup>
  <ItemGroup>
    <SrcFiles Include="$(SourceRoot)one.txt" />
  </ItemGroup>


  <Target Name="Build">
    <Message Text="SrcFiles: @(SrcFiles)" />
    <Message Text="Appending to item" />
    <CreateItem Include="$(SourceRoot)two.txt">
      <Output ItemName="SrcFiles" TaskParameter="Include" />
    </CreateItem>
    <Message Text="SrcFiles: @(SrcFiles)" />

  </Target>

</Project>
```

In this file, I initially declared the SrcFiles item to include only the one.txt file, and then inside the Build target I used the CreateItem task to also include the two.txt file. I have used Message tasks to send the item to the attached loggers. To see the behavior of this, take a look at Figure 3-8.

```
C:\Data\MSBuildExamples\Fundamentals>msbuild Dynamic04.proj /t:Build /nologo
Build started 6/8/2008 1:56:34 PM.
Project "C:\Data\MSBuildExamples\Fundamentals\Dynamic04.proj" on node 0 (Build
target(s)).
  SrcFiles: C:\Data\MSBuildExamples\Fundamentals\src\one.txt
  Appending to item
  SrcFiles: C:\Data\MSBuildExamples\Fundamentals\src\one.txt;C:\Data\MSBuildExa
  mples\Fundamentals\src\two.txt
Done Building Project "C:\Data\MSBuildExamples\Fundamentals\Dynamic04.proj" (Bu
ild target(s)).


Build succeeded.
    0 Warning(s)
    0 Error(s)
```

FIGURE 3-8 Build target on Dynamic04.proj

As expected, the SrcFiles initially printed with only one file, and then the two.txt file was appended to it. To demonstrate the usage of the AdditionalMetadata parameter, take a look at the contents of the following Dynamic06.proj file.

```
<Project xmlns="http://schemas.microsoft.com/developer/msbuild/2003">
  <Target Name="Demo">
    <CreateItem Include="proj1.proj"
                AdditionalMetadata="Type=demo">
      <Output ItemName="Projects" TaskParameter="Include"/>
    </CreateItem>
    <CreateItem Include="proj2.proj"
                AdditionalMetadata="Type=sample">
      <Output ItemName="Projects" TaskParameter="Include"/>
    </CreateItem>
    <CreateItem Include="proj3.proj"
                AdditionalMetadata="Type=reference">
      <Output ItemName="Projects" TaskParameter="Include"/>
    </CreateItem>

    <Message Text="Projects: %(Projects.Identity) %(Projects.Type)"/>
  </Target>

</Project>
```

In the Demo target, a new Item type, Projects, is created and populated with three values; proj1.proj, proj2.proj, and proj3.proj. Each of these values has an associated additional metadata value, Type, assigned as well. An additional metadata value is associated with each of these values, which is the Type metadata. Now that we have covered dynamic properties and items, let's discuss how to include other files into your build process.

Property and Item Evaluation

When the MSBuild engine begins to process a build file, it is evaluated in a top-down fashion in a multi-pass manner. These passes are described in order in the following list.

0. Load all environment and global properties
1. Evaluate properties and imports processing imports as encountered
2. Evaluate item definitions
3. Evaluate items

4. Evaluate using tasks
5. Start build and reading targets

The first step is numbered 0 because it doesn't pertain to processing the file but is important in its evaluation. The first pass (numbered 1) is to populate all static properties and to process all import statements. As an import statement is encountered the contents of the import file are duplicated inline into the current project file. When an import is encountered, the current directory is temporarily set to the directory where the imported file resides, for use when processing imports found within the imported file. This affects only during the processing of the import statement. This is performed to ensure that import elements are processed correctly. For relative paths in items, the directory of the invoked MSBuild file is always used. This current directory is not maintained while any targets in the imported files are executed. We will discuss the directory issue later in this chapter. We will first take a look at properties and items.

In this section, we will focus on the process in which properties and items are populated. Then in the next section we will take a look at importing external files. As stated previously, MSBuild will process your file in multiple passes. The first pass is to process all imports and properties. These items are evaluated as they are encountered. Following this, items are evaluated. You should note that if you create a property that references an item, the value of the property is evaluated when it is used. What this means is that at the time you reference the property, the item reference is evaluated and expanded. So if the item changes, so can the property. To start our discussion of property and item evaluation, we will work our way through a very simple case. Take a look at the following Eval01.proj file.

```
<Project
  xmlns="http://schemas.microsoft.com/developer/msbuild/2003"
  DefaultTargets="PrintInfo">

  <PropertyGroup>
    <PropOne>one</PropOne>
    <PropTwo>$(PropThree)</PropTwo>
    <PropThree>three</PropThree>
    <PropFour>$(PropThree)</PropFour>
  </PropertyGroup>

  <Target Name="PrintInfo">
    <Message Text="PropOne: $(PropOne)" />
    <Message Text="PropTwo: $(PropTwo)" />
    <Message Text="PropThree: $(PropThree)" />
    <Message Text="PropFour: $(PropFour)" />
  </Target>
</Project>
```

Since all of these properties do not depend on items, we would expect all of them to be evaluated at the same time from top to bottom. Two properties in this file, which are in bold above, depend on the value of PropThree. One of the properties, PropTwo, occurs before PropThree, and the other, PropFour, occurs after PropThree. In the only target, PrintInfo, we simply print the values for each of these four properties. This printout is shown in Figure 3-9.

```
C:\Data\MSBuildExamples\Fundamentals>msbuild Eval01.proj /t:PrintInfo /nologo
Build started 6/11/2008 12:38:35 AM.
Project "C:\Data\MSBuildExamples\Fundamentals\Eval01.proj" on node 0 (PrintInfo
 target(s)).
  PropOne: one
  PropTwo:
  PropThree: three
  PropFour: three
Done Building Project "C:\Data\MSBuildExamples\Fundamentals\Eval01.proj" (Print
Info target(s)).

Build succeeded.
    0 Warning(s)
    0 Error(s)
```

FIGURE 3-9 PrintInfo target on Eval01.proj

In the result shown here, take note of two things. The first noticeable item is that PropTwo doesn't have a value; this is because PropThree did not have a value when it was populated. The other significant observation here is that PropFour was successfully populated with the value from PropThree. This is because the declaration of PropFour occurs after the definition for PropThree. Now let's take a look at the same example, using items instead of properties. The following contents are taken from the Eval02.proj file.

```
<Project
  xmlns="http://schemas.microsoft.com/developer/msbuild/2003"
  DefaultTargets="PrintInfo">

  <ItemGroup>
    <ItemOne Include="One" />
    <ItemTwo Include="@(ItemThree)" />
    <ItemThree Include="Three" />
    <ItemFour Include="@(ItemThree)" />
  </ItemGroup>

  <Target Name="PrintInfo">
    <Message Text="ItemOne: @(ItemOne)" />
    <Message Text="ItemTwo: @(ItemTwo)" />
    <Message Text="ItemThree: @(ItemThree)" />
    <Message Text="ItemFour: @(ItemFour)" />
  </Target>
</Project>
```

This example simply replaced all the properties in the previous file with items. Since they are all items, they will be evaluated in a similar manner as the properties were in the previous example. The output, as you might expect, is the same as the previous one as well, so it is not listed a second time. Instead, we will look at properties and items together.

For a slightly more interesting example, we will take a look at what happens when we introduce properties and items together. You will find the contents of a new example in the following Eval03.proj file. As you look at this, try to guess what the output of the PrintInfo target will be for this file.

```
<Project
  xmlns="http://schemas.microsoft.com/developer/msbuild/2003"
  DefaultTargets="PrintInfo">

  <PropertyGroup>
    <OutputPathCopy>$(OutputPath)</OutputPathCopy>
  </PropertyGroup>
```

```
  <ItemGroup>
    <OutputPathItem Include="$(OutputPath)" />
  </ItemGroup>

  <PropertyGroup>
    <Configuration>Debug</Configuration>
    <OutputPath>bin\$(Configuration)\</OutputPath>
  </PropertyGroup>

  <Target Name="PrintInfo">
    <Message Text="Configuration: $(Configuration)" />
    <Message Text="OutputPath: $(OutputPath)"/>
    <Message Text="OutputPathCopy: $(OutputPathCopy)" />
    <Message Text="OutputPathItem: @(OutputPathItem)" />
  </Target>

</Project>
```

The two important elements in the project file are the first property and item declared, the OutputPathCopy and OutputPathItem respectively. Both of these are declared before the property on which both depend. That property is the OutputPath property. In the PrintInfo target, all the properties and the single item are printed out. You will find the results of that target in Figure 3-10.

```
C:\Data\MSBuildExamples\Fundamentals>msbuild Eval03.proj /t:PrintInfo /nologo
Build started 6/11/2008 1:26:51 AM.
Project "C:\Data\MSBuildExamples\Fundamentals\Eval03.proj" on node 0 (PrintInfo
 target(s)).
  Configuration: Debug
  OutputPath: bin\Debug\
  OutputPathCopy:
  OutputPathItem: bin\Debug\
Done Building Project "C:\Data\MSBuildExamples\Fundamentals\Eval03.proj" (Print
Info target(s)).


Build succeeded.
    0 Warning(s)
    0 Error(s)
```

FIGURE 3-10 PrintInfo result on Eval03.proj

As mentioned previously, the interesting pieces of this are the OutputPathCopy property and the OutputPathItem item. If you take a look at the preceding figure, you can see that the value was placed into the OutputPathItem but not into the OutputPathCopy. This is because the item's final value was evaluated after the OutputPath property was declared. This is because the OutputPath property doesn't depend on an item. This section should have given you a good idea of how properties and items are evaluated by MSBuild. We'll now discuss how you can import other files.

Importing Files

MSBuild natively supports importing project files or targets. In fact, this is how Visual Studio builds your projects. In this section, we will see how this works and how you can take advantage of it in your build process. To reuse the contents of other files you must use the *Import* element. This element must be placed directly inside the *Project* element, at the same level as a Target. You specify the file that is to be imported by using the *Project* attribute. The only other attribute that can be placed on the *Import* element is the *Condition* attribute, as with most other MSBuild elements. These are the only two attributes that can be specified for the Import element. If you take a look at any C# project created by Visual Studio you will find the following declaration:

```
<Import Project="$(MSBuildToolsPath)\Microsoft.CSharp.targets" />
```

This imports the Microsoft.CSharp.targets file; the reserved property MSBuildToolsPath is used to resolve the full path to this file. This file is created by Microsoft to fully describe the build process for C# projects. Other managed projects have their own build scripts that are imported into their own project files. The Microsoft.CSharp.targets file, like Microsoft.VisualBasic.targets (used for VB.NET projects), describes all the steps to build the project while the actual project file describes what is being built. These files then import the shared file Microsoft.Common.targets, which contains the common steps to build managed projects. This explains why there is not a single target in project files generated by Visual Studio. All the targets required to build managed projects are imported from another file. We will now move on to discuss how to import external files.

When MSBuild processes an import statement, the current working directory is set to the directory of the imported project file. This is necessary to correctly resolve the location of paths declared in import elements or inside the *UsingTask* element. In addition, the imported file is then expanded in line at the location where the *Import* element occurs. This can be visualized by the image shown in Figure 3-11.

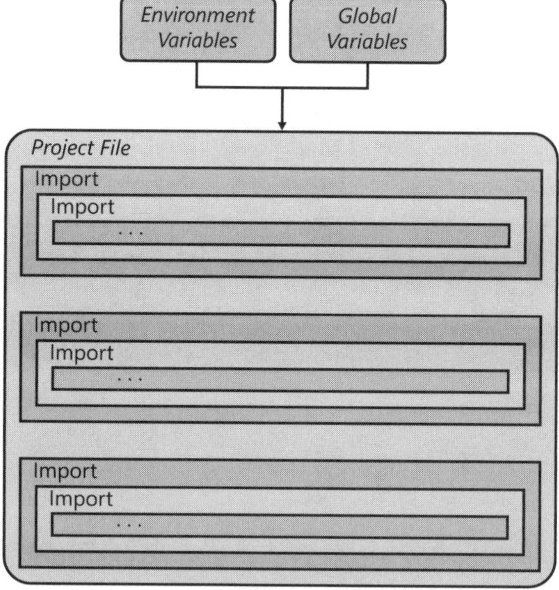

FIGURE 3-11 Project file import visualization

When the MSBuild engine processes a build file, it builds a representation of it in memory. When files are imported, the in-memory representation is made to include the contents of the imported file. We will now take a look at how Visual Studio behaves in building your managed projects by reviewing the contents of the following two MSBuild files, Import01.proj and Import01.targets.

```
<!-- Import01.proj -->
<Project xmlns="http://schemas.microsoft.com/developer/msbuild/2003"
         DefaultTargets="All">

  <PropertyGroup>
    <SourceRoot>$(MSBuildProjectDirectory)\src\</SourceRoot>
    <Configuration>Debug</Configuration>
  </PropertyGroup>
  <ItemGroup>
    <SourceFiles Include="$(SourceRoot)\*" />
  </ItemGroup>

  <Import Project="$(MSBuildProjectDirectory)\Import01.targets" />

  <Target Name="PrintOutputPath">
    <Message Text="OutputPath: $(OutputPath)" />
    <Message Text="MSBuildProjectFile: $(MSBuildProjectFile)" />
  </Target>
  <Target Name="All"
          DependsOnTargets="PrintInfo;PrintOutputPath" />
</Project>

<!--  Import01.targets -->
<Project xmlns="http://schemas.microsoft.com/developer/msbuild/2003">

  <Target Name="PrintInfo">
    <Message Text="SourceRoot: $(SourceRoot)" />
    <Message Text="Configuration: $(Configuration)" />
    <Message Text="SourceFiles: @(SourceFiles)" />
  </Target>

  <PropertyGroup>
    <OutputPath>bin\$(Configuration)\</OutputPath>
  </PropertyGroup>

</Project>
```

In this example, the Import01.proj imports the Import01.targets file; the import statement has been highlighted here. This is a simplified view of how managed projects are built. With managed projects, the project file that is generated by Visual Studio defines all the properties and items to be built, and an imported file defines how to build those values. So in this example, Imports01.proj (project file) represents the project file created by Visual Studio and the Import01.targets (targets file) represents the build file that is imported by those generated projects, based on the language this file changes. Back to the example, the project file defines a few properties as well as an item. Along with these, the target PrintOutputPath is defined, which prints out the value for the OutputPath, which is defined in the targets file. The targets file defines the aforementioned property and defines a target, PrintInfo, which prints out the values for those items defined in the project file. I will execute both targets, PrintInfo and PrintOutputPath, by executing the All target. The results of this are shown in Figure 3-12.

```
C:\Data\MSBuildExamples\Fundamentals>msbuild Import01.proj /t:All /nologo
Build started 6/15/2008 10:33:48 PM.
Project "C:\Data\MSBuildExamples\Fundamentals\Import01.proj" on node 0 (All tar
get(s)).
  SourceRoot: C:\Data\MSBuildExamples\Fundamentals\src\
  Configuration: Debug
  SourceFiles: C:\Data\MSBuildExamples\Fundamentals\src\\four.txt;C:\Data\MSBui
  ldExamples\Fundamentals\src\\one.txt;C:\Data\MSBuildExamples\Fundamentals\src
  \\three.txt;C:\Data\MSBuildExamples\Fundamentals\src\\two.txt
PrintOutputPath:
  OutputPath: bin\Debug\
  MSBuildProjectFile: Import01.proj
Done Building Project "C:\Data\MSBuildExamples\Fundamentals\Import01.proj" (All
 target(s)).


Build succeeded.
    0 Warning(s)
    0 Error(s)
```

FIGURE 3-12 Import01.proj results

Here are some things to note:

1. All items and properties defined in Imports01.proj **before** the *Import* element are available to Import01.targets.
2. All items and properties defined in Imports01.targets are available to Import01.proj **after** the *Import* element.
3. All properties and targets are defined from top to bottom, and the last definition that occurs is the value that persists.
4. Targets are executed after all items, properties, and imports are evaluated.

Because of the first item in the previous list, the target PrintInfo successfully was able to print out the values for the properties and items in Import01.proj. Because of second item in the previous list, the target PrintOutputPath was able to get the value for the OutputPath that was defined in Import01.targets. The third point was not demonstrated here, but it is important to understand it. Any file can define any property except reserved properties, and any target it desires. Because a property and targets can have only one definition, the last definition encountered is the value that will be used to build the project. The last point listed, that targets begin execution after all static items and properties are processed, is very important as well. By the time any target is executed, the MSBuild engine has already completed creating its in-memory representation of the build script. This means that when a target executes, it has no connection back to the file that contains it. It could have been defined in any file that was imported.

We will now examine another set of files that will help us further understand how build files behave when importing other files. This example will be demonstrated by two new files,

Import01.proj and Import02.targets. In this example, the Import02.targets file is stored in a subfolder named Import. The following sample shows the complete definition of both of these files.

```
<!-- Import02.proj -->
<Project xmlns="http://schemas.microsoft.com/developer/msbuild/2003"
         DefaultTargets="All">

  <Target Name="PrintPath">
    <Message Text="MSBuildProjectFullPath: $(MSBuildProjectFullPath)" />
  </Target>

  <Import Project="Import\Import02.targets" />

  <Target Name="All"
          DependsOnTargets="PrintPath;PrintPathImport;PrintCompile" />
</Project>

<!-- Import02.targets -->
<Project xmlns="http://schemas.microsoft.com/developer/msbuild/2003">

  <ItemGroup>
    <Compile Include="Class1.cs" />
  </ItemGroup>

  <Target Name="PrintPathImport">
    <Message Text="MSBuildProjectFullPath: $(MSBuildProjectFullPath)" />
  </Target>

  <Target Name="PrintCompile">
    <Message Text="Compile: @(Compile)" />
    <Message Text="Compile.Fullpath: @(Compile->'%(Fullpath)','%0a%0d')" />
  </Target>

</Project>
```

Both these files contain a target that prints the value of the MSBuildProjectFullPath reserved property. This is to demonstrate the fact that all the properties and items, including built-in properties, have defined values before those targets execute. Also in the imported file, an item is defined Compile, which includes a single file Class1.cs. This file resides in the same folder as the Import02.targets. Can you guess what the results of the `PrintCompile` target would be? If you execute all these targets, the results would be what are shown in Figure 3-13.

```
C:\Data\MSBuildExamples\Fundamentals>msbuild Import02.proj /t:All /nologo
Build started 6/15/2008 11:30:48 PM.
Project "C:\Data\MSBuildExamples\Fundamentals\Import02.proj" on node 0 (All tar
get(s)).
  MSBuildProjectFullPath: C:\Data\MSBuildExamples\Fundamentals\Import02.proj
PrintPathImport:
  MSBuildProjectFullPath: C:\Data\MSBuildExamples\Fundamentals\Import02.proj
PrintCompile:
  Compile: Class1.cs
  Compile.Fullpath: C:\Data\MSBuildExamples\Fundamentals\Class1.cs
Done Building Project "C:\Data\MSBuildExamples\Fundamentals\Import02.proj" (All
 target(s)).


Build succeeded.
    0 Warning(s)
    0 Error(s)
```

FIGURE 3-13 Import02.proj result

If you take a look at the results shown in Figure 3-12, you can see that the value for the MSBuildProjectFullPath property evaluates to the same value regardless of the file that contains the target that prints it. This exemplifies the fact that the file that contains a target has no effect on the values for properties and items. Currently there is **no** property like $(MSBuildFile) that would evaluate to the file that the property is actually expanded in. Currently it is only possible to get the outer project file name.

The imported file also contains another target, PrintCompile, which prints out the value for the Compile item defined in that file. The file that is included in the item Compile is the Class1.cs file. This file resides in the same folder as the Import folder. If you look at the Import02.targets file it is obvious that the Compile item is attempting to include that Class1.cs file. The printed value for that path to that file does not place it in the Import folder. Instead it references the folder of the outermost file, the Import02.proj file. If an imported file declares items to files, it will always be defined relative to the file that the MSBuild process starts with. If you need to declare items in files that will be imported, they should be defined using properties that are defined in the importing file. Now we have covered how to import external files in some detail. Throughout the remainder of this text we will be using this technique. We'll now move on to discuss how you can extend the build process for managed projects.

Extending the Build Process

MSBuild aims to expose the build process and to allow users to completely customize the process. MSBuild does indeed achieve both of these goals, and does a good job of it! We will now take a close look at that build process and see how it can be extended.

When you create a managed project using Visual Studio, toward the bottom of the project file you will find an import statement such as the following one, which was taken from a C# project.

```
<Import Project="$(MSBuildToolsPath)\Microsoft.CSharp.targets" />
```

This statement imports another known file that defines **how** C# projects are built. This project file is shipped along with MSBuild, which is delivered as a part of the .NET Framework. The contents of the project files created by Visual Studio define only properties and items; there are no targets included in that file. All the targets for building managed projects are contained in those shared files provided with MSBuild. If you need to extend the build process you can do so by modifying project file itself. The three most common ways to extend the build process for managed projects are:

1. PreBuildEvent and PostBuildEvent
2. Override BeforeBuild, AfterBuild, and similar targets
3. Target injection

These types of extensions are listed in order of ease of use. In versions of Visual Studio prior to 2005 the only way to extend the build process was to define a command, such as a batch file or external program, that would be executed before or after the build was completed. These are the pre-build event and post-build event respectively. These "events" are implemented using plain MSBuild properties and targets; there is no event construct in MSBuild files. These build events are still supported in current versions of Visual Studio, for backward compatibility and because the Visual Studio UI already supports this concept. You can enter these commands in Visual Studio on the projects' properties page, in the build tab. A screen shot is shown in Figure 3-14.

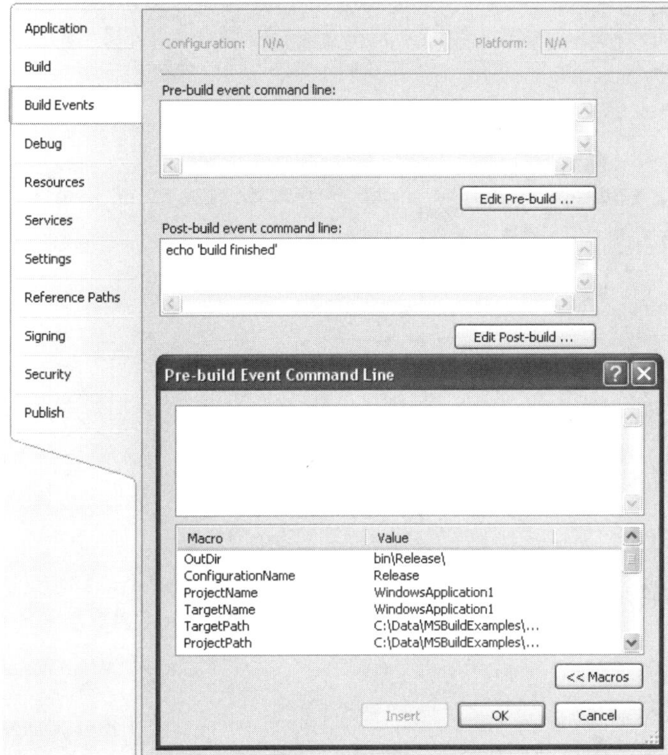

FIGURE 3-14 Build events in Visual Studio

From the UI shown in Figure 3-14, you can insert a set of commands that will be executed before or after the build executes. This is captured in MSBuild simply as a property; the two properties that are used to capture these values are PreBuildEvent and PostBuildEvent. These properties will be defined in the project file itself. This method is the simplest method to extend the build process, but also the least powerful. I would suggest avoiding this technique. A better approach would be one of the two other MSBuild techniques. We will now discuss the second option.

After the PreBuildEvent and PostBuildEvent properties, the next option is to override existing targets that were created as extension points. Previously I showed that the C# projects import a project file named Microsoft.CSharp.targets; other managed languages define their own shared file. All of these files will then import another file, Microsoft.Common.targets. This file, which contains all the common elements in building managed projects, defines many targets that were created simply to be overridden. For example, if you take a look at a project file created by Visual Studio you will see a comment like the following.

```
<!-- To modify your build process, add your task inside one of
     the targets below and uncomment it.
     Other similar extension points exist,
     see Microsoft.Common.targets.
<Target Name="BeforeBuild">
</Target>
<Target Name="AfterBuild">
</Target>
-->
```

These and other targets are defined as empty targets in the `Microsoft.Common.targets` file. The following list shows 14 such targets:

- BeforeBuild
- AfterBuild
- BeforeRebuild
- AfterRebuild
- BeforeResolveReferences
- AfterResolveReferences
- BeforeResGen
- AfterResGen
- BeforeCompile
- AfterCompile
- BeforeClean
- AfterClean
- BeforePublish
- AfterPublish

All of these targets are simply extension points and will be executed at the appropriate time. If you define a target with the same name **after** the import element, then your target will override the default empty target. For example, the following snippet was taken from the sample WindowsApplication1.csproj.

```
<Project DefaultTargets="Build"
xmlns="http://schemas.microsoft.com/developer/msbuild/2003" ToolsVersion="3.5">
   ...

  <Import Project="$(MSBuildToolsPath)\Microsoft.CSharp.targets" />
<!-- To modify your build process, add your task inside one of
     the targets below and uncomment it.
     Other similar extension points exist,
     see Microsoft.Common.targets.
<Target Name="BeforeBuild">
</Target>
<Target Name="AfterBuild">
</Target>
-->
  <Target Name="AfterBuild">
    <Message Text="Build has completed!" Importance="high" />
  </Target>

  ...

</Project>
```

In the preceding snippet, the AfterBuild target was defined to invoke the Message task with the statement "Build has completed!" If you build this you will see the message printed to the console after the project has been built. If you do not see the message when you are building in Visual Studio, you may need to increase the verbosity used by Visual Studio. This is defined in the Options dialog under the Project and Solutions->Build and Run node. Now that we have seen this method, we'll take a look at the last method.

The option just described is a great way to extend the build process, and I highly recommend using it. The only problem with this technique is that only one AfterBuild, or any of those targets listed previously, can be defined at once. Because of this, if two or more imports are processed that define the same target, then the previous definition will be overridden. So if you are creating reusable build scripts, this technique is not suitable. Instead, the target injection technique must be used.

Target injection is the most flexible and the best choice when extending the build process. It is also the least intuitive and most difficult method as well. With that being said, it is pretty easy once you see how it works. If you take a look at the Microsoft.Common.targets, the file that is at the core of building managed projects, you will see targets defined like the one that follows.

```
<Target
    Name="Build"
    Condition=" '$(_InvalidConfigurationWarning)' != 'true' "
    DependsOnTargets="$(BuildDependsOn)"
    Outputs="$(TargetPath)" />
```

If you take a look at this target you will quickly notice that it doesn't actually do anything—it's an empty target. You might wonder, what is the purpose of creating a target that doesn't do anything? It is true that this target itself doesn't perform any work. What it does do is specify a set of targets that must be executed before it is. These targets are placed in the *DependsOnTargets* attribute as $(BuildDependsOn). Immediately above the declaration for the Build target is the following property declaration.

```
<PropertyGroup>
    <BuildDependsOn>
        BeforeBuild;
        CoreBuild;
        AfterBuild
    </BuildDependsOn>
</PropertyGroup>
```

This specifies the value for the BuildDependsOn property, which is a list of targets that must be executed before the Build target is allowed to execute. It is no coincidence that these target names are placed into a property instead of declared inline in the Target element. The reason they were placed inside a property was as an extension point. Because they are placed in a property, you can override the value, thereby extending the build process. We will now take a look at how we can inject a target inside the build process. Using the Build target as an example. When you utilize these properties, odds are that you don't want to simply override the value for BuildDependsOn, but add to it. From the samples I have created a Windows Forms project named WindowsApplication1.csproj. Inside that project file you will find the following statement:

```
<Project DefaultTargets="Build"
         xmlns="http://schemas.microsoft.com/developer/msbuild/2003"
         ToolsVersion="3.5">
...

  <Import Project="$(MSBuildToolsPath)\Microsoft.CSharp.targets" />

  <PropertyGroup>
    <BuildDependsOn>
      $(BuildDependsOn);
      CustomAfterBuild
    </BuildDependsOn>
  </PropertyGroup>

  <Target Name="CustomAfterBuild">
    <Message Text="Inside CustomAfterBuild target"
             Importance="high" />
  </Target>
...
</Project>
```

In the preceding snippet, you see that the Microsoft.CSharp.targets file is imported, which then imports Microsoft.Common.targets. The Microsoft.Common.targets file defines the BuildDependsOn property, so it is available after that import statement. **After** the *Import* element, you can see that the BuildDependsOn property was redeclared. It is very important that this declaration comes after the *Import* element. If you declared a value for

BuildDependsOn before the *Import* element, then it would simply be overwritten in the imported file. As stated previously in this chapter, that last definition for a property is the one that is used.

Looking back at the declaration for BuildDependsOn just shown, you can see that the new value for the property is declared using the value for the property itself! If you append to a dependency property by referencing the current value, you do not have to worry if the current value is empty. In this case the resulting dependency property will have extra semi-colons which is not a problem. What this notation does is allow you to take an existing property and append, or prepend, to it. In this case we have appended the target CustomAfterBuild to the BuildDependsOn property. When MSBuild begins to process the Build target, it will first execute all targets in the TargetDependsOn list, and therefore execute the list of targets we specified. We can see if this works by simply building the WindowsApplication1.csproj file. The definition for the CustomAfterBuild target Follows. The results of the command `msbuild.exe WindowsApplication1.csproj` are shown in Figure 3-15.

```
C:\Data\MSBuildExamples\WindowsApplication1>msbuild WindowsApplication1.csproj /
nologo
Build started 6/16/2008 9:32:40 PM.
Project "C:\Data\MSBuildExamples\WindowsApplication1\WindowsApplication1.csproj
" on node 0 (default targets).
  No resources are out of date with respect to their source files. Skipping res
  ource generation.
CoreCompile:
Skipping target "CoreCompile" because all output files are up-to-date with resp
ect to the input files.
_CopyAppConfigFile:
Skipping target "_CopyAppConfigFile" because all output files are up-to-date wi
th respect to the input files.
CopyFilesToOutputDirectory:
  WindowsApplication1 -> C:\Data\MSBuildExamples\WindowsApplication1\bin\Debug\
  WindowsApplication1.exe
PostBuildEvent:
  'build finished'
AfterBuild:
  Build has completed!
CustomAfterBuild:
  Inside CustomAfterBuild target
```

FIGURE 3-15 Target Injection on Build

From the results, you can see that we were able to successfully inject our target into this process. After looking through the Microsoft.Common.targets file, I was able to find several dependency properties that are available for your use. Those are listed in Table 3-2, in the order in which they are defined in that file starting from the top.

TABLE 3-2 Predefined Target Dependency Properties

BuildDependsOn	CreateSatelliteAssembliesDependsOn
CoreBuildDependsOn	PrepareForRunDependsOn
RebuildDependsOn	UnmanagedRegistrationDependsOn
RunDependsOn	CleanDependsOn
PrepareForBuildDependsOn	CoreCleanDependsOn
GetFrameworkPathsDependsOn	PostBuildEventDependsOn
PreBuildEventDependsOn	PublishDependsOn
UnmanagedUnregistrationDependsOn	PublishOnlyDependsOn

TABLE 3-2 Predefined Target Dependency Properties

BuildDependsOn	CreateSatelliteAssembliesDependsOn
ResolveReferencesDependsOn	PublishBuildDependsOn
GetRedistListsDependsOn	BuiltProjectOutputGroupDependsOn
ResolveAssemblyReferencesDependsOn	DebugSymbolsProjectOutputGroupDependsOn
PrepareResourcesDependsOn	DocumentationProjectOutputGroupDependsOn
PrepareResourceNamesDependsOn	SatelliteDllsProjectOutputGroupDependsOn
ResGenDependsOn	SourceFilesProjectOutputGroupDependsOn
CoreResGenDependsOn	ContentFilesProjectOutputGroupDependsOn
CompileLicxFilesDependsOn	SGenFilesOutputGroupDependsOn
CompileDependsOn	

As you can see, there are many places where you can place customizations to the build process in an unobtrusive, safe, and supported manner. The names of these properties are for the most part self-explanatory. I will not expand on these here but if you need more information you should go directly to the source, the Microsoft.Common.targets file. You should also know that the files Microsoft.CSharp.targets and other files for managed languages do define a few other dependency properties that can be used. They will not be listed here. Throughout this text we will be using this procedure, so you will become familiar with it.

In this and the previous chapter, a lot of material was covered, and I don't expect you to master it by simply reading these chapters. Mastery can be achieved only by using these ideas in your own MSBuild scripts. The remainder of the book will use these chapters as a basis on which to craft your knowledge of MSBuild. In these two chapters, we have covered 90 percent of what you need to know to make MSBuild do what you need 90 percent of the time. The rest of the material in the book will make up for the gaps that were left out here, and define how you customize your build process.

Part II
Customizing MSBuild

In this part:

Chapter 4

Custom Tasks

MSBuild is shipped with many built-in tasks, and there are many tasks that are available by third parties. Even with these there may be times where you need to write your own task. In this chapter, we will take a look at how custom tasks are created and used. In the next chapter, we will cover custom loggers. Before you create a new task you should make sure that you cannot reuse an already existing task to fulfill your needs. Here is a list of open source task repositories where you can find MSBuild tasks:

- MSBuild Extension Pack *http://www.codeplex.com/MSBuildExtensionPack*
- Microsoft SDC Tasks *http://www.codeplex.com/sdctasks*
- MSBuild Community Tasks *http://msbuildtasks.tigris.org*

Custom tasks allow you to write .NET code that can be used in your build process. Custom tasks have all the same abilities that the built-in tasks have. Until this chapter we have created only MSBuild project files; in this chapter we will focus primarily on how your tasks can be written to be effectively used with MSBuild.

Custom Task Requirements

Essentially the only requirement of a custom task is to implement the Microsoft.Build.Framework.ITask interface. This interface contains two properties and one method. The class diagram for that interface is shown in Figure 4-1.

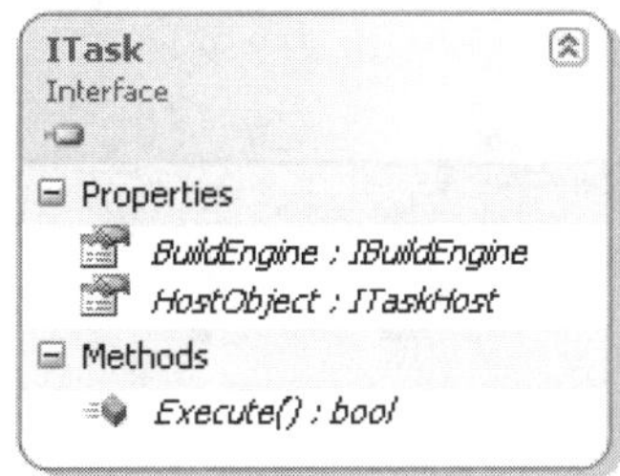

FIGURE 4-1 ITask interface

The two properties BuildEngine and HostObject will be set by the MSBuild engine itself. These will be set when the task is constructed by the MSBuild engine. The contract for the *Execute* method is that if it returns true, then the task was a success; otherwise it is treated as a failure. Except in disastrous cases, such as running out of memory, the task should not throw an exception. If a problem occurs, it should log an error and then return false.

Creating Your First Task

As many other texts do, we will create a Hello World example. This simple example, which follows, was taken from the `HelloWorld.cs` file.

```
public class HelloWorld : ITask
{
    public IBuildEngine BuildEngine
    { get; set; }
    public ITaskHost HostObject
    { get; set; }

    public bool Execute()
    {
        // set up support for logging
        TaskLoggingHelper loggingHelper = new TaskLoggingHelper(this);
        loggingHelper.LogMessageFromText(
           "Hello MSBuild", MessageImportance.High);

        return true;
    }
}
```

In this first example, we have created a `HelloWorld` task that outputs the message *Hello MSBuild* to the loggers attached to MSBuild. This is achieved by using an instance of the *TaskLoggingHelper* class. In this case, we have directly implemented the `ITask` interface. The only piece that we are really interested in is the implementation of the *Execute* method. Despite this being pretty simple, I will show you an even simpler way to create this task, but we will first take a look at how we can integrate this task into an MSBuild project file, HelloWorldExample.proj, which follows.

```
<Project
  xmlns="http://schemas.microsoft.com/developer/msbuild/2003"
  DefaultTargets="Demo">

  <UsingTask AssemblyFile="$(MSBuildProjectDirectory)\..\Examples.Tasks.dll"
             TaskName="HelloWorld" />

  <Target Name="Demo">
    <HelloWorld />
  </Target>
</Project>
```

When you create a new task you have to declare that you are going to use it. This is achieved by the *UsingTask* element. The *UsingTask* element has only a few possible attributes, which are summarized in Table 4-1.

TABLE 4-1 UsingTask Attributes

Name	Description
TaskName	The class name of the task that is to be used. If there is a naming conflict, this value should be specified using the full namespace. If there is a conflict, then unexpected results might occur. This is a required property.
AssemblyFile	Specifies the location of the assembly that contains the task to be loaded. This must be a full path. This will result in the assembly being loaded by the System.Reflection.Assembly.LoadFrom method. Either this attribute or `AssemblyName` must be used, but not both. Of the two, AssemblyFile is the most used parameter.
AssemblyName	Name of the assembly that contains the task to be loaded. Using this property will result in the assembly being loaded by the System.Reflection.Assembly.Load method. You would use this if your tasks assembly is in the GAC. If you are deploying a task assembly publicly, you generally should put it in the GAC.

In this example, the UsingTask references the Example.Tasks.dll in the parent directory. This is because the project file is placed in a folder in the output directory. This will be explained in more detail later in this chapter. After you have declared that you are going to reference the task, with *UsingTask* element, you are free to invoke the task inside any targets declared after that point. The preceding sample file shows a single target, Demo. This target executes the task with the statement `<HelloWorld />`. Since this task doesn't have any inputs or outputs we do not need to specify any attributes or children in the XML. This is all that is required to invoke this task. The result of this executing the Demo target from this build file is shown in Figure 4-2.

```
C:\Data\MSBuildExamples\Examples.Tasks\bin\Debug\Samples>msbuild HelloWorldExamp
le.proj /t:Demo /nologo
Build started 7/8/2008 1:11:43 AM.
Project "C:\Data\MSBuildExamples\Examples.Tasks\bin\Debug\Samples\HelloWorldExa
mple.proj" on node 0 (Demo target(s)).
  Hello MSBuild!!!!
Done Building Project "C:\Data\MSBuildExamples\Examples.Tasks\bin\Debug\Samples
\HelloWorldExample.proj" (Demo target(s)).


Build succeeded.
    0 Warning(s)
    0 Error(s)
```

FIGURE 4-2 HelloWorld.proj execution

As you can see from Figure 4-2, the Hello World message was successfully printed on the console.

Even though this example was pretty simple, it can be even simpler by using the classes *Microsoft.Build.Utilities.Task, Microsoft.Build.Utilities.ToolTask,* and *Microsoft.Build.Utilities .AppDomainIsolatedTask.* Typically, when you create a new task, you should extend one of these classes instead of implementing the interface yourself, unless you must extend another class. Table 4-2 shows a brief description that can help you decide which of these classes to extend.

TABLE 4-2 Common Task Abstract Classes

Class Name	When to Extend
Task	Most MSBuild tasks will extend this class. This class should be extended whenever your task does not wrap an executable.
ToolTask	Extend this class when you are creating a task that will wrap a call to an .exe file. It includes all the functionally of the *Task* class, because it derives from it, but adds support for running external programs.
AppDomainIsolatedTask	When you need your task to be loaded in its own app domain, then you should use this as your base class. A typical reason to derive from this class is if you need to use a task that is contained in an assembly that was created during the executing build process. Deriving from this class will mean that the task will be loaded in a new App Domain, which will be unloaded after you're done. It is uncommon to derive from this class.

When you extend one of these classes, all you have to do is implement the *Execute* method. The abstract class will create the required properties in the ITask interface. In the case of the Hello World example, we would pick the Task class to extend. We can create a new task, HelloWorld2. This new, simpler, implementation is shown as follows.

```
public class HelloWorld2 : Task
{
    public override bool Execute()
    {
        Log.LogMessageFromText("Hello MSBuild from Task!", MessageImportance.High);
        return true;
    }
}
```

In this new implementation, the only requirement is to implement the *Execute* method. By using one of these abstract classes we can focus on what the task is supposed to accomplish. Also, you may have noticed that logging the Hello World statement is different from the previous implementation. This is because those helper classes also define a property, Log, which is of the type Microsoft.Build.Utilities.TaskLoggingHelper, which makes logging much easier. Now that we have briefly described how to create simple MSBuild tasks, we will discuss how values can be passed into and out of MSBuild tasks. Later in this chapter, we'll discuss how to extend the *ToolTask* class.

Task Input/Output

When you create custom MSBuild tasks they will most likely need to accept some input and/or provide some output values. Inside your task these are implemented with normal .NET properties that may be decorated with attributes. Don't confuse these with MSBuild properties. We will first examine a very simple example and then move on to discuss more realistic tasks. Building on the HelloWorld2 task, I've created a new task, HelloWorld3, which accepts two input parameters. Those input parameters are FirstName and LastName. The definition of the HelloWorld3 task is shown as follows.

```
public class HelloWorld3 : Task
{
    [Required]
    public string FirstName
    { get; set; }

    public string LastName
    { get; set; }

    public override bool Execute()
    {
        Log.LogMessage(string.Format("Hello {0} {1}", FirstName, LastName));

        return true;
    }
}
```

As you can see, both of the properties here were defined as any other .NET property would be. You may have noticed that the FirstName property has a *Required* (Microsoft.Build.Framework.Required) attribute attached to it. As the name states, this is a property that is required to be set before the task is allowed to be executed. This is checked by MSBuild itself. If a user attempts to invoke a task without providing values for all required parameters, then the task will fail.

Any property that has a writeable property is available as an MSBuild input parameter. There are some limitations on the type, but we will discuss that later in this chapter. Now we can see how we can provide values to these custom input parameters from an MSBuild project file; see the following example, which is taken from HelloWorld3Example.proj.

```
<Project DefaultTargets="Demo"
         xmlns="http://schemas.microsoft.com/developer/msbuild/2003">
  <UsingTask AssemblyFile="$(MSBuildProjectDirectory)\..\Examples.Tasks.dll"
             TaskName="HelloWorld3" />

  <Target Name="Demo">
    <HelloWorld3 FirstName="Mike" LastName="Murphy" />
  </Target>
</Project>
```

When you provide values as input into an MSBuild task, you will always provide those values using XML attributes, where the attribute name is the name of the .NET property and the attribute value is the value that the .NET property should be set to. From this example, we can see that the *FirstName* and *LastName* attributes correspond to the names of the .NET properties that we created in the task previously. If you execute the Demo target in this MSBuild file, you would see the result shown in Figure 4-3.

```
C:\Data\MSBuildExamples\Examples.Tasks\bin\Debug\Samples>msbuild HelloWorld3Exam
ple.proj /nologo
Build started 7/10/2008 12:30:16 AM.
Project "C:\Data\MSBuildExamples\Examples.Tasks\bin\Debug\Samples\HelloWorld3Ex
ample.proj" on node 0 (default targets).
  Hello Mike Murphy
Done Building Project "C:\Data\MSBuildExamples\Examples.Tasks\bin\Debug\Samples
\HelloWorld3Example.proj" (default targets).


Build succeeded.
    0 Warning(s)
    0 Error(s)
```

FIGURE 4-3 HelloWorld3 example

As we expected, the values were successfully passed into that task and were then passed to the console logger. Now we can see how to pass a value from a task back to the calling MSBuild project file. Once again I've modified the previous task and created a new one, HelloWorld4, which exposes an output property named Message. The class is shown as follows:

```
public class HelloWorld4 : Task
{
    [Required]
    public string FirstName
    { get; set; }

    public string LastName
    { get; set; }

    [Output]
    public string Message
    { get; set; }

    public override bool Execute()
    {
        Message = string.Format("Fullname: {0} {1}", FirstName, LastName);
        Log.LogMessage(string.Format("Hello {0} {1}", FirstName, LastName));

        return true;
    }
}
```

Just like inputs, outputs are simply .NET properties. Output properties must be decorated with the *Microsoft.Build.Framework.Output* attribute. When you extract a value from a task you will always use an *Output* element as a child of the task node itself. An example of this is demonstrated in the following sample, HelloWorld4Example.proj.

```
<Project DefaultTargets="Demo"
         xmlns="http://schemas.microsoft.com/developer/msbuild/2003">
  <UsingTask AssemblyFile="$(MSBuildProjectDirectory)\..\Examples.Tasks.dll"
             TaskName="HelloWorld4" />

  <Target Name="Demo">
```

```
    <HelloWorld4 FirstName="Mike" LastName="Murphy">
      <Output PropertyName="PropFromTask" TaskParameter="Message" />
    </HelloWorld4>

    <Message Text ="From task: $(PropFromTask)" />

  </Target>
</Project>
```

If the task you are using has multiple outputs, then you can declare multiple *Output* elements. The *Output* element has three attributes, in addition to the *Condition* attribute, which are briefly outlined in Table 4-3.

TABLE 4-3 Output Element Attributes

Attribute	Description
TaskParameter	This is the name of the .NET property that you are accessing the value of. This is a required parameter.
PropertyName	The name of the MSBuild property in which the value should be placed. Either this or ItemName must be used, but not both.
ItemName	The name of the MSBuild item in which the value should be placed. Either this or PropertyName must be used, but not both.

In the HelloWorld4 example, we are outputting the value of the Message property on the task into an MSBuild property named PropFromTask. This is why we use the *PropertyName* attribute instead of *ItemName.* This syntax takes getting used to, but is easy to use after that. Now let's take a look at a more realistic task that performs some real work.

All of the custom tasks that we have discussed thus far were variations of the HelloWorld task. We will now take a look at a few tasks that are actually useful in your own build scripts. We will start with the GetDate task. This is a task that returns the current date in a specified format. This task is shown in the following code block.

```
public class GetDate : Task
{
    public string Format
    { get; set; }

    [Output]
    public string Date
    { get; private set; }

    public override bool Execute()
    {
        DateTime now = DateTime.Now;
        Date = now.ToString(Format, null);
        return true;
    }
}
```

This task defines an optional input parameter, Format. (This is an optional parameter because it is not decorated with the *Required* attribute.) A single output property is declared, named Date, which is a string representation of the time in which the task was invoked. We can see this used in the following GetDateExample.proj file.

```
<Project xmlns="http://schemas.microsoft.com/developer/msbuild/2003"
         DefaultTargets="Demo">

  <UsingTask AssemblyFile="$(MSBuildProjectDirectory)\..\Examples.Tasks.dll"
    TaskName="GetDate" />

  <Target Name="Demo">
    <GetDate>
      <Output PropertyName="DateUnformatted" TaskParameter="Date" />
    </GetDate>

    <GetDate Format="yyyyMMdd.hh.ss">
      <Output PropertyName="DateValue" TaskParameter="Date" />
    </GetDate>

    <PropertyGroup>
      <FolderName>$(MSBuildProjectName)_$(DateValue)</FolderName>
    </PropertyGroup>

    <Message Text="DateUnformatted value: $(DateUnformatted)" />
    <Message Text="DateValue value: $(DateValue)" />
    <Message Text="FolderName value: $(FolderName)" />
  </Target>

</Project>
```

In this example, we are invoking the `GetDate` task twice, once without specifying a format and the other with a format passed in. The values are stored in MSBuild properties named DateUnformatted and DateValue, and then these values are passed to the `Message` task. The result of this build file is shown in Figure 4-4.

```
C:\Data\MSBuildExamples\Examples.Tasks\bin\Debug\Samples>msbuild GetDateExample.
proj /nologo
Build started 7/10/2008 1:41:37 AM.
Project "C:\Data\MSBuildExamples\Examples.Tasks\bin\Debug\Samples\GetDateExampl
e.proj" on node 0 (default targets).
  DateUnformatted value: 7/10/2008 1:41:37 AM
  DateValue value: 20080710.01.37
  FolderName value: GetDateExample_20080710.01.37
Done Building Project "C:\Data\MSBuildExamples\Examples.Tasks\bin\Debug\Samples
\GetDateExample.proj" (default targets).


Build succeeded.
    0 Warning(s)
    0 Error(s)
```

FIGURE 4-4 GetDate example

In this demonstration, we have shown how we can pass values into and out of the task.

To recap, when you pass a value into a task it is always passed in as an attribute on the task's element. Output values will be exposed to the build script by using an *Output* element as a child of the *Task* element. We will now move on to discuss what types are supported.

Supported Task Input and Output Types

Task inputs and outputs are the only means by which a project file can communicate with a task. This is by design, so that it is easy to see what information is passed into and out of the task by reading the project file. When you create values that can be passed into and out of tasks, there are a variety of types that are supported. Since XML is the representation that all MSBuild scripts are stored in, all values must be able to be converted to and from a string. As mentioned in Chapter 2, "MSBuild Deep Dive, Part 1,"there are fundamentally two types of values that are supported by MSBuild: scalar values and vector values. For vector values an **array** of acceptable scalar types is allowed. Table 4-4 summarizes what types are supported to be passed through MSBuild tasks.

TABLE 4-4 Types Supported for MSBuild Inputs and Outputs

Type	Description
String	String values are simply passed back and forth directly, no conversion necessary.
ITaskItem	This interface (Microsoft.Build.Framework.ITaskItem) is a part of MSBuild itself. It is typically used when referencing files and for item value members. If an MSBuild task needs to deal with items as input or output, then they should be exposed by ITaskItem properties. It will allow you to pass items with metadata on them to the task; it also allows the task to set or modify metadata on the item and then return those items back into the build process.
Value types	MSBuild will allow you to pass value types back and forth from task to script. The conversion support is limited to subclasses of ITaskItem and those types that the *System.Convert.ChangeType* method is able to convert from and to strings. Those types are: bool, byte, char, DateTime, Decimal, Double, int, long, sbyte, short, Single, uint, ulong, ushort Arrays of these types are acceptable as well. When using the bool type, acceptable values include: "true", "false", "on", "off", "yes" and "no", and when used with the ! operator, such as "!true".

In the tasks that we have created thus far, we have shown only task inputs and outputs using string values. From the Value Types listed in Table 4-4, you can see that there are many other types of values that we can pass through into and out of tasks. When you create task properties of any supported type you don't have to worry about the conversion between string and the actual type. The MSBuild engine will take care of this automatically. The most interesting type listed in Table 4-4 is the ITaskItem type. This is shipped with MSBuild, in the *Microsoft.Build.Framework* assembly, and is heavily used in tasks. In the next task we will demonstrate using objects of this type.

The next sample we will discuss is the TempFile task. This task creates a temp file and returns its locations to the calling build script. The location value is passed as the property TempFilePath, which is declared as an ITaskItem. The class definition is shown as follows.

```
public class TempFile : Task
{
    [Output]
    public ITaskItem TempFilePath
```

```
    { get; private set; }

    public override bool Execute()
    {
        string path = System.IO.Path.GetTempFileName();

        TempFilePath = new TaskItem(path);
        return true;
    }
}
```

Inside the *Execute* method we get the full path to a new temporary file, and create a new TaskItem object that refers to it and set it to the TempFilePath property. The *TaskItem* class is the class that you should use when you have to create new objects that implement ITaskItem. The constructor being called defined is TaskItem(string itemSpec). The itemSpec (item specification) parameter is the representation of the value passed in the *Include* attribute in an MSBuild file. After the value for TempFilePath is set, the task returns true to indicate that the task completed without errors. You can see this task being used in the corresponding sample file, TempFileExample.proj, as follows:

```
<Project xmlns="http://schemas.microsoft.com/developer/msbuild/2003"
         DefaultTargets="Demo">

  <UsingTask AssemblyFile="$(MSBuildProjectDirectory)\..\Examples.Tasks.dll"
           TaskName="TempFile" />

  <Target Name="Demo">
    <TempFile>
      <Output ItemName="TestFile" TaskParameter="TempFilePath" />
    </TempFile>

    <Message Text="TestFile: @(TestFile)" />
    <Message Text="TestFile.Filename: @(TestFile->'%(Filename)')" />
    <Message Text="TestFile.Extension: @(TestFile->'%(Extension)')" />

  </Target>

</Project>
```

As with every custom task, we first declare that we are going to be using the task with a UsingTask statement. This makes the TempFile task available for use. In the example the value from the task is placed into an item named TestFile, then a few messages are sent to the logger. The output of the Demo target is shown in Figure 4-5.

As can be seen from this sample, the task successfully created a temp file and returned its path back to the calling MSBuild file. Since we place the value from the task into an item, we could retrieve values for metadata of that item as well. In the TempFile task the TempFilePath was declared as an ITaskItem, which is the preferred method. If a consuming MSBuild script places a value into an item, it is automatically converted into a representation using ITaskItem. So in this example the difference is trivial, but you should generally use ITaskItem when you expect to expose properties to be items in consuming scripts.

```
C:\Data\MSBuildExamples\Examples.Tasks\bin\Debug\Samples>msbuild TempFileExample
.proj /nologo
Build started 7/11/2008 1:32:02 AM.
Project "C:\Data\MSBuildExamples\Examples.Tasks\bin\Debug\Samples\TempFileExamp
le.proj" on node 0 (default targets).
  TestFile: C:\Documents and Settings\Ibrahim\Local Settings\Temp\tmp2B8.tmp
  TestFile.Filename: tmp2B8
  TestFile.Extension: .tmp
Done Building Project "C:\Data\MSBuildExamples\Examples.Tasks\bin\Debug\Samples
\TempFileExample.proj" (default targets).


Build succeeded.
    0 Warning(s)
    0 Error(s)
```

FIGURE 4-5 TempFile task demonstration

Using objects that are ITaskItems is preferred because you are able to pass a richer object to and from a task. Objects of this type can have metadata associated with it, which the task can interact with. We will discuss this concept in more detail later in the next section.

Using Arrays with Task Inputs and Outputs

We have now discussed various topics about passing values into and out of tasks; one of the only issues that we have not discussed is passing vector values into and out of tasks. We will discuss that now, by examining a real MSBuild task. This task was taken from my open source task repository, Sedodream Tasks, which is available at Codeplex at http://www.*codeplex.com/sedodream*. The task that we will demonstrate is the Move task. You may have noticed that out of the box there is a copy task and a delete task, but there is no move task, so this task will fit that need. This task was designed to work similar to the Copy task in the sense that it has a similar set of inputs, outputs, and behavior. The properties that are declared by the task are shown in the following code snippet.

```
[Required]
public ITaskItem[] SourceFiles
{ get; set; }

public ITaskItem[] DestinationFiles
{ get; set; }

public ITaskItem DestinationFolder
{ get; set; }

[Output]
public ITaskItem[] MovedFiles
{ get; private set; }

[Output]
public long[] FileLengths
{ get; private set; }
```

From these properties, there are three that are declared as arrays of ITaskItem objects and the remaining as a scalar ITaskItem. These could have been created using `string[]`, but this would limit the information that we could gather from the values. Specifically, a string object cannot have any metadata associated with it, whereas ITaskItem objects can. You will find an example of the usage of this task in the following file, MoveExample.proj.

```
<Project xmlns="http://schemas.microsoft.com/developer/msbuild/2003"
         DefaultTargets="Demo">

  <UsingTask AssemblyFile="$(MSBuildProjectDirectory)\..\Examples.Tasks.dll"
             TaskName="Move" />

  <PropertyGroup>
    <SampleFilesPath>$(MSBuildProjectDirectory)\sampleFiles\</SampleFilesPath>
    <DestPath>$(MSBuildProjectDirectory)\dest\</DestPath>
  </PropertyGroup>

  <ItemGroup>
    <SampleFiles Include="$(SampleFilesPath)**\*.txt"
                 Exclude="$(SourceFolder)**\.svn\**\*" />
  </ItemGroup>

  <Target Name="Demo">
    <Move SourceFiles="@(SampleFiles)"
          DestinationFiles=
          "@(SampleFiles->'$(DestPath)%(RecursiveDir)%(Filename)%(Extension)')">
    </Move>
  </Target>

</Project>
```

In this example, we create a new item, SampleFiles, and pass that into the SourceFiles property for the Move task. The value for DestinationFiles is a transformation of the SourceFiles item. When you use tasks that have inputs that should have a one-to-one correspondence, it is common for one of them to be a transformation of the other. This is what is shown here. Previously we mentioned that the ITaskItem type of objects can have metadata; we will now discuss that in more detail. In the code for a custom task you can use the methods *GetMetadata* and *SetMetadata* to get and set the values for an item's metadata respectfully. We will see this at work in the sample task I created, MetadataExample.

In order to demonstrate clearly how you can use metadata on items passed into and out of custom tasks, I have created a sample task, MetadataExample, that demonstrates this. This task is very simple and is shown in its entirety as follows.

```
public class MetadataExample : Task
{
    [Required]
    public ITaskItem[] ServerList
    { get; set; }
```

```
    [Output]
    public ITaskItem[] Result
    { get; set; }

    public override bool Execute()
    {
        if (ServerList.Length > 0)
        {
            Result = new TaskItem[ServerList.Length];

            for(int i=0; i<Result.Length; i++)
            {
                ITaskItem item = ServerList[i];
                ITaskItem newItem = new TaskItem(item.ItemSpec);
                string fullpath = item.GetMetadata("Fullpath");

                newItem.SetMetadata("ServerName", item.GetMetadata("Name"));
                newItem.SetMetadata("DropLoc", item.GetMetadata("DropLocation"));

                newItem.SetMetadata("IpAddress", string.Format("127.0.0.{0}", i+10));
                Result[i] = newItem;
            }
        }
        return true;
    }
}
```

In this task we have two properties, both of which are declared as ITaskItem[]. The ServerList is a required input parameter and Result is the output parameter. In the *Execute* method we get some values from the metadata and use it to populate values into the Result item. We can see this in action in the following MetadataExample01.proj file.

```
<Project xmlns="http://schemas.microsoft.com/developer/msbuild/2003"
         DefaultTargets="Demo">

  <UsingTask AssemblyFile="$(MSBuildProjectDirectory)\..\Examples.Tasks.dll"
           TaskName="MetadataExample" />

  <PropertyGroup>
    <ConfigFileRoot>$(MSBuildProjectDirectory)\sampleConfigFiles\</ConfigFileRoot>
  </PropertyGroup>
  <ItemGroup>
    <Server Include="$(ConfigFileRoot)server1.app.config">
      <Name>server1</Name>
      <DropLocation>D:\Drops\</DropLocation>
    </Server>
    <Server Include="$(ConfigFileRoot)server2.app.config">
      <Name>server2</Name>
      <DropLocation>E:\Builds\Drops\</DropLocation>
    </Server>
    <Server Include="$(ConfigFileRoot)server3.app.config">
      <Name>server3</Name>
      <DropLocation>D:\Data\DropDir\</DropLocation>
    </Server>
```

```
    <Server Include="$(ConfigFileRoot)server4.app.config">
      <Name>server4</Name>
      <DropLocation>D:\Projects\DropLocation\</DropLocation>
    </Server>
  </ItemGroup>


  <Target Name="Demo">

    <MetadataExample ServerList="@(Server)">
      <Output ItemName="ServerIpList" TaskParameter="Result" />
    </MetadataExample>

    <Message Text="ServerIpList: @(ServerIpList)" />

    <Message
      Text="Server: %(ServerIpList.ServerName)
  %(ServerIpList.DropLoc)
  %(ServerIpList.IpAddress)" />
  </Target>

</Project>
```

In this project file, we have created an item named Server and attached a value for Name and DropLocation metadata for each item. Inside the Demo target of this project file, we invoke the MetadataExample task and pass in the Server item. Then we place the output of the task into an item named ServerIpList with the *Output* element. Finally we print a message to display the custom metadata values that the task set. If you execute this project file, you would see the results shown in Figure 4-6.

```
C:\Data\MSBuildExamples\Examples.Tasks\bin\Debug\Samples>msbuild MetadataExample
01.proj /nologo
Build started 7/12/2008 1:42:34 PM.
Project "C:\Data\MSBuildExamples\Examples.Tasks\bin\Debug\Samples\MetadataExamp
le01.proj" on node 0 (default targets).
  ServerIpList: C:\Data\MSBuildExamples\Examples.Tasks\bin\Debug\Samples\sample
  ConfigFiles\server1.app.config;C:\Data\MSBuildExamples\Examples.Tasks\bin\Deb
  ug\Samples\sampleConfigFiles\server2.app.config;C:\Data\MSBuildExamples\Examp
  les.Tasks\bin\Debug\Samples\sampleConfigFiles\server3.app.config;C:\Data\MSBu
  ildExamples\Examples.Tasks\bin\Debug\Samples\sampleConfigFiles\server4.app.co
  nfig
  Server: server1
    D:\Drops\
    127.0.0.10
  Server: server2
    E:\Builds\Drops\
    127.0.0.11
  Server: server3
    D:\Data\DropDir\
    127.0.0.12
  Server: server4
    D:\Projects\DropLocation\
    127.0.0.13
Done Building Project "C:\Data\MSBuildExamples\Examples.Tasks\bin\Debug\Samples
\MetadataExample01.proj" (default targets).

Build succeeded.
    0 Warning(s)
    0 Error(s)
```

FIGURE 4-6 Using metadata

If you look at the results shown here, you can see that we were able to successfully pass metadata into and out of a task. Note that once an item value has been passed to a task any modifications to it are not reflected back into the MSBuild file. So if you use the *SetMetadata* method on an item that was passed into the task by an input, it will **not** be reflected back in the calling MSBuild file. Now that we have discussed all you need to know to pass values in and out of tasks, we will discuss extending the ToolTask class, which we briefly touched on earlier.

Extending ToolTask

There are many instances in which you need to invoke an .exe file in your build process. There is a task, the Exec task, which allows you to execute any command. This works great and is used throughout the MSBuild community. If you find yourself executing the same .exe on several occasions, then it may be worth writing a custom task to execute the command. Custom tasks that wrap up executables have many advantages to simply using the Exec task. Some of those benefits are outlined in the following list.

- **Ease of use** Since custom tasks have specific properties for inputs and outputs, they are very easy to use.
- **Better input validation** You can write .NET code to validate the parameters that the script is requesting be sent to the executable.
- **Easier path resolution** Sometimes you may not know where the .exe file resides. You may have to search the registry or examine a set of folders. This is typically performed more easily in code than in an MSBuild script.
- **Pre- and post-processing** Because you are creating a custom task, you can perform actions before and/or after the execution of the executable.
- **Parsing stdout and stderr** The ToolTask class can detect errors and warnings from messages that are sent into the stdout and stderr streams.
- **Enables task execution skipping** By overriding the *SkipTaskExecution* method, you can programmatically determine if the task should be skipped.

When you have decided to write a custom task to wrap an executable file you should consider extending the *ToolTask* class. This class, which is in the *Microsoft.Build.Utilities* assembly, was designed specifically for this. The class diagram for the *ToolTask* abstract class is shown in Figure 4-7, which was generated with the MSBuild 3.5 assemblies.

As shown in the previous diagram and the text, the *ToolTask* class extends the task class. This class implements the Execute method from the task class, but it does define one abstract method and one abstract property that need to be implemented. Those are the `GenerateFullPathToTool` method and the ToolName property. There are many other methods and properties that are relevant in this class, and we will discuss some of those now. We will discuss only the methods and properties that you are likely to interact with.

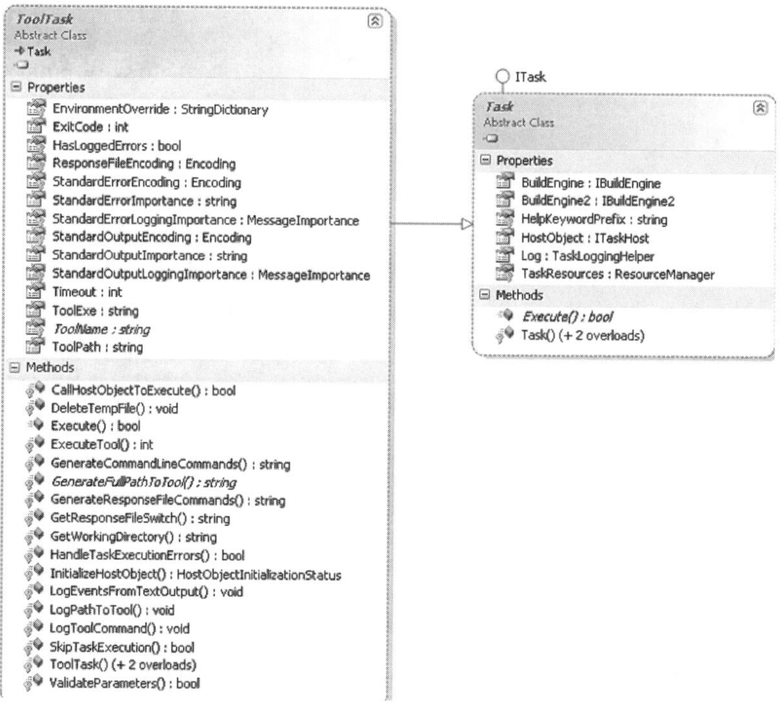

FIGURE 4-7 *ToolTask* class diagram

ToolTask Methods

- ***ExecuteTool*** This is the method called that will execute the tool based on the values from the input parameters.
- ***GenerateFullPathToTool*** You will have to implement this method. The return value, as the name suggests, is the full path to the tool that you are executing.
- ***DeleteTempFile (New with 3.5)*** This is simply a helper method that can be used to delete files. The advantage of using this is that it doesn't fail the build if the file can't be deleted; it only warns and continues.
- ***GenerateCommandLineCommands*** This is used to generate any parameters that are passed to the command. The return value will be appended to the full tool path for the command that will be executed. This value, along with the response file, if provided, is passed to the System.Diagnostics.ProcessStartInfo(string,string) constructor as the arguments command.
- ***GenerateResponseFileCommands*** If your tool accepts a response file for initialization, then you can return a string that contains the values that should be contained in a response file sent to the tool. These commands will be written to a temporary file and then passed to the tool. When you use this method you may also need to override the

GetResponseFileSwitch method. A typical reason for preferring a response file is that you can pass many parameters. If you pass parameters you are typically limited to 8 Kb, imposed by cmd.exe.

- ***GetResponseFileSwitch*** If the tool that you are invoking accepts a response file, then you need to override this method if you want to supply a response file to it. If the tool simply accepts the file path as the response file, then you do not need to override this method; that is the default behavior. If the tool requires a switch to process the response file, then override this method to create the switch to be passed to the tool.
- ***GetWorkingDirectory*** If you need to specify the working directory of the tool, then override this method to override the working directory to use. If null is returned from this method, then the current directory will be used as the working directory. This is the default behavior.
- ***HandleTaskExecutionErrors*** This method will be called after the command completes with a non-zero exit code. The return value of this method is used as the return value of the task itself. If you have a scenario where you would like to conditionally ignore certain exit codes, then you can override this method and examine the exit code and decide to return true or false. There exist tools that return non-zero exit codes even when the tool succeeds. If you return true, then the build will proceed as if there were no error.
- ***SkipTaskExecution*** The return value of this method will determine if the command should actually be executed. If this method returns false, then the task will be executed; otherwise it will not. If the task execution is skipped due to the return value of this method, it will not be treated as an error but as an intended response. The default implementation of this method simply returns false. You can use this opportunity to do custom dependency checking, and skip the task if everything is up to date.
- ***ValidateParameters*** This is an empty method that can be used to validate any input parameters that have been passed to the task. If this method returns false, then the task will automatically fail. By default, this method simply returns true. If your task accepts inputs, then you can place your input validation in this method and it will be called by the default implementation of the *Execute* method. If the *Execute* method is overridden, then this validation method should be called near the beginning of the process.

ToolTask Properties

- **EnvironmentOverride** In this dictionary you can place any values that will override environment variables. For example you could override the TEMP or PATH environment variables. These overrides will affect only the tool that is executed by the task, not the entire build process.
- **ExitCode** Contains the exit code of the tool. This is an MSBuild Output property so its value will be available to build files using the task.

- **ResponseFileEncoding** Contains the encoding that should be used to write out the response file. The default value for this is System.Text.Encoding.UTF8.
- **StandardErrorEncoding** Contains the encoding value that should used for error output. The default value for this is the default encoding of the system running the task.
- **StandardErrorImportance** Contain the MessageImportance level that tool errors will be logged at. The default value for this is MessageImportance.High.
- **StandardErrorLoggingImportance** Contains the MessageImportance level for messages sent to the standard error stream, the default value for this is MessageImportance.Normal.
- **StandardOutputEncoding** Contains the encoding of the standard output stream. The default value for this is the default value of the machine running the task.
- **StandardOutputImportance** Contains the encoding of the standard output stream. The default value for this is MessageImportance.Normal.
- **StandardOutputLoggingImportance** Contains the MessageImportance level that messages sent to the standard output will be logged at. The default value for this is MessageImportance.Low.
- **Timeout** Contains the amount of the time that the task will be allowed to run. If the task exceeds the initial value,set prior to execution, then it will be stopped, and the task will fail. This value is in milliseconds.
- **ToolExe (New with 3.5)** This serves as an alternative to the ToolName property. The problem with the ToolName property is that it is read-only so there is no option to change the name of the .exe; this property introduces that option. If this is specified it will take precedence over ToolName.
- **ToolName** Contains the name of the executable file to run. This should not include the path, just the name of the actual executable file. If ToolExe is specified, then that value is used in place of this.
- **ToolPath** Contains the full path to the folder where the tool is located. If this property returns a value, then the result from the *GenerateFullPathToTool* method is ignored.

The MSBuild team has created this helper class to ensure that wrapping an existing .exe is very simple. This is because there are many preexisting tools that can be very useful during the build process. If you are writing a task that will invoke an executable, you should extend this base class so you can focus on what is important and not on the plumbing of calling it.

In order to demonstrate how we can effectively use this class, I will create a new task that wraps up an .exe that is delivered with Visual Studio. This exe is the MakeZipExe.exe executable. Before we take a look at the task that will be created for this executable let's take a look at the usage for this tool, as shown in Figure 4-8.

```
C:\Data\MSBuildExamples\Examples.Tasks\bin\Debug\Samples>makezipexe
Microsoft (R) Zip File to Exe converter version 1.0
Copyright (C) Microsoft Corporation 2005. All rights reserved.

Usage:
        -zipfile:filename
                Path to the zip file to turn into an exe.
        -output:filename
                Path to the .exe file to generate. If this is not specified,
                then an .exe file with the same name as the input file (but
                with the .exe extension) will be used.
        -overwrite
                Overwrite the output the file if it exists.
        -?
                This help screen.
```

FIGURE 4-8 MakeZipExe.exe usage

This tool has only a few parameters that can be provided but is certainly a useful tool, so it should pose as a good demonstration task. From the usage of the tool we can see that we should create three properties that will be sent to the tool. Those properties are Zipfile, OutputFile, and Overwrite. The only required property will be Zipfile, because this is the only required parameter by the tool itself. Now we can take a look at the following task definition.

```
public class MakeZipExe : ToolTask
{
    private const string ExeName = "makezipexe.exe";

    public MakeZipExe()
    {
        Overwrite = false;
    }

    [Required]
    public ITaskItem Zipfile { get; set; }
    public ITaskItem OutputFile { get; set; }
    public bool Overwrite { get; set; }

    protected override bool ValidateParameters()
    {
        base.Log.LogMessageFromText("Validating arguments", MessageImportance.Low);

        if (!File.Exists(Zipfile.GetMetadata("FullPath")))
        {
            string message = string.Format("Missing ZipFile: {0}", Zipfile);
            base.Log.LogError(message, null);
            return false;
        }
        if (File.Exists(OutputFile.GetMetadata("FullPath")) && !Overwrite)
        {
            string message = string.Format("Output file {0}, Overwrite false.",
                OutputFile);
            base.Log.LogError(message, null);
            return false;
        }

        return base.ValidateParameters();
    }
```

```
protected override string GenerateFullPathToTool()
{
    string path = ToolPath;
    // If ToolPath was not provided by the MSBuild script try to find it.
    if (string.IsNullOrEmpty(path))
    {
        string regKey = @"SOFTWARE\Microsoft\VisualStudio\9.0\Setup\VS";
        using (RegistryKey key = Registry.LocalMachine.OpenSubKey(regKey))
        {
            if (key != null)
            {
                string keyValue =
                    key.GetValue("EnvironmentDirectory", null).ToString();
                path = keyValue;
            }
        }
    }
    if (string.IsNullOrEmpty(path))
    {

        using (RegistryKey key = Registry.LocalMachine.OpenSubKey
            (@"SOFTWARE\Microsoft\VisualStudio\8.0\Setup\VS"))
        {
            if (key != null)
            {
                string keyValue =
                    key.GetValue("EnvironmentDirectory", null).ToString();
                path = keyValue;
            }
        }

    }
    if (string.IsNullOrEmpty(path))
    {
        Log.LogError("VisualStudio install directory not found",
            null);

        return string.Empty;
    }
    string fullpath = Path.Combine(path, ToolName);
    return fullpath;
}

protected override string GenerateCommandLineCommands()
{
    StringBuilder sb = new StringBuilder();
    if (Zipfile != null)
    {
        sb.Append(
            string.Format("-zipfile:{0} ",
            Zipfile.GetMetadata("FullPath")));
    }
    if (OutputFile != null)
    {
        sb.Append(
            string.Format("-output:{0} ",
            OutputFile.GetMetadata("FullPath")));
    }
```

```
        if (Overwrite)
            sb.Append("-overwrite:true ");

        return sb.ToString();
    }
    protected override string ToolName
    {
        get { return ExeName; }
    }
}
```

One of the things to take note of here is the usage of ITaskItem. Previously in this chapter, we mentioned that you should try to employ objects of this type for properties that refer to files and directories. This task overrides the abstract ToolName property to return the name of the file to be executed. Along with this property, three methods—*ValidateParameters, GenerateFullPathToTool,* and *GenerateCommandLineCommands*—are overridden. In most implementations extending ToolTask, these methods will be found. *ValidateParameters* is used to validate the input provided from the calling script and to throw meaningful errors for invalid input. *GenerateFullPathToTool,* is an abstract method and must be implemented by the concrete class. *GenerateCommandLineCommands* is the method that will be called to determine what values will be passed into the command as parameters. If you have a task that doesn't accept any parameters, then you do not need to implement this method. If you noticed, we did not have to define the *Execute* or *ExecuteTool* methods; this is because the ToolTask implements these methods by calling the other methods declared in this class. Now we can see how this task can be used.

Using this task is no different from using a task that extends Task or directly implements ITask. You have to declare that you are interested in using the task with the UsingTask statement and then invoke it in a target. I have created the following example file, MakeZipExeExample.proj.

```
<Project xmlns="http://schemas.microsoft.com/developer/msbuild/2003"
         DefaultTargets="Demo">

  <UsingTask AssemblyFile="$(MSBuildProjectDirectory)\..\Examples.Tasks.dll"
           TaskName="MakeZipExe" />

  <Target Name="Demo">
    <MakeZipExe ZipFile="Sample.zip"
                OutputFile="Sample.exe">
    </MakeZipExe>
  </Target>
</Project>
```

In this simple execution of the task, we invoke the MakeZipExe task inside the Demo target. We specify the zipfile that should be the source for the self-extracting zipfile and where the output needs to be written to. If you execute the Demo target you will see that the Sample.exe file is successfully created. In the results captured in Figure 4-9, I increased the verbosity of the console logger to "detailed" in order to display the relevant messages.

```
C:\Data\MSBuildExamples\Examples.Tasks\bin\Debug\Samples>msbuild MakeZipExeExamp
le.proj /t:demo /v:d /nologo
Build started 7/15/2008 12:51:42 AM.
Project "C:\Data\MSBuildExamples\Examples.Tasks\bin\Debug\Samples\MakeZipExeExa
mple.proj" on node 0 (demo target(s)).
Building with tools version "2.0".
Target "Demo" in file "C:\Data\MSBuildExamples\Examples.Tasks\bin\Debug\Samples
\MakeZipExeExample.proj" from project "C:\Data\MSBuildExamples\Examples.Tasks\b
in\Debug\Samples\MakeZipExeExample.proj":
Using "MakeZipExe" task from assembly "C:\Data\MSBuildExamples\Examples.Tasks\b
in\Debug\Samples\..\Examples.Tasks.dll".
Task "MakeZipExe"
  Validating arguments
  Command:
  C:\Program Files\Microsoft Visual Studio 9.0\Common7\IDE\makezipexe.exe -zipf
  ile:C:\Data\MSBuildExamples\Examples.Tasks\bin\Debug\Samples\Sample.zip -outp
  ut:C:\Data\MSBuildExamples\Examples.Tasks\bin\Debug\Samples\Sample.exe
  The "MakeZipExe" task is using "makezipexe.exe" from "C:\Program Files\Micros
  oft Visual Studio 9.0\Common7\IDE\makezipexe.exe".
  Microsoft (R) Zip File to Exe converter version 1.0
  Copyright (C) Microsoft Corporation 2005. All rights reserved.

  exe file generation successful.
Done executing task "MakeZipExe".
Done building target "Demo" in project "MakeZipExeExample.proj".
Done Building Project "C:\Data\MSBuildExamples\Examples.Tasks\bin\Debug\Samples
\MakeZipExeExample.proj" (demo target(s)).


Build succeeded.
    0 Warning(s)
    0 Error(s)
```

FIGURE 4-9 MakeZipExe task demonstration

From the image in Figure 4-9, we can see that the MakeZipExe tool was successfully discovered, and invoked with the expected parameters. Also the result file, Sample.exe, was correctly created. Now that we have introduced how you can quickly and effectively create custom MSBuild tasks that wrap command line tools, we'll move on to discuss the little-known topic of debugging MSBuild tasks.

Debugging Tasks

When you write custom MSBuild tasks you are writing managed code, and hooking into an existing process, the MSBuild engine. Even though MSBuild tasks are very easy to write, you will inevitably run into times when they do not behave as you expect. This will be the case especially when you are writing complex tasks. When this time arrives you will need to debug your tasks, which we discuss in this section.

When you need to debug your custom MSBuild tasks, you will find that there are primarily three ways to debug these tasks. Ultimately the goal when debugging tasks is to have all the tools available when one is debugging .NET applications. We should be able to use Visual Studio to debug custom tasks. Following are three ways that you can debug tasks.

1. Examine the content of the log
2. Use Debugger.Launch() to prompt for debugger attachment
3. Start MSBuild as an External Program, and debug normally

The first technique, examining the log, is obviously the simplest but will also provide the least amount of information. Also, it is not an interactive process; you simply examine the log file that was generated. You can increase the number of messages you task logs to discover more about its behavior, and you can increase the verbosity of the loggers. If you set the verbosity to be "diagnostic," then all properties and items are dumped by the logger. With that being said, let's discuss the other methods.

We will now discuss the second option, the *Debugger.Launch()* method. When you are trying to debug an MSBuild task, one technique that I have seen employed is to add the statement System.Diagnostics.Debugger.Launch(). Typically you will place this statement inside the *Execute* method. When this statement is encountered, you will be prompted about attaching a debugger to the process. After this you can start executing the build script that you would like to debug that invokes the task you are trying to debug. You should be prompted with a dialog similar to the one shown in the Figure 4-10.

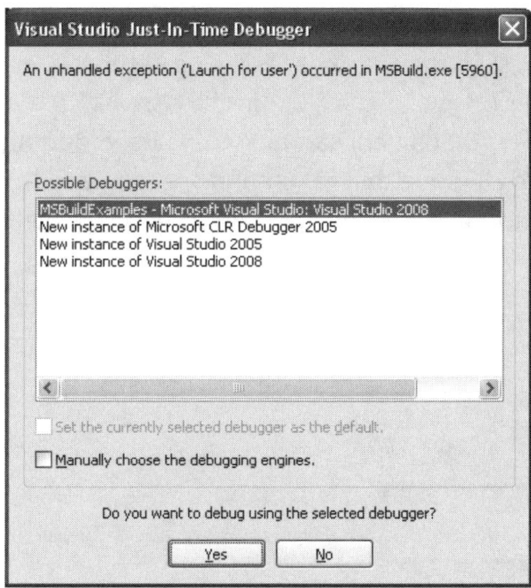

FIGURE 4-10 Debugger selection dialog

From this dialog you can choose Visual Studio as the debugger. Following this, you can set breakpoints, step into methods, and all the other benefits you are accustomed to, with the exception of Edit and Continue. This is a great technique to employ, but it has at least the following drawbacks:

- You have to change the task (adding a Debugger.Launch() statement)
- No support for Edit and Continue

The way to get around these issues is to employ the last method, Start MSBuild as an External Program. Once you create a task and a build script that exercises the task you can use Visual Studio to start the MSBuild.exe executable on the specified build script and to use the debugger to debug it. This is similar to but not exactly the same as the previous approach. In the Debug pane of the Project properties you will see an option to Start External Program; this is the option that we will use. I will show you how to achieve this by debugging a task contained in the samples, the MetadataExample task that we discussed earlier.

Normally when I am writing tasks I create a set of sample MSBuild scripts that can be used to exercise and demonstrate the task usage of the task. If it is possible I place these samples in the project that contains the project itself in a dedicated directory. The reason for this is that it allows me to be able to maintain the task and the samples in one place. Another reason is that it makes it a little simpler to debug the tasks. For sample scripts I set the files to be copied to the output directory. The reason you will want to do so also is so you can execute the MSBuild scripts in their output folders and know that you are using the latest version of the task. In the samples this folder is named *Samples*. This is why you have seen UsingTask statements such as:

```
<UsingTask
    AssemblyFile="$(MSBuildProjectDirectory)\..\Examples.Tasks.dll"
     TaskName="AspnetRegsql"/>
```

In this example, we know that we will be executing this script from the output directory and it is contained in a directory named *Samples*. So the *Example.Tasks.dll* assembly is located in the directory above the current project; this is why I use the '`..`' in the *AssemblyFile* attribute. Another advantage of taking this approach is that if your sample scripts need dummy files to go along with them, you can place them all inside that folder and set the Copy to Output Directory appropriately. You can set the attribute directly inside Visual Studio in the Properties grid. You can see this in Figure 4-11.

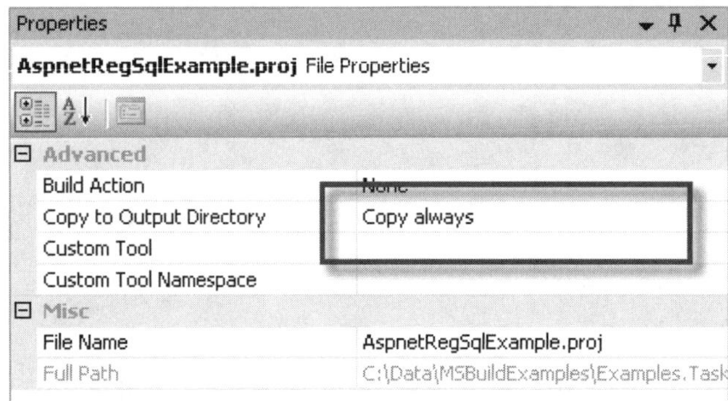

FIGURE 4-11 Copy to Output Directory

In this figure, I have set the *Copy to Output Directory* value to be *Copy always*, but you could also set it to *Copy if newer*; either should work. Now we can debug the MetadataExample task. I will use the following MetadataExample01.proj file to demonstrate this.

```
<Project xmlns="http://schemas.microsoft.com/developer/msbuild/2003"
         DefaultTargets="Demo">

  <UsingTask AssemblyFile="..\Examples.Tasks.dll"
           TaskName="MetadataExample" />

  <PropertyGroup>
    <ConfigFileRoot>$(MSBuildProjectDirectory)\sampleConfigFiles\</ConfigFileRoot>
  </PropertyGroup>
```

```
<ItemGroup>
  <Server Include="$(ConfigFileRoot)server1.app.config">
    <Name>server1</Name>
    <DropLocation>D:\Drops\</DropLocation>
  </Server>
  <Server Include="$(ConfigFileRoot)server2.app.config">
    <Name>server2</Name>
    <DropLocation>E:\Builds\Drops\</DropLocation>
  </Server>
  <Server Include="$(ConfigFileRoot)server3.app.config">
    <Name>server3</Name>
    <DropLocation>D:\Data\DropDir\</DropLocation>
  </Server>
  <Server Include="$(ConfigFileRoot)server4.app.config">
    <Name>server4</Name>
    <DropLocation>D:\Projects\DropLocation\</DropLocation>
  </Server>
</ItemGroup>


<Target Name="Demo">

  <MetadataExample ServerList="@(Server)">
    <Output ItemName="ServerIpList" TaskParameter="Result" />
  </MetadataExample>

  <Message Text="ServerIpList: @(ServerIpList)" />

  <Message Text="Server: %(ServerIpList.ServerName)
%(ServerIpList.DropLoc)
%(ServerIpList.IpAddress)" />
</Target>

</Project>
```

For the project that contains this task, in this case Examples.Tasks, go to the properties page for the project by selecting Properties from the Project menu. On the debug tab we have to specify that we want to invoke MSBuild, which will turn load our assembly when it detects the UsingTask statement referencing it. The following list describes three settings that you should be aware of.

- **Start External Program** You should select this value and provide the full path to the msbuild.exe file. Make sure to pick the correct version of MSBuild you are intending to use. These files are located in the directory %Windows%\Microsoft.NET\Framework\v2.0.50727\ and %Windows%\Microsoft.NET\Framework\v3.5\ for MSBuild 2.0 and MSBuild 3.5 respectively.
- **Command Line Arguments** Here you should place the path to the MSBuild sample file that invokes the task that you are trying to debug. Also you can provide any properties or other switches to the msbuild.exe executable. I typically also attach

a FileLogger in case I might need to examine it to determine what was happening before, or after, the task was invoked. For instance, you may need to examine the log to determine what other targets were executed.

- **Working Directory** You should set this to the full path where the sample script lies, which should be under the output directory of the tasks' project itself.

You should note that these values are not stored in the project file but in the user file, so if you are working in a team it should not affect any of the others working with you. You can see the value that I set this to for the MetadataExample task in Figure 4-12.

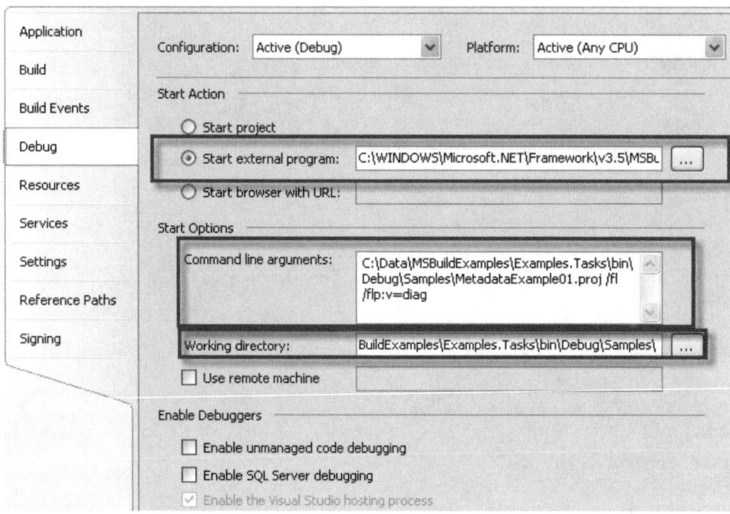

FIGURE 4-12 Project properties

Here I've highlighted the areas listed previously. In this example, I am using MSBuild 3.5 on the MetadataExample01.proj file. After you have set these values correctly, all you have to do is set breakpoints where you want to stop and then hit F5! From there you can step through the task and use all the tools that Visual Studio makes available to you.

Now we have covered everything you need to know to efficiently and effectively write custom MSBuild tasks. In this chapter, we have discussed how to get started writing tasks, handling task input and output, what task base classes are available, debugging tasks, and more. Writing custom MSBuild tasks is one way to extend MSBuild itself; the other way is to write custom loggers. In the next chapter we will cover custom loggers in detail. Following that chapter we will start the MSBuild cookbook section.

Chapter 5

Custom Loggers

We have identified that there are two ways to extend MSBuild: by custom tasks and custom loggers. In the previous chapter, we covered custom tasks; in this chapter, we will discuss custom loggers. We'll start by discussing what loggers are available out of the box and how they can be used. After that we'll take a look at what it takes to write and use a new custom logger. Now let's get started.

Overview

One of the most important aspects of a build tool is its logging support. You can create the best build tool ever, but if the logging mechanism doesn't meet the needs of consumers then it will never be used. MSBuild has a great deal of flexibility with respect to loggers. There are two loggers that are shipped with MSBuild: the console logger and the file logger. We will cover these two loggers in the next two sections. A logger is an object that can accept and respond to build events. For example, throughout this book we have been sending messages to the loggers using the Message task.

The Message task has two properties: Text and Importance. The Text property contains the message that is to be logged, and the Importance a value indicating the priority of the message. When this task is executed the MSBuild engine will raise an event on each attached logger sending both pieces of information. Individual loggers are allowed to interpret how messages with high importance versus those with low importance are to be handled. This importance level, along with the verbosity setting for the logger, typically determines how the message is logged. Each logger can have its own verbosity setting, which plays a role in what messages are logged and how. In the case of the console logger, messages with high importance are highlighted, whereas those with low importance are suppressed when the verbosity setting is set to normal, the default value.

We can now take a look at how different messages are passed through to the console logger using the Message task. The next block contains the content of the Logging01.proj project file.

```
<Project xmlns="http://schemas.microsoft.com/developer/msbuild/2003"
         DefaultTargets="Demo"
         ToolsVersion="3.5">
  <Target Name="Demo">
    <Message Text="high importance message" Importance="high" />
    <Message Text="normal importance message" Importance="normal" />
    <Message Text="low importance message" Importance="low" />
  </Target>

</Project>
```

In this project file the single target, Demo, contains three calls to the Message task. Each task has a different setting for the importance setting. If you execute the command `msbuild Logging01.proj /t:Demo` the result will be what is shown in the following figure.

```
C:\Data\MSBuildExamples\Fundamentals>msbuild Logging01.proj /t:Demo /nologo
Build started 10/14/2008 10:56:53 PM.
Project "C:\Data\MSBuildExamples\Fundamentals\Logging01.proj" on node 0 (Demo t
arget(s)).
  high importance message
  normal importance message
Done Building Project "C:\Data\MSBuildExamples\Fundamentals\Logging01.proj" (De
mo target(s)).

Build succeeded.
    0 Warning(s)
    0 Error(s)
```

FIGURE 5-1 Message importance demonstration 1

In Figure 5-1, you will see that only the messages with high importance and normal importance are shown. The message with a low-importance level is suppressed. This is a decision made by the console logger, based on the importance of the message as well as the verbosity setting of the logger. Also notice the message with high importance is printed in a more noticeable color. In the next section, we will cover the console logger in detail. For now let's just say that the extra command line `switch /clp:v=d` increases the verbosity setting of the console logger. If you execute the command `msbuild Logging01.proj /t:Demo /clp:v=d`, then the result would be what is shown in Figure 5-2.

```
C:\Data\MSBuildExamples\Fundamentals>msbuild Logging01.proj /t:Demo /clp:v=d /no
logo
Build started 10/14/2008 11:15:46 PM.
Project "C:\Data\MSBuildExamples\Fundamentals\Logging01.proj" on node 0 (Demo t
arget(s)).
Building with tools version "3.5".
Target "Demo" in file "C:\Data\MSBuildExamples\Fundamentals\Logging01.proj" fro
m project "C:\Data\MSBuildExamples\Fundamentals\Logging01.proj":
Using "Message" task from assembly "Microsoft.Build.Tasks.v3.5, Version=3.5.0.0
, Culture=neutral, PublicKeyToken=b03f5f7f11d50a3a".
Task "Message"
  high importance message
Done executing task "Message".
Task "Message"
  normal importance message
Done executing task "Message".
Task "Message"
  low importance message
Done executing task "Message".
Done building target "Demo" in project "Logging01.proj".
Done Building Project "C:\Data\MSBuildExamples\Fundamentals\Logging01.proj" (De
mo target(s)).

Build succeeded.
    0 Warning(s)
    0 Error(s)
```

FIGURE 5-2 Message importance demonstration 2

From the results shown in Figure 5-2, you can see that there is much more information logged to the console compared to Figure 5-1. Not only is the low importance message logged but much more information as well. When the Message task is executed an event is raised. This is not the only event that is raised related to logging. There are many other types of events that will be raised. We will cover those types during the discussion on creating custom loggers. We will now discuss the two loggers that are shipped with MSBuild.

Console Logger

When you invoke msbuild.exe the console logger will be attached by default; you can disable this by using the `/noconsolelogger (/noconlog)` switch. You can set the verbosity of the console logger using the `/verbosity (/v)` switch when using msbuild.exe. The defined values for the verbosity are shown in Table 5-1.

TABLE 5-1 Logger Verbosity

Long Name	Short Name
Quiet	q
Minimal	m
Normal	n
Detailed	d
Diagnostic	diag

When you are specifying the verbosity for either of these loggers you can use the long name or the short name. A common practice is to set the verbosity of the console logger to Minimal and attach file loggers with higher verbosities. That way, the console shows the progress and errors/warnings, and a log file is available for diagnosis. The console logger accepts only a few parameters and they are outlined in Table 5-2. The parameters are passed by the `/consoleloggerparameters (/clp)` switch.

TABLE 5-2 ConsoleLogger Parameters

Name	Description
PerformanceSummary	When passed as a parameter, the console logger will output messages that show the amount of time spent building tasks, targets, and projects. If you are trying to profile long running builds this may be very useful.
NoSummary	When passed, this suppresses the errors and warnings summary that is typically displayed at the end of the log.
NoItemAndPropertyList	Indicates to not display the values for properties and items that are typically shown at the start of the build log when using the diagnostic verbosity setting.
Verbosity*	Overrides the verbosity for the console logger.
Summary*	Shows errors and warnings summary at the end of the log.
ErrorsOnly*	Shows only errors.
WarningsOnly*	Shows only warnings.
ShowCommandLine*	Shows TaskCommandLineEvent messages. This is raised when the *TaskLoggingHelper.LogCommandLine* method is invoked.
ShowTimestamp*	Displays a timestamp to every message.
ShowEventId*	Displays the event ID for started, finished, and message events.

TABLE 5-2 ConsoleLogger Parameters

Name	Description
ForceNoAlign*	Does not align the text to the size of the console buffer.
DiableMPLogging*	Disables the multiprocessor logging style of output when running in non-multiprocessor mode.
EnableMPLogging*	Enables the multiprocessor logging style even when running in non-multiprocessor mode. This logging style is on by default.

* denotes parameters new with .NET 3.5.

When you are using the console logger you will typically not need to pass any of these parameters with the exception of the verbosity parameter. In the previous section, the command `msbuild Logging01.proj /t:Demo /clp:v=d` was demonstrated to increase the verbosity of the console logger. Now we know that the `/clp:v=d` switch sets the verbosity of the console logger to detailed. You can pass additional parameters by separating them with a semicolon. For example, the previous command could have been `msbuild Logging01 .proj /t:Demo /nologo /clp:v=d;ShowEventId;Summary;PerformanceSummary`. Now let's take a look at the file logger.

File Logger

The other logger that is shipped with MSBuild is the file logger, which logs messages to a file. With MSBuild 3.5 a new set of command line switches are provided to attach a file logger. We will first discuss the 3.5 syntax then the 2.0 syntax. In order to attach a file logger you can use the /fl switch and the /flp switch to specify its parameters, similar to the /clp switch. For example, you can use the command `msbuild Logging01.proj /fl` to attach a file logger without specifying any parameters. You can also use /fl[n] and /flp[n] where n ranges from 1 to 9 in order to attach additional file loggers. When you use these switches /flp1 corresponds to /fl1 and /flp4 o /fl4. If you specify parameters using /flp[n] then the /fl[n] is implied, so it is optional, so if you pass /flp4 then you do not have to pass /fl4 as well.

The command `msbuild Logging01.proj /fl /fl1 /fl2 /fl3` will attach four file loggers. These will produce four different logs: msbuild.log, msbuild1.log, msbuild2.log, and msbuild3.log. When you don't specify a file name then the default is msbuild[n].log where [n] corresponds to /fl[n]. Since we didn't specify any parameters they would all log the same content. We will cover the available parameters after we discuss the 2.0 syntax.

If you are using .NET 2.0 you have to use the /logger (/l) switch to attach the file logger. The syntax for that is switch is `/l:<LoggerClassName>,<LoggerAssembly>[;LoggerParameters]`.

The values in that syntax are described as:

- **LoggerClassName** The name of the class that contains the logger. A partial or full namespace is acceptable but not required.
- **LoggerAssembly** The assembly that obtains the logger. This can either be the path to the assembly or the assembly name.
- **LoggerParameters** The string that should be passed to the logger as the value for the Parameters property. This is passed to the logger **exactly** as declared. These must be interpreted by the logger itself.

In order to attach the file logger in MSBuild 2.0 you will use the syntax `/l:FileLogger,Microsoft.Build.Engine[,LoggerParameters]`. The LoggerParameters value is an optional string that will be passed to the file logger. Here is an example for building the Overview01.proj with a file logger attached to the build process: `msbuild Overview01.proj /l:FileLogger,Microsoft.Build.Engine`.

When you are using MSBuild 2.0, the default verbosity of the file logger is Normal; in .NET 3.5 it is Detailed. In order to change the verbosity level you can pass it as a value in the parameters. We will discuss this after we take a look at the available parameters. Now that we have described how to attach the file logger to a build process, take a look at all the parameters that can be sent to the file logger, as described in Table 5-3.

TABLE 5-3 FileLogger Parameters

Parameter name	Description
Append	If an existing log file exists, it will be appended to instead of overwritten. You do not need to specify a value for this parameter; its existence will set it. In fact, if you specify a value, even false, it will be ignored! Default value is false.
Encoding	Used to specify the encoding that will be used to write the log file. This is interpreted by the `System.Text.Encoding.GetEncoding(string)` method. Default value is the default encoding for the system.
Logfile	Specifies the path to where the log file will be written. Default value is msbuild.log.
Verbosity	Used to specify the value for the verbosity of the logger. This uses the same values as mentioned previously. Default value is Normal for 2.0 and Detailed for 3.5.

Note Along with these values, all parameters for the ConsoleLogger can be provided as well.

The parameters listed in Table 5-3 are available for both MSBuild 2.0 and MSBuild 3.5. When using MSBuild 3.5 you specify the parameter using the /flp switch. You can set the verbosity to diagnostic by `msbuild Overview01.proj /fl /flp:v=diag`. The same for 2.0 syntax is `msbuild Overview01.proj /l:FileLogger,Microsoft.Build.Engine;v=diag`.

Building on the previous example, the command to attach a file logger that logs in diagnostic mode to a file named overview.log would be `msbuild Overview01.proj /fl /flp:Verbosity=diag;logfile=overview.log in 3.5 syntax`. In 2.0 syntax that would be `msbuild Overview01.proj /l:FileLogger,Microsoft.Build.Engine;Verbosity=diag;logfile=overview.log`. You should note that when you are using MSBuild you are free to attach any number of loggers as you desire; you can even attach more than one instance of the same logger. For example, a common scenario is to attach a file logger reading only errors and warnings, minimal verbosity, and another at a higher verbosity. This is a good idea because the log on minimal verbosity can be used to quickly determine where build errors occur, and the other(s) can be used to determine how to resolve them. The syntax to use for that would be `msbuild Overview01.proj /l:FileLogger,Microsoft.Build.Engine;Verbosity=m;logfile=overview.minimal.log /l:FileLogger,Microsoft.Build.Engine;Verbosity=d;logfile=overview.detailed.log`. If you were using 3.5 you could use the shorter syntax for only one of the two loggers; the other would have to use the longer /l syntax. Now that we have discussed the pre-existing loggers, let's move on to discuss creating custom loggers.

ILogger Interface

Before we can discuss how to create new loggers, we must first take a look at what loggers are. A logger is any object that implements the ILogger (Microsoft.Build.Framework.ILogger) interface. This is a simple interface; it contains only two properties and two methods. The class diagram for this interface is shown in Figure 5-3.

The Verbosity property determines the level of detail that should be included in the log. If the verbosity is set by using the `/verbosity (/v)` switch on msbuild.exe, then this value is passed to each attached logger, but it can be overridden by parameters passed to individual loggers as well. The values for this are (in the order of least detail to most): Minimal, Quiet, Normal, Detailed, and Diagnostic. It is up to the writer of the logger to interpret what these values mean and how they change what events are being logged.

The Parameters property is a string property that contains all the parameters that are sent to the logger. It is also the responsibility of the logger to parse the string for individual values. Typically the string that is passed is parsed by loggers as key-value pairs separated by

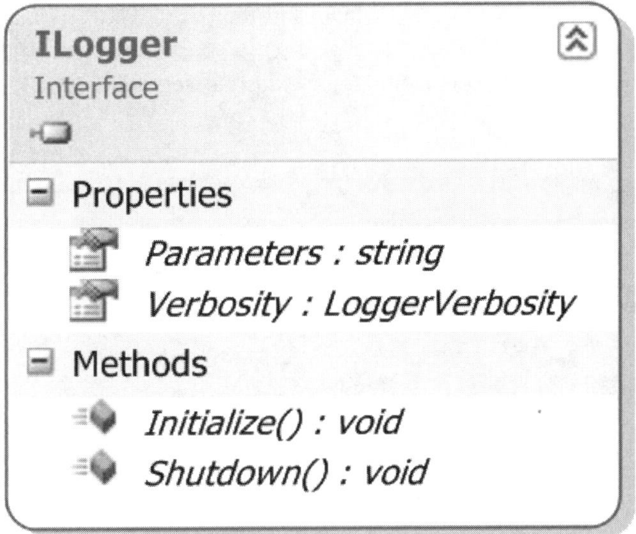

FIGURE 5-3 ILogger interface

a semicolon. Loggers do not currently have the strongly-typed properties interface that tasks do. Instead, they are passed by the properties string directly, and have to parse it themselves. We will now discuss creating custom loggers.

Creating Custom Loggers

There are three ways to create a new custom logger:

1. Implement the ILogger interface
2. Extend the abstract Microsoft.Build.Utilities.Logger class
3. Extend an existing logger

In Figure 5-3, we showed the ILogger interface, which all loggers must implement. The abstract Logger class has been provided to serve as a base class for new loggers. This class implements all the requirements of the ILogger interface except overriding the *Initialize* method, which is left to subclasses. The third option is most likely the simplest; all you have to do is extend an existing logger and override a specific behavior. We will see how to utilize all three methods in this chapter.

We will first take a look at implementing the ILogger interface. We previously discussed the Parameters and Verbosity properties so will now look at the *Initialize* method. The signature for this method is `void Initialize(Microsoft.Build.Framework.IEventSource eventSource)`. This method is called by the MSBuild engine before the build process begins. The passed-in object, `EventSource`, can be used to register build events that the logger is interested in. The event source is a class that contains a number of events, one per logging message type. By registering an event handler for these events, we get access to the event when it is raised by the MSBuild engine. Those events are summarized in Table 5-4.

TABLE 5-4 IEventSource Build Events

Name	Description
MessageRaised	Raised when a build registers a message.
WarningRaised	Raised when a warning occurs.
ErrorRaised	Raised when a build error occurs.
BuildStarted	Raised when the build starts.
BuildFinished	Raised when the build is completed.
ProjectStarted	Raised when a project is starting to build.
ProjectFinished	Raised when a project is finished building.
TargetStarted	Raised when a target is started.
TargetFinished	Raised when a target is finished building.
TaskStarted	Raised when a task is starting to execute.
TaskFinished	Raised when a task is finished executing.
AnyEventRaised	Raised when any build event occurs. In other words, all events raise their specific handler, and then raise an AnyEvent. If you have a simple logger, you can just subscribe to AnyEventRaised only.
CustomEventRaised	Raised when a custom build event occurs. This is used when an event doesn't fall into any other category, for instance the ExternalProjectStarted event.
StatusEventRaised	Raised when a status event occurs. Status events include build started, build finished, target started, target finished, etc.

Custom loggers can attach handlers to as many or as few of these build events as they choose. Each of these event handlers passes a specific subclass of BuildEventArgs. For example, a TargetStarted event will be passed a BuildTargetStarted event argument. The class diagram for this class is shown in Figure 5-4.

The event arguments that are passed to each individual event handler will all contain at least this information; some will contain even more data. The BuildWarningEventArgs object contains additional information that helps identify where in the build script the warning was raised.

The samples contain the complete source to the IndentFileLogger. This is a very simple logger that maintains logs messages with indentation depending on when the message was received. This is implemented using an int that keeps track of the current indentation. When a started event (e.g., ProjectStarted, TargetStarted, etc.) is encountered the indent level is increased. Conversely, when a finished event is encountered then the indent level is decreased. The reason for discussing this logger is not the implementation, but how the

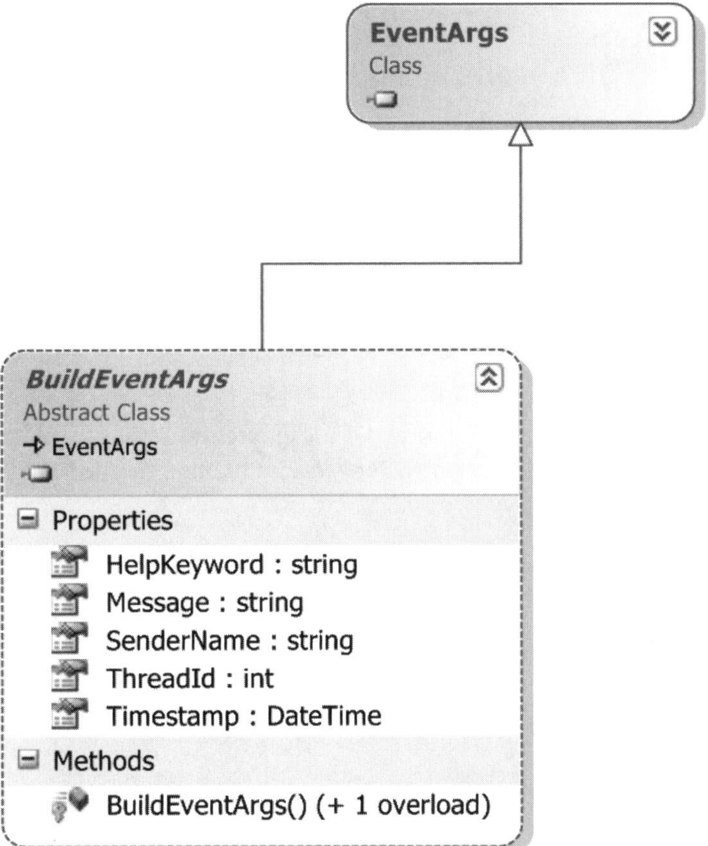

FIGURE 5-4 BuildEventArgs class diagram

results are logged to demonstrate the order in which these events are raised. When building the sample solution with this logger attached, the first section of the log is shown as follows. Note some lines were truncated to fit this page.

```
BuildMessage:Using solution cache file "..\..\..\..\MSBuildExamples.sln.cache" ...
BuildStarted:Build started.
  ProjectStarted:Project "MSBuildExamples.sln" (default targets):
    BuildMessage:Building with tools version "3.5".
    TargetStarted:Target "ValidateSolutionConfiguration" in project "MSBuildExamples.sln"
      BuildMessage:Task "Error" skipped, due to false condition; ...
      BuildMessage:Task "Warning" skipped, due to false condition; ...
      BuildMessage:Using "Message" task from assembly ...
      TaskStarted:Task "Message"
        BuildMessage:Building solution configuration ...
        TaskFinished:Done executing task "Message".
      TargetFinished:Done building target ...
    TargetStarted:Target "ValidateToolsVersions" ...
      BuildMessage:Task "Error" skipped, due to false ...
      TargetFinished:Done building target "ValidateToolsVersions" ...
    TargetStarted:Target "Build" in project "MSBuildExamples.sln"
```

```
BuildMessage:Using "MSBuild" task from assembly ...
TaskStarted:Task "MSBuild"
  BuildMessage:Global Properties:
  BuildMessage:  Configuration=Debug
```

The IndentFileLogger starts each log message with the event type that raised it. From the preceding output you can see the order in which these events are raised. BuildStarted will be followed by ProjectStarted, then TargetStarted and any task related events inside of that. Messages, errors, warnings, and status events can be raised at any point during the build process. We will move on to discuss creating custom loggers by taking a look at a very simple logger, the HelloLogger.

The HelloLogger will not accept any parameters and it will ignore the Verbosity setting. We will leave that for other examples later in this chapter. The *Initialize* method for this logger is shown as follows.

```
public void Initialize(IEventSource eventSource)
{
    // always writes to a log with this name
    string logFile = "hello.log";
    if (File.Exists(logFile))
    { File.Delete(logFile); }

    // initialize the writer
    writer = new StreamWriter(logFile);
    writer.AutoFlush = true;
    //this writer must be closed in the Shutdown() method

    // register to the events you are interested in here
    eventSource.AnyEventRaised +=
        new AnyEventHandler(AnyEventRaised);
    eventSource.BuildStarted +=
        new BuildStartedEventHandler(BuildStarted);
    eventSource.BuildFinished +=
        new BuildFinishedEventHandler(BuildFinished);
    eventSource.CustomEventRaised +=
        new CustomBuildEventHandler(CustomEvent);
    eventSource.ErrorRaised +=
        new BuildErrorEventHandler(ErrorRaised);
    eventSource.MessageRaised +=
        new BuildMessageEventHandler(MessageRaised);
    eventSource.ProjectStarted +=
        new ProjectStartedEventHandler(ProjectStarted);
    eventSource.ProjectStarted +=
        new ProjectStartedEventHandler(ProjectFinished);
    eventSource.StatusEventRaised +=
        new BuildStatusEventHandler(StatusEvent);
    eventSource.TargetStarted +=
        new TargetStartedEventHandler(TargetStarted);
    eventSource.TargetFinished +=
        new TargetFinishedEventHandler(TargetFinished);
    eventSource.TaskStarted +=
        new TaskStartedEventHandler(TaskStarted);
```

```
        eventSource.TaskFinished +=
            new TaskFinishedEventHandler(TaskFinished);
        eventSource.WarningRaised +=
            new BuildWarningEventHandler(WarningRaised);
    }
```

In this method, we first initialize the writer to the file that will contain the contents of the log. Following that, we attach an event handler to all the available build events. Even though each event is assigned a distinct handler in this logger, each delegate performs the same operation, `writer.WriteLine(GetLogMessage(e));`. In the next code snippet, you can see the definition for the ILogger parameters, the *Shutdown* method, and a couple helper methods. From the event handlers, the BuildStarted event handler is shown for brevity and lack of repetition; the other event handlers are not shown but they are a replica of the *BuildStarted* method. The full source is available with the code samples for this text.

```
void BuildStarted(object sender, BuildStartedEventArgs e)
{ writer.WriteLine(GetLogMessage("BuildStarted",e)); }

/// <summary>
/// This is set by the MSBuild engine
/// </summary>
public string Parameters
{ get; set; }

/// <summary>
/// Called by MSBuild engine to give you a chance to
/// perform any cleanup
/// </summary>
public void Shutdown()
{
    // close the writer
    if (writer != null)
    {
        writer.Flush();
        writer.Close();
        writer = null;
    }
}

public LoggerVerbosity Verbosity
{ get; set; }

protected string GetLogMessage(string eventName, BuildEventArgs e)
{
    if (string.IsNullOrEmpty(eventName)){ throw new ArgumentNullException("eventName"); }

    string eMessage = string.Format("{0}\t{1}\t{2}",
        eventName,
        FormatString(e.Message),
        FormatString(e.HelpKeyword)
        );
    return eMessage;
}
```

```
protected string FormatString(string str)
{
    string result = string.Empty;
    if (!string.IsNullOrEmpty(str))
    {
        result = str.Replace("\t", "    ")
            .Replace("\r\n", "\r\n\t\t\t\t");
    }
    return result;
}
```

From the previous snippet, we can see that the Verbosity and Parameters properties are implemented even though they are not used. Inside the *Shutdown* method is where the writer to the log file is closed out. The only other elements in this class are a couple of helper methods to get the log message from a build event argument as well as a method to format the message for the logger. From the folder `MSBuildExamples\Examples.Loggers\bin\Debug\Samples\` the command to build the `Unittest.Proj1.csproj` with the HelloLogger attached would be `msbuild.exe ..\..\..\..\unittest\Unittest.Proj1\Unittest.Proj1.csproj -l:HelloLogger,..\Examples.Loggers.dll`. If you execute this command you will see a file, hello.log, written to the working directory. This is the log created by this logger. A portion of this log is shown next with some of the lines truncated.

```
MessageRaised    Overriding target "SatelliteDllsProjectOutputGroup" in project ...
AnyEventRaised   Overriding target "SatelliteDllsProjectOutputGroup" in project ...
BuildStarted     Build started.
StatusEvent      Build started.
AnyEventRaised   Build started.
ProjectStarted   Project "Unittest.Proj1.csproj" (default targets):
ProjectFinished  Project "Unittest.Proj1.csproj" (default targets):
StatusEvent      Project "Unittest.Proj1.csproj" (default targets):
AnyEventRaised   Project "Unittest.Proj1.csproj" (default targets):
MessageRaised    Building with tools version "3.5".
AnyEventRaised   Building with tools version "3.5".
TargetStarted    Target "_CheckForInvalidConfigurationAndPlatform" in project ...
StatusEvent      Target "_CheckForInvalidConfigurationAndPlatform" in project ...
AnyEventRaised   Target "_CheckForInvalidConfigurationAndPlatform" in project ...
MessageRaised    Task "Error" skipped, due to false condition; ...
AnyEventRaised   Task "Error" skipped, due to false condition; ...
MessageRaised    Task "Warning" skipped, due to false condition; ...
AnyEventRaised   Task "Warning" skipped, due to false condition; ...
MessageRaised    Using "Message" task from assembly ...
AnyEventRaised   Using "Message" task from assembly ...
TaskStarted      Task "Message"
StatusEvent      Task "Message"
AnyEventRaised   Task "Message"
MessageRaised    Configuration=Debug
AnyEventRaised   Configuration=Debug
TaskFinished     Done executing task "Message".
```

From the log file we can see that the HelloLogger successfully logged the build process as expected. Now that we've shown an example of creating a completely new MSBuild logger, we'll move on to discuss employing one of the other methods of creating custom loggers mentioned previously.

Extending the Logger Abstract Class

The definition for an MSBuild logger is that it implements the ILogger interface. You don't need to implement this interface directly; you can extend the Logger abstract class instead. When you extend this class, you need to provide the definition only for the *Initialize* method. The class diagram for the Logger class is shown in Figure 5-5.

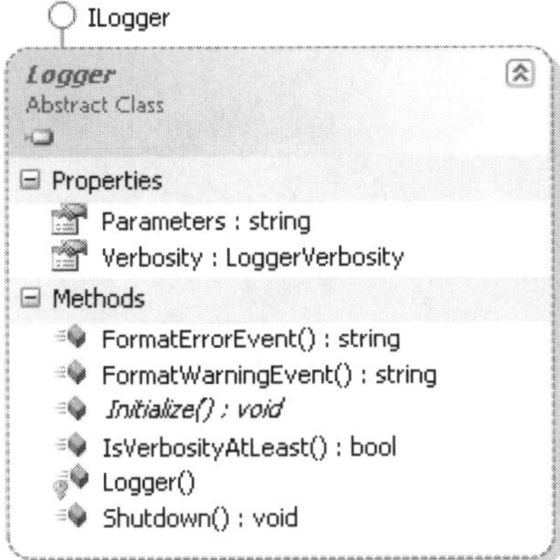

FIGURE 5-5 Logger class diagram

From Figure 5-5 you can see that there are three helper methods that can be used to help the logging process. Those methods are summarized in Table 5-5.

TABLE 5-5 Logger Helper Methods

Name	Description
FormatErrorEvent	This can be used to format a BuildErrorEventArgs object into a readable string.
FormatWarningEvent	This can be used to format a BuildWarningEventArgs object into a readable string.
IsVerbosityAtLeast	Can be used to determine if the current verbosity setting of the logger is greater than the value passed in.

We will now create a simple logger that extends the Logger class and that makes use of both the Verbosity and Parameters. This logger builds on the previous example and is called HelloLogger2.

The HelloLogger2 logger will parse the parameters as well as use the verbosity setting to determine what messages should be placed in the log file. In this logger, the *Initialize* method has changed a little bit; the most significant change is that the method InitializeParameters is called. The next snippet contains this method and a few supporting methods. In the snippet I have bolded a few key elements that we will discuss.

```
public override void Initialize(IEventSource eventSource)
{
    // parse the values passed in as parameters
    InitializeParameters();

    if (string.IsNullOrEmpty(LogFile))
    {
        //apply default log name here
        LogFile = "hello2.log";
    }

    if (File.Exists(LogFile))
    { File.Delete(LogFile); }

    // initialize the writer
    writer = new StreamWriter(LogFile);

    // register to the events you are interested in here
    eventSource.BuildStarted +=
        new BuildStartedEventHandler(BuildStarted);
    eventSource.BuildFinished +=
        new BuildFinishedEventHandler(BuildFinished);
    eventSource.CustomEventRaised +=
        new CustomBuildEventHandler(CustomEvent);
    eventSource.ErrorRaised +=
        new BuildErrorEventHandler(ErrorRaised);
    eventSource.MessageRaised +=
        new BuildMessageEventHandler(MessageRaised);
    eventSource.ProjectStarted +=
        new ProjectStartedEventHandler(ProjectStarted);
    eventSource.ProjectStarted +=
        new ProjectStartedEventHandler(ProjectFinished);
    eventSource.TargetStarted +=
        new TargetStartedEventHandler(TargetStarted);
    eventSource.TargetFinished +=
        new TargetFinishedEventHandler(TargetFinished);
    eventSource.TaskStarted +=
        new TaskStartedEventHandler(TaskStarted);
    eventSource.TaskFinished +=
        new TaskFinishedEventHandler(TaskFinished);
    eventSource.WarningRaised +=
        new BuildWarningEventHandler(WarningRaised);
}
/// <summary>
/// Read values form <c>Parameters</c> string and populate
/// other properties.
/// </summary>
```

```
protected virtual void InitializeParameters()
{
    try
    {
        if (!string.IsNullOrEmpty(Parameters))
        {
            // Parameters string should be in the format:
            //  Prop1=value1;Prop2=value2;Prop3=value;...
            foreach (string paramString in
                this.Parameters.Split(new char[] {';'}))
            {
                // now we have Prop1=value1
                string[] keyValue =
                    paramString.Split(new char[] {'='});
                if (keyValue == null || keyValue.Length < 2)
                {
                    continue;
                }
                // keyValue[0] = Prop1
                // keyValue[1] = value1
                this.ProcessParam(keyValue[0].ToLower(), keyValue[1]);
            }
        }
    }
    catch (Exception e)
    {
        throw new LoggerException(
            string.Format(
                "Unable to initialize parameters; message={0}",
                e.Message),
                e);
    }
}

/// <summary>
/// Method that will process the parameter value.
/// If either <code>name</code> or
/// <code>value</code> is empty then this parameter
/// will not be processed.
/// </summary>
/// <param name="name">name of the paramater</param>
/// <param name="value">value of the parameter</param>
protected virtual void ProcessParam(string name, string value)
{
    try
    {
        if (!string.IsNullOrEmpty(name) &&
            !string.IsNullOrEmpty(value))
        {
            switch (name.Trim().ToUpper())
            {
                case ("LOGFILE"):
                case ("L"):
                    this.LogFile = value;
                    break;
```

```
                case ("VERBOSITY"):
                case ("V"):
                    ProcessVerbosity(value);
                    break;
            }
        }
    }
    catch (Exception e)
    {
        string message = string.Format(
            "Unable to process parameters;[name={0}, value={1}] message={2}",
            name, value, e.Message);
        throw new LoggerException(message, e);
    }
}

/// <summary>
/// This will set the verbosity level from the parameter
/// </summary>
/// <param name="level"></param>
protected virtual void ProcessVerbosity(string level)
{
    if (!string.IsNullOrEmpty(level))
    {
        switch (level.Trim().ToUpper())
        {
            case ("QUIET"):
            case ("Q"):
                this.Verbosity = LoggerVerbosity.Quiet;
                break;

            case ("MINIMAL"):
            case ("M"):
                this.Verbosity = LoggerVerbosity.Minimal;
                break;

            case ("NORMAL"):
            case ("N"):
                this.Verbosity = LoggerVerbosity.Normal;
                break;

            case ("DETAILED"):
            case ("D"):
                this.Verbosity = LoggerVerbosity.Detailed;
                break;

            case ("DIAGNOSTIC"):
            case ("DIAG"):
                this.Verbosity = LoggerVerbosity.Diagnostic;
                break;
        }
    }
}
```

From the bold lines, this first is inside the *InitializeParameters* method, which calls the *ProcessParam* method for each parameter passed in. Once the Parameters string has been parsed we have to interpret what it contains. The *InitializeParameters* method splits the string into an array of strings containing key-value pairs. As mentioned previously, the format of the Parameters string is entirely up to the logger. By convention I have chosen to separate elements by a semicolon and to specify name-values in the format `<name>=<value>`. Unless you have a specific requirement that would not allow this, you should do the same.

The next highlight is on the usage of the LoggerException. This is a special type of exception that the MSBuild engine specifically handles. MSBuild loggers should throw this type of exception instead of any other exceptions. When this exception is thrown it gives the MSBuild engine a chance to gracefully shut down the process. Once this exception is caught, the *Shutdown* method on all attached loggers will be called before the msbuild.exe process exits. If any other type of exception is thrown, MSBuild considers this a bug in the logger and logs the call stack to the console to help you to fix the bug.

The final item highlighted is the *ProcessVerbosity* method. This method is called inside the *ProcessParam* method to initialize the value for the verbosity. If a logger supports its own verbosity setting, one other than the current verbosity for the entire build, then it must do so through the parameters string. If you remember from previously, the default verbosity setting is determined from the /verbosity (/v) switch for msbuild.exe. This logger is able to have a different verbosity if a Verbosity (V) value is passed through the parameters string. If you create your own logger you should be able to reuse the definition of this method to take care of this parameter for you.

We have now discussed how the parameters are parsed, so we can take a look at how the verbosity influences what log messages are sent to the log file. I based the types of messages that were being logged on messages that the console logger logs. There are two types of messages that you always want to log: Errors and Warnings. The next code snippet contains the handlers for these two events as well as the BuildStarted and BuildFinished handlers.

```
void ErrorRaised(object sender, BuildErrorEventArgs e)
{
    // always write out errors
    writer.WriteLine(GetLogMessage("ErrorRaised", e));
}
void WarningRaised(object sender, BuildWarningEventArgs e)
{
    // always log warnings
    writer.WriteLine(GetLogMessage("WarningRaised", e));
}
void BuildStarted(object sender, BuildStartedEventArgs e)
{
    if (IsVerbosityAtLeast(LoggerVerbosity.Normal))
    {
        writer.WriteLine(GetLogMessage("BuildStarted", e));
    }
}
void BuildFinished(object sender, BuildFinishedEventArgs e)
{
    if (IsVerbosityAtLeast(LoggerVerbosity.Normal))
    {
        writer.WriteLine(GetLogMessage("BuildFinished", e));
    }
}
```

In the previous snippet, you can see that the errors and warnings are always written to the log, as previously mentioned. The BuildStarted and BuildFinished events are not always written to the log. These messages should be passed only if the verbosity is set to Normal or higher. This is accomplished by the bold "if" statements. If the events are paired, for instance BuildStarted and BuildFinished, you should make sure that the required verbosity for both messages is the same. In the previous snippet, both handlers check to see that the verbosity is set to Normal or higher. Of all the event handlers in this logger, the only handler that is a bit different is the MessageRaised event. The definition for that handler is shown in the next snippet.

```
void MessageRaised(object sender, BuildMessageEventArgs e)
{
    bool logMessage = false;

    switch (e.Importance)
    {
        case MessageImportance.High:
            logMessage = IsVerbosityAtLeast(LoggerVerbosity.Minimal);
            break;
        case MessageImportance.Normal:
            logMessage = IsVerbosityAtLeast(LoggerVerbosity.Normal);
            break;
        case MessageImportance.Low:
            logMessage = IsVerbosityAtLeast(LoggerVerbosity.Detailed);
            break;
        default:
            throw new LoggerException(
                string.Format(
                "Unrecognized value for MessageImportance: [{0}]",
                e.Importance));
    }

    if (logMessage)
    {
        writer.WriteLine(GetLogMessage("MessageRaised", e));
    }
}
```

The reason why this event handler is different from the others is that the BuildMessageEventArgs has an importance associated with it. Because of this we have to examine the verbosity as well as the importance set for the message. This event is raised by the Message task, through an instance of the `Microsoft.Build.Utilities.TaskLoggingHelper` class. The value for the importance on the event argument comes from the Importance parameter passed to the Message task. Using this logger is similar to using the previous logger. In the next image, you can see how we attach the HelloLogger2 with a log file named unittest.diag.log and a Verbosity setting of Diagnostic.

```
C:\Data\MSBuildExamples\unittest\Unittest.Proj1>msbuild Unittest.Proj1.csproj /t
:Rebuild /l:HelloLogger2,..\..\Examples.Loggers\bin\Debug\Examples.Loggers.dll;l
ogfile=unittest.diag.log.;v=diag /nologo
Build started 7/30/2008 12:22:31 AM.
Project "C:\Data\MSBuildExamples\unittest\Unittest.Proj1\Unittest.Proj1.csproj"
 on node 0 (Rebuild target(s)).
  Deleting file "C:\Data\MSBuildExamples\unittest\Unittest.Proj1\bin\Debug\Unit
  test.Proj1.dll".
  Deleting file "C:\Data\MSBuildExamples\unittest\Unittest.Proj1\bin\Debug\Unit
  test.Proj1.pdb".
  Deleting file "C:\Data\MSBuildExamples\unittest\Unittest.Proj1\bin\Debug\nuni
  t.framework.dll".
  Deleting file "C:\Data\MSBuildExamples\unittest\Unittest.Proj1\bin\Debug\nuni
  t.framework.xml".
  Deleting file "C:\Data\MSBuildExamples\unittest\Unittest.Proj1\obj\Debug\Reso
  lveAssemblyReference.cache".
  Deleting file "C:\Data\MSBuildExamples\unittest\Unittest.Proj1\obj\Debug\Unit
  test.Proj1.dll".
  Deleting file "C:\Data\MSBuildExamples\unittest\Unittest.Proj1\obj\Debug\Unit
  test.Proj1.pdb".
_CopyFilesMarkedCopyLocal:
  Copying file from "..\..\contrib\nunit2.2\nunit.framework.dll" to "bin\Debug\
  nunit.framework.dll".
  Copying file from "..\..\contrib\nunit2.2\nunit.framework.xml" to "bin\Debug\
  nunit.framework.xml".
CopyFilesToOutputDirectory:
  Copying file from "obj\Debug\Unittest.Proj1.dll" to "bin\Debug\Unittest.Proj1
  .dll".
  Unittest.Proj1 -> C:\Data\MSBuildExamples\unittest\Unittest.Proj1\bin\Debug\U
  nittest.Proj1.dll
  Copying file from "obj\Debug\Unittest.Proj1.pdb" to "bin\Debug\Unittest.Proj1
  .pdb".
Done Building Project "C:\Data\MSBuildExamples\unittest\Unittest.Proj1\Unittest
.Proj1.csproj" (Rebuild target(s)).


Build succeeded.
    0 Warning(s)
    0 Error(s)
```

FIGURE 5-6 HelloLogger2 usage

We can see that the logger was successfully attached to the build process, and the expected log file was indeed created. Now that we have covered many details of creating custom loggers, we'll see how we can extend the ConsoleLogger to create new loggers.

Extending Existing Loggers

In the previous section, we saw how we could create new loggers by implementing the ILogger interface and extending the Logger abstract class. The only other method to create a new logger is to extend an existing logger. We'll now see how to accomplish this by extending the console logger. The console logger can be used as a basis for various loggers, not just those that log to the console. You may be surprised to find out that the FileLogger class extends the ConsoleLogger class! Some reasons you should consider extending this class are outlined here.

- **Ease of Creation** From the three methods listed previously for creating new loggers, extending an existing logger is the easiest method.
- **Automatic Indentation** The console logger already has a sophisticated means for indenting the log messages to logically group log messages, as well as implementing rules to know when to show certain events. It's quite a lot of work to make a logger produce output that looks good. When you extend the console logger, you can get this functionality.
- **Consistent Verbosity Interpretation** Because you are extending the console logger, you can let it determine what log messages need to be logged based on the verbosity setting instead of doing it manually.

Because of the advantages of extending the console logger, you should give it strong consideration before you implement the same logic. The console logger has five properties, which are summarized in Table 5-6.

TABLE 5-6 ConsoleLogger Properties

Name	Type	Description
Parameters	string	The property that contains the parameter string that was passed to the logger.
ShowSummary	bool	If true, then a summary of errors and warnings will be passed to the logger.
SkipProjectStartedText	bool	If true, then the log message stating that a project that is beginning to build is not passed to the logger.
Verbosity	Microsoft.Build. Framework, LoggerVerbosity	Determines the amount of detail that should be contained in the log. Possible values; quiet (q), minimal (m), normal (n), detailed (d), and diagnostic (diag).
WriteHandler	delegate	The delegate that will be called to physically write log statements. In custom implementations that are not logging to the console, you will need to override this property.

The values for the properties listed in the preceding outline will affect what statements will be logged and how they will be logged. For example, if your logger should never show the summary text, then you should set the value for ShowSummary to false and not allow it to be overridden. The most interesting property is the WriteHandler property. This is the delegate that will be called to place the messages into the log. The declaration for this delegate is `public delegate void WriteHandler(string message)`. If the console logger determines that a message should be logged, based on event and verbosity, then this delegate is invoked to perform the write into the log. If you are creating a new logger to write to a destination other than the console, you will have to override this value. This is performed in the CustomFileLogger, which we'll now take a look at.

The CustomFileLogger is a new custom logger that, as its name suggests, writes its log to a file. It extends the ConsoleLogger and overrides the WriteHandler to achieve this. Earlier we stated the indentation is taken care of by the base class. When you override the *WriteHandler* method the indentation has already been placed in the output. All the WriteHandler can do is write the text of the log message. You cannot access the current indent level. The properties of this logger, as well as the *Initialize* and *Shutdown* methods, are shown in the next snippet.

```
protected string LogFile { get; set; }
protected bool Append { get; set; }
protected StreamWriter FileWriter {get;set;}
```

```
public override void Initialize(Microsoft.Build.Framework.IEventSource eventSource)
{
    // default value
    Append = false;

    ParseCustomParameters();
    base.Initialize(eventSource);

    if (string.IsNullOrEmpty(LogFile))
    {
        // default value
        LogFile = "custom.build.log";
    }

    FileWriter = new StreamWriter(LogFile, Append);
    FileWriter.AutoFlush = true;

    base.WriteHandler = new WriteHandler(HandleWrite);
}

public override void Shutdown()
{
    base.Shutdown();
    if (FileWriter != null)
    {
        FileWriter.Close();
        FileWriter = null;
    }
}
```

In the *Initialize* method, you can see that it calls ParseCustomParameters, which will extract the values that have been passed through the logger's parameters. We will see this method shortly. In addition to this, the important items in that method are: base.Initialize is called, the file writer is initialized, and WriterHandler is overridden to point to the *HandleWrite* method. In the *Shutdown* method, the file writer is closed out to ensure that the stream is closed gracefully. Now we can take a look at how the parameters are parsed out; the related methods are shown here.

```
public virtual void ParseCustomParameters()
{
    if (!string.IsNullOrEmpty(Parameters))
    {
        string[] paramPairs = Parameters.Split(';');
        for (int i = 0; i < paramPairs.Length; i++)
        {
            if (paramPairs[i].Length > 0)
            {
                string[] paramPair = paramPairs[i].Split('=');
                if (!string.IsNullOrEmpty(paramPair[0]))
                {
                    if (paramPair.Length > 1)
                    {
                        ApplyParam(paramPair[0], paramPair[1]);
                    }
```

```
                    else
                    {
                        ApplyParam(paramPair[0], null);
                    }
                }
            }
        }
    }
}

public virtual void ApplyParam(string paramName, string paramValue)
{
    if (!string.IsNullOrEmpty(paramName))
    {
        string paramNameUpper = paramName.ToUpperInvariant();
        switch (paramNameUpper)
        {
            case "LOGFILE":
            case "L":
                LogFile = paramValue;
                break;
            case "VERBOSITY":
            case "V":
                Verbosity = GetLoggerVerbosityFrom(paramValue);
                break;
            case "APPEND":
                if (string.Compare(paramValue, "true", true) == 0)
                {
                    Append = true;
                }
                else
                {
                    Append = false;
                }
                break;
        }
    }
}

protected LoggerVerbosity GetLoggerVerbosityFrom(string verbosityStr)
{
    if (string.IsNullOrEmpty(verbosityStr))
    { throw new ArgumentNullException("verbosityStr"); }

    string verbosityUpper = verbosityStr.ToUpperInvariant();
    LoggerVerbosity? result = null;
    switch (verbosityUpper)
    {
        case "QUIET":
        case "Q":
            result = LoggerVerbosity.Quiet;
            break;
```

```
            case "MINIMAL":
            case "M":
                result = LoggerVerbosity.Minimal;
                break;
            case "NORMAL":
            case "N":
                result = LoggerVerbosity.Normal;
                break;
            case "DETAILED":
            case "D":
                result = LoggerVerbosity.Detailed;
                break;
            case "DIAGNOSTIC":
            case "DIAG":
                result = LoggerVerbosity.Diagnostic;
                break;
            default:
                result = null;
                break;
        }

        if (!result.HasValue)
        {
            throw new LoggerException(
                string.Format("Invalid value for Verbosity: {0}",
                    verbosityStr));
        }
        else
        {
            return result.Value;
        }
    }
```

Inside the *ParseCustomParameters* method I have bold two lines of code. The first bold line, `string[] paramPairs = Parameters.Split(';')`, splits up the string based on ";" characters. This creates an array of strings that contain key-value pairs in the format <name>=<value>. The other bold line is `string[] paramPair = paramPairs[i].Split('=')`. This separates the key-value string into a key and value; then these values are interpreted by the *ApplyParam* method. I point these statements out to reinforce the fact that the logger itself is completely responsible for parsing and interpreting what the values in the string mean. Even the value for the verbosity is not automatically processed by the Logger class.

Now that we have seen how the CustomFileLogger was created, we can see how to use it. In order to attach this logger, as with any custom logger, we will use the /l (/logger) switch on the msbuild.exe. We can see an example of attaching this logger in Figure 5-7, which shows the beginning of a build with this logger. The command for this from the Examples. Loggers\bin\Debug\Samples\ is

```
msbuild ..\..\..\..\Examples.Tasks\Examples.Tasks.csproj /t:Rebuild
/l:CustomFileLogger,..\Examples.Loggers.dll,
```

```
C:\Data\MSBuildExamples\Examples.Loggers\bin\Debug\Samples>msbuild ..\..\..\..\E
xamples.Tasks\Examples.Tasks.csproj /t:Rebuild /l:CustomFileLogger,..\Examples.L
oggers.dll /nologo
Build started 8/6/2008 12:35:05 AM.
Project "C:\Data\MSBuildExamples\Examples.Tasks\Examples.Tasks.csproj" on node
0 (Rebuild target(s)).
  Deleting file "C:\Data\MSBuildExamples\Examples.Tasks\bin\Debug\Samples\JSLin
  t\broswer01.js".
  Deleting file "C:\Data\MSBuildExamples\Examples.Tasks\bin\Debug\Samples\JSLin
  t\fail01.js".
  Deleting file "C:\Data\MSBuildExamples\Examples.Tasks\bin\Debug\Samples\JSLin
  t\pass01.js".
  Deleting file "C:\Data\MSBuildExamples\Examples.Tasks\bin\Debug\Samples\JSLin
  t\temp_jslint.js".
  Deleting file "C:\Data\MSBuildExamples\Examples.Tasks\bin\Debug\Samples\sampl
  eFiles\four.txt".
  Deleting file "C:\Data\MSBuildExamples\Examples.Tasks\bin\Debug\Samples\sampl
  eFiles\one.txt".
  Deleting file "C:\Data\MSBuildExamples\Examples.Tasks\bin\Debug\Samples\sampl
  eFiles\sub\sub_four.txt".
  Deleting file "C:\Data\MSBuildExamples\Examples.Tasks\bin\Debug\Samples\sampl
  eFiles\sub\sub_one.txt".
```

FIGURE 5-7 CustomFileLogger usage example

In Figure 5-7 we can see that the build for the Example.Tasks project is invoked with the new custom logger attached to the process. Since the build successfully started we know that MSBuild was able to create a new instance of the logger and attach it to the process. If you repeat this command you will see that a new log file, custom.build.log, has been created. Since we didn't specify a value for LogFile, the default value is used, which is custom.build.log. As shown with the file logger, it is useful to attach multiple loggers to the build process. In order to do so, you simply use multiple /l switches. You can see this in action in Figure 5-8. The command here is

```
msbuild ..\..\..\..\Examples.Tasks\Examples.Tasks.csproj /t:Rebuild
/l:CustomFileLogger,..\Examples.Loggers.dll;v=m;logfile=custom.minimal.log
/l:CustomFileLogger,..\Examples.Loggers.dll;v=diag;logfile=custom.diag.log
```

```
C:\Data\MSBuildExamples\Examples.Loggers\bin\Debug\Samples>msbuild ..\..\..\..\E
xamples.Tasks\Examples.Tasks.csproj /t:Rebuild /l:CustomFileLogger,..\Examples.L
oggers.dll;v=m;logfile=custom.minimal.log /l:CustomFileLogger,..\Examples.Logger
s.dll;v=diag;logfile=custom.diag.log /nologo
Build started 8/6/2008 12:49:54 AM.
Project "C:\Data\MSBuildExamples\Examples.Tasks\Examples.Tasks.csproj" on node
0 (Rebuild target(s)).
  Deleting file "C:\Data\MSBuildExamples\Examples.Tasks\bin\Debug\Samples\JSLin
  t\broswer01.js".
  Deleting file "C:\Data\MSBuildExamples\Examples.Tasks\bin\Debug\Samples\JSLin
  t\fail01.js".
  Deleting file "C:\Data\MSBuildExamples\Examples.Tasks\bin\Debug\Samples\JSLin
  t\pass01.js".
  Deleting file "C:\Data\MSBuildExamples\Examples.Tasks\bin\Debug\Samples\JSLin
  t\temp_jslint.js".
  Deleting file "C:\Data\MSBuildExamples\Examples.Tasks\bin\Debug\Samples\sampl
  eFiles\four.txt".
  Deleting file "C:\Data\MSBuildExamples\Examples.Tasks\bin\Debug\Samples\sampl
  eFiles\one.txt".
```

FIGURE 5-8 Attaching multiple CustomFileLoggers

The MSBuild command demonstrated in Figure 5-8 shows how we can attach two instances of the CustomFileLogger to the build process. One is set to a Minimal verbosity setting and the other to Diagnostic mode. The file custom.minimal.log will be used to quickly identify errors and warnings, and the custom.diagnostic.log file can be used to diagnose the build process. With this content we have now covered extending existing loggers, which was the third of the three options for creating new custom loggers. Extending the console logger in this fashion is a good idea, but it does have some limitations. The most difficult limitation to deal with for some loggers is the fact that you are simply logging lines of text; you don't really have an idea of the state of the process.

This is because the console logger is handling this and then simply calling into the WriteHandler to handle writing text to the log file. One example where you would need to know which event caused messages to be logged would be if you were using XmlLogger. In order to create the correct XML element you need to know what build event occurred. We will see how to do this now.

FileLoggerBase and XmlLogger

In order to demonstrate a realistic logger that doesn't extend ConsoleLogger, I will show you the XmlLogger. The full source for this logger is available at my open source MSBuild project, *codeplex.com/sedodream*, as well as in the samples provided with this text. By default, MSBuild will create a text-based log, but if you are going to feed this log to other applications for processing or presentation it might be easier if you had an XML-based log. Since one doesn't ship with MSBuild, you can write your own. In this section we will do just that.

Before we get into the implementation of the XmlLogger take a look at the output from the logger shown next. The command executed from the Examples.Loggers\bin\Debug\ directory is:

```
msbuild ..\..\..\Fundamentals\Properties04.proj /l:XmlLogger,Examples.Loggers.dll
```

The resulting XML file is shown in the next snippet.

```
<MSBuild>
  <Build Started="10/16/2008 11:13:35 PM"
         Verbosity="Normal"
         Finished="10/16/2008 11:13:35 PM"
         Succeeded="True">
    <Message>Build started.</Message>
    <Project Name="C:\Data\MSBuildExamples\Fundamentals\Properties04.proj"
             Message="Project &quot;Properties04.proj&quot; (default targets):"
             Started="10/16/2008 11:13:35 PM" Finished="10/16/2008 11:13:35 PM">
      <Target Started="10/16/2008 11:13:35 PM"
              Name="PrintAssemblyInfo"
              Message=
            "Target &quot;PrintAssemblyInfo&quot; in project &quot;Properties04
                  .proj&quot;"
              Finished="10/16/2008 11:13:35 PM"
              Succeeded="True">
        <Task Started="10/16/2008 11:13:35 PM"
              Name="Message"
              Finished="10/16/2008 11:13:35 PM">
          <Message Importance="Normal">Temp: C:\DOCUME~1\Ibrahim\LOCALS~1\Temp
          </Message>
        </Task>
        <Task Started="10/16/2008 11:13:35 PM"
              Name="Message"
              Finished="10/16/2008 11:13:35 PM">
          <Message Importance="Normal">Windir: C:\WINDOWS</Message>
        </Task>
```

```
        <Task Started="10/16/2008 11:13:35 PM" Name="Message"
              Finished="10/16/2008 11:13:35 PM">
          <Message Importance="Normal">
            VS80COMNTOOLS: c :\Program Files\Microsoft Visual Studio 9.0\Common7\
                  Tools\
          </Message>
        </Task>
        <Task Started="10/16/2008 11:13:35 PM" Name="Message"
              Finished="10/16/2008 11:13:35 PM">
          <Message Importance="Normal">
            VS90COMNTOOLS: c:\Program Files\Microsoft Visual Studio 9.0\Common7\Tools\
          </Message>
        </Task>
      </Target>
    </Project>
    <Message>Build succeeded.</Message>
  </Build>
</MSBuild>
```

We will start our discussion by taking a look at the XmlLoggers base class FileLoggerBase. This is an abstract class that I have written to assist in the creation of file-based loggers. In Figure 5-9, you will find a class diagram for the XmlLogger.

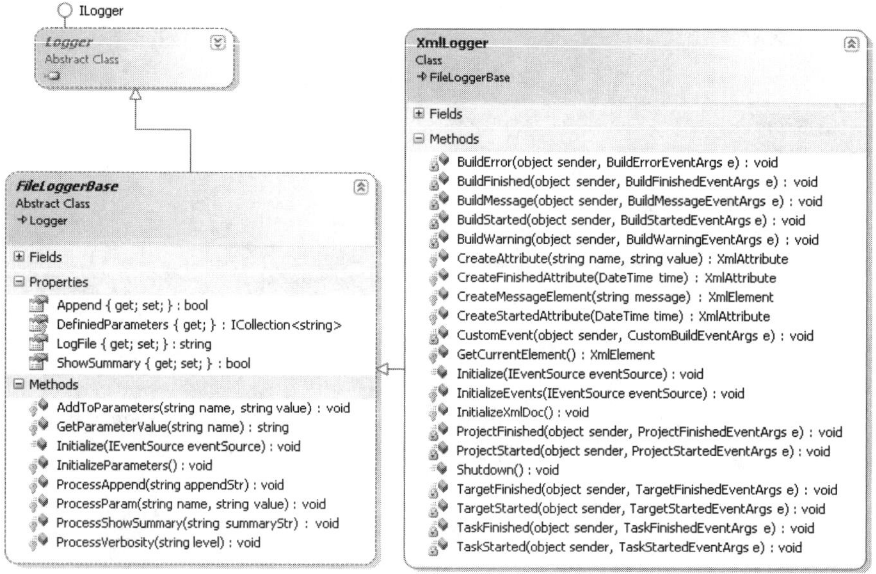

FIGURE 5-9 XmlLogger class diagram

From the class diagram we can see that the FileLoggerBase class extends from the Microsoft.Build.Utilities.Logger class. The FileLoggerBase class adds some common functionality that will make creating loggers easier; most notably it will read the values for the parameters shown in Table 5-7.

TABLE 5-7 FileLoggerBase Known Properties

Parameter Name	Description
LogFile	The name of the file to which the log should be written.
Verbosity	The verbosity setting for the logger. These can be specified by full name or short name.
Append	Value that determines if the file should be appended to, if it exists, or overwritten. If false, then the file will be overwritten if it exists.
ShowSummary	Value that determines if a summary should be displayed in the log. It is up to each concrete logger to determine how this affects the behavior of the application.

When parameters are passed to the logger on the command line, they are made available in the Parameters property in the ILogger interface. This property is a string and needs to be parsed by each logger. The FileLoggerBase will parse parameters that are passed in the format `paramName=value;paramName2=value2;`.... This is performed when the *Initialize* method is called. Now that we have discussed what the FileLoggerBase basically takes care of, let's take a look at the XmlLogger implementation.

The XmlLogger uses a set of stacks to keep track of what needs to be written out to the Xml document at the end of the build. The following example shows the definition of the *Initialize* method in the XmlLogger.

```
public override void Initialize(IEventSource eventSource)
{
        errorList = new List<string>();
        warningList = new List<string>();

        buildElements = new Stack<XmlElement>();
        projectElements = new Stack<XmlElement>();
        targetElements = new Stack<XmlElement>();
        taskElements = new Stack<XmlElement>();
        buildTypeList = new Stack<BuildType>();

        // apply default values
        LogFile = "build.log.xml";
        Append = false;
        ShowSummary = false;

        // have base init the parameters
        base.Initialize(eventSource);

        this.InitializeEvents(eventSource);

        this.InitializeXmlDoc();
}
```

In this method, we let the FileLoggerBase class take care of parsing the logger parameters, after which the class fields are initialized. In the *InitializeEvents* method, the build event handlers are registered with the IEventSource. The following example shows the definition of the *InitializeEvents* method.

```
protected void InitializeEvents(IEventSource eventSource)
{
    try
    {
        eventSource.BuildStarted +=
            new BuildStartedEventHandler(this.BuildStarted);
        eventSource.BuildFinished +=
            new BuildFinishedEventHandler(this.BuildFinished);
        eventSource.ProjectStarted +=
            new ProjectStartedEventHandler(this.ProjectStarted);
        eventSource.ProjectFinished +=
            new ProjectFinishedEventHandler(this.ProjectFinished);
        eventSource.TargetStarted +=
            new TargetStartedEventHandler(this.TargetStarted);
        eventSource.TargetFinished +=
            new TargetFinishedEventHandler(this.TargetFinished);
        eventSource.TaskStarted +=
            new TaskStartedEventHandler(this.TaskStarted);
        eventSource.TaskFinished +=
            new TaskFinishedEventHandler(this.TaskFinished);
        eventSource.ErrorRaised +=
            new BuildErrorEventHandler(this.BuildError);
        eventSource.WarningRaised +=
            new BuildWarningEventHandler(this.BuildWarning);
        eventSource.MessageRaised +=
            new BuildMessageEventHandler(this.BuildMessage);
    }
    catch (Exception e)
    {
        string message = string.Format(
            "Unable to initialize events; message={0}",
            e.Message);
        throw new LoggerException(message, e);
    }
}
```

In the preceding snippet, you will notice in the catch block that it converts the Exception to one of type LoggerException. This is important because if your logger raises another exception, then it will be difficult to identify the logger as the reason for the build failure. Of the 14 events defined in the Microsoft.Build.Framework.IEventSource interface, the XmlLogger registers to receive notification of 11 events. Figure 5-10 shows a class diagram for the IEventSource interface, which lists all the available build events. Table 5-4 includes specific information regarding these events.

After the events are registered with the event source, the logger will move on to initialize the Xml document itself in the *InitializeXmlDoc* method. Since we have discussed how this logger is initialized, we can move on to take a look at a few of the handlers themselves. In the

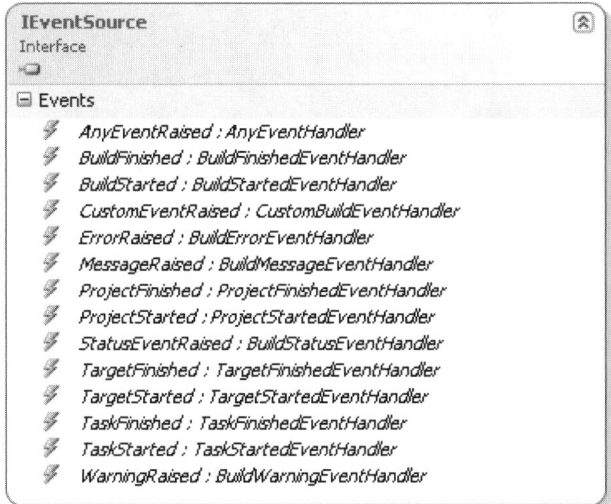

FIGURE 5-10 IEventSource interface

following example, you will see the definition for the BuildStarted and ProjectStarted events. In production code, exceptions would be properly handled.

```
void BuildStarted(object sender, BuildStartedEventArgs e)
{
    buildTypeList.Push(BuildType.Build);

    XmlElement buildElement = xmlDoc.CreateElement("Build");

    rootElement.AppendChild(buildElement);
    buildElement.Attributes.Append(
        CreateStartedAttribute(e.Timestamp));
    buildElement.Attributes.Append(
        CreateAttribute("Verbosity", this.Verbosity.ToString()));

    if (this.Parameters != null &&
        base.IsVerbosityAtLeast(LoggerVerbosity.Detailed))
    {
        // log all the parameters that were passed to the logger
        XmlElement paramElement =
            xmlDoc.CreateElement("LoggerParameters");
        buildElement.AppendChild(paramElement);
        foreach (string current in DefiniedParameters)
        {
            XmlElement currentElement =
                xmlDoc.CreateElement("Parameter");
            currentElement.InnerText =
                current + "=" + GetParameterValue(current);
            paramElement.AppendChild(currentElement);
        }
    }
```

```
    buildElement.AppendChild(CreateMessageElement(e.Message));

    buildElements.Push(buildElement);
}

void ProjectStarted(object sender, ProjectStartedEventArgs e)
{
    buildTypeList.Push(BuildType.Project);

    XmlElement projectElement = xmlDoc.CreateElement("Project");
    projectElements.Push(projectElement);

    buildElements.Peek().AppendChild(projectElement);

    projectElement.Attributes.Append(
        CreateAttribute("Name", e.ProjectFile));

    projectElement.Attributes.Append(
        CreateAttribute("Message", e.Message));
    projectElement.Attributes.Append(
        CreateStartedAttribute(e.Timestamp));

    if (base.IsVerbosityAtLeast(LoggerVerbosity.Detailed))
    {
        projectElement.Attributes.Append(
            CreateAttribute("SenderName", e.SenderName));
    }

    if (base.IsVerbosityAtLeast(LoggerVerbosity.Diagnostic))
    {
        XmlElement propertiesElement =
            xmlDoc.CreateElement("Properties");
        projectElement.AppendChild(propertiesElement);

        foreach (DictionaryEntry current in e.Properties)
        {
            if (current.Equals(null) ||
                current.Key == null ||
                string.IsNullOrEmpty(current.Key.ToString()) ||
                current.Value == null ||
                string.IsNullOrEmpty(current.Value.ToString()))
            {
                continue;
            }
            XmlElement newElement =
                xmlDoc.CreateElement(current.Key.ToString());
            newElement.InnerText = current.Value.ToString();
            propertiesElement.AppendChild(newElement);
        }
    }
}
```

As was stated previously, each logger must interpret what the logger verbosity means. In the two preceding methods, you can see that in a few locations the verbosity is checked before actions are performed. An example of attaching the XmlLogger to a build is shown in Figure 5-11.

```
C:\Data\MSBuildExamples\Examples.Loggers\bin\Debug\Samples>msbuild ..\..\..\..\E
xamples.Tasks\Examples.Tasks.csproj /t:Rebuild /nologo /l:XmlLogger,..\Examples.
Loggers.dll;v=detailed;logfile=build.detailed.xml
Build started 8/7/2008 1:59:42 AM.
Project "C:\Data\MSBuildExamples\Examples.Tasks\Examples.Tasks.csproj" on node
0 (Rebuild target(s)).
  Deleting file "C:\Data\MSBuildExamples\Examples.Tasks\bin\Debug\Samples\JSLin
  t\broswer01.js".
  Deleting file "C:\Data\MSBuildExamples\Examples.Tasks\bin\Debug\Samples\JSLin
  t\fail01.js".
  Deleting file "C:\Data\MSBuildExamples\Examples.Tasks\bin\Debug\Samples\JSLin
  t\pass01.js".
  Deleting file "C:\Data\MSBuildExamples\Examples.Tasks\bin\Debug\Samples\JSLin
  t\temp_jslint.js".
  Deleting file "C:\Data\MSBuildExamples\Examples.Tasks\bin\Debug\Samples\sampl
  eFiles\four.txt".
  Deleting file "C:\Data\MSBuildExamples\Examples.Tasks\bin\Debug\Samples\sampl
  eFiles\one.txt".
  Deleting file "C:\Data\MSBuildExamples\Examples.Tasks\bin\Debug\Samples\sampl
  eFiles\sub\sub_four.txt".
  Deleting file "C:\Data\MSBuildExamples\Examples.Tasks\bin\Debug\Samples\sampl
```

FIGURE 5-11 XmlLogger

In the build command shown in the Figure 5-11, the XmlLogger was attached to the build process. The parameters for that instance specified that the verbosity be set to Detailed and that the log file be placed at build.detailed.xml. This was indeed the behavior and can be confirmed by executing this same statement. Now that we have examined the XmlLogger, we can move on to briefly discuss debugging custom loggers.

Debugging Loggers

Custom loggers are very easy to write and for the most part are easy to implement. Even still, if you are creating new loggers you may need to debug the behavior. Debugging custom loggers is very similar to debugging custom tasks. Just like debugging custom tasks, in the next list you will find three methods that can be used to debug loggers:

1. Examine the contents of the log
2. Debugger.Launch()
3. Start MSBuild as External Program

The simplest and least informative approach is the first one, which entails simply examining the contents of the log to determine the behavior of the logger. If you decide to use this technique, you may want to set the verbosity of the logger to either Detailed or Diagnostic, if possible. This method can be used only for very simple issues and for those that allow the logger to be properly initialized. If there is an initialization error when creating a logger the build process is aborted and no log is written. Unlike the other approaches, this is non-interactive and there is no debugger. For the other two techniques, the Visual Studio debugger will be used.

In second option, the Debugger.Launch() technique, is that when the statement is executed, a dialog will be shown to attach a debugger once you attach Visual Studio to the build process. This dialog is shown in Figure 5-12.

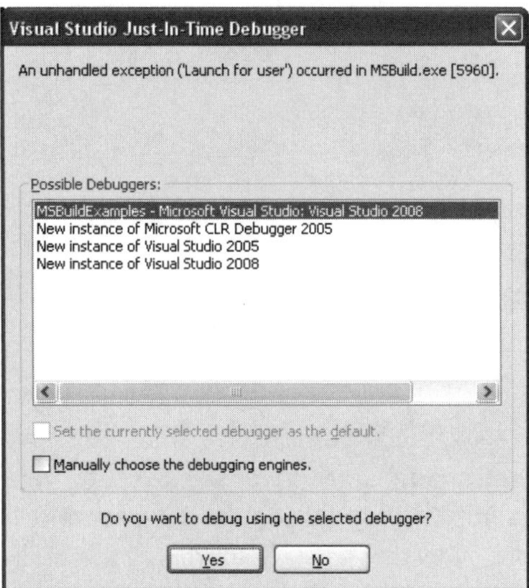

FIGURE 5-12 Debugger selection dialog

After you have completed this, Visual Studio will be attached to the process and it will stop at any breakpoints you set. Normal debugging will continue from here. The pros and cons of this approach were covered in the previous chapter, so they will not be repeated here.

The last approach, Starting MSBuild as an External Process, is the same as covered in the previous chapter, but we will quickly review here as well. For the project that contains the logger, you can change the Debug Start Action. All the settings can be set on the Properties page for the Project under the Debug tab. On this tab there are three values that you will need to fill in: Start External Program, Command Line Arguments, and Working Directory. The value for Start External Program should contain the full path to the executable that you want to run; in this case the full path to msbuild.exe. The Command Line Arguments value should contain the project file to build, the statement to attach the logger, and any other properties that you want to pass. The working directory should be set to any known directory, but ideally to a directory under the output folder for the project. This may simplify the project file used for debugging. For a more detailed description of these, you can refer back to Chapter 4, "Custom Tasks." A sample set of properties to debug the CustomFileLogger is shown in Figure 5-13.

The values that were discussed previously are highlighted in Figure 5-12. Now we have discussed the three main ways that you can debug custom MSBuild loggers.

As you've seen in this chapter, creating MSBuild loggers is very easy and very powerful. We have covered a lot of material in this chapter, including creating loggers, passing values to loggers, extending existing loggers, and debugging loggers. If you need to create new MSBuild loggers you should now have a great arsenal with which to do so. The best way to learn how to create good loggers is by creating loggers. I strongly suggest simply diving in

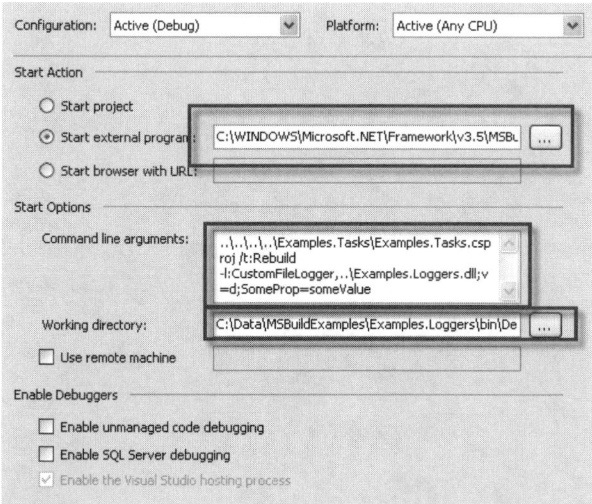

FIGURE 5-13 Debug settings for CustomFileLogger

and getting started with creating loggers. If you are using .NET 3.5 you should note that there is a new kind of logger that you can create, Distributed Loggers, which was intended for multiprocessor builds. These types of loggers are more complex and suitable for only a limited set of applications, so we will not cover them in this book. In the next chapter, we will cover two very important but very elusive topics: Batching and Incremental Building. Knowing these will turn good build scripts into great ones.

Part III

Advanced MSBuild Topics

In this part:

Chapter 6

Batching and Incremental Builds

Batching and incremental building are two very important yet potentially confusing topics. In this chapter, we will describe these two topics in great detail. Batching, at a high level, allows you to repeatedly perform an action over a set of inputs. Incremental building is a process that enables MSBuild to determine when target outputs are already up to date and can be skipped. These two topics are advanced and closely related to each other. After you read this chapter you will be able to take your build scripts to the next level.

Batching Overview

Typically during a build process you deal with many files, and very often you need to handle files that are categorized. For instance, you have files that are sent to the compiler, files that are resources, files that are references, and so on. Because of how common this is, MSBuild has a construct that is designed for this. Since MSBuild is a declarative language, as opposed to an imperative one, there must be a way to describe the operation you desire and let MSBuild take care of the looping for you. This concept is referred to as batching. Batching is an advanced topic that can be confusing, but is very powerful. Batching is a mechanism for placing items into groups, also referred to as batches, based on matching metadata. Batching always occurs on metadata; items with the same value for batched metadata will reside in the same batch. You can think of these batches as buckets; each bucket represents a set of files with the same values for the batched metadata. There are two kinds of batching, task batching and target batching. Task batching is where you execute a given task once per batch, and target batching is where a target is executed once per batch. Task batching is far more useful in practice. Note that batches are not required to contain more than one item; many times they include only one.

They say a picture is worth a thousand words—perhaps a snippet is as well. So let's take a look at the following example for a clearer explanation. This is taken from the file Batching01.proj.

```
<Project xmlns="http://schemas.microsoft.com/developer/msbuild/2003">
  <PropertyGroup>
    <SourceFolder>src\</SourceFolder>
  </PropertyGroup>

  <ItemGroup>
    <SourceFiles Include="$(SourceFolder)*.txt" />
  </ItemGroup>

  <Target Name="TaskBatching">
    <!-- Transforms items into single string -->
    <Message Text="--------------------------------------------" />
```

```
    <Message Text="Not batched @(SourceFiles->'%(FullPath)')" />
    <!-- Invokes message task per each batch -->
    <Message Text="------------------------------------------" />
    <Message Text="Batched %(SourceFiles.FullPath)" />
  </Target>
</Project>
```

In this project, we declare the SourceFiles item to include all files ending in .txt located in the src folder. The following image depicts the file/folder structure in which the project file is located.

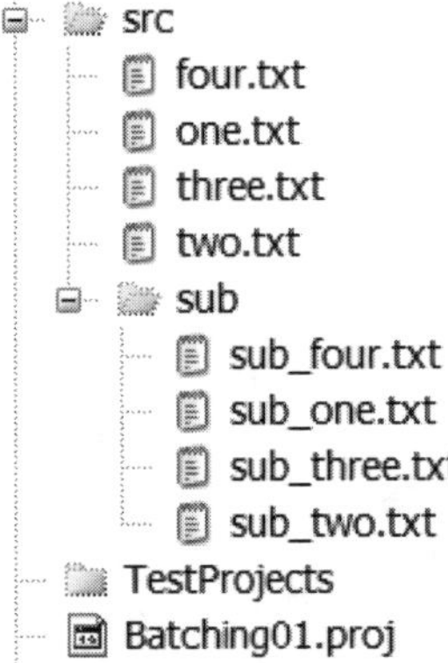

FIGURE 6-1 Directory structure

From the preceding image we can expect that the SourceFiles item will contain the four files in the src folder. Inside the TaskBatching target you can see that we simply invoke the message task a few times. We can examine the output closely and describe where the batching is occurring. The result is shown in Figure 6-2.

```
Build started 5/10/2008 1:51:53 PM.
Project "C:\Data\MSBuildExamples\Batching\Batching01.proj" on node 0 (TaskBatch
ing target(s)).
  ------------------------------------------
  Not batched C:\Data\MSBuildExamples\Batching\src\four.txt;C:\Data\MSBuildExam
  ples\Batching\src\one.txt;C:\Data\MSBuildExamples\Batching\src\three.txt;C:\D
  ata\MSBuildExamples\Batching\src\two.txt
  ------------------------------------------
  Batched C:\Data\MSBuildExamples\Batching\src\four.txt
  Batched C:\Data\MSBuildExamples\Batching\src\one.txt
  Batched C:\Data\MSBuildExamples\Batching\src\three.txt
  Batched C:\Data\MSBuildExamples\Batching\src\two.txt
Done Building Project "C:\Data\MSBuildExamples\Batching\Batching01.proj" (TaskB
atching target(s)).


Build succeeded.
    0 Warning(s)
    0 Error(s)
```

FIGURE 6-2 TaskBatching target result

From the previous output, the most important thing to notice is that the statement `<Message Text="Not batched @(SourceFiles->'%(FullPath)')" />` resulted in a single invocation of the Message task. This is obvious because the prefix *Not batched* is presented only once. On the other hand, the other statement, `<Message Text="Batched %(SourceFiles.FullPath)" />`, resulted in the Message task being executed four times, once for each file. To be correct, it is once per batch, where the batch is defined by the metadata FullPath for SourceFiles. Because the FullPath value will be unique for each file, it creates batches that contain only one item. To describe this in a diagram, you can think of a target (without batching) as shown in Figure 6-3.

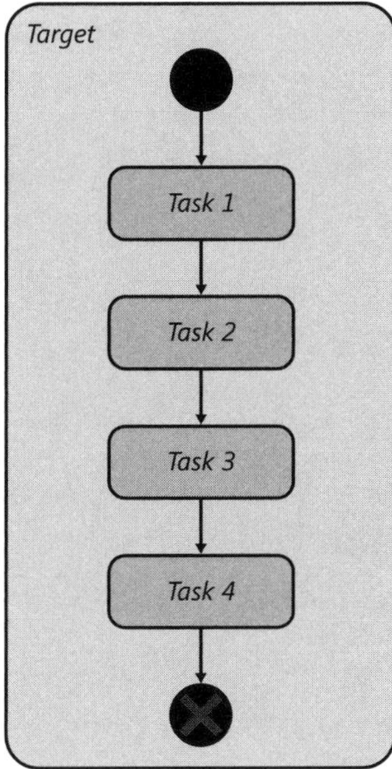

FIGURE 6-3 Target (without batching) visualization diagram

In unbatched targets, each task is executed one after another until all the tasks have been executed. In contrast to this, when a batched task is encountered, the batches are created, and then each batch is passed to the task and executed. Note that the execution of this is not performed in parallel, each batch is processed one by one. After each batch has been processed, execution continues. This is shown in Figure 6-4.

As shown in Figure 6-4 the MSBuild engine will automatically create the batches and pass the items into the task that is being batched. In the previous example we created batches with only one item. Now let's take a little closer look at how batches work. We will first examine task batching and then move on to target batching.

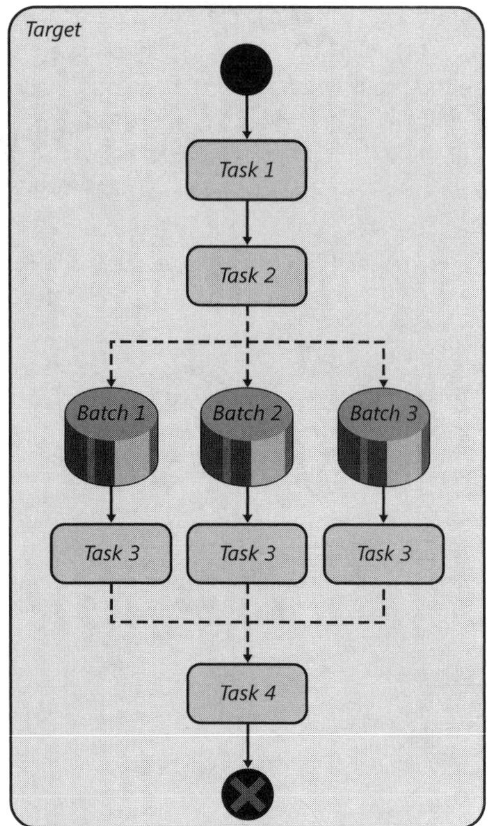

FIGURE 6-4 Target (with batching) visualization diagram

Task Batching

As stated previously, task batching is the process of invoking the same individual task multiple times, each time with a subset of the original input items, where the input is defined by the batches created for the task. See the following example, which is contained in the Batching02.proj file.

```
<Project xmlns="http://schemas.microsoft.com/developer/msbuild/2003">
  <PropertyGroup>
    <SourceFolder>src\</SourceFolder>
  </PropertyGroup>

  <ItemGroup>
    <SourceFiles Include="$(SourceFolder)one.txt">
      <CopyToOutputDirectory>Always</CopyToOutputDirectory>
    </SourceFiles>
    <SourceFiles Include="$(SourceFolder)two.txt">
      <CopyToOutputDirectory>PreserveNewest</CopyToOutputDirectory>
    </SourceFiles>
```

```
    <SourceFiles Include="$(SourceFolder)three.txt">
      <CopyToOutputDirectory>Always</CopyToOutputDirectory>
    </SourceFiles>
    <SourceFiles Include="$(SourceFolder)four.txt">
      <CopyToOutputDirectory>PreserveNewest</CopyToOutputDirectory>
    </SourceFiles>
  </ItemGroup>

  <Target Name="TaskBatching">
    <!-- Transforms items into single string -->
    <Message Text="--------------------------------------------" />
    <Message Text="Not batched @(SourceFiles->'%(CopyToOutputDirectory)')" />
    <!-- Invokes message task once per each batch -->
    <Message Text="--------------------------------------------" />
    <Message Text="Batched %(SourceFiles.CopyToOutputDirectory)" />
  </Target>

  <Target Name="TargetBatching" Outputs="%(SourceFiles.CopyToOutputDirectory)">
    <Message Text="CopyToOutputDirectory: %(SourceFiles.CopyToOutputDirectory)" />
    <Message Text="@(SourceFiles)" />
  </Target>

</Project>
```

In this example, we first declare one item, SourceFiles, with four elements. Each element has the metadata CopyToOutputDirectory specified. Two elements have CopyToOutputDirectory set to Always, and the other two have it set to PreserveNewest. We'll examine the result of the TaskBatching target. This target, which is a copy of the previous example, invokes the Message task for the SourceFiles item once without batching, and once with batching using the CopyToOutputDirectory item metadata. In Figure 6-5 you will find the result of executing this target.

```
C:\Data\MSBuildExamples\Batching>msbuild Batching02.proj /nologo
Build started 11/1/2008 3:30:05 PM.
Project "C:\Data\MSBuildExamples\Batching\Batching02.proj" on node 0 (default t
argets).
  --------------------------------------------
  Not batched Always;PreserveNewest;Always;PreserveNewest
  --------------------------------------------
  Batched Always
  Batched PreserveNewest
Done Building Project "C:\Data\MSBuildExamples\Batching\Batching02.proj" (defau
lt targets).


Build succeeded.
    0 Warning(s)
    0 Error(s)
```

FIGURE 6-5 TaskBatching target result

The output is interesting. In the first invocation we can see that the values for the CopyToOutputDirectory metadata were simply appended to each other and passed to the Message task, as expected. In the last invocation we can see that the expression `%(SourceFiles.CopyToOutputDirectory)` was evaluated into two distinct values, Always and PreserveNewest, and the Message task was invoked only once for each of those values.

Now that we have described batching and looked at some trivial examples, we will take a look at some more realistic applications of batching. The following example, TaskBatching.proj, will take a set of files and then copy those files to a set of directories.

```
<Project xmlns="http://schemas.microsoft.com/developer/msbuild/2003">
  <PropertyGroup>
    <SourceFolder>src\</SourceFolder>
    <DestFolder>dest\</DestFolder>
  </PropertyGroup>

  <ItemGroup>
    <SourceFiles Include="$(SourceFolder)*.txt" />
    <Dest Include="$(DestFolder)One" />
    <Dest Include="$(DestFolder)Two" />
    <Dest Include="$(DestFolder)Three" />
    <Dest Include="$(DestFolder)Four" />
    <Dest Include="$(DestFolder)Five" />
  </ItemGroup>

  <Target Name="CopyAll">
    <!-- Task batching to copy files -->
    <Copy SourceFiles ="@(SourceFiles)"
          DestinationFolder="%(Dest.FullPath)" SkipUnchangedFiles="false" />
    <!-- Task batching to print message -->
    <Message Text="Fullpath: %(Dest.FullPath)" />
  </Target>

</Project>
```

In this example, we have defined two properties, SourceFolder and DestFolder. The SourceFolder contains the path to the folder that contains all the files that we would like to copy. The directory structure is the same as that shown in Figure 6-1. The DestFolder property contains the top-level path to the folder where the files will be copied into—actually, into folders under the DestFolder. From that file, take a look at the following item declaration.

```
<ItemGroup>
  <SourceFiles Include="$(SourceFolder)*.txt" />
  <Dest Include="$(DestFolder)One" />
  <Dest Include="$(DestFolder)Two" />
  <Dest Include="$(DestFolder)Three" />
  <Dest Include="$(DestFolder)Four" />
  <Dest Include="$(DestFolder)Five" />
</ItemGroup>
```

This creates the item SourceFiles, which contains all the files that are to be copied. Then it declares the item Dest, which contains a list of folders, under DestFolder. This is an example of using an item that doesn't point to a list of files. In this case it points to a list of directories. You can use an item for any list-based value, not only files and directories. Now let's zero in on the statement:

```
<Copy SourceFiles ="@(SourceFiles)"
      DestinationFolder="%(Dest.FullPath)" SkipUnchangedFiles="false" />
```

> **Note** SkipUnchangedFiles is set to false only for demonstrative purposes, to ensure that every file is copied each time.

In this task declaration, the expression `%(Dest.FullPath)` will cause the Copy task to be invoked once per batch, where the batches are created by an expansion of the FullPath metadata of the Dest item. Since the FullPath is unique it will be executed once per element in Dest, so this expression is equivalent to the following set of statements.

```
<Copy SourceFiles="@(SourceFiles)"
      DestinationFiles="$(DestFolder)One" SkipUnchangedFiles="false" />
<Copy SourceFiles="@(SourceFiles)"
      DestinationFiles="$(DestFolder)Two" SkipUnchangedFiles="false" />
<Copy SourceFiles="@(SourceFiles)"
      DestinationFiles="$(DestFolder)Three" SkipUnchangedFiles="false" />
<Copy SourceFiles="@(SourceFiles)"
      DestinationFiles="$(DestFolder)Four" SkipUnchangedFiles="false" />
<Copy SourceFiles="@(SourceFiles)"
      DestinationFiles="$(DestFolder)Five" SkipUnchangedFiles="false" />
```

So we would expect all the files in SourceFiles to be copied into each of the four folders in DestFolder. The output of executing the CopyAll target is shown in Figure 6-6.

```
C:\Data\MSBuildExamples\Batching>msbuild TaskBatching.proj /t:CopyAll /nologo
Build started 10/17/2008 12:50:44 AM.
Project "C:\Data\MSBuildExamples\Batching\TaskBatching.proj" on node 0 (CopyAll
 target(s)).
  Copying file from "src\four.txt" to "C:\Data\MSBuildExamples\d\One\four.txt".
  Copying file from "src\one.txt" to "C:\Data\MSBuildExamples\d\One\one.txt".
  Copying file from "src\three.txt" to "C:\Data\MSBuildExamples\d\One\three.txt
  ".
  Copying file from "src\two.txt" to "C:\Data\MSBuildExamples\d\One\two.txt".
  Copying file from "src\four.txt" to "C:\Data\MSBuildExamples\d\Two\four.txt".
  Copying file from "src\one.txt" to "C:\Data\MSBuildExamples\d\Two\one.txt".
  Copying file from "src\three.txt" to "C:\Data\MSBuildExamples\d\Two\three.txt
  ".
  Copying file from "src\two.txt" to "C:\Data\MSBuildExamples\d\Two\two.txt".
  Copying file from "src\four.txt" to "C:\Data\MSBuildExamples\d\Three\four.txt
  ".
  Copying file from "src\one.txt" to "C:\Data\MSBuildExamples\d\Three\one.txt".
  Copying file from "src\three.txt" to "C:\Data\MSBuildExamples\d\Three\three.t
  xt".
  Copying file from "src\two.txt" to "C:\Data\MSBuildExamples\d\Three\two.txt".
  Copying file from "src\four.txt" to "C:\Data\MSBuildExamples\d\Four\four.txt"
  .
  Copying file from "src\one.txt" to "C:\Data\MSBuildExamples\d\Four\one.txt".
  Copying file from "src\three.txt" to "C:\Data\MSBuildExamples\d\Four\three.tx
  t".
  Copying file from "src\two.txt" to "C:\Data\MSBuildExamples\d\Four\two.txt".
  Copying file from "src\four.txt" to "C:\Data\MSBuildExamples\d\Five\four.txt"
  .
  Copying file from "src\one.txt" to "C:\Data\MSBuildExamples\d\Five\one.txt".
  Copying file from "src\three.txt" to "C:\Data\MSBuildExamples\d\Five\three.tx
  t".
  Copying file from "src\two.txt" to "C:\Data\MSBuildExamples\d\Five\two.txt".
  Fullpath: C:\Data\MSBuildExamples\d\One
  Fullpath: C:\Data\MSBuildExamples\d\Two
  Fullpath: C:\Data\MSBuildExamples\d\Three
  Fullpath: C:\Data\MSBuildExamples\d\Four
  Fullpath: C:\Data\MSBuildExamples\d\Five
Done Building Project "C:\Data\MSBuildExamples\Batching\TaskBatching.proj" (Cop
yAll target(s)).


Build succeeded.
    0 Warning(s)
    0 Error(s)
```

FIGURE 6-6 CopyAll target result

From Figure 6-6 we can see that each file in the SourceFiles item was indeed copied to the individual directories defined in DestFolder. If you set the verbosity of the logger to Detailed you will see that the Copy task was executed five times. Now that we have discussed TaskBatching, we will move on to discuss TargetBatching.

Target Batching

Target batching is similar to task batching in that an operation is invoked once per batch. Task batching is the process of invoking an individual task once per batch; target batching is executing a target once per batch. Target batching is driven entirely by the Outputs attribute of the target. Based on the batches created, the target is executed once per batch. Target batching is not used very much in practice, but task batching is. Take a look at the following file, TargetBatching01.proj, for a simple example.

```
<Project xmlns="http://schemas.microsoft.com/developer/msbuild/2003">
  <PropertyGroup>
    <SourceFolder>src\</SourceFolder>
  </PropertyGroup>

  <ItemGroup>
    <SourceFiles Include="$(SourceFolder)*.txt" />
  </ItemGroup>

  <Target Name="PrintMessage"
          Outputs="%(SourceFiles.Fullpath)">
    <Message Text="PrintMessage started" />
    <Message Text="@(SourceFiles)" />
  </Target>
</Project>
```

In the target PrintMessage, the value %(SourceFiles.FullPath) in the Output attribute means that the batches will be created using the FullPath metadata of the SourceFiles item. Then these batches will be used to represent the SourceFiles item. During each of the resulting target executions, as the batches are referred to using the @(SourceFiles) item, it no longer contains all items, but instead a subset of the original item list being used with each batch. Take a look at the result of executing the PrintMessage target shown in Figure 6-7.

From the result shown in Figure 6-7 we can see that PrintMessage target was indeed invoked once per batch—that is, four times—for SourceFiles. Also note that when target batching occurs, only the items in each batch are available when the item itself is referenced. For example, in the PrintMessage target the Message task is actually passed @(SourceFiles), but only the files in the batch are printed.

```
Build started 5/11/2008 10:44:08 PM.
Project "C:\Data\MSBuildExamples\Batching\TargetBatching01.proj" on node 0 (Pri
ntMessage target(s)).
  PrintMessage started
  C:\Data\MSBuildExamples\Batching\src\four.txt
PrintMessage:
  PrintMessage started
  C:\Data\MSBuildExamples\Batching\src\one.txt
PrintMessage:
  PrintMessage started
  C:\Data\MSBuildExamples\Batching\src\three.txt
PrintMessage:
  PrintMessage started
  C:\Data\MSBuildExamples\Batching\src\two.txt
Done Building Project "C:\Data\MSBuildExamples\Batching\TargetBatching01.proj"
(PrintMessage target(s)).


Build succeeded.
    0 Warning(s)
    0 Error(s)
```

FIGURE 6-7 PrintMessage target result

Now that we have a better idea of target batching, we will examine an example that is a little easier to relate to. The following TargetBatching02.proj file demonstrates how to build a solution file for each of the defined configurations.

```
<Project xmlns="http://schemas.microsoft.com/developer/msbuild/2003">
  <PropertyGroup>
    <SourceRoot>$(MSBuildProjectDirectory)\TestProjects\</SourceRoot>
  </PropertyGroup>

  <ItemGroup>
    <BuildFile Include="$(SourceRoot)TestProj1.sln" />
    <Config Include="Debug configuration">
      <Configuration>Debug</Configuration>
    </Config>
    <Config Include="Release configuration">
      <Configuration>Release</Configuration>
    </Config>
  </ItemGroup>

  <Target Name="BuildAll"
          Outputs="%(Config.Configuration)">

    <Message Text="Start building for configuration: %(Config.Configuration)" />
    <MSBuild Projects="@(BuildFile)"
             Properties="Configuration=%(Config.Configuration)"
             Targets="Rebuild" />
  </Target>
</Project>
```

The solution file is referenced in the BuildFile item. The other item, Config, defines the values for the configuration that should be used. These values are defined in the Configuration metadata. The BuildAll target is the one that builds the solution for each defined configuration. The batching is achieved by the attribute Outputs="%(Config.Configuration)". The Outputs attribute is also related to Incremental Building which is discussed later in this chapter. Target batching is a different use of this attribute. So the BuildAll target will be executed once per unique value of the Configuration metadata for the Config item, which is Debug and Release. If you execute the command `msbuild TargetBatching02.proj /t:BuildAll` you will notice that the target BuildAll is indeed invoked once for Debug and then for Release. This configuration value is passed through to the build file using the MSBuild tasks' Properties parameter. We have now provided an overview of task and target batching; the next section will describe the behavior of build scripts when combining task and target batching.

Combining Task and Target Batching

In this section, we will demonstrate ways to use task and target batching together. In this discussion, we will examine the following sample project file, Batching04.proj.

```
<Project xmlns="http://schemas.microsoft.com/developer/msbuild/2003">
  <ItemGroup>
    <Server Include="Server1">
      <Type>2008</Type>
      <Name>SVR01</Name>
      <AdminContact>Sayed Ibrahim Hashimi</AdminContact>
    </Server>
    <Server Include="Server2">
      <Type>2003</Type>
      <Name>SVR02</Name>
      <AdminContact>Sayed Y. Hashimi</AdminContact>
    </Server>
    <Server Include="Server3">
      <Type>2008</Type>
      <Name>SVR03</Name>
      <AdminContact>Nicole Woodsmall</AdminContact>
    </Server>
    <Server Include="Server4">
      <Type>2003</Type>
      <Name>SVR04</Name>
      <AdminContact>Keith Tingle</AdminContact>
    </Server>
  </ItemGroup>

  <Target Name="TaskBatching">
    <Message Text="%40(Server->'%25(Name)'): @(Server->'%(Name)')" />
    <Message Text="===========================================" />
    <!--
      Task Batching here using the Name metadata.
      Notice that Message task is invoked once per unique batch
      The same applies for %(Server.Type) below.
    -->
```

```
    <Message Text="%25(Server.Name): %(Server.Name)" />
    <Message Text="==========================================" />
    <Message Text="%25(Server.Type): %(Server.Type)" />
    <Message Text="==========================================" />
  </Target>

  <!--
   NOTE: Others targets defined here.
  -->
</Project>
```

This previous listing does not contain the full source for the project file; a few targets were not shown yet. Instead they will be shown on their own later in this section. In this target, we have declared an item, Server, which contains references to four servers each with three values for custom metadata. The custom metadata defined are Type, Name, and AdminContact. Following that there are four targets, which we will examine in detail now. The TaskBatching target demonstrates task batching once again. The first message statement, `<Message Text="%40(Server->'%25(Name)'): @(Server->'%(Name)')" />`, is a statement that does not start batching, because that syntax results in the Server item being transformed into a single string then passed to the Message task. This was inserted to print out the values to the logger. Following that, we first batch using the Name metadata with `<Message Text="%25(Server.Name): %(Server.Name)" />` and similarly with the Type metadata value. You can see the results of the TaskBatching target with the command `msbuild Batching04.proj /t:TaskBatching` in Figure 6-8.

```
C:\Data\MSBuildExamples\Batching>msbuild Batching04.proj /t:TaskBatching /nologo

Build started 11/1/2008 3:44:07 PM.
Project "C:\Data\MSBuildExamples\Batching\Batching04.proj" on node 0 (TaskBatch
ing target(s)).
  @(Server->'%(Name)'): SVR01;SVR02;SVR03;SVR04
  ==========================================
  %(Server.Name): SVR01
  %(Server.Name): SVR02
  %(Server.Name): SVR03
  %(Server.Name): SVR04
  ==========================================
  %(Server.Type): 2008
  %(Server.Type): 2003
  ==========================================
Done Building Project "C:\Data\MSBuildExamples\Batching\Batching04.proj" (TaskB
atching target(s)).


Build succeeded.
    0 Warning(s)
    0 Error(s)
```

FIGURE 6-8 Result of TaskBatching target

From the result shown in Figure 6-8 we can see that, as expected, there were four batches created for the Server.Name property and two distinct groups created from the Server.Type value. To reiterate: When the batching is performed, MSBuild will identify the unique values in the batching expression and create the required groups. Now we will move on to the targets that involve target batching.

In the next snippet, the TargetBatching01 target is declared which is also defined inside the Batching04.proj file. Other sections of this file were shown previously.

```
<Target Name="TargetBatching01" Outputs="%(Server.Name)">
  <Message Text="===== TargetBatching01 ============" />
  <Message Text="%25(Server.Name): %(Server.Name)" />
  <Message Text="%25(Server.Type): %(Server.Type)" />
  <Message Text="Server: @(Server)" />
  <Message Text="===================================" />
</Target>
```

The TargetBatching01 target creates batches with the Server.Name property. This is due to the attribute Outputs="%(Server.Name)" being present. When we execute this target we would expect that it is executed once for each unique value for Server.Name. Since each name value is defined as being unique we should see this target executed four times. The result is shown in Figure 6-9.

```
Build started 5/13/2008 11:41:01 PM.
Project "C:\Data\MSBuildExamples\Batching\Batching04.proj" on node 0 (TargetBat
ching01 target(s)).
  ===== TargetBatching01 ============
  %(Server.Name): SVR01
  %(Server.Type): 2008
  Server: Server1
  ===================================
TargetBatching01:
  ===== TargetBatching01 ============
  %(Server.Name): SVR02
  %(Server.Type): 2003
  Server: Server2
  ===================================
TargetBatching01:
  ===== TargetBatching01 ============
  %(Server.Name): SVR03
  %(Server.Type): 2008
  Server: Server3
  ===================================
TargetBatching01:
  ===== TargetBatching01 ============
  %(Server.Name): SVR04
  %(Server.Type): 2003
  Server: Server4
  ===================================
Done Building Project "C:\Data\MSBuildExamples\Batching\Batching04.proj" (Targe
tBatching01 target(s)).


Build succeeded.
    0 Warning(s)
    0 Error(s)
```

FIGURE 6-9 TargetBatching01 result

We can see that the target was indeed executed four times, once for each Server item, because the Server.Name value is unique. The TargetBatching02 target is a carbon copy of the TargetBatching01 target, with the exception of the Output attribute. The TargetBatching02 target node contains the attribute Outputs="%(Server.Type)", which means that we will execute that target once for each unique set of value for the Type metadata on the Server item. The result of this target invocation is shown in Figure 6-10.

```
Build started 5/13/2008 11:50:55 PM.
Project "C:\Data\MSBuildExamples\Batching\Batching04.proj" on node 0 (TargetBat
ching02 target(s)).
  ===== TargetBatching02 ============
  %(Server.Name): SVR01
  %(Server.Name): SVR03
  %(Server.Type): 2008
  Server: Server1;Server3
  ==================================
TargetBatching02:
  ===== TargetBatching02 ============
  %(Server.Name): SVR02
  %(Server.Name): SVR04
  %(Server.Type): 2003
  Server: Server2;Server4
  ==================================
Done Building Project "C:\Data\MSBuildExamples\Batching\Batching04.proj" (Targe
tBatching02 target(s)).


Build succeeded.
    0 Warning(s)
    0 Error(s)
```

FIGURE 6-10 TargetBatching02 target

In the TargetBatching01 target, each target was executing with a context of a single value for the Server item. This is because the batching produced batches with only one item. In this sample, we are batching over the Type metadata, which has two unique values, among four different item values. If you look at the previous result, you can see that the statement `<Message Text="%25(Server.Name): %(Server.Name)" />` produces two values to be printed. This is because there are two items in both of the batches. This is an example of target batching on Server.Type, and task batching on Server.Name. In the next section, we will discuss multi-value batches in more detail.

Multi-batching

When you get started with batching it takes time to understand its behavior, and even more effort to utilize it effectively. Batching over multiple values requires a deep understanding of how batching works. In this section we will take a closer look at batching, mostly through a series of examples.

We will first examine what the behavior is when we perform task batching with two different items. When a batched statement is encountered, MSBuild will create unique batches based on the **item itself** and the value for the metadata. What this means is that when you are using qualified batching statements, no batch will contain references to more than one item.

A qualified batching statement is one that declares the item type as well as the metadata name. It is possible to batch without specifying the item type inside the %(EXPRESSION); we cover this in the "Batching Using Shared Metadata" section. In the next snippet, you will find the contents of the Batching05.proj file. The complete source is not shown here; a few targets are shown later in this section.

```
<Project xmlns="http://schemas.microsoft.com/developer/msbuild/2003">
  <ItemGroup>
    <!-- Test1 items -->
    <Test1 Include="One">
      <a>A1</a>
      <b>B</b>
      <c>C</c>
    </Test1>
    <Test1 Include="Two">
      <a>A</a>
      <b>B1</b>
      <c>C</c>
    </Test1>
    <Test1 Include="Three">
      <a>A1</a>
      <b>B1</b>
      <c>C1</c>
    </Test1>
    <!-- Test2 items -->
    <Test2 Include="Four">
      <a>A</a>
      <b>B1</b>
      <c>C1</c>
    </Test2>
    <Test2 Include="Five">
      <a>A1</a>
      <b>B</b>
      <c>C2</c>
    </Test2>
    <Test2 Include="Six">
      <a>A</a>
      <b>B</b>
      <c>C2</c>
    </Test2>
  </ItemGroup>

  <Target Name="Task01">
    <Message Text="%25(Test1.a): %(Test1.a)" />
    <Message Text="---------------------------------------" />
    <Message Text="%25(Test2.a): %(Test2.a)" />
    <Message Text="---------------------------------------" />
    <Message Text=
      "%25(Test1.a): %(Test1.a) || %25(Test2.a): %(Test2.a)" />
  </Target>

  <!--
   NOTE: Others targets defined here.
  -->
</Project>
```

In this project file, there are two items declared, Test1 and Test2, both of which have metadata values for a, b, and c. In the Task01 target, the values for the "a" metadata are batched first separately, then together. The result from executing this target, shown in Figure 6-11, might be different from what you expect.

```
C:\Data\MSBuildExamples\Batching>msbuild Batching05.proj /fl /t:Task01 /nologo
Build started 10/17/2008 10:27:37 PM.
Project "C:\Data\MSBuildExamples\Batching\Batching05.proj" on node 0 (Task01 ta
rget(s)).
  %(Test1.a): A1
  %(Test1.a): A
  ----------------------------------------
  %(Test2.a): A
  %(Test2.a): A1
  ----------------------------------------
  %(Test1.a): A1 || %(Test2.a):
  %(Test1.a): A || %(Test2.a):
  %(Test1.a):  || %(Test2.a): A
  %(Test1.a):  || %(Test2.a): A1
Done Building Project "C:\Data\MSBuildExamples\Batching\Batching05.proj" (Task0
1 target(s)).


Build succeeded.
    0 Warning(s)
    0 Error(s)
```

FIGURE 6-11 Batching05.proj Task01 result

As you can see from the result in Figure 6-11, both items have the values A and A1 for the "a" metadata. When they are batched together with the statement `<Message Text="%25(Test1.a): %(Test1.a) || %25(Test2.a): %(Test2.a)"/>` the result is that the Message task is invoked four times, twice for values on Test1 and twice for the values on Test2. When there are values for Test1, the values for Test2 are empty, and vice versa. This is why the message task outputs values for only Test1 or Test2 but never for both at once. We can get a better perspective of target batching by examining the result from the Target01. The Target01 target is shown in the next snippet and it is defined in the Batching05.proj as well.

```
<Target Name="Target01"
        Outputs="%(Test1.a)%(Test2.a)">
  <Message Text="%25(Test1.a): %(Test1.a) "/>
  <Message Text="%25(Test1.Identity) %(Test1.Identity)" />
  <Message Text="----------------------------------------" />
  <Message Text="%25(Test2.a): %(Test2.a)" />
  <Message Text="%25(Test2.Identity) %(Test2.Identity)" />
</Target>
```

The result of executing this target is shown in Figure 6-12. In this example, I also print the value for the Identity metadata, which shows which items are included in the batch.

From the result shown in Figure 6-12, you can see that the Target01 target was executed four times, just as was the Message task of the previous example. Also just as the previous invocation, when a value existed for Test1, there was none for Test2. We can now take a look at batching to build multiple configurations.

```
C:\Data\MSBuildExamples\Batching>msbuild Batching05.proj /t:Target01 /nologo
Build started 10/17/2008 10:35:24 PM.
Project "C:\Data\MSBuildExamples\Batching\Batching05.proj" on node 0 (Target01
target(s)).
  %(Test1.a): A1
  %(Test1.Identity) One
  %(Test1.Identity) Three
  ------------------------------------------------------------
  %(Test2.a):
  %(Test2.Identity)
Target01:
  %(Test1.a): A
  %(Test1.Identity) Two
  ------------------------------------------------------------
  %(Test2.a):
  %(Test2.Identity)
Target01:
  %(Test1.a):
  %(Test1.Identity)
  ------------------------------------------------------------
  %(Test2.a): A
  %(Test2.Identity) Four
  %(Test2.Identity) Six
Target01:
  %(Test1.a):
  %(Test1.Identity)
  ------------------------------------------------------------
  %(Test2.a): A1
  %(Test2.Identity) Five
Done Building Project "C:\Data\MSBuildExamples\Batching\Batching05.proj" (Targe
t01 target(s)).

Build succeeded.
    0 Warning(s)
    0 Error(s)
```

FIGURE 6-12 Batching05.proj TargetEx01 result

Using Batching to Build Multiple Configurations

There are many situations when you might need to build a set of projects for a set of defined configuration values. We'll examine how to do this now. The basic idea here is that you'll use the MSBuild task in order to build each project while passing in the Configuration property value. All the values for the configuration should be placed in an item so they can be expanded using batching. The contents of the Batching06.proj file are shown in the next snippet.

```
<Project xmlns="http://schemas.microsoft.com/developer/msbuild/2003"
         ToolsVersion="3.5">
  <PropertyGroup>
    <SourceRoot>TestProjects\</SourceRoot>
    <OutputRoot>..\BUILD\BuildTemp\</OutputRoot>
  </PropertyGroup>

  <ItemGroup>
    <AllConfigurations Include="Debug configuration">
      <Configuration>Debug</Configuration>
    </AllConfigurations>
    <AllConfigurations Include="Release configuration">
      <Configuration>Release</Configuration>
    </AllConfigurations>

    <OutputPath Include="$(OutputRoot)One\">
      <Path>$(OutputRoot)One\</Path>
    </OutputPath>
```

```
    <OutputPath Include="$(OutputRoot)Two\">
      <Path>$(OutputRoot)Two\</Path>
    </OutputPath>
  </ItemGroup>

  <ItemGroup>
    <Projects Include="$(SourceRoot)TestProj1\TestProj1.csproj" />
    <Projects Include="$(SourceRoot)TestProj2\TestProj2.csproj" />
    <Projects Include="$(SourceRoot)TestProj3\TestProj3.csproj" />
  </ItemGroup>

  <!-- Show an example of the Configuration batching deal -->
  <Target Name="Task01">
    <!-- Build each project for each defined configuration -->
    <MSBuild Projects="@(Projects)"
             Properties="Configuration=%(AllConfigurations.Configuration)"
             Targets="Rebuild"
             ToolsVersion="3.5"
             />
  </Target>

  <!--
   NOTE: Others targets defined here.
  -->

</Project>
```

In this file there are two noteworthy items: Projects and AllConfigurations, described as follows.

- Projects: contains a list of projects that should be built.
- AllConfigurations: contains the values for all the configurations that should be used during the build process.

The Task01 target shown in the previous snippet demonstrates task batching. This target builds all the projects for the defined configuration values. This is achieved by calling the MSBuild task and passing in all the projects to be built along with the value for the configuration. If you take a look at MSBuild task invocation, it uses the notation @(Projects), which will send a list of projects to a single MSBuild task. The beginning of the build process for the Task01 target is shown in Figure 6-13.

From the result shown in Figure 6-13, you can see that the TestProj1 started building and then the TestProj2 started to build after that. If the full log were shown here you would see that the TestProj3 project then started building. Figure 6-13 shows that the configuration used for the build was Debug. The remainder of the build not shown in Figure 6-13 is building using Release as the Configuration value. This works because the only value used for batching was %(AllConfigurations.Configuration).

```
C:\Data\MSBuildExamples\Batching>msbuild Batching06.proj /t:Task01 /nologo
Build started 10/17/2008 11:00:20 PM.
Project "C:\Data\MSBuildExamples\Batching\Batching06.proj" on node 0 (Task01 ta
rget(s)).
Project "C:\Data\MSBuildExamples\Batching\Batching06.proj" (1) is building "C:\
Data\MSBuildExamples\Batching\TestProjects\TestProj1\TestProj1.csproj" (2) on n
ode 0 (Rebuild target(s)).
  Deleting file "C:\Data\MSBuildExamples\Batching\TestProjects\TestProj1\bin\De
  bug\TestProj1.exe".
  Deleting file "C:\Data\MSBuildExamples\Batching\TestProjects\TestProj1\bin\De
  bug\TestProj1.pdb".
  Deleting file "C:\Data\MSBuildExamples\Batching\TestProjects\TestProj1\obj\De
  bug\TestProj1.Properties.Resources.resources".
  Deleting file "C:\Data\MSBuildExamples\Batching\TestProjects\TestProj1\obj\De
  bug\TestProj1.csproj.GenerateResource.Cache".
  Deleting file "C:\Data\MSBuildExamples\Batching\TestProjects\TestProj1\obj\De
  bug\TestProj1.exe".
  Deleting file "C:\Data\MSBuildExamples\Batching\TestProjects\TestProj1\obj\De
  bug\TestProj1.pdb".
CoreResGen:
  Processing resource file "Properties\Resources.resx" into "obj\Debug\TestProj
  1.Properties.Resources.resources".
CopyFilesToOutputDirectory:
  Copying file from "obj\Debug\TestProj1.exe" to "bin\Debug\TestProj1.exe".
  TestProj1 -> C:\Data\MSBuildExamples\Batching\TestProjects\TestProj1\bin\Debu
  g\TestProj1.exe
  Copying file from "obj\Debug\TestProj1.pdb" to "bin\Debug\TestProj1.pdb".
Done Building Project "C:\Data\MSBuildExamples\Batching\TestProjects\TestProj1\
TestProj1.csproj" (Rebuild target(s)).

Project "C:\Data\MSBuildExamples\Batching\Batching06.proj" (1) is building "C:\
Data\MSBuildExamples\Batching\TestProjects\TestProj2\TestProj2.csproj" (3) on n
ode 0 (Rebuild target(s)).
  Deleting file "C:\Data\MSBuildExamples\Batching\TestProjects\TestProj2\bin\De
  bug\TestProj2.exe".
  Deleting file "C:\Data\MSBuildExamples\Batching\TestProjects\TestProj2\bin\De
  bug\TestProj2.pdb".
  Deleting file "C:\Data\MSBuildExamples\Batching\TestProjects\TestProj2\obj\De
  bug\TestProj2.Properties.Resources.resources".
  Deleting file "C:\Data\MSBuildExamples\Batching\TestProjects\TestProj2\obj\De
  bug\TestProj2.csproj.GenerateResource.Cache".
  Deleting file "C:\Data\MSBuildExamples\Batching\TestProjects\TestProj2\obj\De
  bug\TestProj2.exe".
  Deleting file "C:\Data\MSBuildExamples\Batching\TestProjects\TestProj2\obj\De
  bug\TestProj2.pdb".
CoreResGen:
  Processing resource file "Properties\Resources.resx" into "obj\Debug\TestProj
  2.Properties.Resources.resources".
CopyFilesToOutputDirectory:
  Copying file from "obj\Debug\TestProj2.exe" to "bin\Debug\TestProj2.exe".
  TestProj2 -> C:\Data\MSBuildExamples\Batching\TestProjects\TestProj2\bin\Debu
  g\TestProj2.exe
  Copying file from "obj\Debug\TestProj2.pdb" to "bin\Debug\TestProj2.pdb".
Done Building Project "C:\Data\MSBuildExamples\Batching\TestProjects\TestProj2\
TestProj2.csproj" (Rebuild target(s)).
```

FIGURE 6-13 Batching06.proj Task01 result

For a more complicated variation of the previous example, we will use an example where you need to build a set of projects for all the defined configurations, and you need to set the output path for each configuration to a different location. We can achieve this by a careful application of target batching. The next snippet, taken from Batching06.proj, contains the Target02 target which demonstrates this.

```
<Target Name="Target01"
        Outputs="%(AllConfigurations.Configuration)">
  <!-- Build each project for each defined configuration -->
  <MSBuild Projects="@(Projects)"
           Properties="Configuration=%(AllConfigurations.Configuration)"
           Targets="Rebuild"
           ToolsVersion="3.5"
           />
</Target>
<Target Name="Target02" Outputs="%(Projects.Identity)">
  <PropertyGroup>
    <_CurrentProjectFilename>%(Projects.Filename)</_CurrentProjectFilename>
    <_CurrentProjectFullpath>%(Projects.Fullpath)</_CurrentProjectFullpath>
    <_CurrentOutputPath>$(OutputRoot)$(_CurrentProjectFilename)\</_CurrentOutputPath>
  </PropertyGroup>
```

```
  <MSBuild Projects="$(_CurrentProjectFullpath)"
    Properties="Configuration=%(AllConfigurations.Configuration);
      OutputPath=$(_CurrentOutputPath)%(AllConfigurations.Configuration)\"
    Targets="Rebuild"
    ToolsVersion="3.5"
    />
</Target>
```

The previoius snippet contains two targets, which both build for all configurations. The Target02 target also specifies the output path. We will focus on Target02. In this target, I have chosen to batch with the Projects item instead of the AllConfigurations item. This is because I will need to use some other metadata values from the Projects, such as the filename. To accommodate for the change, I then batch the MSBuild task over all values for AllConfigurations. In that target, you will notice properties defined as

```
<PropertyGroup>
  <_CurrentProjectFilename>%(Projects.Filename)</_CurrentProjectFilename>
</PropertyGroup>
```

This takes the current value for the Filename for Projects item and places it into the property named _CurrentProjectFilename. Since we are batching the target on Projects.Identity we know that the evaluation of that statement will be processed over only a single item value. This is needed because the statement `%(Projects.Identity)` cannot directly be used in the MSBuild task invocation. If this had been done, the task invocation would have been batched using two items, Projects and AllConfigurations. As stated previously, each batch will contain only one value. Because we need the value of Projects and AllConfigurations we create properties to refer to needed Projects values and use those instead. In the MSBuild task used in that target, we are passing the Configuration property as well as the OutputPath property. So we will build for all configurations, and we override the output path while doing so. If we build that target, the result would be similar to that shown in Figure 6-14.

From the result shown in Figure 6-14, you can see that the TestProj1 started building first for Debug, then Release. Following that, the TestProj2 project began building. We'll now move on to discuss another form of batching that was briefly mentioned before, batching using multiple expressions.

Batching Using Multiple Expressions

Thus far we have covered different ways of batching but none of them have shown the behavior if there are multiple batching expressions for the same item. When you have multiple batching statements for the same item such as `<Message Text="Type: %(Server.Type) Env: %(Server.Env)"/>` then the MSBuild engine will create unique batches based on all metadata being batched. Below you will find the Batching10.proj file; some targets were removed to be discussed later in this section.

```
C:\Data\MSBuildExamples\Batching>msbuild Batching06.proj /t:Target02 /nologo
Build started 10/17/2008 11:23:14 PM.
Project "C:\Data\MSBuildExamples\Batching\Batching06.proj" on node 0 (Target02
target(s)).
Project "C:\Data\MSBuildExamples\Batching\Batching06.proj" (1) is building "C:\
Data\MSBuildExamples\Batching\TestProjects\TestProj1\TestProj1.csproj" (2) on n
ode 0 (Rebuild target(s)).
  Deleting file "C:\Data\MSBuildExamples\Batching\TestProjects\BUILD\BuildTemp\
  TestProj1\Debug\TestProj1.exe".
  Deleting file "C:\Data\MSBuildExamples\Batching\TestProjects\BUILD\BuildTemp\
  TestProj1\Debug\TestProj1.pdb".
  Deleting file "C:\Data\MSBuildExamples\Batching\TestProjects\TestProj1\obj\De
  bug\TestProj1.Properties.Resources.resources".
  Deleting file "C:\Data\MSBuildExamples\Batching\TestProjects\TestProj1\obj\De
  bug\TestProj1.csproj.GenerateResource.Cache".
  Deleting file "C:\Data\MSBuildExamples\Batching\TestProjects\TestProj1\obj\De
  bug\TestProj1.exe".
  Deleting file "C:\Data\MSBuildExamples\Batching\TestProjects\TestProj1\obj\De
  bug\TestProj1.pdb".
CoreResGen:
  Processing resource file "Properties\Resources.resx" into "obj\Debug\TestProj
  1.Properties.Resources.resources".
CopyFilesToOutputDirectory:
  Copying file from "obj\Debug\TestProj1.exe" to "..\BUILD\BuildTemp\TestProj1\
  Debug\TestProj1.exe".
  TestProj1 -> C:\Data\MSBuildExamples\Batching\TestProjects\BUILD\BuildTemp\Te
  stProj1\Debug\TestProj1.exe
  Copying file from "obj\Debug\TestProj1.pdb" to "..\BUILD\BuildTemp\TestProj1\
  Debug\TestProj1.pdb".
Done Building Project "C:\Data\MSBuildExamples\Batching\TestProjects\TestProj1\
TestProj1.csproj" (Rebuild target(s)).

Project "C:\Data\MSBuildExamples\Batching\Batching06.proj" (1) is building "C:\
Data\MSBuildExamples\Batching\TestProjects\TestProj1\TestProj1.csproj" (2:2) on
 node 0 (Rebuild target(s)).
  Deleting file "C:\Data\MSBuildExamples\Batching\TestProjects\BUILD\BuildTemp\
  TestProj1\Release\TestProj1.exe".
  Deleting file "C:\Data\MSBuildExamples\Batching\TestProjects\BUILD\BuildTemp\
  TestProj1\Release\TestProj1.pdb".
  Deleting file "C:\Data\MSBuildExamples\Batching\TestProjects\TestProj1\obj\Re
  lease\TestProj1.Properties.Resources.resources".
  Deleting file "C:\Data\MSBuildExamples\Batching\TestProjects\TestProj1\obj\Re
  lease\TestProj1.csproj.GenerateResource.Cache".
  Deleting file "C:\Data\MSBuildExamples\Batching\TestProjects\TestProj1\obj\Re
  lease\TestProj1.exe".
  Deleting file "C:\Data\MSBuildExamples\Batching\TestProjects\TestProj1\obj\Re
  lease\TestProj1.pdb".
CoreResGen:
  Processing resource file "Properties\Resources.resx" into "obj\Release\TestPr
  oj1.Properties.Resources.resources".
CopyFilesToOutputDirectory:
  Copying file from "obj\Release\TestProj1.exe" to "..\BUILD\BuildTemp\TestProj
  1\Release\TestProj1.exe".
  TestProj1 -> C:\Data\MSBuildExamples\Batching\TestProjects\BUILD\BuildTemp\Te
  stProj1\Release\TestProj1.exe
  Copying file from "obj\Release\TestProj1.pdb" to "..\BUILD\BuildTemp\TestProj
  1\Release\TestProj1.pdb".
Done Building Project "C:\Data\MSBuildExamples\Batching\TestProjects\TestProj1\
TestProj1.csproj" (Rebuild target(s)).

Project "C:\Data\MSBuildExamples\Batching\Batching06.proj" (1) is building "C:\
Data\MSBuildExamples\Batching\TestProjects\TestProj2\TestProj2.csproj" (3) on n
ode 0 (Rebuild target(s)).
  Deleting file "C:\Data\MSBuildExamples\Batching\TestProjects\BUILD\BuildTemp\
```

FIGURE 6-14 Batching06.proj TargetEx02 result

```
<Project xmlns="http://schemas.microsoft.com/developer/msbuild/2003">
  <ItemGroup>
    <Server Include="Server1">
      <Type>2008</Type>
      <Name>SVR01</Name>
      <AdminContact>Sayed Ibrahim Hashimi</AdminContact>
      <Env>PROD</Env>
    </Server>
    <Server Include="Server2">
      <Type>2003</Type>
      <Name>SVR02</Name>
      <AdminContact>Sayed Y. Hashimi</AdminContact>
      <Env>UAT</Env>
    </Server>
    <Server Include="Server3">
      <Type>2008</Type>
      <Name>SVR03</Name>
      <AdminContact>Nicole Woodsmall</AdminContact>
      <Env>PROD</Env>
    </Server>
```

```
    <Server Include="Server4">
      <Type>2003</Type>
      <Name>SVR04</Name>
      <AdminContact>Keith Tingle</AdminContact>
      <Env>DEV</Env>
    </Server>
  </ItemGroup>

  <Target Name="PrintTypeEnv">
    <!-- Batches over Type and Env -->
    <Message Text="Type: %(Server.Type) Env: %(Server.Env)"/>
  </Target>

  <!--
  NOTE: Others targets defined here.
  -->
</Project>
```

The PrintTypeEnv target uses batching for the Type and Env metadata from the Server item list. In this case, the batches will be formed by unique combinations of Type and Env metadata. If you execute the command `msbuild Batching10.proj /t:PrintTypeEnv` the result would be what is shown in Figure 6-15.

```
C:\Data\MSBuildExamples\Batching>msbuild Batching10.proj /t:PrintTypeEnv /nologo

Build started 11/1/2008 5:10:38 PM.
Project "C:\Data\MSBuildExamples\Batching\Batching10.proj" on node 0 (PrintType
Env target(s)).
  Type: 2008 Env: PROD
  Type: 2003 Env: UAT
  Type: 2003 Env: DEV
Done Building Project "C:\Data\MSBuildExamples\Batching\Batching10.proj" (Print
TypeEnv target(s)).

Build succeeded.
    0 Warning(s)
    0 Error(s)
```

FIGURE 6-15 PrintTypeEnv target results

In this case, there are three unique combinations of the Type and Env metadata, there are two item values with Type=2008 and Env=PROD. Because of this the Message task was invoked three times. This behavior is a little different from the examples in the Multi-batching section. In that section there were multiple batches created because different metadata was used from different item lists. In this case we are using multiple metadata values from the same item list.

Below you will find the other targets from the Batching10.proj file which were omitted from the previously shown snippet.

```
<Target Name="PrintTypeName">
  <!-- Batches over Type and Name -->
  <Message Text="Type: %(Server.Type) Name: %(Server.Name)"/>
</Target>
<Target Name="PrintTypeNameEnv">
  <!-- Batches over Type, Name and Env -->
  <Message Text="Type: %(Server.Type) Name: %(Server.Name) Env: %(Server.Env)"/>
</Target>
```

These two targets also demonstrate batching with multiple values from the same item. Take a look at the results of the command `msbuild Batching10.proj /t:PrintTypeName;PrintTypeNameEnv` shown in Figure 6-16.

```
C:\Data\MSBuildExamples\Batching>msbuild Batching10.proj /t:PrintTypeName;PrintT
ypeNameEnv /nologo
Build started 11/1/2008 5:20:02 PM.
Project "C:\Data\MSBuildExamples\Batching\Batching10.proj" on node 0 (PrintType
Name;PrintTypeNameEnv target(s)).
  Type: 2008 Name: SVR01
  Type: 2003 Name: SVR02
  Type: 2008 Name: SVR03
  Type: 2003 Name: SVR04
PrintTypeNameEnv:
  Type: 2008 Name: SVR01 Env: PROD
  Type: 2003 Name: SVR02 Env: UAT
  Type: 2008 Name: SVR03 Env: PROD
  Type: 2003 Name: SVR04 Env: DEV
Done Building Project "C:\Data\MSBuildExamples\Batching\Batching10.proj" (Print
TypeName;PrintTypeNameEnv target(s)).

Build succeeded.
    0 Warning(s)
    0 Error(s)
```

FIGURE 6-16 PrintTypeName and PrintTypeNameEnv target results

In the first target PrintTypeName, the batching is using the Type and Name metadata values. Since the Name metadata is unique, we would expect that the Message task be executed once for each value in the Server item list. From the results shown in Figure 6-16, you can see that this is indeed the case. This also hold true for the PrintTypeNameEnv target, which extends the first target by also batching on the Env metadata value. There is no limit on the number of metadata values that can be used for a task. Now we will take a look at why MSBuild allows batching expressions to be expressed without an item list name.

Batching Using Shared Metadata

The concept of shared metadata is loosely defined; it is a set of metadata that is common across more than one item type. For example, in VB.NET and C# project files many different items can have a value for the DependentUpon metadata. There are scenarios in which you would like to batch using different item types that have identical metadata—that is batching using shared metadata.

In all the examples we have discussed thus far, we have always qualified the item type in the batching expression. For example, we recently used the expression %(Projects.Identity). In this expression, the item type was Projects and we were batching on the Identity metadata. Consider this example: As you create projects in Visual Studio, several item types allow a value for the CopyToOutputDirectory value. Some item types that support this include EmbeddedResource, Compile, Content, and so on. Instead of handling each set of files individually, it would be ideal if we could act on them all at once. You can do this by declaring a metadata expression without the item type. You will see this in the following Batching07.proj file.

```
<Project xmlns="http://schemas.microsoft.com/developer/msbuild/2003"
         ToolsVersion="3.5"
         DefaultTargets="PrintInfo">
  <ItemGroup>
    <None Include="None01.txt">
      <CopyToOutputDirectory>PreserveNewest</CopyToOutputDirectory>
    </None>
    <None Include="None02.txt">
      <CopyToOutputDirectory>Always</CopyToOutputDirectory>
    </None>
    <None Include="None03.txt;None4.txt">
      <CopyToOutputDirectory>PreserveNewest</CopyToOutputDirectory>
    </None>
    <Compile Include="src01.cs;src02.cs;src03.cs">
      <CopyToOutputDirectory>PreserveNewest</CopyToOutputDirectory>
    </Compile>
    <Compile Include="src04.cs;src05.cs">
      <CopyToOutputDirectory>Always</CopyToOutputDirectory>
    </Compile>
  </ItemGroup>

  <Target Name="PrintInfo">
    <Message Text="%(CopyToOutputDirectory): @(None) @(Compile)" />
    <Message Text="====" />
    <Message Text="PreserveNewest: @(Compile) @(None)"
             Condition="'%(CopyToOutputDirectory)'=='PreserveNewest'" />
    <Message Text="Always: @(Compile) @(None)"
             Condition="'%(CopyToOutputDirectory)'=='Always'" />
  </Target>
</Project>
```

Inside the PrintInfo target, the Message task is invoked with the expression `%(CopyToOutputDirectory)`. The CopyToOutputDirectory metadata is being referenced without an item type specified. When this is the case, at least one item type must be passed to the task so that the MSBuild engine knows what item type(s) to use for batching. In this case, the Message task is referencing the None and Compile items, so it will create unique batches for CopyToOutputDirectory consisting of items from both None and Compile item types. You can see the result of executing this target in Figure 6-17.

```
C:\Data\MSBuildExamples\Batching>msbuild Batching07.proj /t:PrintInfo /nologo
Build started 9/17/2008 7:36:40 PM.
Project "C:\Data\MSBuildExamples\Batching\Batching07.proj" on node 0 (PrintInfo
 target(s)).
  PreserveNewest: None01.txt;None03.txt;None4.txt src01.cs;src02.cs;src03.cs
  Always: None02.txt src04.cs;src05.cs
  ====
  PreserveNewest: src01.cs;src02.cs;src03.cs None01.txt;None03.txt;None4.txt
  Always: src04.cs;src05.cs None02.txt
Done Building Project "C:\Data\MSBuildExamples\Batching\Batching07.proj" (Print
Info target(s)).


Build succeeded.
    0 Warning(s)
    0 Error(s)
```

FIGURE 6-17 Common metadata batching, example 1

From the result shown in Figure 6-17, we can see that the statement `<Message Text="%(CopyToOutputDirectory): @(None) @(Compile)"/>` was executed once for the value PreserveNewest and once for Always. Also during the batching, values from both None and Compile item types were placed in the same batch. Because of this we can create steps in our build process that don't discriminate based on an item type; only on one of its metadata values. If you do use this, you must ensure that every value in each referenced item type has declared the used metadata value. For example, if the example in Figure 6-17 had an additional ItemGroup declaration before the PrintInfo target, such as

```
<ItemGroup>
  <Compile Include="src06.cs" />
</ItemGroup>,
```

then the target would fail with the error message shown in Figure 6-18.

```
C:\Data\MSBuildExamples\Batching>msbuild Batching07.proj /t:PrintInfo /nologo
Build started 9/17/2008 7:43:59 PM.
Project "C:\Data\MSBuildExamples\Batching\Batching07.proj" on node 0 (PrintInfo
 target(s)).
C:\Data\MSBuildExamples\Batching\Batching07.proj(28,5): error MSB4096: The item
 "src06.cs" in item list "Compile" does not define a value for metadata "CopyTo
OutputDirectory". In order to use this metadata, either qualify it by specifyi
ng %(Compile.CopyToOutputDirectory), or ensure that all items in this list defi
ne a value for this metadata.
Done Building Project "C:\Data\MSBuildExamples\Batching\Batching07.proj" (Print
Info target(s)) -- FAILED.

Build FAILED.

"C:\Data\MSBuildExamples\Batching\Batching07.proj" (PrintInfo target) (1) ->
(PrintInfo target) ->
  C:\Data\MSBuildExamples\Batching\Batching07.proj(28,5): error MSB4096: The it
em "src06.cs" in item list "Compile" does not define a value for metadata "Copy
ToOutputDirectory". In order to use this metadata, either qualify it by specif
ying %(Compile.CopyToOutputDirectory), or ensure that all items in this list de
fine a value for this metadata.

    0 Warning(s)
    1 Error(s)
```

FIGURE 6-18 Common metadata batching error

This is one difference in behavior from the batching methods we discussed previously. In all previous cases, if an item value did not have the specified metadata value defined, it would be treated as empty. In this case it causes the build to fail. If you need to use this type of batching but you are not sure if all the item values have a defined the metadata, then you may have to provide a default value. You can use the new *ItemDefintionGroup* element to provide this for you. The following Batching08.proj file demonstrates this behavior.

```
<Project xmlns="http://schemas.microsoft.com/developer/msbuild/2003"
         ToolsVersion="3.5"
         DefaultTargets="PrintInfo">
  <ItemGroup>
    <None Include="None01.txt">
      <CopyToOutputDirectory>PreserveNewest</CopyToOutputDirectory>
    </None>
    <None Include="None02.txt">
      <CopyToOutputDirectory>Always</CopyToOutputDirectory>
    </None>
    <None Include="None03.txt;None4.txt">
      <CopyToOutputDirectory>PreserveNewest</CopyToOutputDirectory>
    </None>
    <Compile Include="src01.cs;src02.cs;src03.cs">
      <CopyToOutputDirectory>PreserveNewest</CopyToOutputDirectory>
    </Compile>
```

```
    <Compile Include="src04.cs;src05.cs">
      <CopyToOutputDirectory>Always</CopyToOutputDirectory>
    </Compile>
  </ItemGroup>

  <ItemGroup>
    <Compile Include="src06.cs" />
  </ItemGroup>

  <ItemDefinitionGroup>
    <Compile>
      <CopyToOutputDirectory>Never</CopyToOutputDirectory>
    </Compile>
  </ItemDefinitionGroup>

  <Target Name="PrintInfo">
    <ItemGroup>
      <Compile Include="src07.cs" />
      <Compile Include="src08.cs">
        <CopyToOutputDirectory>Always</CopyToOutputDirectory>
      </Compile>
    </ItemGroup>

    <Message Text="%(CopyToOutputDirectory): @(None) @(Compile)" />
    <Message Text="====" />
    <Message Text="PreserveNewest: @(Compile) @(None)"
             Condition="'%(CopyToOutputDirectory)'=='PreserveNewest'" />
    <Message Text="Always: @(Compile) @(None)"
             Condition="'%(CopyToOutputDirectory)'=='Always'" />
    <Message Text="Never: @(Compile) @(None)"
             Condition="'%(CopyToOutputDirectory)'=='Never'" />
  </Target>
</Project>
```

This file declares a few values for the Compile item type that have not defined the CopyToOutputDirectory metadata value. A default value is provided via the ItemDefinitionGroup declaration. I've highlighted the changed regions. The result of executing the PrintInfo target in this file is shown in Figure 6-19.

```
C:\Data\MSBuildExamples\Batching>msbuild Batching08.proj /t:PrintInfo /nologo
Build started 9/17/2008 11:08:10 PM.
Project "C:\Data\MSBuildExamples\Batching\Batching08.proj" on node 0 (PrintInfo
 target(s)).
  PreserveNewest: None01.txt;None03.txt;None4.txt src01.cs;src02.cs;src03.cs
  Always: None02.txt src04.cs;src05.cs;src08.cs
  Never:  src06.cs;src07.cs
  ====
  PreserveNewest: src01.cs;src02.cs;src03.cs None01.txt;None03.txt;None4.txt
  Always: src04.cs;src05.cs;src08.cs None02.txt
  Never: src06.cs;src07.cs
Done Building Project "C:\Data\MSBuildExamples\Batching\Batching08.proj" (Print
Info target(s)).


Build succeeded.
    0 Warning(s)
    0 Error(s)
```

FIGURE 6-19 Common metadata batching, example 2

From this result, we can see that the default value was successfully applied and we were able to use batching with unique values of the common metadata value.

Another method of achieving the same result would be to use the ability to dynamically update an item's metadata value using the ItemGroup inside a target. The following Batching09.proj file removes the *ItemDefinitionGroup* element and replaces its functionality with this other technique.

```
<Project xmlns="http://schemas.microsoft.com/developer/msbuild/2003"
         ToolsVersion="3.5"
         DefaultTargets="PrintInfo">
  <ItemGroup>
    <None Include="None01.txt">
      <CopyToOutputDirectory>PreserveNewest</CopyToOutputDirectory>
    </None>
    <None Include="None02.txt">
      <CopyToOutputDirectory>Always</CopyToOutputDirectory>
    </None>
    <None Include="None03.txt;None4.txt">
      <CopyToOutputDirectory>PreserveNewest</CopyToOutputDirectory>
    </None>
    <Compile Include="src01.cs;src02.cs;src03.cs">
      <CopyToOutputDirectory>PreserveNewest</CopyToOutputDirectory>
    </Compile>
    <Compile Include="src04.cs;src05.cs">
      <CopyToOutputDirectory>Always</CopyToOutputDirectory>
    </Compile>
  </ItemGroup>

  <ItemGroup>
    <Compile Include="src06.cs" />
  </ItemGroup>

  <Target Name="PrintInfo">
    <ItemGroup>
      <Compile Include="src07.cs" />
      <Compile Include="src08.cs">
        <CopyToOutputDirectory>Always</CopyToOutputDirectory>
      </Compile>
    </ItemGroup>

    <ItemGroup>
      <Compile Condition="'%(Compile.CopyToOutputDirectory)'==''">
        <CopyToOutputDirectory>Never</CopyToOutputDirectory>
      </Compile>
    </ItemGroup>

    <Message Text="%(CopyToOutputDirectory): @(None) @(Compile)" />
    <Message Text="====" />
    <Message Text="PreserveNewest: @(Compile) @(None)"
             Condition="'%(CopyToOutputDirectory)'=='PreserveNewest'" />
    <Message Text="Always: @(Compile) @(None)"
             Condition="'%(CopyToOutputDirectory)'=='Always'" />
    <Message Text="Never: @(Compile) @(None)"
             Condition="'%(CopyToOutputDirectory)'=='Never'" />
  </Target>
</Project>
```

In this demonstration, I have highlighted in bold the text that has changed. You can see that the *ItemGroup* element is used inside the PrintInfo target. In this case, we are providing a value for the CopyToOutputDirectory metadata if its value is empty. This is implemented with task batching and as a condition. The difference between this approach and the ItemDefinitionGroup approach is this: The ItemDefinitionGroup will provide a true default value, in the sense that it applies even for item values defined later in the build process, whereas the replacement approach modifies only currently defined item values. We will now move on to discuss incremental building, another great feature of MSBuild, which is little known.

Incremental Building

As products grow into giants, so do their build times. For a large code base, a build time of a few hours is not uncommon. Knowing this, there must be a way to ensure that only components that have changed, or depend on changed components, be built. This is accomplished through incremental building. Incremental building allows the MSBuild engine to determine which targets can be skipped, or even partially skipped. This then enables faster build times in most cases. In this section, we will discuss how you can take advantage of this in your own build scripts.

We have seen in target batching that the Output parameter of the *Target* element contains the batching statement. On the *Target* element there is also an Input parameter; when both of these values are present, Incremental Building is enabled. In this case, the MSBuild engine will examine the timestamps of the input files and compare them to the timestamps of the files provided in the outputs value. If the outputs were created after the inputs, then the target is skipped. We can now take a look at this in action.

The Incremental01.proj file demonstrates incremental building. It copies a set of files from one location to another. If the files are up to date then the target which performs the copy is skipped. This file is shown next.

```
<Project xmlns="http://schemas.microsoft.com/developer/msbuild/2003"
         ToolsVersion="3.5">
  <PropertyGroup>
    <SourceFolder>$(MSBuildProjectDirectory)\src\</SourceFolder>
    <DestFolder>$(MSBuildProjectDirectory)\dest\</DestFolder>
  </PropertyGroup>

  <ItemGroup>
    <SourceFiles Include="$(SourceFolder)*.txt" />
  </ItemGroup>

  <Target Name="CopyFilesToDest"
     Inputs="@(SourceFiles)"
     Outputs="@(SourceFiles->'$(DestFolder)%(RecursiveDir)%(Filename)%(Extension)')">
    <Copy SourceFiles="@(SourceFiles)"
      DestinationFiles=
        "@(SourceFiles->'$(DestFolder)%(RecursiveDir)%(Filename)%(Extension)')" />
  </Target>
```

```
  <Target Name="CleanDestFolder">
    <CreateItem Include="$(DestFolder)**\*">
      <Output ItemName="_FilesToDelete" TaskParameter="Include" />
    </CreateItem>
    <Delete Files="@(_FilesToDelete)" />
  </Target>
</Project>
```

In this build script, we have declared two targets, CopyFilesToDest and CleanDestFolder. The important target here is CopyFilesToDest target. The inputs for that target are specified as `@(SourceFiles)`, and outputs as `@(SourceFiles->'$(DestFolder)%(RecursiveDir)%(Filename)%(Extension)')`, which is a transformation of the SourceFiles item. If the files in the output location are newer than the source files, then we would expect this target to be skipped. The CleanDestFolder target can be used to delete the output files. Take a look at the result of the command `msbuild Incremental01.proj /t:CleanDestFolder;CopyFilesToDest.` The result would be what is shown in Figure 6-20.

```
C:\Data\MSBuildExamples\Batching>msbuild Incremental01.proj /t:CleanDestFolder;C
opyFilesToDest /nologo
Build started 8/12/2008 12:54:18 AM.
Project "C:\Data\MSBuildExamples\Batching\Incremental01.proj" on node 0 (CleanD
estFolder;CopyFilesToDest target(s)).
  Deleting file "C:\Data\MSBuildExamples\Batching\dest\four.txt".
  Deleting file "C:\Data\MSBuildExamples\Batching\dest\one.txt".
  Deleting file "C:\Data\MSBuildExamples\Batching\dest\three.txt".
  Deleting file "C:\Data\MSBuildExamples\Batching\dest\two.txt".
CopyFilesToDest:
  Copying file from "C:\Data\MSBuildExamples\Batching\src\four.txt" to "C:\Data
  \MSBuildExamples\Batching\dest\four.txt".
  Copying file from "C:\Data\MSBuildExamples\Batching\src\one.txt" to "C:\Data\
  MSBuildExamples\Batching\dest\one.txt".
  Copying file from "C:\Data\MSBuildExamples\Batching\src\three.txt" to "C:\Dat
  a\MSBuildExamples\Batching\dest\three.txt".
  Copying file from "C:\Data\MSBuildExamples\Batching\src\two.txt" to "C:\Data\
  MSBuildExamples\Batching\dest\two.txt".
Done Building Project "C:\Data\MSBuildExamples\Batching\Incremental01.proj" (Cl
eanDestFolder;CopyFilesToDest target(s)).


Build succeeded.
    0 Warning(s)
    0 Error(s)
```

FIGURE 6-20 CopyFilesToDest result 1

In this example, I purposefully deleted all the output files before the CopyFilesToDest target is called. I do this to ensure that the target is called, which can be seen in the result in Figure 6-20. From that output we can see that the files were successfully copied from the source location to the destination. Now what would happen if we ran that target again, without first calling the CleanDestFolder target? The result is shown in Figure 6-21.

```
C:\Data\MSBuildExamples\Batching>msbuild Incremental01.proj /t:CopyFilesToDest /
nologo
Build started 8/12/2008 1:19:56 AM.
Project "C:\Data\MSBuildExamples\Batching\Incremental01.proj" on node 0 (CopyFi
lesToDest target(s)).
Skipping target "CopyFilesToDest" because all output files are up-to-date with
respect to the input files.
Done Building Project "C:\Data\MSBuildExamples\Batching\Incremental01.proj" (Co
pyFilesToDest target(s)).


Build succeeded.
    0 Warning(s)
    0 Error(s)
```

FIGURE 6-21 CopyFilesToDest result 2

As the result shows, the target was successfully skipped because all the outputs were up to date with respect to the inputs. This basic implementation serves as the basis for incremental building, and is the key to efficient build scripts. The targets shipped by Microsoft to build managed projects use incremental building extensively. If you make modifications to the build, your targets should also support this when possible. If you extend the build process for a managed project to use custom targets that create files, you should also make sure those files are deleted when the project is cleaned. We will take a look at this specific example in Chapter 8, "Practical Applications, Part 1." It's very important that your incremental build works properly—that is, that it does not touch any files. This is not only because it makes your life easier as a developer, but also because it's highly antisocial in the context of a larger build: subsequent (correctly authored) build steps will be triggered to run because you touched those files. Sometimes inputs and outputs alone will not enable you to properly implement incremental builds. For example, if a task operates on files that have transitive dependencies, for example C++ header files, then you may not be able to (or don't want to) list all of them in inputs and outputs. In this scenario, you must bypass the inputs and outputs list and let the task do the timestamp checking for itself before it is run. The GenerateResource task behaves in this manner because .resx files can refer to other files.

Partially Building Targets

When incremental building is utilized you may run into times when a target is up to date for some files but not all. You shouldn't have to completely rebuild the target simply to take care of a few files, and indeed, you do not—MSBuild will take care of this for you automatically. This is called partially building targets.

The best way to describe how partial building works is to demonstrate it. We'll start by examining the build script shown in the next snippet.

```
<Project xmlns="http://schemas.microsoft.com/developer/msbuild/2003"
         ToolsVersion="3.5" DefaultTargets="CopyFilesToDest">
  <PropertyGroup>
    <SourceFolder>src\</SourceFolder>
    <DestFolder>dest\</DestFolder>
  </PropertyGroup>

  <ItemGroup>
    <SourceFiles Include="$(SourceFolder)*.txt" />
  </ItemGroup>

  <Target Name="CopyFilesToDest"
     Inputs="@(SourceFiles)"
     Outputs="@(SourceFiles->'$(DestFolder)%(RecursiveDir)%(Filename)%(Extension)')">
    <Copy SourceFiles="@(SourceFiles)"
      DestinationFiles=
       "@(SourceFiles->'$(DestFolder)%(RecursiveDir)%(Filename)%(Extension)')" />
  </Target>
```

```
  <Target Name="CleanDestFolder">
    <CreateItem Include="$(DestFolder)**\*">
      <Output ItemName="_FilesToDelete" TaskParameter="Include" />
    </CreateItem>
    <Delete Files="@(_FilesToDelete)" />
  </Target>

  <Target Name="DeleteSomeRandomFiles">
    <CreateItem Include="$(DestFolder)One.txt;$(DestFolder)Three.txt">
      <Output ItemName="_PartialFilesToDelete" TaskParameter="Include" />
    </CreateItem>
    <Delete Files="@(_PartialFilesToDelete)" />
  </Target>
</Project>
```

This script, Incremental02.proj, is a modification of the previous example from Incremental01.proj. The change is the addition of a new target, DeleteSomeRandomFiles. This target will clean out some of the files in the dest folder but not all of them. Assuming that the CopyFilesToDest target has been run previously without being cleaned, the result of the command `msbuild Incremental02.proj /t: DeleteSomeRandomFiles;CopyFilesToDest` is shown in Figure 6-22.

```
C:\Data\MSBuildExamples\Batching>msbuild Incremental02.proj /t:DeleteSomeRandomF
iles,CopyFilesToDest /nologo
Build started 10/18/2008 12:01:14 AM.
Project "C:\Data\MSBuildExamples\Batching\Incremental02.proj" on node 0 (Delete
SomeRandomFiles;CopyFilesToDest target(s)).
  Deleting file "dest\One.txt".
  Deleting file "dest\Three.txt".
CopyFilesToDest:
Building target "CopyFilesToDest" partially, because some output files are out
of date with respect to their input files.
Copying file from "src\one.txt" to "dest\one.txt".
Copying file from "src\three.txt" to "dest\three.txt".
Done Building Project "C:\Data\MSBuildExamples\Batching\Incremental02.proj" (De
leteSomeRandomFiles;CopyFilesToDest target(s)).

Build succeeded.
    0 Warning(s)
    0 Error(s)
```

FIGURE 6-22 Partially building targets

If you take a look at the result shown in Figure 6-22, you will see the message `Building target "CopyFilesToDest" partially, because some output files are out of date with respect to their input files.` Since the DeleteSomeRandomFiles target deleted only a few of the generated files, the ones that were not deleted were still up to date. So those files do not need to be rebuilt. MSBuild automatically recognized this and executed only the CopyFilesToDest for the outdated inputs. Following that statement you can see that two files were copied to the destination location. Since some of the files were up to date, the batch that was sent to the CopyFilesToDest target contained only the out-of-date files. When the inputs and outputs contain the same number of values, MSBuild will match input to output in a 1:1 fashion. For example, it will assume that the first value in the input corresponds to the first value of the output, and the second input value to the second output value, and so on. Using this process, MSBuild is able to determine specifically what set of inputs are out of date with respect to outputs, and process only those item values. Typically you will not have to be concerned with partial building because MSBuild will take care of it, but you should be aware of it.

In this chapter, we have covered an advanced technique—batching. Batching will allow you to create build scripts that take full advantage of the MSBuild engine. When you create build scripts you should remember that batching is available, and put it to use when necessary. Along with batching we have discussed incremental building, which allows for drastically reduced build times for most builds. For any complex build scripts, incremental building must be implemented. Now that we have covered batching and incremental building, in the next chapter we will take a look at how you external tools can be used in the build process. We will discuss some guidelines for using external tools, as well as show how to correctly integrate a few tools.

Chapter 7

External Tools

MSBuild has been around since Visual Studio 2005 (.NET 2.0), so it is still a somewhat new technology. Sometimes, when there's no specific MSBuild task that provides the functionality you need, you'll need to use one of the many existing tools that can and should be used to assist in build and deployments. Some of the most commonly used tools include FxCop, StyleCop, NUnit, and so on. In this chapter I will describe how external tools can be effectively consumed by MSBuild. We'll examine a few commonly used tools and discuss how to integrate them into your build process. We'll first describe how these can simply be invoked in build scripts and then describe a way to create reusable targets files for tools. Also, we will discuss some guidelines for reusable build scripts.

Exec Task

The simplest method to invoke an existing tool is by using the Exec task. This task is shipped with MSBuild. It can be used to execute any program or command. This is the task that is used to execute the PreBuild and PostBuild events as well. There are several properties on this task, which are summarized in Table 7-1.

TABLE 7-1 Exec Task Properties

Name	Description
Command	The command that is to be executed. This is the only **required** parameter.
WorkingDirectory	Specifies the working directory.
Timeout	Specifies the timeout, in milliseconds. After the amount of time specified has passed, the command will be terminated. By default there is no timeout, so a command will be allowed to execute indefinitely.
ExitCode	Output property containing the exit code returned by the execute command.
IgnoreExitCode	If true, then the Exec task will not fail the build based on the exit code. Otherwise the build is failed for any non-zero exit code. Currently there is a bug related to this in which, if this value is set to true and an error message has been logged, the build should fail but doesn't.

TABLE 7-1 Exec Task Properties

Name	Description
Outputs	An input/output parameter that contains the output items from the task. This is not set by the Exec task itself but made available to be set by the consumer. This parameter is needed only for output inferral. When a target is skipped MSBuild tries to create all the properties and items that the target would have created if it had run. For custom tasks this is possible only if the output is also an input. So this should be set to whatever the outputs for the executed command would be, if the task were run, so that MSBuild can properly determine dependencies. This is output inferral. By exposing the outputs as an input as well, output inferral is supported. Generally you will not have to worry about this.
StdErrEncoding	An input/output parameter that specifies the encoding that is used for the standard error stream. The default value is almost always sufficient; it is the current OEM encoding or else ANSI. These possible values are code page names for the desired encoding, for example UTF-8 and UTF-32.
StdOutEncoding	An input/output parameter that specifies the encoding that is used for the standard output stream. These possible values are code page names for the desired encoding, for example UTF-8 and UTF-32.
IgnoreStandardErrorWarningFormat*	If true, the output is not examined for **standard** errors and warnings.
CustomErrorRegularExpression*	If provided, this will be the regular expression pattern used to determine if an error occurred. MSBuild will attempt to examine the output of the executing tool for errors and warnings. For standard compliant tools this is automatic. For tools that do not log using the standard conventions (e.g., GCC compiler), then you can provide an expression to detect the errors. Also, you may need to provide an expression for the CustomWarningRegularExpression parameter. Typically you should use this in conjunction with the IgnoreStandardErrorWarningFormat parameter.
CustomWarningRegularExpression*	If provided, this will be the regular expression pattern used to determine that a warning occurred. See the note in the CustomErrorRegularExpression description about how MSBuild processes the executables output. Typically you should use this in conjunction with the IgnoreStandardErrorWarningFormat parameter.

* denotes new parameters new with .NET 3.5.

The most commonly used Exec properties are Command, IgnoreExitCode, and WorkingDirectory. In the next code fragment you will see a very simple usage of this task. This is from the Exec01.proj file in the Fundamentals directory.

```
<Project xmlns="http://schemas.microsoft.com/developer/msbuild/2003"
         ToolsVersion="3.5">
  <Target Name="Demo">
    <Exec Command="echo Hello MSBuild" />
  </Target>
</Project>
```

In this demonstration we are simply invoking the echo command to pass a message to the console. When you use the Exec task, the contents of the command are placed in a .cmd file and passed to cmd.exe for execution. We can verify that this was successfully executed by examining the result shown in Figure 7-1.

```
C:\Data\MSBuildExamples\Fundamentals>msbuild Exec01.proj /t:Demo /fl /nologo
Build started 9/7/2008 6:14:38 PM.
Project "C:\Data\MSBuildExamples\Fundamentals\Exec01.proj" on node 0 (Demo targ
et(s)).
  Hello MSBuild
Done Building Project "C:\Data\MSBuildExamples\Fundamentals\Exec01.proj" (Demo
target(s)).


Build succeeded.
    0 Warning(s)
    0 Error(s)
```

FIGURE 7-1 Exec result

From the result shown in Figure 7-1 we can see that the Exec task successfully executed the provided command and the message was successfully sent to the console. You should use the Exec task to invoke an executable when a task doesn't exist to invoke it for you. For example, you should use the Exec task to invoke svcutil.exe, from the Windows SDK, but not the csc.exe because the Csc task wraps the csc.exe executable. A few of the reasons why custom tasks are easier to use is that they can expose a specific set of properties that the tool can use, the output may be cleaner, and the task may be able to discover where the .exe is located. Many existing build processes are captured in non-MSBuild scripts, and the Exec task can be used to invoke those scripts. By doing this you can slowly migrate your build process to MSBuild, instead of employing an "all or nothing" approach.

One common usage of the Exec task, especially when using MSBuild 2.0, is to invoke the attrib command. This command can be used to change a file's attributes. When applications are under development, many files are marked as read-only, due to the source control provider. This is great for development, but sometimes causes problems for a build process that might copy and replace files with other ones. If you are using MSBuild 3.5 the Copy task now has a property OverwriteReadOnlyFiles, which can be used to bypass the copy read-only file problem. With MSBuild 2.0 you would have to change the file's attribute to be writeable.

An example of this would be replacing resource files at build time, or replacing Javascript files for Web projects. The following Exec02.proj file contains an example demonstrating using the attrib command.

```
<Project xmlns="http://schemas.microsoft.com/developer/msbuild/2003"
         ToolsVersion="3.5">
  <ItemGroup>
    <SrcFiles Include="src\*" />
  </ItemGroup>
  <Target Name="Demo">
    <Message Text="SrcFiles: @(SrcFiles)" />
    <Message Text="%0a%0dMaking files Readonly" Importance="high" />
    <!-- Make SrcFiles Readonly -->
    <Exec Command="attrib %(SrcFiles.Identity) +R" />

    <!-- Display the attributes -->
    <Exec Command="attrib %(SrcFiles.Identity)" />

    <Message Text="%0a%0dMaking files writeable" Importance="high" />
    <!-- Make SrcFiles Writeable -->
    <Exec Command="attrib %(SrcFiles.Identity) -R" />

    <!-- Display the attributes -->
    <Exec Command="attrib %(SrcFiles.Identity)" />
  </Target>
</Project>
```

This file declares a single item, SrcFiles, and a single target, Demo. Inside the Demo target the attrib command is used to apply the read-only flag, display file attributes, remove read-only attribute, and finally display the attributes a last time. The result of invoking this build script is captured in Figure 7-2.

```
C:\Data\MSBuildExamples\Fundamentals>msbuild Exec02.proj /t:Demo /fl /nologo
Build started 9/7/2008 7:29:43 PM.
Project "C:\Data\MSBuildExamples\Fundamentals\Exec02.proj" on node 0 (Demo targ
et(s)).
  SrcFiles: src\four.txt;src\one.txt;src\three.txt;src\two.txt

Making files read-only
  A    R     C:\Data\MSBuildExamples\Fundamentals\src\four.txt
  A    R     C:\Data\MSBuildExamples\Fundamentals\src\one.txt
  A    R     C:\Data\MSBuildExamples\Fundamentals\src\three.txt
  A    R     C:\Data\MSBuildExamples\Fundamentals\src\two.txt

Making files writeable
  A          C:\Data\MSBuildExamples\Fundamentals\src\four.txt
  A          C:\Data\MSBuildExamples\Fundamentals\src\one.txt
  A          C:\Data\MSBuildExamples\Fundamentals\src\three.txt
  A          C:\Data\MSBuildExamples\Fundamentals\src\two.txt
Done Building Project "C:\Data\MSBuildExamples\Fundamentals\Exec02.proj" (Demo
target(s)).


Build succeeded.
    0 Warning(s)
    0 Error(s)
```

FIGURE 7-2 Exec02.proj result

As you can see, the attrib command was successfully invoked to set and clear the read-only flag. Now that the read-only attribute has been cleared we are free to copy any file on top of this one. Another common usage of the Exec task is to interact with source control providers. With more common source control providers you may be able to find custom tasks, but tasks for all providers are not available. You may have to use the Exec task to perform the operation for you. We will now conclude our discussion of the Exec task and move on to cover the MSBuild task.

MSBuild Task

When you are building products there will be many instances where you simply want to build an existing MSBuild file. This could be an MSBuild file that you authored or one that was created by a third party tool for you. Of course you could use the Exec task to perform this, but a better option is to use the MSBuild task. This is another task that is delivered along with MSBuild itself. As the name suggests, it will invoke MSBuild on the specified file(s). Some of the advantages of using this task instead of the Exec task include increased performance, better integration, and ease of use. The properties for this task are outlined in Table 7-2.

TABLE 7-2 MSBuild Task Properties

Name	Description
BuildInParallel	If true, then the projects will be built in parallel if possible. The default value for this is false. The Microsoft.Common.targets file passes a default value of true for this property when using the MSBuild task.
Projects	Project file(s) to be built. If you specify more than one, either pass it in as an item list or as a semicolon delimited list.
Properties	Optional semicolon delimited list of properties in the format <**n**>=<**v**> where **<n>** is the name of the property and **<v>** is the value. These are global properties and treated the same as properties passed to the msbuild.exe command using the /property (/p) switch. You can also add properties using the Properties or AdditionalProperties project item metadata.
RebaseOutputs	If this is true, then any relative paths from the built projects' Target outputs will be adjusted to that of the calling project. The default value for this is false.
RunEachTargetSeparately	If true, then each target will be executed independently of the other targets in the Target property. If not building in parallel, then each project will be built once for each target. If building in parallel, then all projects will be built together for each target. If an error occurs during a target and this is set to false, subsequent targets are allowed to execute instead of the entire task execution terminated. The default value for this is false. It is more efficient to leave this value as false; otherwise the engine will be called to build each target in turn, rather than giving it a list.
SkipNonexistentProjects*	If this is set to true, then if a project doesn't exist it is skipped instead of raising an error. The default value for this is false.

TABLE 7-2 MSBuild Task Properties

Name	Description
StopOnFirstFailure	If this is set to true and an error occurs, the task invocation will be stopped. The default value for this is false. If set to false and you are building projects A and B, and A fails, project B will begin building. If you are building targets t1 and t2, if t1 fails, then t2 will start.
TargetAndPropertyListSeparators*	Can be used to change the default semicolon separator for properties and targets.
TargetOutputs	Output parameter that contains the outputs from the specified targets that were built.
Targets	Specifies the target(s) to be built. If providing more than one value, then it should be a semicolon delimited list just as when using the /target (/t) switch with msbuild.exe.
ToolsVersion	Determines which version of tools will be used to build the project. Valid values are 2.0, and 3.5. The default value is 2.0. This determines the version of the tasks and targets that are used to build your project. Note that Microsoft.Common .targets also has a property named TargetFrameworkVersion that can be used to target other framework versions. These are not the same. TargetFrameworkVersion is a regular property used by the common Microsoft targets files. If your ToolsVersion is 2.0 then the TargetFrameworkVersion must be 2.0 as well.
UnloadProjectsOnCompletion*	If this is set to true, then when a project has finished building it will be removed from memory. Once a project is unloaded it cannot be loaded again. If you are building many projects, then you should set this to true if possible so MSBuild doesn't consume too many resources. The behavior of this is subtle and difficult to use correctly. You should set this only if it is absolutely necessary. In the next version of MSBuild this will be transparent.
UseResultsCache*	This enables the outputs of a built target to be cached. When the results are cached a project can be unloaded while the outputs still available as if the project was not unloaded. If you are setting the UnloadProjectsOnCompletion to true, then this should be set to true as well. The default value for this is true. Similar to UnloadProjectsOnCompletion, you should not set this property unless you have no other option.

* denotes new parameters new with .NET 3.5.

From the properties listed in Table 7-2, the most commonly used are Projects, Targets, Properties, and TargetOutputs. We will demonstrate the usage of all these properties in this section. The following snippet shows the contents of two project files; MSBuildTask01.proj and MSBuildTask01_external.proj, which is located in the Fundamentals directory.

MSBuildTask01.proj

```
<Project xmlns="http://schemas.microsoft.com/developer/msbuild/2003"
         ToolsVersion="3.5"
         DefaultTargets="Demo">

  <Target Name="Demo">
    <Message Text="Inside Demo target" />
    <MSBuild Projects="MSBuildTask01_external.proj"
             Targets="PrintMessage" />
  </Target>

</Project>
```

MSBuildTask01_external.proj

```
<Project xmlns="http://schemas.microsoft.com/developer/msbuild/2003"
         ToolsVersion="3.5">

  <Target Name="PrintMessage">
    <Message Text="Hello MSBuild" />
  </Target>
</Project>
```

The MSBuildTask01.proj file contains a single target Demo. This is the one that we will be invoking from the MSBuild command line. This target uses the MSBuild task to call the PrintMessage target contained in the MSBuildTask01_external.proj file. If you executed the command `msbuild.exe MSBuildTask01.proj /t:Demo` the result would be what is shown in Figure 7-3.

```
C:\Data\MSBuildExamples\Fundamentals>msbuild MSBuildTask01.proj /t:Demo /nologo
Build started 11/8/2008 7:19:29 PM.
Project "C:\Data\MSBuildExamples\Fundamentals\MSBuildTask01.proj" on node 0 (De
mo target(s)).
  Inside Demo target
Project "C:\Data\MSBuildExamples\Fundamentals\MSBuildTask01.proj" (1) is buildi
ng "C:\Data\MSBuildExamples\Fundamentals\MSBuildTask01_external.proj" (2) on no
de 0 (PrintMessage target(s)).
  Hello MSBuild
Done Building Project "C:\Data\MSBuildExamples\Fundamentals\MSBuildTask01_exter
nal.proj" (PrintMessage target(s)).

Done Building Project "C:\Data\MSBuildExamples\Fundamentals\MSBuildTask01.proj"
 (Demo target(s)).


Build succeeded.
    0 Warning(s)
    0 Error(s)
```

FIGURE 7-3 MSBuildTask01.proj result

From the results shown in Figure 7-3 you can see that the PrintMessage target was called using the MSBuild task from the Demo target. Now that we have seen how to use the MSBuild task, we'll take a look at how we can send properties into a project.

When you invoke the MSBuild task, the properties and items of the calling MSBuild file are **not** passed through to the projects by the MSBuild task. This is by design. You can pass property values using the Properties parameter of the MSBuild task. You cannot pass items through, but you can use Properties to initialize items inside the project being built. These properties are global properties. They are treated in the same manner as properties that are passed into msbuild.exe using the /p switch; that is, they cannot be overwritten by static values declared in the project file that will be processed by the MSBuild task. Building a project with a different set of Properties causes it to build again; it has a different identity. Building a project with the same set of properties causes the build to be skipped. In the following code section you will find the contents of the MSBuildTask02.proj file, which is a modified version of the previous example.

```
<Project xmlns="http://schemas.microsoft.com/developer/msbuild/2003"
         ToolsVersion="3.5"
         DefaultTargets="Demo">

  <Target Name="Demo">
    <Message Text="Inside Demo target" />
    <MSBuild Projects="$(MSBuildProjectFullPath)"
             Targets="PrintMessage"
             Properties="SourceName=PrintMessage Target"
             />
  </Target>

  <Target Name="PrintMessage">
    <Message Text="Hello MSBuild from: $(SourceName)" />
  </Target>
</Project>
```

The difference between this example and the previous is that in this example a value for SourceName is passed by the Properties parameter. As stated in Table 7-2, properties should be passed in the format <n>=<v>. In this case the name of the property that we are passing is SourceName and the value is "PrintMessage target". If we were to pass more than one value we would have to delimit the name-value pairs with a semicolon. You can see the result of building the Demo target of this file in Figure 7-4.

```
C:\Data\MSBuildExamples\Fundamentals>msbuild MSBuildTask02.proj /t:Demo /fl /nol
ogo
Build started 9/8/2008 11:28:32 PM.
Project "C:\Data\MSBuildExamples\Fundamentals\MSBuildTask02.proj" on node 0 (De
mo target(s)).
  Inside Demo target
Project "C:\Data\MSBuildExamples\Fundamentals\MSBuildTask02.proj" (1) is buildi
ng "C:\Data\MSBuildExamples\Fundamentals\MSBuildTask02.proj" (1:2) on node 0 (P
rintMessage target(s)).
  Hello MSBuild from: PrintMessage Target
Done Building Project "C:\Data\MSBuildExamples\Fundamentals\MSBuildTask02.proj"
 (PrintMessage target(s)).

Done Building Project "C:\Data\MSBuildExamples\Fundamentals\MSBuildTask02.proj"
 (Demo target(s)).


Build succeeded.
    0 Warning(s)
    0 Error(s)
```

FIGURE 7-4 MSBuildTask02.proj result

As you can see from the result shown in Figure 7-4, the SourceName property was successfully passed from the calling file into the project being built. We can now move on to take a look at a more realistic example.

A very common scenario is creating an MSBuild file that will be used as the "master" build file. What this means is that you will have one MSBuild file that is responsible for building a set of project files, as well as any other steps before, after, or between project builds. You can achieve this by using the MSBuild task. The next example, taken from MSBuildTask03.proj, uses the MSBuild task to build two sample Unittest projects. The full source for this file in shown in the following example.

```
<Project xmlns="http://schemas.microsoft.com/developer/msbuild/2003"
         ToolsVersion="3.5"
         DefaultTargets="BuildAll">
  <PropertyGroup>
    <UnitTestSrcRoot>..\unittest\</UnitTestSrcRoot>
  </PropertyGroup>
  <ItemGroup>
    <UnitTestProjects
      Include="$(UnitTestSrcRoot)Unittest.Proj1\Unittest.Proj1.csproj" />
    <UnitTestProjects
      Include="$(UnitTestSrcRoot)Unittest.Proj2\Unittest.Proj2.csproj" />
  </ItemGroup>

  <PropertyGroup>
    <!-- BuildAll convention used here but these could be named anything. -->
    <BuildAllDependsOn>
      BeforeBuildAll;
      CoreBuildAll;
      AfterBuildAll
    </BuildAllDependsOn>
  </PropertyGroup>
  <Target Name="BuildAll" DependsOnTargets="$(BuildAllDependsOn)" />

  <Target Name="CoreBuildAll">
    <MSBuild Projects="@(UnitTestProjects)"
             Targets="Rebuild;"
             Properties="Configuration=Release">
      <Output ItemName="unitTestBuildOutputs" TaskParameter="TargetOutputs" />
    </MSBuild>

    <Message Text="unitTestBuildOutputs:%0a%0d@(unitTestBuildOutputs,'%0a%0d')" />
  </Target>

  <Target Name="BeforeBuildAll">
    <Message Text="Before BuildAll" Importance="high" />
  </Target>

  <Target Name="AfterBuildAll">
    <Message Text="After BuildAll" Importance="high" />
  </Target>
</Project>
```

In this project I have defined an item, UnitTestProjects, which contains the two projects that are to be built. These projects are built inside the CoreBuildAll target using the MSBuild task. If you take a look at that task invocation, you will see that we are building the Release configurations of the specified projects. Also you can see that we're placing the output value from the TargetOutputs parameter into the unitTestBuildOutputs item. The TargetOutputs value will expose any values defined as Outputs on **explicitly** called targets. In this case we are explicitly calling only the Rebuild target. If you take a look at the definition for that target, from the Microsoft.Common.targets file, you will see what is contained in the next snippet.

```
<Target
    Name="Rebuild"
    Condition=" '$(_InvalidConfigurationWarning)' != 'true' "
    DependsOnTargets="$(RebuildDependsOn)"
    Outputs="$(TargetPath)" />
```

This target has defined the Outputs value to be $(TargetPath), which is a property pointing to the location of the output file. This will be the value that is transferred into the unitTestBuildOutputs item. You will see that I have defined a target to be executed before and after the project is built, using BeforeBuildAll and AfterBuildAll. You can see this in action by executing the command `msbuild MSBuildTask03.proj /t:BuildAll`. The last bit of the result of this is shown in Figure 7-5.

```
_CopyFilesMarkedCopyLocal:
  Copying file from "..\..\contrib\nunit2.2\nunit.framework.dll" to "bin\Releas
  e\nunit.framework.dll".
  Copying file from "..\..\contrib\nunit2.2\nunit.framework.xml" to "bin\Releas
  e\nunit.framework.xml".
CopyFilesToOutputDirectory:
  Copying file from "obj\Release\Unittest.Proj1.dll" to "bin\Release\Unittest.P
  roj1.dll".
  Unittest.Proj1 -> C:\Data\MSBuildExamples\unittest\Unittest.Proj1\bin\Release
  \Unittest.Proj1.dll
  Copying file from "obj\Release\Unittest.Proj1.pdb" to "bin\Release\Unittest.P
  roj1.pdb".
Done Building Project "C:\Data\MSBuildExamples\unittest\Unittest.Proj1\Unittest
.Proj1.csproj" (Rebuild target(s)).

Project "C:\Data\MSBuildExamples\Fundamentals\MSBuildTask03.proj" (1) is buildi
ng "C:\Data\MSBuildExamples\unittest\Unittest.Proj2\Unittest.Proj2.csproj" (3)
on node 0 (Rebuild target(s)).
  Deleting file "C:\Data\MSBuildExamples\unittest\Unittest.Proj2\bin\Release\Un
  ittest.Proj2.dll".
  Deleting file "C:\Data\MSBuildExamples\unittest\Unittest.Proj2\bin\Release\Un
  ittest.Proj2.pdb".
  Deleting file "C:\Data\MSBuildExamples\unittest\Unittest.Proj2\bin\Release\nu
  nit.framework.dll".
  Deleting file "C:\Data\MSBuildExamples\unittest\Unittest.Proj2\bin\Release\nu
  nit.framework.xml".
  Deleting file "C:\Data\MSBuildExamples\unittest\Unittest.Proj2\obj\Release\Un
  ittest.Proj2.dll".
  Deleting file "C:\Data\MSBuildExamples\unittest\Unittest.Proj2\obj\Release\Un
  ittest.Proj2.pdb".
_CopyFilesMarkedCopyLocal:
  Copying file from "..\..\contrib\nunit2.2\nunit.framework.dll" to "bin\Releas
  e\nunit.framework.dll".
  Copying file from "..\..\contrib\nunit2.2\nunit.framework.xml" to "bin\Releas
  e\nunit.framework.xml".
CopyFilesToOutputDirectory:
  Copying file from "obj\Release\Unittest.Proj2.dll" to "bin\Release\Unittest.P
  roj2.dll".
  Unittest.Proj2 -> C:\Data\MSBuildExamples\unittest\Unittest.Proj2\bin\Release
  \Unittest.Proj2.dll
  Copying file from "obj\Release\Unittest.Proj2.pdb" to "bin\Release\Unittest.P
  roj2.pdb".
Done Building Project "C:\Data\MSBuildExamples\unittest\Unittest.Proj2\Unittest
.Proj2.csproj" (Rebuild target(s)).

CoreBuildAll:
  unitTestBuildOutputs:
C:\Data\MSBuildExamples\unittest\Unittest.Proj1\bin\Release\Unittest.Proj1.d
  ll
C:\Data\MSBuildExamples\unittest\Unittest.Proj2\bin\Release\Unittest.Proj2.d
  ll
AfterBuildAll:
  After BuildAll
Done Building Project "C:\Data\MSBuildExamples\Fundamentals\MSBuildTask03.proj"
 (BuildAll target(s)).


Build succeeded.
    0 Warning(s)
    0 Error(s)
```

FIGURE 7-5 MSBuildTask03.proj result

From the result captured in Figure 7-5, you can see that both unittests were successfully built using the MSBuild task. Furthermore, you can see that the result assemblies were placed into the unitTestBuildOutputs item as expected. Now we have demonstrated how we can utilize the MSBuild task in order to build child projects. You should note that if you want to take advantage of the multiprocessor support that MSBuild 3.5 has, you must invoke msbuild.exe using the /maxcpucount (/m) switch, and when using the MSBuild task you should set the BuildInParallel to true. The MSBuild task also supports a set of known metadata that can be used during the build process: Properties, AdditionalProperties, and ToolsVersion. For a complete discussion on this, see Appendix A, "New Features in MSBuild 3.5."

Thus far we have discussed the Exec task and the MSBuild task. Now we'll move on to discuss error message formats. If you have many projects that will utilize the same tools then you should create reusable scripts to make integration of the tools simpler.

MSBuild and Visual Studio Known Error Message Formats

When a tool is executed that outputs some text, MSBuild will examine the text for errors and warnings. There is a known format that many tools use to report these messages. By default MSBuild will examine the text, and report errors and/or warnings based on the output. This behavior can be changed, or disabled, by using these parameters on the Exec task: IgnoreStandardErrorWarningFormat, CustomErrorRegularExpression, and CustomWarningRegularExpression. Most of the content here is based on an entry from the MSBuild Team blog, and is used with their permission.

Take a look at the following four messages, which are all properly formatted and will be recognized by MSBuild and Visual Studio.

```
Main.cs(17,20): warning CS0168: The variable 'foo' is declared but never used

C:\dir1\foo.resx(2) : error BC30188: Declaration expected.

cl : Command line warning D4024 : unrecognized source file type 'foo.cs', object ...

error CS0006: Metadata file 'System.dll' could not be found.
```

These messages conform to the special five-part format shown in Figure 7-6. The order of these parts is important and should not change.

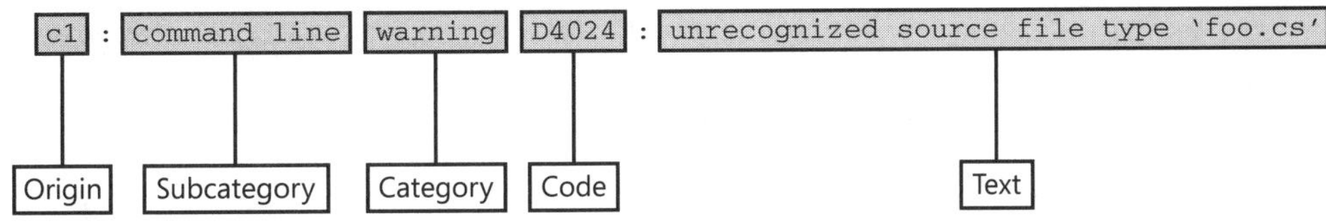

FIGURE 7-6 Known message format

Now we will describe each of the components of this format:

- **Origin (Required)** Origin can be blank. If present, the origin is usually a tool name, such as "cl" in one of the examples. But it could also be a filename, such as "Main.cs" shown in another example. If it is a filename, then it must be an absolute or a relative filename, followed by an optional parenthesized line/column information in one of the following forms:

  ```
  (line) or (line-line) or (line-col) or (line,col-col) or (line,col,line,col)
  ```

  Lines and columns start at 1 in a file; that is, the beginning of a file is 1, and the leftmost column is 1. If the Origin is a tool name, then it must not change based on locale; that is, it needs to be locale neutral.
- **Subcategory (Optional)** Subcategory is used to classify the category itself further, and should not be localized.
- **Category (Required)** Category must be either "error" or "warning". Case does not matter. As with origin, category must not be localized.
- **Code (Required)** Code identifies an application-specific error code / warning code. The Code must not be localized and it must not contain spaces.
- **Text** User-friendly text that explains the error, and must be localized if you cater to multiple locales.

When MSBuild calls command line tools (for instance, csc.exe or vbc.exe), it looks at the output emitted by the tool to the standard out and standard error streams. Any lines that match the error format that I just described will be treated specially; that is, lines that are recognized as errors or warnings will be turned into build errors and warnings respectively.

To see the real benefit of this, you have to be building from within Visual Studio. Because MSBuild treats these messages specially, they get logged as first-class warnings and errors in the Visual Studio task list. If the Origin specifies line/column information, then double clicking on the message will take you to the source of the error in the offending file.

Creating Reusable Build Elements

When you are integrating tools into your build process that serve as key elements in a build, then you should consider creating reusable elements that can be consumed by various products. Creating reusable build elements is different, and more difficult, than the content we have covered thus far. When you are creating these scripts there are a few rules that you should follow. We will point out how the scripts that we create in this chapter adhere to the guidelines outlined in the following list.

1. Needs to be self-contained
2. Process needs to be transparent and extensible to the consumer

3. Overridable behavior
4. A contract should be defined and validated

The first rule "Needs to be self-contained," means that all the necessary steps to perform the desired actions are captured in the defined script. This does not mean that the script cannot make assumptions (these are covered by rule #4), but it does mean that the tool's build script cannot modify values of the calling build script. For example, if you have a build script for public use that defines how to invoke FxCop, then the FxCop script file should not change the value for the BuildDependsOn property even though this is tempting. Instead, the importing build script should place the FxCop target(s) into that property.

The second consideration, "Process needs to be transparent and extensible to the consumer," means that the entire process needs to be able to be modified to suit the needs of the caller. For example, similar to the Microsoft.Common.targets, target dependency lists should be exposed as properties so consumers can extend them to inject their own targets. For example, the Microsoft.Common.targets contains properties such as BuildDependsOn, CompileDependsOn, ResolveReferencesDependsOn, PrepareResourceNamesDependsOn, and many others. By exposing such properties, callers can easily change the process of the script itself. There are a few weak points in the technique, which are outlined as follows.

1. The target must explicitly define its DependsOnTargets value in a property.
2. If the property is carelessly overwritten, unexpected results will occur.
3. You can only prepend or append; you cannot inject a step in the middle.

Because of these limitations, this solution is not ideal either, but it is better than any other option currently available. You'll be happy to know that with MSBuild 4.0 all of these limitations will be lifted with a new construct.

The third rule, "Overridable behavior," is for the most part built into MSBuild. This is because every target that is imported into a file can be overridden by simply redeclaring that target at some point after the Import statement that initially defines it. Because of this, you should be wary of creating MSBuild scripts that have targets with an excessive number of task invocations. Just as when you write code, when your targets grow too large, then they should be refactored.

Now we can move on to the final guideline, "A contract should be defined and validated." Of all the rules, this is the one that is most interesting. Thinking in terms of .NET there are interfaces, and in WCF there is an OperationContract. Unfortunately, MSBuild doesn't have a clear method of defining a contract between a consumer and a provider. Despite this limitation, we need a way to declare an agreement between these two parties, and that agreement should be validated. In reusable .targets files, the data are always provided by the caller and the essential behavior is always described by the callee. Because the callee needs to know what data to act upon, the correct properties and items need to be made available to it. Also, the validation logic can be placed inside a target, which is called before the essential actions are performed. If you are validating static items, then you can place these validation targets inside the InitialTargets declaration. We will see this implemented in all the target files in this chapter. When you are creating target files, there is a convention that you should be aware of and make sure to follow. That is to prefix with an underscore all properties, items, and target names that should be considered internal implementation details. By doing so, you are letting the caller know that its behavior is subject to change or might even be removed in newer versions. A future version of MSBuild might support some type of scoping mechanism that can be used to work around this issue. This convention is followed by all target files provided by Microsoft. Now that we have outlined some guidelines, we can take a look at what it takes to integrate some specific tools into our build process.

NUnit

If you are not familiar with NUnit, it is an open source unit testing framework. It is very similar to the unit testing tools that are available in the team versions of Visual Studio, which have specific tasks and targets. You can learn more about NUnit at its homepage, *nunit.org*. NUnit is not the only alternative to Visual Studio tests; another tool is xUnit.net, and there are many others. If you are using NUnit to test your applications, then you should automate running NUnit as a part of your build process. There are a few different ways to achieve this. One of the best options is to use the NUnit task that is available from the MSBuild Community Tasks, msbuildtasks.tigris.org. We will first take a look at this task and then describe how to effectively utilize it. Table 7-3 describes the properties that are available on the NUnit task.

TABLE 7-3 NUnit Task Properties

Name	Description
Assemblies	Contains the assemblies that the NUnit task will examine. You can also pass in the full path to a Visual Studio project, if it ends in one of these extensions: .csproj, .vbproj, .vjsproj, or .vcproj. Another option here is to pass an NUnit project file. This is the only **required** input.
IncludeCategory	Specifies the NUnit test case category(ies) that should be executed. If you decorate your test cases with an *NUnit.Framework.Category* attribute, then this feature may be useful. If you are providing multiple values, then they should be separated by a **comma**. This corresponds to the `/include` command line parameter of the nunit-console.exe.
ExcludeCategory	Specifies the NUnit test case category(ies) that should be excluded from test execution. If you are passing more than one value for this, they should be **comma** separated. This corresponds to the `/exclude` command line parameter.
Fixture	This contains the name of the Fixture to test. This corresponds to the `/fixture` command line parameter.
XsltTransformFile	If you need the NUnit result file to be processed by your own XSLT, then provide the full path to that file for this property. This value will correspond to the `/transform` command line parameter.

TABLE 7-3 NUnit Task Properties

Name	Description
OutputXmlFile	This is where the test results XML file will be stored. This is not a required input, but you should always set this. If this is not set, then the file will be placed in a file named TestResult.xml in the working directory. This corresponds to the /xml parameter.
ErrorOutputFile	If provided, this file will be populated with any messages that are sent to the standard error stream. This corresponds to the /err parameter.
WorkingDirectory	This can be used to specify the working directory when invoking the tool.
DisableShadowCopy	By default, NUnit will execute all of your test cases on shadow copies of your assemblies. These are typically contained in the "%temp%\nunit20\ShadowCopyCache\" folder. This behavior can be disabled by providing a value of `true` for this property. This corresponds to the `/noshadow` command line parameter.
ProjectConfiguration	Using this you can specify the value for configuration that the test cases should be run against. This corresponds to the `/config` command line parameter.
TestInNewThread	If a value of true is provided for this property, then the test cases will be executed in their own thread. This corresponds to the /thread parameter.

To demonstrate using this task I have created a simple class containing some test cases, as shown in the following class definition.

```
using System;
using NUnit.Framework;

namespace Unittest.Proj1
{
    [TestFixture]
    public class TestOperators
    {
        [Test]
        public void TestAddition()
        {
            int result = 1 + 1;
            Assert.AreEqual(2, result);

            result = 100 + 1;
            Assert.AreEqual(101, result);

            result = 1005 + (-1);
            Assert.AreEqual(1004, result);
        }
        [Test]
        public void TestSubtraction()
        {
            int result = 1 - 1;
            Assert.AreEqual(0, result);
```

```
                result = 100 - 1;
                Assert.AreEqual(99, result);

                result = 1005 - (-1);
                Assert.AreEqual(1006, result);
            }
        }
}
```

This class is located in the Unittest.Proj1 project. Now we need to create an MSBuild file that can be used to execute the unit tests in that project for us using the NUnit task, shown in the following nunitExample.proj file.

```
<Project xmlns="http://schemas.microsoft.com/developer/msbuild/2003"
         DefaultTargets="UnitTest">

  <Import
    Project=
"$(MSBuildExtensionsPath)\MSBuildCommunityTasks\MSBuild.Community.Tasks.targets" />

  <ItemGroup>
    <UnitTestProjects
      Include="$(MSBuildProjectDirectory)\Unittest.Proj1\Unittest.Proj1.csproj">
    </UnitTestProjects>
  </ItemGroup>

  <PropertyGroup>
    <NUnitResultFile>$(MSBuildProjectDirectory)\nunit-result.xml</NUnitResultFile>
  </PropertyGroup>

  <Target Name="UnitTest">
    <!-- Build all the projects in UnitTestProjects -->
    <MSBuild Projects="@(UnitTestProjects)" />
    <!-- Execute the test cases, if any fail so will the build -->
    <NUnit Assemblies="@(UnitTestProjects)"
           OutputXmlFile="$(NUnitResultFile)"
           />

  </Target>
</Project>
```

In this MSBuild file I have declared the UnitTestProjects item, and included the Unittest.Proj1.csproj file. Also note that the MSBuild.Community.Tasks.Targets file is imported using the MSBuildExtensionsPath reserved property. This property points to the suggested location for third-party targets and tasks. The Import element declared makes the NUnit task, and many others, available for use. They should be located in a directory under that path. This typically points to the folder C:\Program Files\MSBuild. Also there is a related property, MSBuildExtensionsPath32, which is for tasks and targets that have 32- and 64-bit versions. In the UnitTest target, the default target for this file, I first build the project, then invoke the NUnit task against it. In this example I have chosen, for simplicity, to pass the project file as the NUnit input file. The listing shown in Figure 7-7 captures the results of executing this MSBuild file.

```
C:\Data\MSBuildExamples\unittest>msbuild nunitExample.proj /clp:v=n /nologo
Build started 8/23/2008 12:41:28 AM.
Project "C:\Data\MSBuildExamples\unittest\nunitExample.proj" on node 0 (default
 targets).
Project "C:\Data\MSBuildExamples\unittest\nunitExample.proj" (1) is building "C
:\Data\MSBuildExamples\unittest\Unittest.Proj1\Unittest.Proj1.csproj" (2) on no
de 0 (default targets).
  Creating directory "bin\Debug\".
CoreCompile:
Skipping target "CoreCompile" because all output files are up-to-date with resp
ect to the input files.
_CopyFilesMarkedCopyLocal:
  Copying file from "..\..\contrib\nunit2.2\nunit.framework.dll" to "bin\Debug\
  nunit.framework.dll".
  Copying file from "..\..\contrib\nunit2.2\nunit.framework.xml" to "bin\Debug\
  nunit.framework.xml".
CopyFilesToOutputDirectory:
  Copying file from "obj\Debug\Unittest.Proj1.dll" to "bin\Debug\Unittest.Proj1
  .dll".
  Unittest.Proj1 -> C:\Data\MSBuildExamples\unittest\Unittest.Proj1\bin\Debug\U
  nittest.Proj1.dll
  Copying file from "obj\Debug\Unittest.Proj1.pdb" to "bin\Debug\Unittest.Proj1
  .pdb".
Done Building Project "C:\Data\MSBuildExamples\unittest\Unittest.Proj1\Unittest
.Proj1.csproj" (default targets).

UnitTest:
  ..
  Tests run: 2, Failures: 0, Not run: 0, Time: 0.016 seconds


Done Building Project "C:\Data\MSBuildExamples\unittest\nunitExample.proj" (def
ault targets).


Build succeeded.
    0 Warning(s)
    0 Error(s)
```

FIGURE 7-7 NUnitExample.proj passing result

From the output shown, we can see that the Unittest.Proj1.csproj file was built, and then the test cases executed via the NUnit task. If any test cases were to have failed, then the build itself would have failed. To demonstrate this behavior I have added the following failing test case to the TestOperatros class.

```
[Test]
public void TestDivide()
{
    int numerator = 100;
    int divisor = 20;
    int result = numerator / divisor;
    Assert.AreEqual(6, result);
}
```

To see how a failing test would affect the build, I executed the nunitExample.proj one more time. The result is shown in Figure 7-8.

As stated, since there was at least one failing test case, the entire build failed. The failures are also summarized at the end of the build. Now that we've described how we can use the NUnit task, we can take a look at how we can create a reusable targets file to simplify the process of invoking it.

```
C:\Data\MSBuildExamples\unittest>msbuild nunitExample.proj /clp:v=n /nologo
Build started 8/23/2008 12:45:13 AM.
Project "C:\Data\MSBuildExamples\unittest\nunitExample.proj" on node 0 (default
 targets).
Project "C:\Data\MSBuildExamples\unittest\nunitExample.proj" (1) is building "C
:\Data\MSBuildExamples\unittest\Unittest.Proj1\Unittest.Proj1.csproj" (2) on no
de 0 (default targets).
  Creating directory "bin\Debug\".
_CopyFilesMarkedCopyLocal:
  Copying file from "..\..\contrib\nunit2.2\nunit.framework.dll" to "bin\Debug\
  nunit.framework.dll".
  Copying file from "..\..\contrib\nunit2.2\nunit.framework.xml" to "bin\Debug\
  nunit.framework.xml".
CopyFilesToOutputDirectory:
  Copying file from "obj\Debug\Unittest.Proj1.dll" to "bin\Debug\Unittest.Proj1
  .dll".
  Unittest.Proj1 -> C:\Data\MSBuildExamples\unittest\Unittest.Proj1\bin\Debug\U
  nittest.Proj1.dll
  Copying file from "obj\Debug\Unittest.Proj1.pdb" to "bin\Debug\Unittest.Proj1
  .pdb".
Done Building Project "C:\Data\MSBuildExamples\unittest\Unittest.Proj1\Unittest
.Proj1.csproj" (default targets).

UnitTest:
  ..F.
  Tests run: 3, Failures: 1, Not run: 0, Time: 0.047 seconds

  Failures:
  1) Unittest.Proj1.TestOperators.TestDivide :
        expected:<6>
         but was:<5>
     at Unittest.Proj1.TestOperators.TestDivide() in c:\Data\MSBuildExamples\un
  ittest\Unittest.Proj1\TestOperators.cs:line 42

C:\Data\MSBuildExamples\unittest\nunitExample.proj(22,5): error MSB6006: "nunit
-console.exe" exited with code 1.
Done Building Project "C:\Data\MSBuildExamples\unittest\nunitExample.proj" (def
ault targets) -- FAILED.

Build FAILED.

"C:\Data\MSBuildExamples\unittest\nunitExample.proj" (default target) (1) ->
(UnitTest target) ->
  C:\Data\MSBuildExamples\unittest\nunitExample.proj(22,5): error MSB6006: "nun
it-console.exe" exited with code 1.

    0 Warning(s)
    1 Error(s)
```

FIGURE 7-8 NUnitExample.proj failing result

I have created a reusable targets file, nunit.targets, which can be used across products. I will show portions of the file in this chapter but you can see it in its entirety in the sample sources. The following snippet contains some key elements of this file.

```
<Target Name="ValidateNUnitSettings">
  <!-- Validate assumptions that are contracted  -->

  <Error Condition="'$(NUnitOutputDir)'==''"
    Text="NUnitOutputDir property not defined" />

  <Error Condition="'@(NUnitAssemblies)'==''"
    Text="NUnitAssemblies not defined" />
  <Error Condition="'%(NUnitAssemblies.ProjectName)'==''"
    Text="Atleast 1 item in NuitAssemblies doesn't have metadata 'ProjectName' defined." />
  <Error Condition="!Exists('%(NUnitAssemblies.FullPath)')"
    Text="Couldn't locate assembly at: %(NUnitAssemblies.FullPath)" />
</Target>

<PropertyGroup>
  <!-- Declare target dependencies here -->
  <UnitTestDependsOn>
    $(UnitTestDependsOn);
    BeforeUnitTest;
    ValidateNUnitSettings;
    UnitTestCore;
```

```
    DetectNUnitFailures;
    ReportNUnitFailures;
    AfterUnitTest;
  </UnitTestDependsOn>
  <UnitTestCleanDependsOn>
    $(UnitTestCleanDependsOn);
    BeforeUnitTestClean;
    CoreUnitTestClean;
    AfterUnitTestClean;
  </UnitTestCleanDependsOn>
</PropertyGroup>

<Target Name="UnitTest"
   Inputs="%(NUnitAssemblies.Identity)"
   Outputs="@(NUnitAssemblies->'$(NUnitOutputDir)%(ProjectName).UNITTEST.xml')"
   DependsOnTargets="$(UnitTestDependsOn)" />

<Target Name="UnitTestCore" Outputs="%(NUnitAssemblies.Identity)">
  <Message Text="Start UnitTest for @(NUnitAssemblies->'%(Fullpath)')" />

  <MakeDir  Condition="!Exists('$(NUnitOutputDir)')"
            Directories="$(NUnitOutputDir)" />

  <Message
    Condition="'$(GenBuildDebugMode)'=='true'"
    Text="Calling NUnit on:%0a%0d@(NunitAssemblies,'%0a%0d')" />

  <PropertyGroup>
    <NUnitContinueOnError
      Condition="'$(NUnitContinueOnError)'==''">true</NUnitContinueOnError>
  </PropertyGroup>
  <!--
  Don't rely on NUnit stopping build on failed unit test, we have more work after wards
  -->
  <NUnit Assemblies="@(NUnitAssemblies)"
    OutputXmlFile="@(NUnitAssemblies->'$(NUnitOutputDir)%(ProjectName).unittest.xml')"
    ContinueOnError="true">
  </NUnit>

  <ItemGroup>
    <_NUnitReportFiles
      Include="@(NUnitAssemblies->'$(NUnitOutputDir)%(ProjectName).unittest.xml')" />
  </ItemGroup>
</Target>

<Target Name="CleanUnitTest"
        DependsOnTargets="$(UnitTestCleanDependsOn)" />
<Target Name="CoreUnitTestClean">
  <MakeDir Directories="$(NUnitOutputDir)"
           Condition="!Exists('$(NUnitOutputDir)')" />
  <ItemGroup>
    <_OldNUnitResultFiles Include="$(NUnitOutputDir)**\*.unittest.xml" />
    <_OldNUnitResultFiles Include="$(NUnitOutputDir)**\*.FAILED.xml" />
  </ItemGroup>

  <Delete Files="@(_OldNUnitResultFiles)" />
</Target>
```

You can see the contract defined, in MSBuild terms, inside the ValidateNUnitSettings target. This target will be executed before the UnitTest target gets executed; this is because it is contained in the UnitTestDependsOn property value. Inside this target, there are four error statements, each with conditional statements. These conditions define the contract that this file defines. If any of these erroneous conditions is detected, then the execution will fail. The following list describes the details of the contract that are asserted in that target.

1. A property named NUnitOutputDir is defined and not empty
2. An item NUnitAssemblies is defined
3. Each item value in NUnitAssemblies contains a value for ProjectName metadata
4. Each file in NUnitAssemblies exists on disk

By using this contract we have defined how a calling project file will feed data into this file. In return, this file will provide the core behavior required to execute the NUnit test cases contained in the provided assemblies. You should note that when declaring a condition such as `Condition="'$(NUnitContinueOnError )'==''"` you should always wrap each term in quotes. If you do not, you may run into situations where the condition may not evaluate as expected. Now we can see how the other requirements for reusable targets files are achieved in this sample.

All the requirements for using the nunit.targets file are contained in the validation target shown previously. One of the requirements is that a list of assemblies be provided for which NUnit will be executed with. If you were authoring this file, you might be tempted to inject the UnitTest target directly into the BuildDependsOn property. This would make the assumption that the file was being consumed by a typical managed project file and would be a violation of the first rule outlined. The calling MSBuild file is entirely responsible for injecting the UnitTest target into its build, not the other way around. Also, your targets files, which are made publically available, should not override or even assume the existence of targets provided in Microsoft.Common.targets such as BeforeBuild, BeforeCompile, etc.

How does this targets file meet the requirements for transparency and extensibility? That is achieved through the use of dependency properties, namely UnitTestDependsOn and UnitTestCleanDependsOn. These properties are used to define the set of steps to be executed in order for their corresponding targets to be executed. For example, the UnitTest target declares its dependency list as `DependsOnTargets=$(UnitTestDependsOn)`. By using these, we externalize the steps required to execute the UnitTest and CleanUnitTest targets. Now that we've discussed how this targets file meets the requirements laid out previously, we can now examine how to use it.

Now that we've created a reusable targets file for invoking NUnit, we'll see how this can be utilized by calling MSBuild scripts. The following file, UnittestBuild.proj, demonstrates the usage of this file.

```
<Project xmlns="http://schemas.microsoft.com/developer/msbuild/2003"
         DefaultTargets="Build">
  <PropertyGroup>
    <SourceRoot>$(MSBuildProjectDirectory)\</SourceRoot>
```

```
  <UnitTestRoot>$(SourceRoot)</UnitTestRoot>
  <OutDirName>bin\</OutDirName>
  <Configuration>Debug</Configuration>
  <NUnitOutputDir>$(SourceRoot)BuildTemp\</NUnitOutputDir>
  <GenericBuildRoot>$(SourceRoot)\..\BUILD\GenericBuild\</GenericBuildRoot>
</PropertyGroup>

<ItemGroup>
  <UnitTestProjects
    Include="$(UnitTestRoot)\Unittest.Proj1\Unittest.Proj1.csproj">
    <ProjectName>Unittest.Proj1</ProjectName>
  </UnitTestProjects>
  <UnitTestProjects
    Include="$(UnitTestRoot)Unittest.Proj2\Unittest.Proj2.csproj">
    <ProjectName>Unittest.Proj2</ProjectName>
  </UnitTestProjects>
</ItemGroup>

<PropertyGroup>
  <BuildDependsOn>
    $(BuildDependsOn);
    Clean;
    CoreBuild;
    UnitTest
  </BuildDependsOn>
</PropertyGroup>
<Target Name="Build" DependsOnTargets="$(BuildDependsOn)" />
<Target Name="Clean">
  <MSBuild Projects="@(UnitTestProjects)" Targets="Clean" />
</Target>
<Target Name="CoreBuild">
  <!--
    Build the NUnit assemblies & put the
    assemblies in the NUnitAssemblies Item -->
  <MSBuild Projects="@(UnitTestProjects)">
    <Output ItemName="NUnitAssemblies"
            TaskParameter="TargetOutputs" />
  </MSBuild>
</Target>

<PropertyGroup>
  <RebuildDependsOn>
    $(RebuildDependsOn);
    Clean;
    Build
  </RebuildDependsOn>
</PropertyGroup>
<Target Name="Rebuild"
        DependsOnTargets="$(RebuildDependsOn)" />

<!-- The MSBuild Community Tasks must be imported for the nunit.targets file -->
<Import
  Project=
  "$(GenericBuildRoot)Contrib\MSBuildCommunityTasks\MSBuild.Community.Tasks.Targets" />
<!-- Import the nunit.proj file here -->
<Import
  Project="$(GenericBuildRoot)Build\nunit.targets" />
```

```
  <PropertyGroup>
    <UnitTestDependsOn>
      CustomBeforeUnitTest;
      $(UnitTestDependsOn);
    </UnitTestDependsOn>
  </PropertyGroup>

  <Target Name="CustomBeforeUnitTest">
    <Message Text="NUnitAssemblies:%0a%0d@(NUnitAssemblies,'%0a%0d')"
             Importance="high" />
  </Target>
</Project>
```

In this example we have created a sample build file that builds a couple of projects and then sends the resulting assemblies to the NUnit task. I've made bold the text where I declare the UnitTestProjects item, which contains the projects that we are testing. Following that you can see that the UnitTest target is placed into the BuildDependsOn list after the projects are to be built. Inside the CoreBuild target, the NUnitAssemblies item is created using the TargetOutputs of the MSBuild task, which is used to build the projects. Also you can see that we inject the CustomBeforeUnitTest target into the list of targets required to execute before the UnitTest target. You should note that this must be defined after the Import statement for the nunit.targets file. If you build this project file, the result will be what is shown in Figure 7-9; only a portion of the result is shown here to conserve space.

```
CustomBeforeUnitTest:
  NunitAssemblies:
C:\Data\MSBuildExamples\unittest\Unittest.Proj1\bin\Debug\Unittest.Proj1.dll
C:\Data\MSBuildExamples\unittest\Unittest.Proj2\bin\Debug\Unittest.Proj2.dll
UnitTestCore:
  Start UnitTest for C:\Data\MSBuildExamples\unittest\Unittest.Proj1\bin\Debug\
  Unittest.Proj1.dll
  ..
  Tests run: 2, Failures: 0, Not run: 0, Time: 0.016 seconds


UnitTestCore:
  Start UnitTest for C:\Data\MSBuildExamples\unittest\Unittest.Proj2\bin\Debug\
  Unittest.Proj2.dll
  .
  Tests run: 1, Failures: 0, Not run: 0, Time: 0.016 seconds


DetectNUnitFailures:
  Reading Xml Document "C:\Data\MSBuildExamples\unittest\BuildTemp\Unittest.Pro
  j1.unittest.xml".
  XmlRead Result: ""
  _NUnitFailures:
DetectNUnitFailures:
  Reading Xml Document "C:\Data\MSBuildExamples\unittest\BuildTemp\Unittest.Pro
  j2.unittest.xml".
  XmlRead Result: ""
  _NUnitFailures:
UnitTest:
Skipping target "UnitTest" because all output files are up-to-date with respect
 to the input files.
UnitTest:
Skipping target "UnitTest" because all output files are up-to-date with respect
 to the input files.
Done Building Project "C:\Data\MSBuildExamples\unittest\unittestBuild.proj" (de
fault targets).


Build succeeded.
    0 Warning(s)
    0 Error(s)
```

FIGURE 7-9 UnittestBuild.proj result

The test cases in both projects were executed successfully. Since all the test cases passed, the build was allowed to continue. Also you can see that the CustomBeforeUnitTest was successfully injected into the build process at the appropriate time. Now we have demonstrated how we can integrate NUnit into the build process in a reusable means, we'll move on to discuss FxCop.

FxCop

FxCop is a code analysis tool created by Microsoft, which can help identify potential problem areas and can help enforce best practices. We will discuss how we can integrate FxCop into the build process here. Similar to the NUnit task, there also is an FxCop task, also provided by the Microsoft Community Tasks project. We will use this task to execute the FxCop tool against the binaries of our projects. In the following example we will execute FxCop against the Examples.Tasks and Example.Loggers project. Another related tool, which we will not demonstrate here, is StyleCop. StyleCop is a source code analysis tool; it examines the actual source files to ensure that styling guidelines are followed and to spot potential rule violations.

Similar to integrating NUnit, a targets file, fxcop.targets, has been created to take care of the heavy lifting for us. This file also has a validation target, ValidateFxCopSettings, which is shown in the following snippet.

```
<Target Name="ValidateFxCopSettings" DependsOnTargets="SetupFxCopProperties">
  <Error Condition="'@(FxCopAssemblies)'==''"
         Text="%40(FxCopAssemblies) not defined" />
  <Error Condition="!Exists('%(FxCopAssemblies.Fullpath)')"
         Text="Path not found (FxCopAssemblies): [%(FxCopAssemblies.Fullpath)]" />

  <Error Condition="'@(FxCopRuleAssemblies)'==''"
         Text="%40(FxCopRuleAssemblies) not defined" />

  <Error Condition="'$(FxCopContribRoot)'==''"
         Text="%24(FxCopContribRoot) is not defined" />
  <Error Condition="!Exists($(FxCopContribRoot))"
         Text="Path not found(FxCopContribRoot): [$(FxCopContribRoot)]" />

  <Error Condition="'$(FxCopOutputRoot)'==''"
         Text="%24(FxCopOutputRoot) is not defined" />
  <Error Condition="!Exists($(FxCopOutputRoot))"
         Text="Path not found(FxCopOutputRoot): [$(FxCopOutputRoot)]" />
</Target>
```

Based on this target we can see what this file requires for successful integration. The file that consumes the fxcop.targets file, FxCop_Examples.proj, is very similar to the one for the NUnit example and is shown next.

```
<Project xmlns="http://schemas.microsoft.com/developer/msbuild/2003"
         DefaultTargets="Build">
  <PropertyGroup>
    <SourceRoot>$(MSBuildProjectDirectory)\</SourceRoot>
    <GenericBuildRoot>$(SourceRoot)BUILD\GenericBuild\</GenericBuildRoot>
    <ContribRoot>$(GenericBuildRoot)Contrib\</ContribRoot>
    <FxCopOutputRoot>$(SourceRoot)__BuildTemp\FxCopTemp\</FxCopOutputRoot>
    <Configuration>Debug</Configuration>
  </PropertyGroup>

  <PropertyGroup>
    <_TaskOutputRoot>$(SourceRoot)Examples.Tasks\</_TaskOutputRoot>
    <_LoggerOutputRoot>$(SourceRoot)Examples.Loggers\</_LoggerOutputRoot>
  </PropertyGroup>
```

```
<ItemGroup>
  <FxCopProjects
    Include="$(_TaskOutputRoot)Examples.Tasks.csproj">
    <Outputs>$(_TaskOutputRoot)\bin\$(Configuration)\Examples.Tasks.dll</Outputs>
  </FxCopProjects>
  <FxCopProjects
    Include="$(_LoggerOutputRoot)Examples.Loggers.csproj">
    <Outputs>$(_LoggerOutputRoot)bin\$(Configuration)\Examples.Loggers.dll</Outputs>
  </FxCopProjects>

  <FxCopAssemblies Include="@(FxCopProjects->'%(Outputs)')" />
</ItemGroup>

<PropertyGroup>
  <BuildDependsOn>
    $(BuildDependsOn);
    CoreBuild;
    RunFxcop;
  </BuildDependsOn>
  <RebuildDependsOn>
    Clean;
    $(BuildDependsOn)
  </RebuildDependsOn>
</PropertyGroup>
<Target Name="Rebuild" DependsOnTargets="$(RebuildDependsOn)" />
<Target Name="Build" DependsOnTargets="$(BuildDependsOn)" />
<Target Name="Clean">
  <MSBuild Projects="@(FxCopProjects)" Targets="Clean" />
</Target>
<Target Name="CoreBuild"
        Inputs="@(FxCopProjects)"
        Outputs="@(FxCopAssemblies)">
  <MSBuild Projects="@(FxCopProjects)" />
</Target>

<PropertyGroup>
  <CleanDependsOn>
    $(CleanDependsOn);
    CleanFxCop;
  </CleanDependsOn>
</PropertyGroup>
<Target Name="Clean" DependsOnTargets="$(CleanDependsOn)">
  <MSBuild Projects="@(FxCopProjects)" Targets="Clean" />
</Target>
<!-- SDC Tasks Required for fxcop.targets file -->
<Import
  Project=
  "$(ContribRoot)\SDC Tasks - Release 2.1.3155.0\Microsoft.Sdc.Common.tasks" />
<!-- The MSBuild Community Tasks must be imported for the nunit.targets file -->
<Import
  Project=
  "$(ContribRoot)\MSBuildCommunityTasks\MSBuild.Community.Tasks.Targets" />
<Import
  Project="$(GenericBuildRoot)Build\fxcop.targets" />
```

```
  <PropertyGroup>
    <RunFxCopDependsOn>
      $(RunFxCopDependsOn);
      CoreBuild;
      CustomAfterFxCop
    </RunFxCopDependsOn>
  </PropertyGroup>

  <Target Name="CustomAfterFxCop">
    <Message Text="FxCop executed."
             Importance="high" />
  </Target>
</Project>
```

From the sample build script you can see how easy it is to consume this targets file. In the previous snippet I have highlighted a few key areas, some of which we will discuss. Inside the CoreBuild target, the MSBuild task is used to build the projects. It is important to note that the CoreBuild target declares values for both Inputs and Outputs. Because of this the target will support incremental building and will be executed only if it is out of date. This is critical in large builds. Sometimes you may have to make changes to your build to support this, but it is well worth it and is a best practice. The RunFxCop target is injected into the build process by placing it into the list of targets to execute during a build by extending the BuildDependsOn property. Along with this the CustomAfterFxCop target is injected into the list of targets that will be executed after the RunFxCop target executes. We can see the results of building this script in Figure 7-10.

There were a few FxCop errors detected during the build process; because of this the build itself was stopped, as expected. We never have an opportunity to see if the CustomAfterFxCop target executes; therefore, it is not displayed in the previous figure. From the results shown, you can also see that the full path to the FxCop HTML report is passed for developers to use in order to help fix all the FxCop related errors.

Now that we have seen how to use the fxcop.targets file, we can take a closer look at the file itself. The full source is delivered along with the other examples for this book. For this book, we will discuss some of the contents of that file here. In the next snippet you will find the list of targets that make up the dependencies for the RunFxCop target.

```
<PropertyGroup>
  <RunFxCopDependsOn>
    SetupFxCopProperties;
    CopySourceFiles;
    ValidateFxCopSettings;
    BeforeFxCop;
    CoreFxCop;
    DetectFxCopError;
    AfterFxcop
  </RunFxCopDependsOn>
</PropertyGroup>
```

```
  Copying file from "obj\Debug\Interop.IWshRuntimeLibrary.dll" to "bin\Debug\In
  terop.IWshRuntimeLibrary.dll".
Done Building Project "C:\Data\MSBuildExamples\Examples.Tasks\Examples.Tasks.cs
proj" (default targets).

Project "C:\Data\MSBuildExamples\FxCop_Examples.proj" (1) is building "C:\Data\
MSBuildExamples\Examples.Loggers\Examples.Loggers.csproj" (3) on node 0 (defaul
t targets).
  Copying file from "..\contrib\log4net.dll" to "bin\Debug\log4net.dll".
_CopyOutOfDateSourceItemsToOutputDirectory:
  Copying file from "C:\Data\MSBuildExamples\Examples.Loggers\Samples\log4net.m
  sbuild.xml" to "bin\Debug\Samples\log4net.msbuild.xml".
  Copying file from "C:\Data\MSBuildExamples\Examples.Loggers\Samples\SampleSed
  oLogger01.bat" to "bin\Debug\Samples\SampleSedoLogger01.bat".
  Copying file from "C:\Data\MSBuildExamples\Examples.Loggers\Samples\SampleSed
  oLogger02.bat" to "bin\Debug\Samples\SampleSedoLogger02.bat".
CopyFilesToOutputDirectory:
  Copying file from "obj\Debug\Examples.Loggers.dll" to "bin\Debug\Examples.Log
  gers.dll".
  Examples.Loggers -> C:\Data\MSBuildExamples\Examples.Loggers\bin\Debug\Exampl
  es.Loggers.dll
  Copying file from "obj\Debug\Examples.Loggers.pdb" to "bin\Debug\Examples.Log
  gers.pdb".
Done Building Project "C:\Data\MSBuildExamples\Examples.Loggers\Examples.Logger
s.csproj" (default targets).

CoreFxcop:
  FxCop begin analysis on: C:\Data\MSBuildExamples\Examples.Tasks\bin\Debug\Exa
  mples.Tasks.dll;C:\Data\MSBuildExamples\Examples.Loggers\bin\Debug\Examples.L
  oggers.dll
DetectFxCopError:
  FxCop HTML Report File: C:\Data\MSBuildExamples\__BuildTemp\FxCopTemp\fxcopRe
  sult.xml.html
  Reading Xml Document "C:\Data\MSBuildExamples\__BuildTemp\FxCopTemp\\fxcopRes
  ult.xml".
  XmlRead Result: "12"
  Reading Xml Document "C:\Data\MSBuildExamples\__BuildTemp\FxCopTemp\\fxcopRes
  ult.xml".
  XmlRead Result: "110"
  Reading Xml Document "C:\Data\MSBuildExamples\__BuildTemp\FxCopTemp\\fxcopRes
  ult.xml".
  XmlRead Result: "2"
  FxCopCriticalErrors: 12
  FxCopErrors: 110
  FxCopCriticalWarnings: 2
C:\Data\MSBuildExamples\BUILD\GenericBuild\Build\fxcop.targets(122,5): error :
FxCopCriticalErrors detected, count: 12
Done Building Project "C:\Data\MSBuildExamples\FxCop_Examples.proj" (default ta
rgets) -- FAILED.


Build FAILED.

"C:\Data\MSBuildExamples\FxCop_Examples.proj" (default target) (1) ->
(DetectFxCopError target) ->
  C:\Data\MSBuildExamples\BUILD\GenericBuild\Build\fxcop.targets(122,5): error
: FxCopCriticalErrors detected, count: 12

    0 Warning(s)
    1 Error(s)
```

FIGURE 7-10 RunFxCop result

The two most important targets from the previous list are ValidateFxCopSettings and CoreFxCop. The validate target declares the contract for consumers and ensures that it is adhered to, and the CoreFxCop target executes FxCop on the input specified. We have already seen the definition for the ValidateFxCopSettings target; in the following snippet we will see the CoreFxCop target.

```
<Target Name="CoreFxcop"
        Inputs="@(FxCopAssemblies)"
        Outputs="$(FxCopReportFile)">
  <Message Text="FxCop begin analysis on: @(FxCopAssemblies)"
           Importance="high" />
  <Message Text="FxCopReportFile: $(FxCopReportFile)"
            Importance="low" />

  <MSBuild.Community.Tasks.FxCop
    TargetAssemblies="@(FxCopAssemblies)"
    RuleLibraries="@(FxCopRuleAssemblies)"
    AnalysisReportFileName="$(FxCopReportFile)"
    DependencyDirectories="$(ContribRoot)MSBuildCommunityTasks"
```

```
      FailOnError="False"
      ApplyOutXsl="False"
      OutputXslFileName="$(FxCopContribRoot)Xml\FxCopReport.xsl"
      IncludeSummaryReport="true"
      ToolPath="$(FxCopContribRoot)"
      />

    <ItemGroup>
      <_FxCopReportFileItem Include="$(FxCopReportFile)" />
    </ItemGroup>
    <PropertyGroup>
      <_FxCopHtmlReportFile>@(_FxCopReportFileItem->'%(Fullpath).html')</_FxCopHtmlReportFile>
    </PropertyGroup>
    <!-- Create human friendly version -->
    <Xml.XslTransform
      Condition="'@(_FxCopReportFile)'=='' and $(FxCopCreateHtmlReport)==true"
      XmlFile="$(FxCopReportFile)"
      XslFile="$(FxCopTransformFile)"
      ResultFile="$(_FxCopHtmlReportFile)">
    </Xml.XslTransform>

  </Target>
```

This target invokes the FxCop target with the provided values. This invocation results in an XML file being written that contains the results of the analysis. This file is used later in the build process to detect FxCop failures. After the FxCop target completes executing, that same XML file is fed into the XslTransform task, provided by the Microsoft SDC task library, to create a human readable version of the FxCop report. The SDC task library is an open source task repository created by Microsoft. Similar to the CoreBuild target shown earlier, the CoreFxCop target defines values for Inputs and Outputs; this will allow the target to be skipped if all FxCopAssemblies are older than the FxCopReportFile file. The remaining aspects of this file are specific implementation details and will not be discussed here.

In this chapter we have discussed a few different ways that you can invoke tools external to your build process. We have also discussed how you can create reusable build elements for build processes that will be repeated from project to project. This chapter concludes our coverage of MSBuild in this fashion. The next two chapters will take a cookbook style approach to delivering material.

Part IV

MSBuild Cookbook

In this part:

Chapter 8
Practical Applications, Part 1

In the previous chapters, we have presented the material that you will need to extend and customize your build process. Stating how to do something and giving an example of doing it are two entirely different things. In order to provide the most benefit, this chapter, as well as the next, are dedicated to providing practical examples that can be used in your build process. In this chapter, we will discuss examples such as setting an assembly version, handling errors, extending the clean process, and a few more.

Setting the Assembly Version

A common scenario when building projects is the need to set the version information for an assembly. The MSBuild team released a task, the AssemblyInfoTask, a while ago to address this need. This is not the only task that can be used for this purpose; you can find others available in open source task repositories. Along with the task, a targets file was delivered to assist in the consumption of the task. You can download this task, packaged in an MSI, at *http://code.msdn.microsoft.com/AssemblyInfoTaskvers*. When you install this task you will find a new folder created in the folder $(MSBuildExtensionsPath)\Microsoft\AssemblyInfoTask\ that contains all the needed files. You should consider placing the contents of this folder under source control, as is the case with these examples. This way each developer and build machine would not be required to install this MSI. Following this, I placed the following statements inside the Examples.Tasks.csproj.

```
<PropertyGroup>
  <ContribRoot>..\Contrib\</ContribRoot>
</PropertyGroup>
<!-- Assembly Info Related -->
<Import Project="$(ContribRoot)Microsoft\AssemblyInfoTask\Microsoft.VersionNumber.targets"/>

<PropertyGroup>
  <Format>01MMdd</Format>
  <AssemblyBuildNumberFormat>$(Format)</AssemblyBuildNumberFormat>
  <!-- Set AssemblyFileBuildNumberFormat to the same value. -->
  <AssemblyFileBuildNumberFormat>$(Format)</AssemblyFileBuildNumberFormat>
</PropertyGroup>
```

It imports the Microsoft.VersionNumber.targets file and then overrides two properties; AssemblyBuildNumberFormat and AssemblyFileBuildNumberFormat. The default value for these properties is yyMMdd. The maximum value for build numbers is 65,535 (because they are stored as unsigned short); because of this I changed default format to be 01MMdd. You can increment the leading 01 as needed, being careful not to increment past 6. Without this, or a similar override, the versioning task would fail because values such as 080924 are out of bounds. Now all we have to do is build the project and the version information will be taken care of for us. When I built the Example.Tasks project and attached a FileLogger, the following statement was contained in the log.

```
Target "UpdateAssemblyInfoFiles" in file
"C:\Data\MSBuildExamples\Contrib\Microsoft\AssemblyInfoTask\Microsoft.VersionNumber.targets"
from project "C:\Data\MSBuildExamples\Examples.Tasks\Examples.Tasks.csproj":
Building target "UpdateAssemblyInfoFiles" completely.
Output file "obj\Debug\Examples.Tasks.dll" does not exist.
Using "AssemblyInfo" task from assembly
        "C:\Data\MSBuildExamples\Contrib\Microsoft\AssemblyInfoTask\assemblyinfotask.dll".
Task "AssemblyInfo"
  Updating assembly info for Properties\AssemblyInfo.cs
        Updating major version to 1
        Updating minor version to 0
        Update method is DateString
        Updating build number to 010913
        Update method is AutoIncrement
        Updating revision number to 03
        Final assembly version is 1.0.010913.03
        Updating major version to 1
        Updating minor version to 0
        Update method is DateString
        Updating build number to 010913
        Update method is AutoIncrement
        Updating revision number to 03
        Final assembly version is 1.0.010913.03
Done executing task "AssemblyInfo".
```

From the log statement, you can see that the version properties were set twice, once for assembly version and again for file version. If you examined the assembly you would see that these properties were indeed set as reported. In this example, I did not override any other properties that could be set by the task, but there are many others. Take a look at the documentation provided along with the download for more information regarding its usage.

If you had placed the Microsoft.VersionNumber.targets into a version-controlled folder you would have had to make the following changes to ensure that it was usable.

```
<ItemGroup>
  <!--<AssemblyInfoFiles Include="**\AssemblyInfo.*"/>-->
  <!-- Modified by Sayed Ibrahim Hashimi
       ensure SVN files are not included -->
  <AssemblyInfoFiles Include="**\AssemblyInfo.*"
                     Exclude="$(SourceFolder)**\.svn\**\*" />
</ItemGroup>

<!-- Import the task -->
<!--<UsingTask
        AssemblyFile="$(APPDATA)\Microsoft\MSBuild\AssemblyInfoTask\AssemblyInfoTask.dll"
        TaskName="AssemblyInfo"/>-->
<!-- Modified by Sayed Ibrahim Hashimi to pick it up
from current directory instead of $(APPDATA) -->
<UsingTask
  AssemblyFile="AssemblyInfoTask.dll"
  TaskName="AssemblyInfo" />
```

Note The AssemblyInfoFiles item declaration used the *Exclude* attribute to filter out any files that may belong to Subversion.

With these changes we can use the targets file and the task without having to install them on all machines on which MSBuild is run. We will revisit this in another example that shows how to set the version properties for more than one project file to the same value. The drawback of using this task is that it modifies a source file, which is a bad practice. One reason is because the source file must be checked out in order to build. A better solution would be to remove the assembly attributes from the AssemblyInfo.cs file and instead have a task that would be executed before the Compile target. This task would then create a new file, in the intermediate folder, that contains the attributes for the assembly and is appended to the Compile item list. Then the file should be appended to the FileWrites list so it can be removed on a clean. For more specific information regarding cleaning see the Extending the Clean example.

Building Multiple Projects

When you are working in a team environment you will typically want a little more control when building your applications than just building the solution. For example, many applications are now using generated code, running code analysis tools, executing test cases, and so on. When you need to create a build process, there are typically two approaches that you can take:

- Write a build file that builds the solution
- Create a build file that builds the projects individually

The main difference between the two is that when you build a solution file you don't have control over what happens as the solution builds each individual project. You can supplement the solution's build process by adding steps before and after the solution is built. If you don't need this fine-grained control over the actual building, then I would suggest that you take this approach. The obvious advantage of using the Solution file is that this is the file used by Visual Studio. So when you use msbuild.exe on a solution file you should get the exact same build that you would within Visual Studio. The major drawback is that solution files are very limited; for example, you cannot change the build process and they can't be nested. In a future version of Visual Studio the solution file will be put into MSBuild format. In this section, we will demonstrate both techniques.

We have discussed the MSBuild task (the one which builds MSBuild projects) in the previous chapter. We will need to utilize this task in order to build the solution and projects. There have been some enhancements to the MSBuild task in version 3.5. The MSBuild task is now able to process properties contained in an item's metadata instead of just accepting values as the Properties input parameter. The following list presents three ways to pass properties into the MSBuild task.

1. As values in the Properties parameter of the MSBuild task
2. Item metadata named Properties
3. Item metadata named AdditionalProperties

The second option will always take precedence over the first, if both are supplied, so only use one or the other. The third option can however be used in conjunction with either the first or the second. Effectively, if a Properties metadata value is found on a project file passed to the MSBuild task, then any properties contained in the Properties input parameter on the MSBuild task itself will be **ignored**. The third option is always appended to either value from the first two options. Take a look at the contents of the following MSBuildTaskProperties.proj file.

```
<Project xmlns="http://schemas.microsoft.com/developer/msbuild/2003"
         ToolsVersion="3.5"
         DefaultTargets="Build">

  <PropertyGroup>
    <ExternalProjectFile>External.proj</ExternalProjectFile>
  </PropertyGroup>

  <ItemGroup>
    <!-- No values for Properties or AdditionalProperties -->
    <Projects Include="$(ExternalProjectFile)" />

    <!-- Only values for Properties -->
    <Projects Include="$(ExternalProjectFile)">
      <Properties>
        Name=One;
        Source=PropertiesMD;
      </Properties>
    </Projects>

    <!-- Only values for AdditionalProperties -->
    <Projects Include="$(ExternalProjectFile)">
      <AdditionalProperties>
        Name=Two;
        Source=AdditionalPropertiesMD;
      </AdditionalProperties>
    </Projects>

    <!-- Values for both Properties and AdditionalProperties -->
    <Projects Include="$(ExternalProjectFile)">
      <Properties>
        Name=Three;
        Source=PropertiesMD;
      </Properties>
```

```
      <AdditionalProperties>
        Name=Three;
        Source=AdditionalPropertiesMD;
      </AdditionalProperties>
    </Projects>
  </ItemGroup>

  <Target Name="Build">
    <!-- Execute the PrintInfo target for all projects in Projects -->
    <MSBuild Properties="Name=propertiesMSBuildTask"
             Projects="@(Projects)"
             Targets="PrintInfo"
             />
  </Target>

</Project>
```

This project will call the PrintInfo target of the External.proj file. This file is shown in the next snippet.

```
<Project xmlns="http://schemas.microsoft.com/developer/msbuild/2003"
         ToolsVersion="3.5"
         DefaultTargets="Build">

  <PropertyGroup>
    <!-- Defaults here -->
    <Name>none</Name>
    <Source>none</Source>
  </PropertyGroup>

  <Target Name="PrintInfo">
    <!-- Prints the values of the Name & Source properties -->
    <Message Text="Name: $(Name)"/>
    <Message Text="Source: $(Source)"/>
  </Target>
</Project>
```

Toward the top of the External.proj project file two properties are declared, Name and Source. We will be overriding these values, but default values were provided in the case that they were not overridden. The MSBuildTaskProperties.proj project file declares an item type, Projects, which contains a list of projects to be built. All the item values point to the External.proj file using the property ExternalProjectFile. If you look at how the Projects items are declared you will see that the four item declarations demonstrate four different ways values can be passed using the Properties and AdditionalProperties metadata. One item contains no values for either, the second only values for Properties, the third only values for AdditionalProperties, and the last has values for both. Inside the Build target we use the MSBuild task to execute the PrintInfo target, which prints the value for the Name and Source properties.

The output shown in Figure 8-1 demonstrates the difference between these three methods of providing properties. From the results you can see that values from both the Properties and AdditionalProperties metadata values were used while building the projects.

```
C:\Data\MSBuildExamples\BUILD>msbuild MSBuildTaskProperties.proj /t:build /fl /n
ologo
Build started 10/25/2008 12:48:43 AM.
Project "C:\Data\MSBuildExamples\BUILD\MSBuildTaskProperties.proj" on node 0 (b
uild target(s)).
Project "C:\Data\MSBuildExamples\BUILD\MSBuildTaskProperties.proj" (1) is build
ing "C:\Data\MSBuildExamples\BUILD\External.proj" (2) on node 0 (PrintInfo targ
et(s)).
  Name: propertiesMSBuildTask
  Source: none
Done Building Project "C:\Data\MSBuildExamples\BUILD\External.proj" (PrintInfo
target(s)).

Project "C:\Data\MSBuildExamples\BUILD\MSBuildTaskProperties.proj" (1) is build
ing "C:\Data\MSBuildExamples\BUILD\External.proj" (2:2) on node 0 (PrintInfo ta
rget(s)).
  Name: One
  Source: PropertiesMD;
Done Building Project "C:\Data\MSBuildExamples\BUILD\External.proj" (PrintInfo
target(s)).

Project "C:\Data\MSBuildExamples\BUILD\MSBuildTaskProperties.proj" (1) is build
ing "C:\Data\MSBuildExamples\BUILD\External.proj" (2:3) on node 0 (PrintInfo ta
rget(s)).
  Name: Two
  Source: AdditionalPropertiesMD;
Done Building Project "C:\Data\MSBuildExamples\BUILD\External.proj" (PrintInfo
target(s)).

Project "C:\Data\MSBuildExamples\BUILD\MSBuildTaskProperties.proj" (1) is build
ing "C:\Data\MSBuildExamples\BUILD\External.proj" (2:4) on node 0 (PrintInfo ta
rget(s)).
  Name: Three
  Source: AdditionalPropertiesMD;
Done Building Project "C:\Data\MSBuildExamples\BUILD\External.proj" (PrintInfo
target(s)).

Done Building Project "C:\Data\MSBuildExamples\BUILD\MSBuildTaskProperties.proj
" (build target(s)).


Build succeeded.
    0 Warning(s)
    0 Error(s)
```

FIGURE 8-1 Build target results

I would suggest using the Properties metadata very carefully because when it is used the values for the Properties parameter on the MSBuild task are completely ignored. If you mistakenly use this and you continue to pass properties directly into the MSBuild task it may be difficult to track down the cause of errors. Using the AdditionalProperties is very safe. When these values are present they take precedence, but values passed directly into the MSBuild task are allowed as well. After we discuss how we can build the projects using the solution file, we will exercise these new behaviors when we build the projects individually. The advantage of using the Properties metadata, or AdditionalProperties, is that you can pass different sets of properties to different projects, whereas using the *Properties* attribute always passes the same global properties to all projects specified in the MSBuild task.

We will start by looking at building a solution file from an MSBuild project using the MSBuild task. One idea when creating a master build file is that you want to perform steps before and after the build. In the next code block, you will find the contents of the ExampleBuild_Sln.proj file.

```
<Project xmlns="http://schemas.microsoft.com/developer/msbuild/2003"
         ToolsVersion="3.5"
         DefaultTargets="FullBuild">

  <PropertyGroup>
    <Root>..\</Root>
    <SourceRoot>$(Root)</SourceRoot>
    <OutputRoot>$(Root)Build\BuildTemp\</OutputRoot>
  </PropertyGroup>
```

```
  <ItemGroup>
    <!-- define all the configurations that we should build -->
    <AllConfigurations Include="Debug" />
    <AllConfigurations Include="Release" />
  </ItemGroup>

  <ItemGroup>
    <SolutionToBuild Include="$(SourceRoot)MSBuildExamples.sln" />
  </ItemGroup>

  <PropertyGroup>
    <FullBuildDependsOn>
      $(FullBuildDependsOn);
      BeforeBuild;
      CoreBuild;
      AfterBuild
    </FullBuildDependsOn>
    <FullRebuildDependsOn>
      $(FullRebuildDependsOn);
      BeforeRebuld;
      Clean;
      FullBuild;
      AfterRebuild
    </FullRebuildDependsOn>
  </PropertyGroup>

  <Target Name="FullBuild"
          DependsOnTargets="$(FullBuildDependsOn)" />
  <Target Name="BeforeBuild">
    <!-- TODO: Get latest source from version control -->
    <!-- TODO: Generate code -->
  </Target>
  <Target Name="AfterBuild">
    <!-- TODO: Unit tests -->
    <!-- TODO: Code Analysis -->
  </Target>

  <Target Name="CoreBuild">
    <MSBuild
      Projects="@(SolutionToBuild)"
      BuildInParallel="true"
      Properties="Configuration=%(AllConfigurations.Identity)" />
  </Target>

  <Target Name="FullRebuild"
          DependsOnTargets="$(FullRebuildDependsOn)" />
  <Target Name="Clean">
    <!-- Clean for each configuration -->
    <MSBuild
      Projects="@(SolutionToBuild)"
      BuildInParallel="true"
      Properties="Configuration=%(AllConfigurations.Identity)"
      Targets="Clean"
      />
  </Target>

</Project>
```

This is the project that is used to build the solution file. In this file the main target, FullBuild, similar to the Microsoft.Common.targets Build target, performs no actions itself. It simply sets up a set of dependent targets to be executed. This list of targets is contained in the FullBuildDependsOn property. I have chosen to do this to make it easier to perform steps before or after the build process. The actual build takes place in the CoreBuild target. In this target, the MSBuild task is invoked on the SolutionToBuild item type. Also you should note that we are specifying the `Properties="Configuration=%(AllConfigurations.Identity)"` so that the correct configuration value is passed to the project. By doing so the MSBuild task will be invoked using task batching for all the values defined in the AllConfigurations item type. In this case, we will build the solution in Debug and Release mode. If you execute the command `msbuild.exe ExampleBuild_Sln.proj` you will see that the solution was indeed built for Debug and Release configuration values.

When you build the solution file you don't have much control over the build process. For example, if you need to set the assembly version by providing values for the AssemblyFileMajorVersion, AssemblyMajorVersion, and other related properties, this cannot be easily achieved because you cannot pass properties to individual projects to be used during the build. In contrast, when building each project this is easily achieved by using the MSBuild task. In the next example, I will build the projects themselves while setting the assembly file version for all projects. The next snippet shows the relevant changes to the previous example. The full source can be found in the ExampleBuild_Projects.proj file.

```
<ItemGroup>
  <!--
  In MSBuild 3.5
  Properties and AdditionalProperties metadata are automatically
  passed when using the MSBuild task.
  If Properties Metaadata exists it takes precedence over and REPLACES
  any value for Properties provided to the MSBuild task itself.
  -->
  <ProjectsToBuild Include="$(SourceRoot)Examples.Loggers\Examples.Loggers.csproj">
    <AdditionalProperties>
      AssemblyFileMajorVersion=2;AssemblyMajorVersion=2;
      AssemblyFileMinorVersion=6;AssemblyMinorVersion=6
    </AdditionalProperties>
  </ProjectsToBuild>
  <ProjectsToBuild Include="$(SourceRoot)Examples.Tasks\Examples.Tasks.csproj">
    <AdditionalProperties>
      AssemblyFileMajorVersion=2;AssemblyMajorVersion=2;
      AssemblyFileMinorVersion=6;AssemblyMinorVersion=6
    </AdditionalProperties>
  </ProjectsToBuild>
  <ProjectsToBuild Include="$(SourceRoot)WindowsApplication1\WindowsApplication1.csproj">
    <AdditionalProperties>
      AssemblyFileMajorVersion=3;AssemblyMajorVersion=3;
      AssemblyFileMinorVersion=91;AssemblyMinorVersion=91
    </AdditionalProperties>
  </ProjectsToBuild>
```

```
  <ProjectsToBuild Include="$(SourceRoot)WindowsApplication2\WindowsApplication2.csproj">
    <AdditionalProperties>
      AssemblyFileMajorVersion=3;AssemblyMajorVersion=3;
      AssemblyFileMinorVersion=91;AssemblyMinorVersion=91
    </AdditionalProperties>
  </ProjectsToBuild>
  <ProjectsToBuild Include="$(UnitTestSourceRoot)Unittest.Proj1\Unittest.Proj1.csproj">
  </ProjectsToBuild>
  <ProjectsToBuild Include="$(UnitTestSourceRoot)Unittest.Proj2\Unittest.Proj2.csproj">
  </ProjectsToBuild>
</ItemGroup>
<Target Name="CoreBuild">
  <MSBuild
    Projects="@(ProjectsToBuild)"
    BuildInParallel="true"
    Properties="Configuration=%(AllConfigurations.Identity)"
    />
</Target>

<Target Name="Clean">
  <!-- Clean for each configuration -->
  <MSBuild
    Projects="@(ProjectsToBuild)"
    BuildInParallel="true"
    Properties=Configuration=%(AllConfigurations.Identity)"
    Targets="Clean"
   />
</Target>
```

In this example, instead of using the SolutionToBuild item a new item, ProjectsToBuild, is declared. This item contains the list of projects that should be built. If you take a look at the declaration you will notice that an AdditionalProperties metadata value is defined for some of the item values. As previously mentioned, if an item that you are passing to the MSBuild task contains metadata values for either Properties or AdditionalProperties, then these will be used as properties while building the project. This is a new feature in MSBuild 3.5. To achieve the same with MSBuild 2.0 you would have to build each project individually and pass the properties in the Properties attribute. When using MSBuild 3.5 one major drawback, besides usability, of this approach is that you would not be able to take advantage of building in parallel. In order for the MSBuild to build projects in parallel, all the projects must be passed into a single instance of the MSBuild task. MSBuild is not able to parallelize multiple declarations of the MSBuild task. Also to take advantage of parallel build you would need to specify that the property BuildInParallel be set to true, as well as invoking msbuild.exe with the /m switch.

The properties defined here for a few of the ProjectsToBuild item values determine what the major and minor version values should be. If you recall from the Setting the Assembly Version sample, these are properties that will be used by the AssemblyInfo task to set the assembly and file version of the created assembly. The command `msbuild ExampleBuild_Projects.proj /t:FullBuild` can be used to build all of the projects. The assemblies with version information also would be correctly stamped with the expected version numbers. I will not display the log here because of its size.

Attaching Multiple File Loggers

We have discussed creating and using loggers in detail in Chapter 5, "Custom Loggers." We mentioned that you could attach several instances of the file logger to the build process by using the notation /fl[n] where [n] is an optional value in the range 1-9. If you use the switch /flp[n] without a corresponding /fl[n] then the corresponding /fl[n] is implied and can be omitted. In that chapter, we didn't expand on why you would want to do so. When a developer is kicking off a build process, a good set of loggers to have attached is outlined in Table 8-1.

TABLE 8-1 Loggers to Attach to a Typical Build

Type	Setting
ConsoleLogger	Verbosity = minimal and display summary
FileLogger	Verbosity = detailed
FileLogger	errorsonly
FileLogger	warningsonly

We purposefully turn down the verbosity of the console logger to show only the most important log messages. This is because it is typically difficult to gain any insight on a decent-sized build from the console logger, as well as for performance reasons. It is much faster to write to a file and then to the console. Builds that write a lot of information to the console take longer than those that do not. This reduced amount of information is fine because we attach a file logger to capture the remaining information into a file, so if needed the results are always available there. There are also two other instances of the file logger suggested, one to capture errors and the other for warnings. This allows the developers to be able to pinpoint specific information about errors and warnings, in order to clear them out. To summarize, there are really two reasons to have logs: to see progress and to diagnose problems. In order to see the progress the build should log to the console as well as have a low verbosity. In order to diagnose problems, the logs need to be written to a file and have detailed information. Take a look at the command shown next, which builds the Examples.Tasks project with the loggers described in Table 8-1.

```
msbuild.exe /clp:verbosity=minimal /clp:summary
/flp:verbosity=detailed;logfile=build.detailed.log
/flp1:errorsonly;logfile=build.errors.log
/flp2:warningsonly;logfile=build.warnings.log
/m /p: BuildInParallel=true
Examples.Tasks.csproj /t:rebuild
```

In the command shown previously, we passed the appropriate parameters to the msbuild.exe to attach the desired loggers. Along with this, we specified the /m switch as well as defined the BuildInParallel value to be true. Because of this, the projects will be built in parallel instead of serially.

Creating a Logger Macro

Because you generally want to attach the same set of loggers to a build process, we need a way to make it easier to attach all the loggers. One way that you might have guessed is to create a batch file; another is to create a DOS macro to perform the same action. A DOS macro is one of the lesser-known features of the command prompt. You can create and manage macros using the DOSKEY command.

We can create a parameterized macro that can automatically attach these loggers for us. In this case, we would need to create a macro with the following command.

```
doskey build=msbuild.exe /clp:verbosity=minimal /clp:summary
/flp:verbosity=detailed;logfile=build.detailed.log
/flp1:errorsonly;logfile=build.errors.log
/flp2:warningsonly;logfile=build.warnings.log
/m /p: BuildInParallel=true
$*
```

The previous command will create a new macro named build that executes msbuild.exe, which is assumed to be on the path, while attaching the loggers declared. You should take note of the usage of the $* symbol. When you invoke a macro, the $* symbol will be replaced with any text following the macro name on the command line. In our previous example, the command would have been simplified to `build Examples.Tasks.csproj /t:rebuild`. In this case, the $* would have been replaced with the value 'Examples.Tasks.csproj /t:rebuild.' Once you create this macro it is very easy to attach the same set of loggers to each build that you perform. One drawback to using a macro is that the macro declaration lasts only for the duration of the command prompt. When the command prompt closes, the macros created in it will no longer be available. You are able to save the macros to a file using a command such as `doskey /macros > FileName`, where FileName is the name of the file to store the macros in. When you start a new command prompt, you can load the macros using the command `doskey /macrofile = FileName`. You could place this file under source control and have developers load it when the command prompt is opened.

Custom Before/After Build Steps in the Build Lab

There are scenarios when you would like to execute a set of steps before or after a build executes, but only on certain machines. For example, on build machines you may want to encrypt config files, or obfuscate your code every time a Visual Studio project is built. The Microsoft.Common.targets file exposes this functionality. Inside that file there are two import statements, one at the very top and the other at the very end, which are:

```
<Import Project="$(CustomBeforeMicrosoftCommonTargets)"
        Condition="Exists('$(CustomBeforeMicrosoftCommonTargets)')"/>

<Import Project="$(CustomAfterMicrosoftCommonTargets)"
        Condition="Exists('$(CustomAfterMicrosoftCommonTargets)')"/>
```

These statements will import a file, if it exists, at the locations contained in the CustomBeforeMicrosoftCommonTargets and CustomAfterMicrosoftCommonTargets if they exist on disk. The default values for these locations are %MSBuildExtensionsPath%\vNNNN\Custom.Before.Microsoft.Common.targets AND %PROGRAM_FILES%\MSBuild\vNNNN\Custom.After.Microsoft.Common.targets, where NNNN is either 2.0 or 3.5 depending on your tools version. If you place an MSBuild file at either of those locations it will be picked up at the appropriate time. If you do create such files, keep in mind that they will be processed by **every** build of a managed Visual Studio project that is executed on that machine. Also it is worth noting that because you can have only one file imported before, or after, it is not typically useful to share various customizations.

You can also override the properties CustomBeforeMicrosoftCommonTargets and CustomAfterMicrosoftCommonTargets to point to other locations. When you override these values you should always provide the full path to the files. If you want the override to be machine-wide then you could create these as environment variables. For a demonstration, I have created the following file, CustomAfter.proj.

```
<Project xmlns="http://schemas.microsoft.com/developer/msbuild/2003"
         ToolsVersion="3.5">
  <!--
  Insert custom steps into the build process
  -->
  <PropertyGroup>
    <BuildDependsOn>
      CustomBefore;
      $(BuildDependsOn);
      CustomAfter;
    </BuildDependsOn>
  </PropertyGroup>

  <Target Name="CustomBefore">
    <Message Text="Inside CustomBefore" Importance="high" />
  </Target>
  <Target Name="CustomAfter">
    <Message Text="Inside CustomAfter" Importance="high" />
  </Target>
</Project>
```

In this file, I extend the build process by injecting the CustomBefore and targets into the build dependency list. From the C:\Data\MSBuildExamples\WindowsApplication4 directory the following command was executed:

```
msbuild WindowsApplication4.csproj
/p:CustomAfterMicrosoftCommonTargets=C:\Data\MSBuildExamples\CustomAfter.proj
```

The end of the build is shown in Figure 8-2.

From Figure 8-2, you can see that the targets were successfully injected into the build process and executed at the appropriate time. I chose to override the CustomAfterMicrosoftCommonTargets property from the command line for this example (because I don't want this to execute with every

```
C:\Data\MSBuildExamples\WindowsApplication4>msbuild WindowsApplication4.csproj /
p:CustomAfterMicrosoftCommonTargets=C:\Data\MSBuildExamples\CustomAfter.proj /no
logo
Build started 10/1/2008 11:45:49 PM.
Project "C:\Data\MSBuildExamples\WindowsApplication4\WindowsApplication4.csproj
" on node 0 (default targets).
  Inside CustomBefore
CoreResGen:
  No resources are out of date with respect to their source files. Skipping res
  ource generation.
CoreCompile:
Skipping target "CoreCompile" because all output files are up-to-date with resp
ect to the input files.
CopyFilesToOutputDirectory:
  WindowsApplication4 -> C:\Data\MSBuildExamples\WindowsApplication4\bin\Debug\
  WindowsApplication4.exe
CustomAfter:
  Inside CustomAfter
Done Building Project "C:\Data\MSBuildExamples\WindowsApplication4\WindowsAppli
cation4.csproj" (default targets).


Build succeeded.
    0 Warning(s)
    0 Error(s)
```

FIGURE 8-2 External build customization demonstration

Visual Studio project build), but you could have placed this file in the previously mentioned location to have it automatically executed. If you do use this procedure, keep in mind that if you need to inject steps into the build process using the technique shown here, you must do this in the After targets file, not the Before targets file. If you override a property such as BuildDependsOn in a file that is imported in the Before targets file, then it will be overridden by the value contained in Microsoft.Common.targets itself.

Handling Errors

As you create project files you may need to perform some custom steps in the case that an error occurs. MSBuild has a specific element that can be used for this exact task. This is the *OnError* element. If you use the *OnError* element it must be the last element found inside the *Target* element that contains it. If this is not the case, then the build will be stopped before any target is executed. Some good examples of when you may want to use this are: to free resources that may have been taken by a previous target, send an email alert that the build has failed, create a work item to track the failed build, or undo checkout The VB.NET/C# build process uses this to run build events that are supposed to be executed on compilation error. Team Build uses the *OnError* element in two places: in the CallCompile and CoreTest targets. If an error occurs, then either the SetBuildBreakProperties or SetTestBreakProperties target is called. Following this the OnBuildBreak target is executed to create a failure work item that will be assigned to a team member. The *OnError* element has a parameter ExecuteTargets, which contains one or more targets that should be executed if the target fails. If you specify more than one target, then the value should be a semicolon delimited list. Targets will be executed in the sequence that they are declared in the ExecuteTargets list. In the file HandleError01.proj, we demonstrate using this element. The contents of this file are shown in the following snippet.

```
<Project xmlns="http://schemas.microsoft.com/developer/msbuild/2003"
         DefaultTargets="Build">
  <Target Name="Build">
```

```
    <!--
    This target simulates a target which fails.
    -->
    <Error Text="An error occurred" />

    <OnError ExecuteTargets="HandleErrors" />
  </Target>

  <Target Name="HandleErrors">

    <Message Text="An error has occurred and the build will fail"
             Importance="high" />

    <!-- TODO: Email error details -->

    <!-- TODO: Create a Work Item for fixing the build -->
  </Target>
</Project>
```

This sample uses the *OnError* element in order to execute the HandleErrors target if an error occurs during the Build target. The Build target uses the Error task to purposefully raise an error during the target. Figure 8-3 contains the results of executing the Build target.

```
C:\Data\MSBuildExamples>msbuild HandleErrors01.proj /t:Build /nologo
Build started 9/20/2008 5:18:57 PM.
Project "C:\Data\MSBuildExamples\HandleErrors01.proj" on node 0 (Build target(s
)).
C:\Data\MSBuildExamples\HandleErrors01.proj(8,5): error : An error occurred
HandleErrors:
  An error has occurrend and the build will fail
Done Building Project "C:\Data\MSBuildExamples\HandleErrors01.proj" (Build targ
et(s)) -- FAILED.

Build FAILED.

"C:\Data\MSBuildExamples\HandleErrors01.proj" (Build target) (1) ->
(Build target) ->
  C:\Data\MSBuildExamples\HandleErrors01.proj(8,5): error : An error occurred

    0 Warning(s)
    1 Error(s)
```

FIGURE 8-3 OnError demonstration

Figure 8-3 shows that the build failed, as expected, when the Error task was called, and the HandleErrors target was called after this error occurred. In this case, I simply sent some text to the log using the Message task, but your error handlers can be much more sophisticated. If there are many instances of the *OnError* element, then they are handled in sequence one after another. If an error occurs inside a target that is handling an error, then another error is logged and the build is stopped. If any other targets were pending to be executed by the *OnError* element, they are abandoned and the build is simply stopped.

Replacing Values in Config Files

There will be many times that you will need to update an applications configuration file at build time. For example, you may need to update a connection string or the logging level. In order to update the configuration, we can use a set of XML-related tasks that is available from the Microsoft SDC Tasks library. You can find these at *http://www.codeplex.com/sdctasks*. In this example, I am going to update the config for the sample WindowsApplication1 project. The contents of the app.config file for that project are shown next.

```
<?xml version="1.0" encoding="utf-8" ?>
<configuration>
  <appSettings>
    <add key="configuration" value="default"/>
    <add key="webUrl" value="http://www.sedodream.com" />
  </appSettings>
</configuration>
```

In this configuration file, I would like to do two things: update the configuration app settings value and add a new setting that will contain an email address that can be used for help. We will have to create a new target, UpdateConfig, to perform these modifications for us. We will also need to inject this target into the build process by placing the following declaration after the Import statement for Microsoft.CSharp.targets.

```
<PropertyGroup>
  <BuildDependsOn>
    $(BuildDependsOn);
    UpdateConfig
  </BuildDependsOn>
</PropertyGroup>
```

The previous statement extends the Build target by appending the UpdateConfig target to its dependency list. Because of this, the UpdateConfig target will be called after the project is built. We introduced this technique in Chapter 4, "MSBuild Fundamentals, Part 2." This target is shown in the following snippet.

```
<Target Name="UpdateConfig" DependsOnTargets="CoreBuild">
  <!-- Create an item that points to the dest config file -->
  <ItemGroup>
    <_DestConfigFile
      Include="@(AppConfigWithTargetPath->'$(OutDir)%(TargetPath)')"/>
  </ItemGroup>
  <PropertyGroup>
    <_UpdateXPath>/configuration/appSettings/add[@key='configuration']</_UpdateXPath>
    <_HelpEmailXPath>/configuration/appSettings/add[@key='helpEmail']</_HelpEmailXPath>
    <_HelpEmail>sayed.hashimi@gmail.com</_HelpEmail>
  </PropertyGroup>
  <Message Text="Updating config file %(_DestConfigFile.FullPath)"
           Importance="low"/>

  <!-- Update existing element -->
  <Xml.ModifyFile
    Path="%(_DestConfigFile.FullPath)"
    AttributeName="value"
    Force="true"
    NewValue="$(Configuration)"
    XPath="$(_UpdateXPath)" />
```

```
  <!--
  First insert a blank element, then use ModifyFile
  to update the value attribute of the element just added
  -->
  <XmlFile.AddElement
    Path="%(_DestConfigFile.FullPath)"
    XPath="/configuration/appSettings"
    Name="add"
    KeyAttributeName="key"
    KeyAttributeValue="helpEmail"
    IgnoreNoMatchFailure="false"
    Force="true" />

  <Xml.ModifyFile
    Path="%(_DestConfigFile.FullPath)"
    AttributeName="value"
    Force="true"
    NewValue="$(_HelpEmail)"
    XPath="$(_HelpEmailXPath)" />
</Target>
```

In this target, I used the AppConfigWithTargetPath item to resolve the full path to the location where the configuration file was being placed after a build has been executed. Specifically, the item's TargetPath metadata value is being used to pinpoint this location. This item is declared in the Microsoft.Common.targets file. The location where the config is finally placed is captured in the _DestConfigFile item. This item and a few properties that are declared in this target all start with an underscore. This is a convention that is used to denote that the element being declared is internal and should not be referenced by others. This convention is followed by all the targets files shipped by Microsoft.

The first notable action in the target is the usage of the ModifyFile task. This task can be used to modify XML files. You can use this task to update existing XML elements by setting the value for an element or setting the value for an attribute. In this case, we want to modify the configuration element `<add key="configuration" value="default"/>` and place the current configuration into value attribute. The XPath to locate this element, which is contained in the _UpdateXPath property, is `/configuration/appSettings/add[@key='configuration']`. This is passed to the ModifyFile task into the XPath input parameter. From the usage of that task you might notice these two values: AttributeName and Force. Because we are passing a value for AttributeName, this signals to the ModifyFile task that we are updating the value for the provide attribute instead of the element itself. If we specify a true value for the Force parameter, this allows the task to write to files that are marked as read-only. Otherwise, if the file to be updated is read-only, an error will occur. For more information about the ModifyFile task, see the SDC task library Web site.

Following this update, we need to insert a new element that contains an email address that can be used for support. This setting should be placed in the helpEmail app setting. In order to achieve this with the SDC tasks, we first need to create a new XML element, using the AddElement task, to contain the value, then update its value using the ModifyFile task.

This two-step process is needed because the AddElement task cannot set the value for an attribute, it can set the value only for the element itself. After these steps are performed, the process has been completed. The following config file results show the Debug configuration.

```
<?xml version="1.0" encoding="utf-8"?>
<configuration>
  <appSettings>
    <add key="configuration" value="Debug" />
    <add key="webUrl" value="http://www.sedodream.com" />
    <add key="helpEmail" value="sayed.hashimi@gmail.com" />
  </appSettings>
</configuration>
```

From the resulting configuration file shown, we can see that we were able to successfully make the needed modifications at build time. You can use a similar technique to assist in automating your own modifications. Another technique for creating or/modifying configuration files is to perform an XSL transformation to generate them. You can use the XslTransform task, which is also a part of the SDC library to perform this. This was briefly demonstrated in Chapter 7, "External Tools," when discussing FxCop.

Extending the Clean

Whenever you extend the build process to generate files you must make sure that those files get cleaned up when the clean process is executed. Two primary ways of performing this are:

- Appending to the FileWrites item list
- Injecting custom targets into the clean process

The Microsoft.Common.targets file maintains a list of files that needs to be removed when the Clean target is executed; this list is the FileWrites list. It is written to disk in the base intermediate output path (i.e., obj\Debug) as the *ProjectFileName*.FileListAbsolute.txt file, where ProjectFileName is the name of the project file, including the extension. You can add values to the FileWrites item list if you need files deleted that were generated by custom steps in your build process. You should never manually edit the *ProjectFileName*.FileListAbsolute.txt file. Take a look at the segment from the WindowsApplication3.csproj file shown next.

```
<PropertyGroup>
  <BuildDependsOn>
    CustomBeforeBuld;
    $(BuildDependsOn);
    CustomAfterBuild
  </BuildDependsOn>
</PropertyGroup>

<Target Name="CustomBeforeBuld">
  <ItemGroup>
    <_UserConfigFile Include="user.config" />
  </ItemGroup>
```

```
  <!-- Since this is before build OutputPath directory may not yet exist -->
  <MakeDir Directories="$(OutputPath)"/>
  <!-- Copy user.config to OutputPath, if it exists -->
  <Copy Condition="Exists('@(_UserConfigFile)')"
        SourceFiles="@(_UserConfigFile)"
        DestinationFiles="@(_UserConfigFile->'$(OutputPath)user.confog')">
    <Output ItemName="_CopiedUserFiles" TaskParameter="CopiedFiles"/>
  </Copy>
  <ItemGroup>
    <FileWrites Include="@(_CopiedUserFiles)"/>
  </ItemGroup>
</Target>
```

Here, we are extending the build process by injecting the CustomBeforeBuild target to be executed before the Build target and the CustomAfterBuild target to be executed after the build. We will show and discuss the CustomAfterBuild shortly. The CustomBeforeBuild target is very straightforward: It copies the file user.config if it exists to the *OutputPath*. Following this the file is appended to the FileWrites item. Because of this, when a clean is executed it would expect that this file would be automatically deleted for us. The results of executing the Clean target are shown in Figure 8-4.

```
C:\Data\MSBuildExamples\WindowsApplication3>msbuild WindowsApplication3.csproj /
t:Clean /nologo
Build started 10/25/2008 2:00:43 AM.
Project "C:\Data\MSBuildExamples\WindowsApplication3\WindowsApplication3.csproj
" on node 0 (Clean target(s)).
  This target is called before the clean begins
CoreClean:
  Deleting file "C:\Data\MSBuildExamples\WindowsApplication3\bin\Debug\user.con
  fog".
  Deleting file "C:\Data\MSBuildExamples\WindowsApplication3\bin\Debug\WindowsA
  pplication3.exe".
  Deleting file "C:\Data\MSBuildExamples\WindowsApplication3\bin\Debug\WindowsA
  pplication3.pdb".
  Deleting file "C:\Data\MSBuildExamples\WindowsApplication3\obj\Debug\WindowsA
  pplication3.Form1.resources".
  Deleting file "C:\Data\MSBuildExamples\WindowsApplication3\obj\Debug\WindowsA
  pplication3.Properties.Resources.resources".
  Deleting file "C:\Data\MSBuildExamples\WindowsApplication3\obj\Debug\WindowsA
  pplication3.csproj.GenerateResource.Cache".
  Deleting file "C:\Data\MSBuildExamples\WindowsApplication3\obj\Debug\WindowsA
  pplication3.exe".
  Deleting file "C:\Data\MSBuildExamples\WindowsApplication3\obj\Debug\WindowsA
  pplication3.pdb".
Done Building Project "C:\Data\MSBuildExamples\WindowsApplication3\WindowsAppli
cation3.csproj" (Clean target(s)).


Build succeeded.
    0 Warning(s)
    0 Error(s)
```

FIGURE 8-4 Clean target results

From the results shown in Figure 8-4, you can see that the user.config file was deleted when we executed the Clean target. This is exactly what we needed. One thing that you should note when using this technique: If your build step adds to the FileWrites item list, it must do so every time it would have written the file, even if it didn't because the file was up to date. For example, the output assembly goes into the FileWrites item list even if the project is up to date in which case the compiler would not have been run.

Since this works so well, you may be wondering why we even would discuss another method. The reason is that this technique has some limitations. Those limitations are:

- Files to be deleted must be under the output path
- You must append to the item early in the build process

The first limitation is straightforward: If the file is not under the output path, it will not be deleted. This is for safety reasons; that way you cannot inadvertently delete files by mistake. The second limitation states that you must append to the FileWrites item early in the build process. More specifically you must append your values to the FileWrites item before the Clean, or IncrementalClean, target executes. When either of these targets gets executed, the clean file, the file that persists the FileWrites item, is written to disk. Despite these limitations there are many cases in which you will be able to effectively use this technique. If you are not able to use this technique then you can extend the clean process itself manually. Another advantage to cleaning manually is that you don't have to predict the files that were written. You can just blow away a whole directory, or use a wildcard expression.

There are some cases when you will be creating or copying files either later in the build process or to locations that are outside the output path that will need to be cleaned up as well. For instance, you may need to copy some of the outputs to different locations. In these cases you will have to inject targets into the clean process to manage this manually.

Extending the clean process manually is similar to how the build process is extended. You have the following options: override an existing blank target such as BeforeClean, or inject a target into the clean process. If you choose the first option you can override either the BeforeClean or AfterClean targets. This is similar to how the BeforeBuild or AfterBuild targets can be overridden as discussed in Chapter 3.

In Visual Studio Project files you will find an import statement similar to the following, which is for C# project files.

```
<Import Project="$(MSBuildToolsPath)\Microsoft.CSharp.targets" />
```

Any customizations to the build or clean process should be declared after this statement to ensure that they are not overwritten. The following snippet shows how we can override the BeforeClean and AfterClean targets.

```
<Target Name="BeforeClean">
  <Message Text="This target is called before the clean begins"/>
  <!-- Place clean customizations here -->
</Target>
<Target Name="AfterClean">
  <Message Text="This target is called after the clean competes"/>
  <!-- Place clean customizations here -->
</Target>
```

When you override either of these two targets they will be called at the appropriate time. If you are creating customizations to a specific project file, this is a great way to go. If you are creating reusable MSBuild scripts then you must chose to inject your targets into the clean process instead of taking this approach. This is because if the same target gets declared more than once, then the last target declared will be the definition that is used. All other target declarations will be ignored.

In order to inject a target into the clean process, the CleanDependsOn property must be extended. This is demonstrated by the following snippet taken from the WindowsApplicaton3.csproj file.

```
<PropertyGroup>
  <CleanDependsOn>
    $(CleanDependsOn);
    CustomClean
  </CleanDependsOn>
</PropertyGroup>
<Target Name="CustomClean">
  <Message Text="Inside CustomClean" Importance="high"/>
  <ItemGroup>
    <_CustomFilesToDelete Include="$(_OutputCopyLocation)**\*"/>
  </ItemGroup>
  <Delete Files="@(_CustomFilesToDelete)"/>
</Target>
```

In this snippet, we are re-declaring the CleanDependsOn property and appending the CustomClean target to its value. By doing so when the Clean target is executed, the CustomClean target will be called at the end of the process. Inside the CustomClean target I create an item, _CustomFilesToDelete, which will contain all the files that need to be deleted. These files are then deleted using the Delete task. Figure 8-5 contains the results of executing the Build target followed by the Clean target.

```
C:\Data\MSBuildExamples\WindowsApplication3>msbuild WindowsApplication3.csproj /
t:Build;Clean /nologo /fl
Build started 9/23/2008 6:48:23 PM.
Project "C:\Data\MSBuildExamples\WindowsApplication3\WindowsApplication3.csproj
" on node 0 (Build;Clean target(s)).
  Processing resource file "Form1.resx" into "obj\Debug\WindowsApplication3.For
  m1.resources".
  Processing resource file "Properties\Resources.resx" into "obj\Debug\WindowsA
  pplication3.Properties.Resources.resources".
CopyFilesToOutputDirectory:
  Copying file from "obj\Debug\WindowsApplication3.exe" to "bin\Debug\WindowsAp
  plication3.exe".
  WindowsApplication3 -> C:\Data\MSBuildExamples\WindowsApplication3\bin\Debug\
  WindowsApplication3.exe
  Copying file from "obj\Debug\WindowsApplication3.pdb" to "bin\Debug\WindowsAp
  plication3.pdb".
CustomAfterBuild:
  _FilesToCopy: bin\Debug\gen.sample.txt;bin\Debug\WindowsApplication3.exe;bin\
  Debug\WindowsApplication3.pdb
  DestFiles: gen.sample.txt;WindowsApplication3.exe;WindowsApplication3.pdb
  Copying file from "bin\Debug\gen.sample.txt" to "bin\Debug\..\..\CustomOutput
  \gen.sample.txt".
  Copying file from "bin\Debug\WindowsApplication3.exe" to "bin\Debug\..\..\Cus
  tomOutput\WindowsApplication3.exe".
  Copying file from "bin\Debug\WindowsApplication3.pdb" to "bin\Debug\..\..\Cus
  tomOutput\WindowsApplication3.pdb".
BeforeClean:
  This target is called before the clean begins
CoreClean:
  Deleting file "C:\Data\MSBuildExamples\WindowsApplication3\bin\Debug\gen.samp
  le.txt".
  Deleting file "C:\Data\MSBuildExamples\WindowsApplication3\bin\Debug\WindowsA
  pplication3.exe".
  Deleting file "C:\Data\MSBuildExamples\WindowsApplication3\bin\Debug\WindowsA
  pplication3.pdb".
  Deleting file "C:\Data\MSBuildExamples\WindowsApplication3\obj\Debug\WindowsA
  pplication3.Form1.resources".
  Deleting file "C:\Data\MSBuildExamples\WindowsApplication3\obj\Debug\WindowsA
  pplication3.Properties.Resources.resources".
  Deleting file "C:\Data\MSBuildExamples\WindowsApplication3\obj\Debug\WindowsA
  pplication3.csproj.GenerateResource.Cache".
  Deleting file "C:\Data\MSBuildExamples\WindowsApplication3\obj\Debug\WindowsA
  pplication3.exe".
  Deleting file "C:\Data\MSBuildExamples\WindowsApplication3\obj\Debug\WindowsA
  pplication3.pdb".
AfterClean:
  This target is called after the clean competes
CustomClean:
  Inside CustomClean
  Deleting file "bin\Debug\..\..\CustomOutput\gen.sample.txt".
  Deleting file "bin\Debug\..\..\CustomOutput\sub\test.txt".
  Deleting file "bin\Debug\..\..\CustomOutput\windows_application3.zip".
  Deleting file "bin\Debug\..\..\CustomOutput\WindowsApplication3.exe".
  Deleting file "bin\Debug\..\..\CustomOutput\WindowsApplication3.pdb".
Done Building Project "C:\Data\MSBuildExamples\WindowsApplication3\WindowsAppli
cation3.csproj" (Build;Clean target(s)).


Build succeeded.
    0 Warning(s)
    0 Error(s)
```

FIGURE 8-5 Extending the clean process

Figure 8-5 shows all the targets that have been used to customize the clean process, namely BeforeClean, AfterClean, and CustomClean. It shows that all were successfully called at the appropriate time and executed as expected. It is easy to forget about cleaning up files that your custom process creates, or copies, but this is very important. If you do not clean up these files correctly, then you may encounter unexpected results during your build process. For instance, targets may continue to be skipped, because of incremental building, even after the clean target has been executed.

In this chapter, we discussed a few very common build customizations such as setting the version for an assembly and extending the clean process. We will continue these types of examples in the next chapter as well. Following that chapter, we will start our Team Build related material.

Chapter 9

Practical Applications, Part 2

In the previous chapter, we started presenting some possible applications of MSBuild that you can use in your own build process. In this chapter, we'll examine some applications geared towards web applications. Some of the examples in this chapter include starting and stopping services, encrypting the web.config file, and compressing JavaScript files.

Starting and Stopping Services

There are several instances where either your build or deployment process relies on services to be running. In these cases, you should ensure that the services are installed and started before they are needed. It's very easy to start and stop services from MSBuild.

You can use the Exec command to execute the command `net start` or `net stop` to start and stop services. A better alternative for this is to use the WindowsService task from the MSBuild Extension Pack. The MSBuild Extension Pack can be found at *http://www.codeplex.com/MSBuildExtensionPack*. Using this task, you can perform many actions relating to services in a unified manner. This task supports these actions: start, stop, install, uninstall, disable, set manual start, set automatic start, check if a service exists, and update service identity. For complete information regarding this task see the documentation provided with the tasks. When you install the MSBuild Extension Pack the documentation file is placed in the same directory as the task assembly, which is typically %Program Files%\ MSBuild\ExtensionPack. The following project file, Services01.proj, demonstrates this task.

```
<Project xmlns="http://schemas.microsoft.com/developer/msbuild/2003"
  ToolsVersion="3.5">

  <!--
  Import the project file that declares the UsingTask statements for
  the MSBuild Extension pack.
  -->
  <Import
    Project="$(MSBuildExtensionsPath)\ExtensionPack\MSBuild.ExtensionPack.tasks"/>

  <Target Name="StartService">
     <!--
      The convention when using the MSBuild Extension Pack is to
      fully qualify the task name to avoid any possible collision with
      other tasks.
     -->
    <MSBuild.ExtensionPack.Computer.WindowsService
      TaskAction="Start"
      ServiceName="aspnet_state" />
```

```
    <!-- Similar to the command -->
    <!-- <Exec Command="net start aspnet_state" IgnoreExitCode="true" /> -->
  </Target>
  <Target Name="StopService">
    <MSBuild.ExtensionPack.Computer.WindowsService
      TaskAction="Stop"
      ServiceName="aspnet_state"/>

    <!-- Similar to the command -->
    <!-- <Exec Command="net stop aspnet_state" IgnoreExitCode="true" /> -->
  </Target>
</Project>
```

This task accepts a TaskAction parameter that describes what action the task is to perform. In order to start a service, the TaskAction should be set to Start and the name of the service, which is required, is provided in the ServiceName parameter. Similarly, to stop a service, Stop should be the TaskAction.

If you execute the command `msbuild Services01.proj /t:StartService;StopService` the result will be what is shown in Figure 9-1.

```
C:\Data\MSBuildExamples\WEB\Misc>msbuild Services01.proj /t:StartService;StopSer
vice /nologo
Build started 10/31/2008 12:38:57 AM.
Project "C:\Data\MSBuildExamples\WEB\Misc\Services01.proj" on node 0 (StartServ
ice;StopService target(s)).
  Starting: aspnet_state - Stopped...
  Started: aspnet_state
StopService:
  Stopping: aspnet_state - Running...
  Please wait, Service state: aspnet_state - StopPending...
  Stopped: aspnet_state
Done Building Project "C:\Data\MSBuildExamples\WEB\Misc\Services01.proj" (Start
Service;StopService target(s)).


Build succeeded.
    0 Warning(s)
    0 Error(s)
```

FIGURE 9-1 Starting and stopping services

In Figure 9-1, the WindowsService task is used to start and then stop the aspnet_state service. You might use this when you deploy a Web application that depends on the ASP.NET state service. When you deploy an application that has dependencies such as services you must make sure that the dependencies along with the application are in a usable state when the deployment has completed.

Web Deployment Project Overview

When you create Web sites and Web applications (both referred to as Web applications from this point) using Visual Studio it is a good idea to also use Web Deployment Projects (WDP) to assist in the deployment of them. WDP is not installed by default with Visual Studio, but is an add-in that you can download for free. You can download it by going to *http://www.microsoft.com/downloads* and searching for WDP. The page name should be listed as "Visual Studio® 2008 Web Deployment Projects." This add-in is supported by Microsoft, and you are encouraged to use it.

The following is a list of features that are provided with the WDP.

- Automatic precompilation with the build process
- WDP files are MSBuild files, so they are extensible
- Various options exist regarding assembly generation, including:
  - Single assembly for all outputs
  - One assembly per folder
  - All pages and control outputs to a single assembly
  - Separate assembly for each page and control output
- Ability to sign assemblies
- Ability to set assembly version

When you are building and debugging your Web applications using Visual Studio you place your markup in one file and the code behind the markup in a separate file. You could take the contents of the directory as is and allow IIS to compile the pages in place. The obvious problem to the approach is that you expose the code for your Web application on the Web server that is running it. Much better is to precompile the application into one or many assemblies and deploy those along with the page files. A WDP can be used for this as well as the other tasks listed previously.

After you have installed the WDP add-in you can create a new WDP in Visual Studio by right-clicking on the desired Web application and selecting Add Web Deployment Project. This will show a dialog that prompts you for the name and location of the Web deployment project. Once you add the project you will see it in the Solution Explorer similar to the one shown in Figure 9-2.

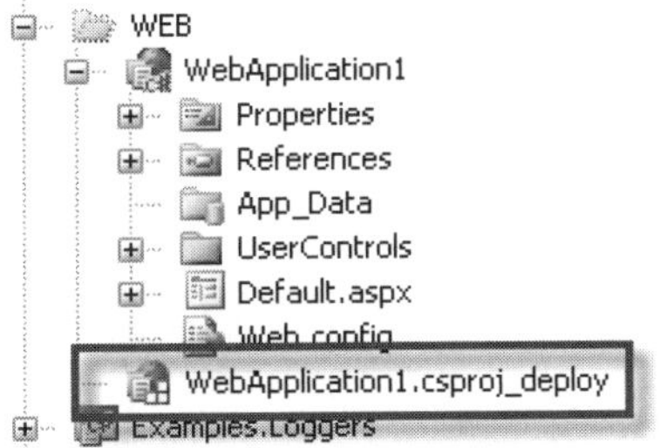

FIGURE 9-2 Web Deployment Project in Solution Explorer

The WDP shows up in Visual Studio as any other project would. When you create WDP projects the name typically ends in_deploy and the extension on the file is .wdproj. Unlike most other project types, there will never be any project items, such as files or folders, placed under this node in Visual Studio. This is just an MSBuild project file, named WebApplication1_01.csproj_deploy.wdproj, with some Visual Studio GUI support. When you build or rebuild the solution, the WDP will also be built. As a best practice, you should disable building WDP projects for Debug configurations, because WDP builds may be lengthy. You can do this from the Configuration Manager in Visual Studio. You can always right-click on the WDP to explicitly build it even if the current configuration is set to Debug. If you double-click on the WDP you will be presented with a dialog that consists of four pages: Compilation, Output Assemblies, Signing, and Deployment. From each of these pages you can assign properties to customize that portion of the deployment process. For instance, take a look at the Output Assemblies page shown in Figure 9-3.

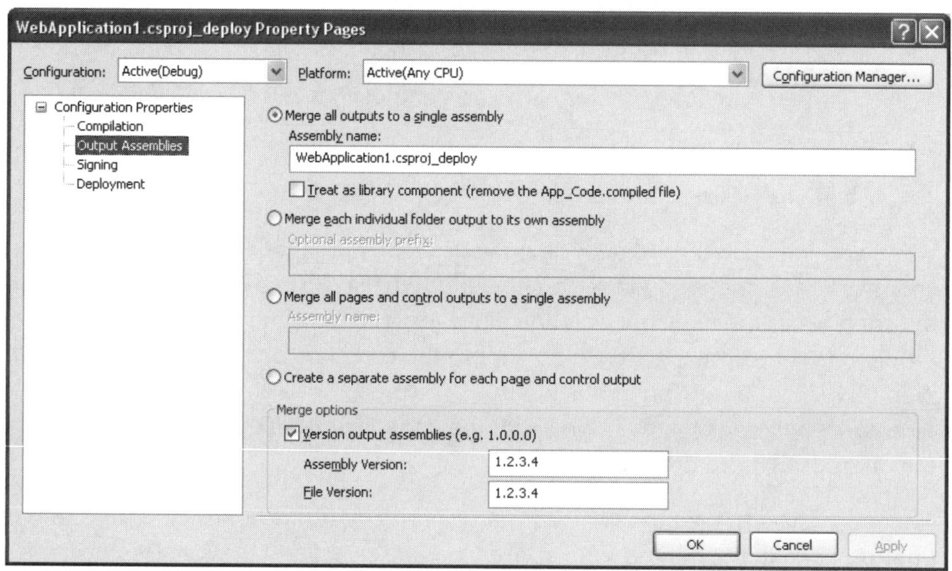

FIGURE 9-3 Web Deployment Project configuration page

From the dialog in Figure 9-3, the options specified are to create one assembly named WebApplication1.csproj_deploy, and the assembly will be stamped the value 1.2.3.4 for both assembly and file version. All the customizations on these pages are stored in the MSBuild project file for the WDP. Note that all the options specified for all four pages are specific to the Configuration and Platform selected in the drop-downs toward the top of the dialog. You can even define new configurations, or platforms, to meet your needs. For instance, you may want to sign your assemblies that are going into production environments but not elsewhere. In this case, you could create a new configuration, Production, that has this setting enabled and configured.

We have discussed what a Web Deployment Project is and the fact that it is an MSBuild file. We will now take a closer look at a WDP file. In order to view the content of a WDP, you can right-click on the WDP node and select Open Project File. The following sample WDP file is taken from WebApplication1_01.csproj_deploy.wdproj.

```
<Project xmlns="http://schemas.microsoft.com/developer/msbuild/2003"
  ToolsVersion="3.5"
  DefaultTargets="Build">
  <PropertyGroup>
    <Configuration
      Condition=" '$(Configuration)' == '' ">Debug</Configuration>
```

```
    <Platform
      Condition=" '$(Platform)' == '' ">AnyCPU</Platform>
    <ProductVersion>9.0.21022</ProductVersion>
    <SchemaVersion>2.0</SchemaVersion>
    <ProjectGuid>{5369651F-4315-41F5-9386-B0B01E2B177C}</ProjectGuid>
    <SourceWebPhysicalPath>..\WebApplication1</SourceWebPhysicalPath>
    <SourceWebProject>
      {72FA2E0D-CF86-4A33-8A83-8567B8FF01EF}|WEB\WebApplication1\WebApplication1.csproj
    </SourceWebProject>
    <SourceWebVirtualPath>/WebApplication1.csproj</SourceWebVirtualPath>
    <TargetFrameworkVersion>v3.5</TargetFrameworkVersion>
  </PropertyGroup>
  <PropertyGroup Condition=" '$(Configuration)|$(Platform)' == 'Debug|AnyCPU' ">
    <DebugSymbols>true</DebugSymbols>
    <OutputPath>.\Debug</OutputPath>
    <EnableUpdateable>false</EnableUpdateable>
    <UseMerge>true</UseMerge>
    <SingleAssemblyName>WebApplication1.csproj_deploy</SingleAssemblyName>
    <UseWebConfigReplacement>false</UseWebConfigReplacement>
    <DeleteAppDataFolder>false</DeleteAppDataFolder>
  </PropertyGroup>
  <PropertyGroup Condition=" '$(Configuration)|$(Platform)' == 'Release|AnyCPU' ">
    <DebugSymbols>false</DebugSymbols>
    <OutputPath>.\Release</OutputPath>
    <EnableUpdateable>true</EnableUpdateable>
    <UseMerge>true</UseMerge>
    <SingleAssemblyName>WebApplication1.csproj_deploy</SingleAssemblyName>
  </PropertyGroup>
  <ItemGroup Condition="'$(Configuration)|$(Platform)' == 'Debug|AnyCPU'">
    <AssemblyAttributes Include="AssemblyFileVersion">
      <Value>1.2.3.4</Value>
    </AssemblyAttributes>
    <AssemblyAttributes Include="AssemblyVersion">
      <Value>1.2.3.4</Value>
    </AssemblyAttributes>
  </ItemGroup>

  <Import
    Project=
"$(MSBuildExtensionsPath)\Microsoft\WebDeployment\v9.0\Microsoft.WebDeployment.targets"
   />

  <PropertyGroup>
    <!-- Customize output location using the OutputPath property -->
    <OutputPath>Out_01\$(Configuration)\</OutputPath>
  </PropertyGroup>
</Project>
```

From the WDP shown you can see that all the values entered through the Visual Studio UI are indeed captured in MSBuild format. Because of this you can easily customize and/or extend the process. In fact, in this example the output path has been customized using the OutputPath property to be Out_01\$(Configuration)\. This file is similar to a C# or VB .NET project in the sense that another file, Microsoft.WebDeployment.targets, which defines the build process, is imported. If you want to get a deeper understanding of the Web Deployment Projects, you should take a look at that file.

I've already mentioned that when you build a solution that contains a WDP, the WDP will also be built automatically, if it is enabled for that Configuration. You can also use msbuild.exe to manually build the WDP as you would any other MSBuild project file. When you build the WDP, you will notice that all the files that are contained in or under the source root for your Web application will be included in the deployment. The source root is captured in the SourceWebPhysicalPath property. This is because WDPs can support either Web sites or Web applications. If you would like to exclude files from being included in the deployment, you can use the ExcludeFromBuild item. For instance, in the WebApplication1_02.csproj_deploy.wdproj file, which extends the previous example, the following customizations have been inserted.

```
<ItemGroup>
   <!-- Use the ExcludeFromBuild item to exclude files from being deployed -->
  <ExcludeFromBuild
    Include="$(SourceWebPhysicalPath)\WebApplication1.csproj" />
  <ExcludeFromBuild
    Include="$(SourceWebPhysicalPath)\WebApplication1.csproj.user" />
  <ExcludeFromBuild
    Include="$(SourceWebPhysicalPath)\CustomOut\**\*" />
  <ExcludeFromBuild
    Include="$(SourceWebPhysicalPath)\**\.svn\**\*" />
</ItemGroup>

<PropertyGroup>
   <!-- Customize output location using the OutputPath property -->
  <OutputPath>Out_02\$(Configuration)\</OutputPath>
</PropertyGroup>
```

In these customizations, the following files will be excluded: the Web applications project file, the Web applications user file, the contents of the CustomOut folder, which is a copy of the bin folder, and any files related to version control. Because the WDP will pick up all files under the SourceWebPhysicalPath directory, this will include any artifacts that are placed there by your source control provider. In the case of Subversion you should exclude those files contained within a .svn folder using the declaration shown previously. Typically a snapshot of the Web directory is made and the build is then processed from that directory. This takes place in the following _CopyBeforeBuild target.

```
<Target Name="_CopyBeforeBuild"
  Condition=" '$(EnableCopyBeforeBuild)' == 'true' or '@(ExcludeFromBuild)' != ''  ">
    <CreateItem Include="$(SourceWebPhysicalPath)\**\*.*"
                Exclude="@(ExcludeFromBuild)">
        <Output ItemName="_WebFiles" TaskParameter="Include" />
    </CreateItem>

    <RemoveDir Directories="$(CopyBeforeBuildTargetPath)" />
    <MakeDir Directories="$(CopyBeforeBuildTargetPath)" />
    <Copy SourceFiles="@(_WebFiles)"
      DestinationFolder=
      "$(CopyBeforeBuildTargetPath)\%(_WebFiles.SubFolder)%(_WebFiles.RecursiveDir)" />
```

```
    <CreateProperty Value="$(CopyBeforeBuildTargetPath)">
        <Output TaskParameter="Value"
                PropertyName="_AspNetCompilerSourceWebPath" />
    </CreateProperty>
</Target>
```

From this target we can see how the ExcludeFromBuild item is used to allow you to filter the files included in the deployment. Also note that at the end of the target the _AspNetCompilerSourceWebPath property is declared to point to the new directory that was just created. Initially it points to the full path of the SourceWebPhysicalPath. This path is passed to the AspNetCompilier task, which a custom task that calls aspnet_compiler.exe. There are also some scenarios in which you may want to remove files from the output Web after the build. In this case you can define an item type to contain these files. Then you can override the AfterBuild target to delete these files. For example, take a look at the following snippet.

```
<ItemGroup>
  <RemoveAfterBuild Include="$(OutputPath)\obj\" />
  <RemoveAfterBuild Include="$(OutputPath)\My Project\" />
</ItemGroup>

<Target Name="AfterBuild">
  <RemoveDir Directories="@(RemoveAfterBuild)" />
</Target>
```

The difference between this approach and the ExcludeFromBuild approach is that these files will be removed after the build process, instead of excluded from it. So if you needed files to be available during your build process but those files are not required by the application to run, then you should use the RemoveAfterBuild approach.

Zipping Output Files, Then Uploading to an Ftp Site

In this sample, the files in the output folder are first compressed into a zip file and then uploaded to an ftp site. This sample uses these tasks from third parties: DateTime, Zip, and FtpUpload. The first task is from the MSBuild Extension Pack and the other two from the MSBuild Community Tasks. The parameters for those tasks are outlined in Tables 9-1, 9-2, and 9-3.

TABLE 9-1 DateTime Task Parameters

Name	Description
TaskAction	Required parameter that describes what action the task should perform. Possible values are Get and GetElapsed. Get will get the current date time in the provided format. GetElapsed will return the elapsed time in the format provided.
Format	Required parameter that contains the DateTime format string.
Start	If the TaskAction is GetElapsed, then this parameter is required. This is the starting DateTime to compute the elapsed time.
End	This is the end point to compute the elapsed amount of time when using the GetElapsed task action. This defaults to the current time.
Result	Output parameter that contains the result of the task.

TABLE 9-2 Zip Task Parameters

Name	Description
Files	Required parameter that contains files to zip.
ZipFileName	Required parameter that is the name of the zip file to be created.
Flatten	Determines if the zip file will have a flat file structure.
WorkingDirectory	The working directory for the task. When using this, a full path should be provided. This will determine the hierarchy of folders and files inside the zip file.
ZipLevel	The level of compression that should be used when creating the zip file. Possible value ranges from 0 to 9. Zero (0) is for no compression and 9 for the best possible compression.
Comment	Optional comment for the zip file.

TABLE 9-3 FtpUpload Task Parameters

Name	Description
LocalFile	Required parameter that is the file that should be uploaded.
RemoteUri	Required parameter that is where the file should be uploaded.
Username	Username to be used when connecting to the ftp site.
Password	Password to be used when connecting to the ftp site
UsePassive	Whether passive mode should be used for the upload, default is false.

In the following snippet, you will find the contents of the ZipOutputFiles target taken from the WebApplication1_ftp01.csproj_deploy.wdproj file.

```
<Target Name="ZipOutputFiles" DependsOnTargets="Build">
  <ItemGroup>
    <_FilesToZip
        Include="$(OutputPath)**\*"
        Exclude="$(OutputPath)obj\**\*;$(OutputPath)bin\Samples\**\*"/>
    <!-- Create an item so we can get full path -->
    <_ZipOutputPathItem Include="$(OutputPath)" />
  </ItemGroup>
  <!--
  Zip task requires that we have the full path
  to the working directory, so create an item
  from OutputPath to get that value.
  -->
  <PropertyGroup>
    <_ZipOutputPathFull>%(_ZipOutputPathItem.Fullpath)</_ZipOutputPathFull>
  </PropertyGroup>

  <!-- Get Date/Time to create unique .zip file name -->
  <MSBuild.ExtensionPack.Framework.DateAndTime
    TaskAction="Get"
    Format="ddMMyyyy_hh_ss">
    <Output TaskParameter="Result" PropertyName="_DateTime" />
  </MSBuild.ExtensionPack.Framework.DateAndTime>

  <ItemGroup>
    <_ZipFile Include="$(OutputPath)..\$(_DateTime)_outputs.zip" />
  </ItemGroup>
```

```
  <MSBuild.Community.Tasks.Zip
    Files="@(_FilesToZip->'%(FullPath)')"
    WorkingDirectory="$(_ZipOutputPathFull)"
    ZipFileName="@(_ZipFile)" />
  <Message Text="OutputPath: $(OutputPath)" />
</Target>
```

Notice that this target has declared that it depends on the Build target, so it will be executed before this target is allowed to begin. The item _FilesToZip is created to contain all the files that should be placed in the zip file. In order to create a unique zip file name, the current date and time will be a part of the zip file name. To get this value the DateAndTime task is used. Then the Zip task is used to create the zip file. Note that the WorkingDirectory is set to the **full path** of the OutputPath folder. This is necessary to create the zip file with the correct hierarchy. The resulting zip file is written to disk in the location contained in the _ZipFile item. Now that the file has been zipped, all that is left is to transfer the file using ftp. The related elements are shown next.

```
<PropertyGroup>
  <FtpFilesDependsOn>
    $(FtpFilesDependsOn);
    Build;
    BeforeFtpFiles;
    ValidateFtpFilesSettings;
    ZipOutputFiles;
    CoreFtpFiles;
    AfterFtpFiles;
  </FtpFilesDependsOn>
</PropertyGroup>
<Target Name="FtpFiles" DependsOnTargets="$(FtpFilesDependsOn)" />
<Target Name="CoreFtpFiles">
  <!-- Ensure _ZipFile is not empty -->
  <Error Condition="'@(_ZipFile)'==''"
         Text="_ZipFile is required" />

  <FtpUpload
    LocalFile="%(_ZipFile.FullPath)"
    RemoteUri="$(FtpRoot)%(_ZipFile.Filename)%(_ZipFile.Extension)"
    Username="$(FtpUsername)"
    Password="$(FtpPassword)"
    UsePassive="true"
    />
</Target>
<Target Name="BeforeFtpFiles" />
<Target Name="AfterFtpFiles" />

<Target Name="ValidateFtpFilesSettings">
  <Error Condition="'$(FtpHost)'==''"
          Text="FtpHost property is required" />
  <Error Condition="'$(FtpUsername)'==''"
         Text="FtpUsername property is required" />
  <Error Condition="'$(FtpPassword)'==''"
         Text="FtpPassword property is required" />
</Target>
```

The target being executed is the FtpFiles target, which depends on the targets contained in the FtpFilesDependsOn property. The main targets contained in that list are: Build, ValidateFtpFilesSettings, ZipOutputFiles, and CoreFtpFiles. The ValidateFtpFilesSettings target ensures that the properties FtpHost, FtpUsername, and FtpPassword are declared. In this example they are passed in to MSBuild from the command line using the /p switch. In the CoreFtp target the FtpUpload task is used to perform the actual upload. You could execute this target using the command `msbuild WebApplication1_ftp01.csproj_deploy.wdproj /t:FtpFiles /fl /p:FtpHost=FTP_HOST;FtpUsernameFTP_USERNAME;ftpPassword= FTP_PASSWORD.` The UPPER_CASE values are values provided by you.

In this chapter, we have introduced the Web Deployment Projects. Some limitations and work-arounds of the WDPs were discussed. Following that, we have covered a few examples that you may be able to use in your current build and deployment process for Web applications. This chapter concludes the MSBuild material. Starting in the next chapter, we'll begin our discussion of Team Foundation Build.

Compressing JavaScript Files

If your Web applications are deploying JavaScript files, then you should process those files through a JavaScript compressor before they are placed on the IIS server. A freely available one, JSMin, can be found at *http://www.crockford.com/javascript/jsmin.html*. JSMin offers significant compression results without modifying the actual source that is executed. Instead it performs noninvasive operations such as: remove comments and remove unnecessary white space. The JSCompress task available as a part of the MSBuildCommunityTasks incorporates JSMin to compress JavaScript files.

The WebApplication1 project from the samples includes a Scripts folder that contains some JavaScript source files. These files were taken from the open source Dojo project, which is available at *http://dojotoolkit.org*. To demonstrate compressing JavaScript take a look at the WDP named WebApplication1_javascript.csproj_deploy.wdproj, which will automatically compress JavaScript files if the Configuration is set to Release. The additions that were made to the file are shown next.

```
<PropertyGroup>
  <!-- aspnet_regiis.exe requires a path without the trailing slash -->
  <_OutputPathNoTrailingSlash>Out_JS01\$(Configuration)</_OutputPathNoTrailingSlash>
  <!-- Customize output location using the OutputPath property -->
  <OutputPath>$(_OutputPathNoTrailingSlash)\</OutputPath>
  <_WebProject>$(SourceWebPhysicalPath)\WebApplication1.csproj</_WebProject>
  <ContribRoot>..\..\BUILD\GenericBuild\Contrib\</ContribRoot>
</PropertyGroup>

  <!-- JSCompress task is contained in MSBuildCommunityTasks -->
<Import
  Project="$(ContribRoot)MSBuildCommunityTasks\MSBuild.Community.Tasks.targets" />
```

```
<PropertyGroup>
  <BuildDependsOn>
  BuildWebProject;
  $(BuildDependsOn);
  CompressJavascript
</BuildDependsOn>
  <EnableJSCompress
    Condition="'$(EnableJSCompress)' == ''
    AND
    '$(Configuration)' == 'Release'">true</EnableJSCompress>
</PropertyGroup>
<Target Name="CompressJavascript">
  <ItemGroup>
    <_JSFilesToCompress Include="$(OutputPath)Scripts\**\*.js" />
  </ItemGroup>
  <Message Text="Compresing Javascript files"
           Condition="'$(EnableJSCompress)' == 'true'" Importance="high" />
  <Message Text="NOT compresing Javascript files"
           Condition="'$(EnableJSCompress)' != 'true'" Importance="high" />
  <JSCompress
    Files="@(_JSFilesToCompress)"
    Condition="'$(EnableJSCompress)' == 'true'" />
</Target>
```

In this sample, the property EnableJSCompress is created and given the default value of true when building the Release configuration. Note that if a value already exists for EnableJSCompress, then it is not overwritten. In this way we can provide a default without overriding any preexisting value. The CompressJavaScript target uses the JSCompress task to compress the JavaScript files contained in the Scripts folder. The available parameters for that task are summarized in Table 9-4.

TABLE 9-4 JSCompress Task Parameters

Name	Description
Files	Input parameter that will contain the list of files to be compressed.
CompressedFiles	Output container containing the list of files that were compressed.
Encoding	The encoding of the files.

In this example, we pass the JavaScript files into the Files parameter using the _JSFilesToCompress item. If you execute the command `msbuild WebApplication1_javascript01.csproj_deploy .wdproj /p:Configuration=Release` then at the end of the build you will notice what is shown in Figure 9-4.

Because of the usage of the JSCompress task, the size of the JavaScript files was reduced from 74.4 Kb to 30.5 Kb. Since Web sites are using more and more JavaScript, compressing the source files will become more important. It is recommended that you allow developers to edit human-friendly files while at the same time automating your deployments to compress the JavaScript files as shown here.

```
  Copying file from ".\TempBuildDir\\Scripts\readme.txt" to "C:\Data\MSBuildExa
  mples\WEB\WebApplication1.csproj_deploy\Out_JS01\Release\\Scripts\readme.txt"
  .
  Updating Web.config <compilation> element debug attribute to 'False'.
  Successfully updated Web.config <compilation> element debug attribute to 'Fal
  se'.
CompressJavascript:
  Compresing Javascript files
  Compressing JavaScript in "Out_JS01\Release\Scripts\back.js".
  Compressing JavaScript in "Out_JS01\Release\Scripts\date.js".
  Compressing JavaScript in "Out_JS01\Release\Scripts\fx.js".
  Compressing JavaScript in "Out_JS01\Release\Scripts\html.js".
  Compressing JavaScript in "Out_JS01\Release\Scripts\i18n.js".
  Compressing JavaScript in "Out_JS01\Release\Scripts\number.js".
Done Building Project "C:\Data\MSBuildExamples\WEB\WebApplication1.csproj_deplo
y\WebApplication1_javascript01.csproj_deploy.wdproj" (default targets).

Build succeeded.
    0 Warning(s)
    0 Error(s)
```

FIGURE 9-4 CompressJavaScript example

Encrypting web.config

There is a built-in tool that you can use to encrypt sections of your web.config file. This tool is aspnet_regiis.exe and it ships with the .NET Framework. It was introduced in .NET 2.0. This tool can be used for many different purposes; in this section we will limit the discussion to using it to encrypt the web.config file.

When a section of the web.config file, or machine.config for that matter, is encrypted using the aspnet_regiis.exe tool, it is done such that the section will be decrypted on the fly during the lifetime of the Web application. The encryption is transparent to the application code. When you use aspnet_regiis.exe to encrypt the configuration file, you will use the -pef switch to indicate what section needs to be encrypted. In this example, we will also use a WDP, an extension of those previously discussed. The WDP file for this example can be found in the WebApplication1_encWebConfig.csproj_deploy.wdproj file. The customizations that were made to the file are shown in the following snippet.

```
<PropertyGroup>
   <!-- aspnet_regiis.exe requires a path without the trailing slash -->
  <_OutputPathNoTrailingSlash>Out_Enc01\$(Configuration)</_OutputPathNoTrailingSlash>
  <!-- Customize output location using the OutputPath property -->
  <OutputPath>$(_OutputPathNoTrailingSlash)\</OutputPath>
  <_WebProject>$(SourceWebPhysicalPath)\WebApplication1.csproj</_WebProject>
</PropertyGroup>

<PropertyGroup>
  <BuildDependsOn>
    BuildWebProject;
    $(BuildDependsOn);
    EncryptWebConfig
  </BuildDependsOn>
</PropertyGroup>
<Target Name="EncryptWebConfig">
  <!-- Get the .NET 2.0 path -->
  <GetFrameworkPath>
    <Output PropertyName="_Net20Path" TaskParameter="FrameworkVersion20Path" />
  </GetFrameworkPath>
```

```
  <PropertyGroup>
    <_AspNetRegIisExe>&quot;$(_Net20Path)\aspnet_regiis.exe&quot;</_AspNetRegIisExe>
    <_pef>-pef &quot;connectionStrings&quot;</_pef>
    <_out>&quot;$(_OutputPathNoTrailingSlash)&quot;</_out>
  </PropertyGroup>
  <Exec Command="$(_AspNetRegIisExe) $(_pef) $(_out)"/>
</Target>
```

As you can see, the build process was extended by injecting the EncryptWebConfig target to the end of the BuildDependsOn target. Inside that target, the GetFrameworkPath task is used to determine where the .NET 2.0 Framework is installed. The properties for that task, which are all outputs, are summarized in Table 9-5.

TABLE 9-5 GetFrameworkPath Parameters

Name	Description
FrameworkVersion11Path	Returns the path for the .NET 1.1 assemblies.
FrameworkVersion20Path	Returns the path for the .NET 2.0 assemblies.
FrameworkVersion30Path	Returns the path for the .NET 3.0 assemblies.
FrameworkVersion35Path	Returns the path for the .NET 3.5 assemblies.
Path	Returns the path for the .NET assemblies being used for the build process.

This example uses the GetFrameworkPath task to determine where .NET 2.0 is installed because the aspnet_regiss.exe is located in that directory. After that the following command is executed.

```
"%Framework2.0%\aspnet_regiis.exe" -pef "connectionStrings"
"C:\Data\MSBuildExamples\WEB\WebApplication1.csproj_deploy\Out_04\Debug".
```

Following that, the original connectionStrings node from the web.config is transformed into

```
<connectionStrings configProtectionProvider="RsaProtectedConfigurationProvider">
  <EncryptedData Type="http://www.w3.org/2001/04/xmlenc#Element"
    xmlns="http://www.w3.org/2001/04/xmlenc#">
    <EncryptionMethod Algorithm="http://www.w3.org/2001/04/xmlenc#tripledes-cbc" />
    <KeyInfo xmlns="http://www.w3.org/2000/09/xmldsig#">
      <EncryptedKey xmlns="http://www.w3.org/2001/04/xmlenc#">
        <EncryptionMethod Algorithm="http://www.w3.org/2001/04/xmlenc#rsa-1_5" />
        <KeyInfo xmlns="http://www.w3.org/2000/09/xmldsig#">
          <KeyName>Rsa Key</KeyName>
        </KeyInfo>
        <CipherData>
          <CipherValue>jHA75XUfC9PK7dyN4nSZZV1jNsTYfOS2BUudEmo8Fl3+vAYxRDkowZJ/g4wU
            hJanj2HCa1nhwHKfBZvaHmlQej9nYnsssYg3vOr89LvAkHoXz4fUclg6ywjWYkyvadqyBog
            S1GRsdwLhtGRgdkeF6I76w40o9wCOkxolFYYara4=</CipherValue>
        </CipherData>
      </EncryptedKey>
    </KeyInfo>
```

```
    <CipherData>
      <CipherValue>YyzhkAEVtYsWIykmXZJqzXeDvVJNGKX/Xk6hcWA+dcITBM/4qYKsBoxx2nn69iEa
      /5hvSoOX1UQFe6fF5YuiziHYOI+n7TNKUJbAt4SIHOwGZYIy72Mbkjw7lmEEPXR01YymocZtnlPbi
      aagNscvuLOoSvfR1zFrb4JNHuUwgIQFjeq3lEMGNzThuqoPjl+Csgmgrbc6EVx9C5jubfUSLiW8UZ
      /raVTu2cHVk+HsljOtwkIUkP6CkcPRiGA3wvfjI1+KMfUaBB5IRIXljjQV2cObgQbgcyZTzA3jyR3
      fSOXpKZzHJ3IYvnOFXTpY/TfB7fHPEg8xOyHZ43cMlf2hCcdlO4RteWT9jSX3rNbvZCS8Y2/81qJH
      AYbZUft1KRgQwLSB/KDep6g=</CipherValue>
    </CipherData>
  </EncryptedData>
</connectionStrings>
```

Now the connection strings have been encrypted. You can encrypt several other sections of the web.config as well. You should encrypt only the sections that contain sensitive information, because encrypted sections do carry a performance penalty when being used by the application. If you are encrypting the web.config on a build server then you have to make sure that the machine key is the same for the build server as the IIS server, otherwise the section(s) will not be successfully unencrypted.

Building Dependent Projects

If you are using a Web Application Project (WAP) as opposed to a Web site, then there is one major flaw in the process followed by the Microsoft.WebDeployment.targets file. The WAP is never built; it is assumed to have already been built. In the case of this example, if the WebApplication1 project was not built and you executed the command `msbuild WebApplication1_01.csproj_deploy.wdproj` the result would be what is shown in Figure 9-5.

```
C:\Data\MSBuildExamples\WEB\WebApplication1.csproj_deploy>msbuild WebApplication
1_01.csproj_deploy.wdproj /fl /nologo
Build started 9/28/2008 3:10:59 PM.
Project "C:\Data\MSBuildExamples\WEB\WebApplication1.csproj_deploy\WebApplicati
on1_01.csproj_deploy.wdproj" on node 0 (default targets).
/WebApplication1.csproj/UserControls/MyCustomUserControl.ascx(1): error ASPPARS
E: Could not load type 'WebApplication1.UserControls.MyCustomUserControl'.
Done Building Project "C:\Data\MSBuildExamples\WEB\WebApplication1.csproj_deplo
y\WebApplication1_01.csproj_deploy.wdproj" (default targets) -- FAILED.


Build FAILED.

"C:\Data\MSBuildExamples\WEB\WebApplication1.csproj_deploy\WebApplication1_01.c
sproj_deploy.wdproj" (default target) (1) ->
(AspNetCompiler target) ->
  /WebApplication1.csproj/UserControls/MyCustomUserControl.ascx(1): error ASPPA
RSE: Could not load type 'WebApplication1.UserControls.MyCustomUserControl'.

    0 Warning(s)
    1 Error(s)
```

FIGURE 9-5 Web Deployment Project failure

Since the WAP is not being built, the AspNetCompiler task fails because it was unable to load a user control that was contained inside the WAP. In order to work around this problem we will have to build the WAP. Additionally we must build the WAP **before** the _CopyBeforeBuild target is executed; otherwise, a copy of the Web files will be created that doesn't contain the built assemblies. Take a look at the following definition of the BuildDependsOn property from Microsoft.WebDeployment.targets.

```
<PropertyGroup>
    <BuildDependsOn>
      _PrepareForBuild;
      _SplitProjectReferencesByType;
```

```
      _ResolveReferences;
      _ResolveProjectReferences;
      ResolveAssemblyReferences;
      _CopyBeforeBuild;
      BeforeBuild;
      AspNetCompiler;
      BeforeMerge;
      AspNetMerge;
      AfterMerge;
      CopyToOutputDir;
      ReplaceWebConfigSections;
      CreateVirtualDirectory;
      AfterBuild
    </BuildDependsOn>
</PropertyGroup>
```

The important thing to notice here is that the BeforeBuild target is positioned **after** the _CopyBeforeBuild target in the dependency list. We cannot use the BeforeBuild target to build the WAP because it needs to be built prior to the copy step. Instead we have to extend the BuildDependsOn property and inject that step at the very beginning. The WebApplication1_03 .csproj_deploy.wdproj demonstrates this, and the snippet is shown next.

```
<PropertyGroup>
   <!-- Customize output location using the OutputPath property -->
  <OutputPath>Out_03\$(Configuration)\</OutputPath>
  <_WebProject>$(SourceWebPhysicalPath)\WebApplication1.csproj</_WebProject>
</PropertyGroup>

<PropertyGroup>
  <BuildDependsOn>
    BuildWebProject;
    $(BuildDependsOn)
  </BuildDependsOn>
</PropertyGroup>

<Target Name="BuildWebProject">
  <MSBuild
    Projects="$(_WebProject)"
    Properties="Configuration=$(Configuration);Platform=$(Platform)" />
</Target>
```

In this file, the BuildDependsOn property has been prepended to contain the BuildWebProject target, which builds the WAP. Now that these customizations have been created, the WAP is not assumed to have been built and each time the WDP project is built the WAP will be built ensuring that it is up to date with respect to the source files. When you are building the solution file you do not have to worry about this because Visual Studio will build the projects in the correct order.

Extending the Clean Process

In an ideal world, extending the clean process would be exactly the same as that shown in the previous chapter. That is, target names would be added to the CleanDependsOn target and the targets would be called automatically when the project was cleaned. Unfortunately, this approach will not work when using WDP. In the following snippet, you will see the definition of the Clean target first from Microsoft.Common.targets (which C# and VB .NET projects use) followed by the Clean target taken from Microsoft.WebDeployment.targets.

```
<!-- From Microsoft.Common.targets -->
<Target
    Name="Clean"
    Condition=" '$(_InvalidConfigurationWarning)' != 'true' "
    DependsOnTargets="$(CleanDependsOn)" />

<!-- From Microsoft.WebDeployment.targets -->
<Target Name="Clean">
  <CreateProperty Value="true">
    <Output TaskParameter="Value" PropertyName="Clean" />
  </CreateProperty>
</Target>
```

The definition of the Clean target from the Microsoft.WebDeployment.targets is missing the critical attribute DependsOnTargets="$(CleanDependsOn)". Because of this we are not able to extend the behavior of the Clean target. You could redeclare the Clean target in your own WDP to include that attribute. This is not recommended because if the WDP team makes changes to the Microsoft.WebDeployment.targets file, you may have to change your WDP files. Instead you are left with creating another target, for example FullClean, which will properly clean the project.

From the previous example, WebApplication1_03.csproj_deploy.wdproj, we need a means to clean the Web project that we are building in the BuildWebProject. This can be accomplished by creating a target FullClean as follows.

```
<PropertyGroup>
  <FullCleanDependsOn>
    $(FullCleanDependsOn);
    Clean;
    CleanWebProject;
  </FullCleanDependsOn>
</PropertyGroup>

<Target Name="FullClean"
        DependsOnTargets="$(FullCleanDependsOn)" />

<Target Name="CleanWebProject">
  <MSBuild
    Projects="$(_WebProject)"
    Properties="Configuration=$(Configuration);Platform=$(Platform)"
    Targets="Clean" />
</Target>
```

In the FullClean target the dependency property, FullCleanDependsOn, is declared to include the Clean target as well as the CleanWebProject. When the project is to be cleaned completely, the FullClean target needs to be called. When creating C# or VB .NET projects, the Clean target is automatically called when the Rebuild target is executed. It would be great if we could have the Rebuild target call the new FullClean target by extending the RebuildDependsOn property as we would for C# or VB .NET projects. Again this will not work for WDPs. As previously mentioned, you will see the definition of the Rebuild target first from Microsoft.Common.targets followed by the definition from Microsoft.WebDeployment.targets.

```
<!-- From Microsoft.Common.targets -->
<Target
    Name="Rebuild"
    Condition=" '$(_InvalidConfigurationWarning)' != 'true' "
    DependsOnTargets="$(RebuildDependsOn)"
    Outputs="$(TargetPath)" />

<!-- From Microsoft.WebDeployment.targets -->
<Target
    Name="Rebuild"
    DependsOnTargets="Clean;$(BuildDependsOn)">
</Target>
```

In this case the Rebuild target has declared the DependsOnTargets property by hard-coding the Clean target name in front the BuildDependsOn property value. The correct approach would have been to place those items in a new property RebuildDependsOn, so consumers could extend the Rebuild target. Since this is not the case you cannot inject the FullClean target into the Rebuild targets dependencies either.

Currently the Web Deployment Projects have some limitations regarding extensibility from consumers, but once you are aware of these limitations you can work around them. In a future version of Web Deployment Projects perhaps these limitations will be corrected. We'll now take a look at how we can further customize these projects.

Deployment Using Web Deployment Projects

There are many approaches to deploying your applications to various environments. In this sample, I'll demonstrate how you can extend the WDP to assist your deployment process. The approach I demonstrate is fairly simplistic and has some limitations, which we will discuss. The following target is taken from the WebApplication1_deploy01.csproj_deploy.wdproj file.

```
<Target Name="DeployToServer" DependsOnTargets="Build">
  <PropertyGroup>
    <_ServerName>sayed_762</_ServerName>
    <_VDirName>Sample01</_VDirName>
    <_ServerDeployPath>\\$(_ServerName)\D$\Stage\$(_VDirName)\</_ServerDeployPath>
    <_ServerLocalPath>D:\Stage\$(_VDirName)\</_ServerLocalPath>
    <_ReplaceExisting>true</_ReplaceExisting>
  </PropertyGroup>

  <!-- Create dir if it doesn't exist -->
  <MakeDir Directories="$(_ServerDeployPath)" />
```

```
  <!-- Copy files -->
  <ItemGroup>
    <_FilesToDeploy
      Include="$(OutputPath)**\*"
      Exclude="$(OutputPath)obj\**\*;$(OutputPath)bin\Samples\**\*" />
  </ItemGroup>

  <Message Text="Copying files to remote server [$(_ServerName)]" />
  <Copy SourceFiles="@(_FilesToDeploy)"
        DestinationFiles=
        "@(_FilesToDeploy->'$(_ServerDeployPath)%(RecursiveDir)%(Filename)%(Extension)')" />

  <CreateVirtualDirectory
    Alias = "$(_VDirName)"
    ServerName ="$(_ServerName)"
    Path = "$(_ServerLocalPath)"
    ReplaceExisting = "$(_ReplaceExisting)" />

</Target>
```

The first thing to notice about the DeployToServer target is that it depends on the Build target. In this target a few properties are first declared that will be used throughout the target. The _ServerName property contains the name of the server that the application is to be deployed to. After the properties are declared, the destination folder is created, if it doesn't already exist, by using the MakeDir task. Then a set of files is copied to the server. Finally the CreateVirtualDirectory task is used to create a virtual directory on the remote machine. The properties of this task are summarized in Table 9-6.

TABLE 9-6 CreateVirtualDirectory Task Parameters

Name	Description
Alias	Required parameter that contains the name of the Virtual Directory to create.
Path	Required parameter that contains the location where the virtual directory will point. This should be a path used on the remote machine, not a path relative to the build machine. For instance D:\Stage\Sample01 and not \\sayed-762\D$\Stage\Sample01.

MetabaseProperties	Any additional metabase properties that should be set can be passed here. The name of the property should be placed in the Include attribute and the value of the property as metadata named Value. For example, the item type VirtualDirectoryMetabaseProperties can be used for this.
	`<ItemGroup>`
	`  <VirtualDirectoryMetabaseProperties`
	`     Include="EnableDirBrowsing">`
	`    <value>true</value>`
	`  </VirtualDirectoryMetabaseProperties>`
	`  <VirtualDirectoryMetabaseProperties`
	`     Include="AccessWrite">`
	`    <value>true</value>`
	`  </VirtualDirectoryMetabaseProperties>`
	`</ItemGroup>`

TABLE 9-6 CreateVirtualDirectory Task Parameters

Name	Description
ReplaceExisting	If set to true, then this will allow any existing virtual directory to be replaced. The default value for this is false.
ServerName	Name of the server on which the virtual directory is being created. This defaults to "localhost."
SiteId	The ID for the Web site on which the virtual directory will be installed. The default value for this is 1. Typically you have to worry about this only if your IIS server is hosting multiple Web sites.

In the example shown previously, the CreateVirtualDirectory task is used to create a virtual directory named Sample01 on the server sayed_762. The contents of this virtual directory are placed at D:\stage\Sample01 on the IIS server. When the command `msbuild WebApplication1_deploy01.csproj_deploy.wdproj /t:DeployToServer` was executed, the files were copied to the remote server and the virtual directory was created.

This sample shows how you can deploy a Web application to a remote server. Every deployment process is different and each has its own pros and cons. This should get you started with your own deployment process. This approach has the following limitations:

- The process running the build must have Administrator rights to the IIS server.
- IIS must have read/write access to the folder where the files are being placed.
- Copying files one by one can be very slow.
- If you encrypt the web.config on the build machine you must make sure that the machine key is the same on the build server as the IIS server.

Because of these limitations this exact approach may not suit your needs, but this should not prevent you from creating your own deployment process using the Web Deployment Projects.

Part V
Team Foundation Build

In this part:

Chapter 10

Team Build Quick Start

MSBuild is a build engine rather than a build automation tool, which is where Team Foundation Build (referred to as Team Build for short) comes in to the picture. Team Build is a component of Microsoft's application life-cycle management tool called Visual Studio Team System. Team Build provides build automation that integrates tightly with the other Visual Studio Team System components such as version control, work-item tracking, testing, and reporting.

Why discuss Team Build in a book primarily about MSBuild? Apart from both being build tools, the good news is that Team Build also uses MSBuild project files to define the build process, so the MSBuild knowledge you've gained in the previous chapters will allow you to extend and customize Team Build's default build process.

Introduction to Team Build

This section discusses the features and architecture of Team Build to familiarize you with its key components and how they relate. These features and components are covered in more depth in later sections.

Team Build Features

Team Build 2008 has a comprehensive set of features that should meet the needs of almost all build automation requirements, and even if it doesn't, it is highly configurable and extensible.

Some of the key features in Team Build 2008 are as follows:

- Provides a default build process suitable for building most .NET applications
- Build process is based on MSBuild and is highly configurable and extensible
- Supports queuing of builds and multiple build machines
- Supports manual, scheduled, and continuous integration builds
- Retention policies for removing old builds
- Integrates with reporting, testing, version control, and work item tracking components of Visual Studio Team System
- Includes an API for automating, extending, and integrating with Team Build

High-Level Architecture

Because Team Build is a component of Visual Studio Team System, it uses an architecture similar to the other components in Visual Studio Team System. A high-level diagram of Team Build's architecture is shown in Figure 10-1.

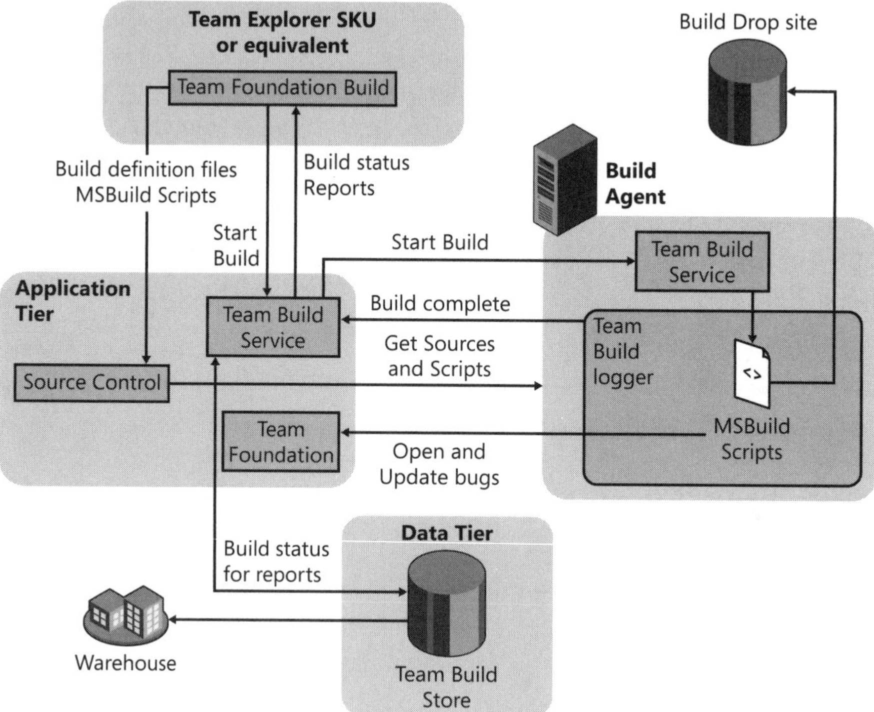

FIGURE 10-1 High-level architecture
Source: MSDN, Team Foundation Build Overview.

The Team Build architecture includes:

- **Team Build client** Visual Studio Team System provides a number of out-of-the-box clients for Team Build, including Team Explorer, which is an add-in for Visual Studio, TfsBuild.exe, which is a command-line client for Team Build, and Team System Web Access, which is a Web interface for Team Build (and other components of Visual Studio Team System). Team Build also has an API that can be used to develop your own clients for Team Build, and that will be discussed in Chapter 11, "Team Build Deep Dive."
- **Build agents** These are machines that will execute the build process. Any machine that has the Team Build service installed on it can be used as a build agent, but a build agent can be associated with only one Team Foundation Server Application Tier (although a Team Foundation Server Application Tier can be associated with multiple build agents).

- **Team Foundation Server application tier** Any Team Build client that wants to communicate with Team Build or with a Build agent does so through Team Foundation Server's application tier. The application tier is implemented as a number of Web services in the Internet Information Server.
- **Team Foundation Server data tier** The data tier for Team Foundation Server is hosted as a number of relational databases in SQL Server. From a Team Build perspective there are two key relational databases, TFSBuild and TFSWarehouse, although Team Build also interacts with databases from other Visual Studio Team System components such as testing, version control, and work item tracking.
- **TFSBuild database** This database stores operational build data such as the list of build agents, build definitions, build queues, build history, etc.
- **TFSWarehouse database** This database stores historical build data for reporting even after it has been purged from the TFSBuild database.
- **Team System cube** This multidimensional OLAP cube is implemented in SQL Server Analysis Services and is populated regularly from the TFSWarehouse database for high-performance reporting.
- **Drop folder** When a build completes the build logs, build outputs (if the build is successful or partially successful) and test results are copied to a shared network folder.

Preparing for Team Build

In this section, we're going to look at the preparations you'll need to make to set up the necessary infrastructure before you start automating your build processes using Team Build.

Build Agents

Assuming you've already set up your Team Foundation Server, the first step is to set up build agents to execute your builds. A build agent is simply a machine that has the Team Build service installed on it.

Although it's technically possible to install Team Build on the same machine as Team Foundation Server, this is not recommended for a number of reasons:

- Compiling software is particularly resource-intensive, and this could be detrimental to the performance of Team Foundation Server.
- Build scripts and unit tests might be written by people who aren't Team Foundation Server administrators, and having these running on the Team Foundation Server could compromise its security, integrity, and stability.
- Build scripts and the projects being compiled often require third-party software or libraries to be installed on the build agent, and installing these on the Team Foundation Server could also compromise its security, integrity, and stability.

Tip The only time you should consider installing Team Build on the same machine as Team Foundation Server is when building a virtual machine for demonstration or testing purposes where it is not practical to have a separate virtual machine acting as the build agent.

What Makes a Good Build Agent?

Now that you've decided that it's not a good idea to install Team Build on your Team Foundation Server, you have to decide where it should be installed. You should take a few factors into account:

- Build agents should be kept as simple as possible. Even minor changes on a build agent can affect the outcome of a build, and if the configuration of a build agent is complex then it increases the chance of discrepancies if a build agent needs to be rebuilt, when adding additional build agents, or when reproducing an old build.
- Build agents should be build agents and nothing else. Running other services on the build agent contradicts the rule that they should be as simple as possible but also results in Team Build having to compete with the other services for resources.
- Builds usually have to read a large amount of data (the source files) from the Team Foundation Server and write a large amount of data (the build outputs) to the drop folder. Because of this the build agent should have fast network access to both of these locations. In Chapter 12, we look at how to configure Team Build to use the Team Foundation Proxy to improve performance when the build agent has limited bandwidth to the Team Foundation Server.
- The build agent needs sufficient disk space to store a copy of the source code and build outputs for each build definition. You should also allow additional disk space for any temporary files during the build process.
- Team Build 2008 has the ability to take advantage of the parallel build functionality introduced in MSBuild 3.5 so multiple processors can improve the performance of your builds.

Although developers can perform builds locally using the Desktop Build functionality, which is discussed later in this chapter, there might be circumstances where Team Build needs to be installed on developers' workstations. This can be particularly useful when developing, testing, and debugging build customizations or to allow developers to run full end-to-end builds on their local machine.

Setting Up a Build Agent

The Team Build installation process is quite simple, but it is recommended that you document the process you use to set up your first build agent so that the process can be repeated if you add additional build agents to your environment in the future.

Installing Prerequisites

Before installing Team Build, the following prerequisites need to be met. These are summarized in Table 10-1.

- You will need a domain account for the Team Build service to run if you choose not to use the NT AUTHORITY\NETWORK SERVICE account. This account doesn't need to be, and shouldn't be, an administrator on either the build agent or the Team Foundation Server, but it does need to be added to the Build Services group of each Team Project that it will execute builds for. See Team Build Security later in this chapter for more information about securing Team Build.
- To execute unit tests, code coverage, or code analysis as part of the build process you will need to install Microsoft Visual Studio Team System for Software Developers on the build agent.
- To execute unit tests compiled using the 8.0 unit testing framework (which shipped with Microsoft Visual Studio Team System 2005), you will need to install Microsoft Visual Studio 2005 for Software Developers.
- To execute automated tests other than unit tests as part of the build process, you will need to install Microsoft Visual Studio Team System for Software Testers on the build agent.
- To build projects that aren't based on MSBuild (such as Visual Studio Deployment Projects), you will need to install the appropriate edition of Microsoft Visual Studio that builds that project type on the build agent.
- You will need any other software or libraries required by your build process or the software you're building. This would include any utilities or MSBuild tasks called by your build process (such as the MSBuild Community Tasks) as well as any GAC references required by the projects you're building (such as the Microsoft Office primary interop assemblies).

TABLE 10-1 Summary of Team Build Prerequisites

Feature	Required Software
Code Analysis	Visual Studio Team System for Software Developers
Code Coverage	Visual Studio Team System for Software Developers
Database Projects	Visual Studio Team System for Database Professionals
Load Testing	Visual Studio Team System for Testers
MSBuild Project Types	.NET Framework SDK

TABLE 10-1 Summary of Team Build Prerequisites

Feature	Required Software
Non-MSBuild Project Types (e.g., Deployment Projects)	Any edition of Visual Studio able to build the specific project type
Third-Party Build Dependencies	The corresponding third-party software
Third-Party GAC References	The corresponding third-party software
Unit Testing	Visual Studio Team System for Software Developers
Running Visual Studio 2005 Unit Tests	Visual Studio Team System 2005 for Software Developers
Visual C++ Projects	Visual Studio
Web Testing	Visual Studio Team System for Testers

Installing Team Build

When installing any Team Foundation Server component, you should download and refer to the latest version of the Team Foundation Server Installation Guide from *http://go.microsoft.com/fwlink/?LinkId=79226*.

The installation process for Team Build is quite simple:

1. Insert the installation media.
2. Select Team Foundation Build from the Team Foundation Server Setup page.
3. Follow the installation wizard.
4. Add the Team Build service account to the Team Project's Build Services security group. Instructions on how to do this can be found in "Team Build Security" later in this chapter.

Note There is one page of the installation wizard that is a little misleading. When you are prompted for the Team Foundation Server Service Account, you are actually being prompted for the domain account to run the Team Build service as, not the Team Foundation Server service account. These should never be the same account; see "Team Build Security" later in this chapter for more information about selecting a Team Build service account and securing Team Build.

Adding the Build Agent to Team Projects

Once Team Build has been installed on a machine, you still need to add the machine as a build agent to each Team Project that is allowed to submit builds to it. This gives you the flexibility of having different build agents for different Team Projects, but you can still add a single build agent to multiple Team Projects.

To add the build agent to a Team Project, do this:

1. Open Microsoft Visual Studio 2008.
2. Open Team Explorer.

3. Expand the Team Project.
4. Right-click Builds, and click Manage Build Agents. This will open the Manage Build Agents dialog shown in Figure 10-2.

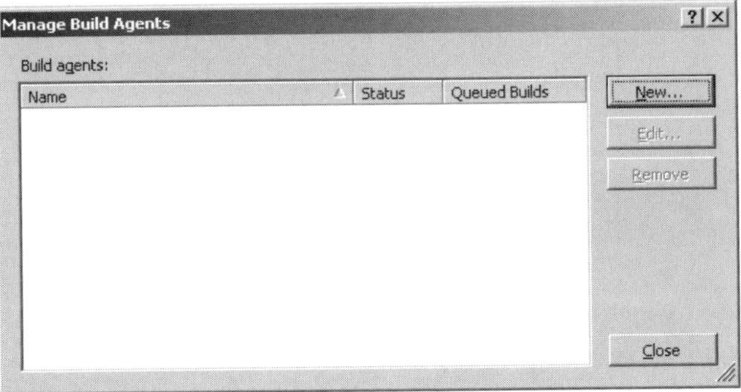

FIGURE 10-2 Manage Build Agents dialog box

5. Click New to open the Build Agent Properties dialog box shown in Figure 10-3.

FIGURE 10-3 Build Agent Properties dialog box

The Display Name and Description fields are used to describe the build agent to developers when working with build queues and history.

The Computer Name field is the host name of the build agent. This will be used by Team Build to communicate with the build agent so the Computer Name should be resolvable from the Team Foundation Server application tier. The Communications Port and Require Secure Channel (HTTPS) fields are used to customize how the Team Foundation Server application tier communicates with the build agent, which is discussed in Chapter 11.

The Working Directory field allows you to specify which directory on the build agent will be used as the working directory during the build. This default working directory is

$(Temp)\$(BuildDefinitionPath), which will use a subdirectory of the Team Build service account's temporary directory named after the Team Project and build definition.

For example, if you have a Team Project called Contoso with a build definition called HelloWorldManual and your Team Build service account is TFSBUILD, then the working directory would be C:\Documents and Settings\TFSBUILD\Local Settings\Temp\Contoso\HelloWorldManual.

You might want to modify the working directory in these scenarios:

- If your build agent has multiple disk partitions, you might want to change the working directory to use one of the additional disk partitions—for example, E:\$(BuildDefinitionPath).
- If the source code or build outputs have a particularly deep directory structure or particularly long file names, you may want to use a shorter path—for example, C:\Build\$(BuildDefinitionId). This is particularly important when building database projects whose naming conventions result in very long filenames.

You should always include $(BuildDefinitionPath) or $(BuildDefinitionId) in your working directory so that multiple build definitions can exist side by side in the build agent's working directory. The properties available in the Working Directory field are listed in Table 10-2.

TABLE 10-2 Working Directory MSBuild Properties

Variable Name	Description
BuildDefinitionPath	Contains the Team Project Name and the Build Definition Name. For example, Contoso\HelloWorldManual.
BuildDefinitionId	Contains the integer identifier for the Build Definition in the Team Build database.
Environment Variable Properties	Each environment variable on the build agent is available as an MSBuild property. For example, $(Temp) expands to C:\Documents and Settings\TFSBUILD\Local Settings\Temp\ if the Team Build service account is TFSBUILD.

The default status of a build agent is Enabled and in this state developers can queue builds on the build agent and it will process them. In the Disabled state, builds can still be queued on the build agent but they won't be processed until its status is changed to Enabled.

The Initializing and Unreachable states are usually set by Team Build automatically when the build agent is still in the process of starting up or can't be reached. If a build agent is in one of the states for a long period of time you may need to manually change the build agent's status back to Enabled for it to start processing builds again.

Finally, the Default button resets the Communications Port, Require Secure Channel (HTTPS), and Working Directory fields back to their default values.

Drop Folder

The final piece of infrastructure that needs to be in place before you create a build definition is a drop folder for the build agent to drop the build logs, build outputs, and test results into.

Because a Team Build environment may have multiple build agents, the drop folder is typically located on a separate network share that all the build agents use. This means that developers, testers, etc. can access the drops from a single central location.

The drop folder is typically a share on a file server of some description but it could just as easily be a Network Attached Storage device or some other shared storage device. There are only a few requirements for the drop folder:

- It must be accessible via a UNC path from all of the build agents.
- The Team Build service account must have Full Control permission to it. This is required for the build agent to be able to drop the build logs and outputs.
- The Team Foundation Server service account must have Full Control permission to it. This is required for developers, testers, or the build process to publish test results.
- It must have sufficient space available to store the number of builds retained by the retention policies you define.

Tip There is nothing worse than builds failing simply because there is not enough space available in the drop location, especially because you don't find this out until the very end of the build process. It is recommended that you set up monitoring of the available space in the drop location so that you are alerted if it falls below a threshold.

Creating a Build Definition

Now that the necessary infrastructure is in place, you can create your first build definition. Build definitions define the information required to execute a build, such as what should be built, what triggers a build, and how long these builds should be retained.

To create a new build definition:

1. Open Microsoft Visual Studio 2008.
2. Open Team Explorer.
3. Expand the Team Project.
4. Right-click Builds, and click New Build Definition.

General

The General tab shown in Figure 10-4 allows you to name the build definition and optionally describe it. The description is displayed when a developer queues the build, so this can be useful to communicate additional information about what the build definition is for.

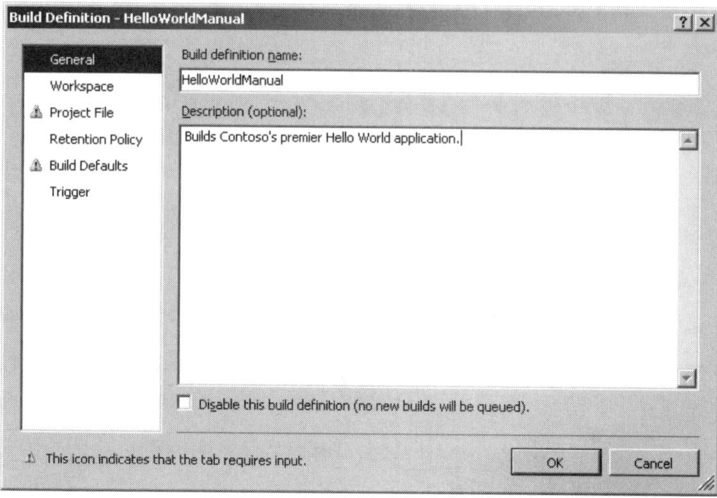

FIGURE 10-4 Build Definition: General

You can also temporarily disable the build definition from here as well, which can be used to prevent developers from queuing builds for obsolete or archived build definitions without having to delete the build definition.

Tip Since the build definition name is often used from the command line and as a part of the build agent's working directory path, it is recommended that you minimize the length of the name (to avoid exceeding maximum path lengths) and avoid unnecessary special characters, including spaces.

Workspace

The Workspace tab shown in Figure 10-5 allows you to define which version control folders Team Build will get to execute the build. You can specify multiple folders to get by adding additional working folder mappings with a status of Active, or you can prevent Team Build from getting a folder by changing the status of the mapping from Active to Cloak, as demonstrated in Figure 10-6, which downloads the Source and Docs folders but not the Docs/Mockups folder.

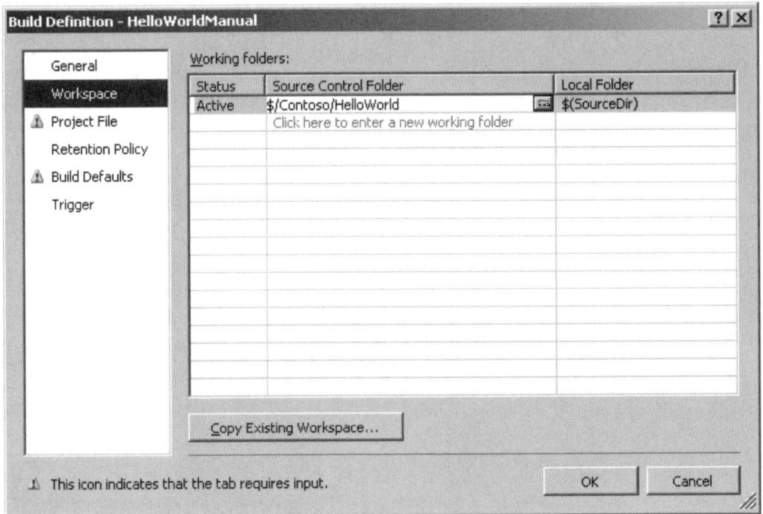

FIGURE 10-5 Build Definition: Workspace

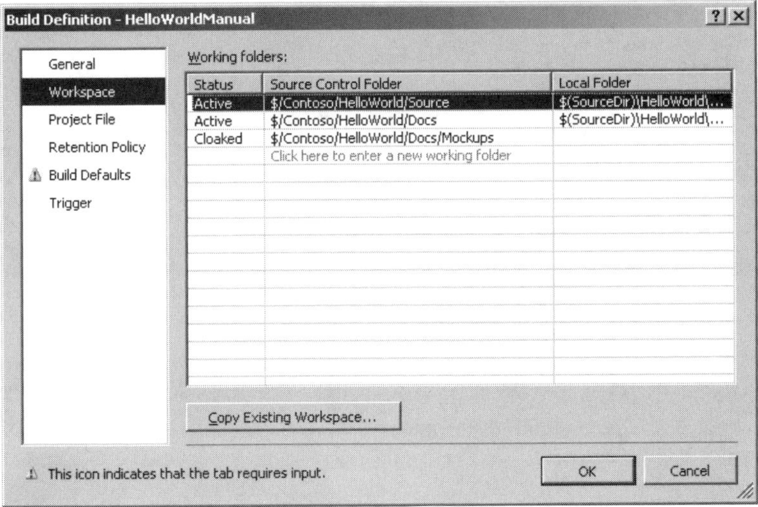

FIGURE 10-6 Build Definition: Workspace (multiple working folders)

By default, any additional mapping you add will be mapped to a local folder with the same name as the source control folder, or you can override this by changing the value in the Local Folder column.

If one of the developers already has a workspace that contains the necessary working folder mappings, you can click the Copy Existing Workspace button to copy the mappings from that workspace into the build definition.

Tip The default working folder mapping in the Workspace tab will download all of the files in the Team Project. If the Team Project contains a large number of files and folders that aren't needed by a build definition, you can significantly improve its performance by mapping only the required folders or by cloaking folders that aren't required.

Project File

Build definitions are linked to an MSBuild project file called TFSBuild.proj that defines the solutions and configurations to be built as well as other build options such as code analysis and testing. This MSBuild project file is also used to customize the Team Build process, which is discussed in detail in Chapter 11.

The Project File tab shown in Figure 10-7 allows you to reuse an existing project file by clicking Browse or create a new TFSBuild.proj project file by clicking Create.

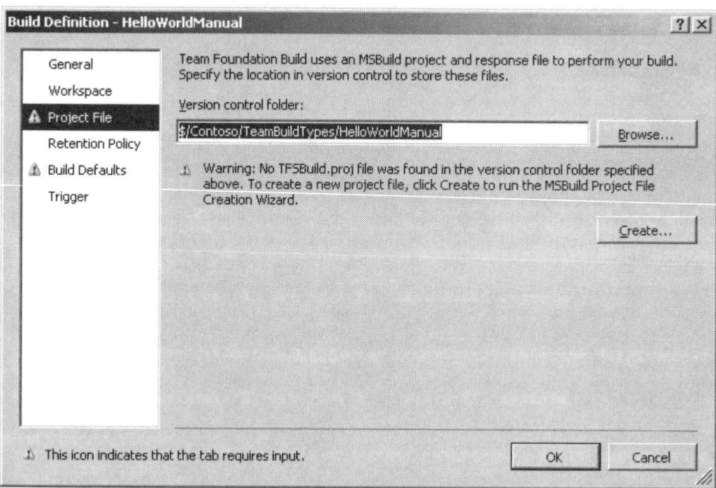

FIGURE 10-7 Build Definition: Project File

Creating a New Project File

The Selections tab shown in Figure 10-8 lists all of the solution files (*.sln) found in the workspace defined on the Workspace tab. You can select multiple solutions, but if there are build order dependencies between them you will need to use the up and down arrows to arrange the solutions into the order that they should be built.

The Configurations tab shown in Figure 10-9 allows you to specify what configurations and platforms should be built for the selected solutions. If you specify multiple entries, then the solutions will be built multiple times, once per entry, and the build outputs placed in separate subfolders of the drop folder. In this example, the solution will be built four times and the build outputs placed in the subfolders Release\x86, Debug\x86, Release\x64, and Debug\x64.

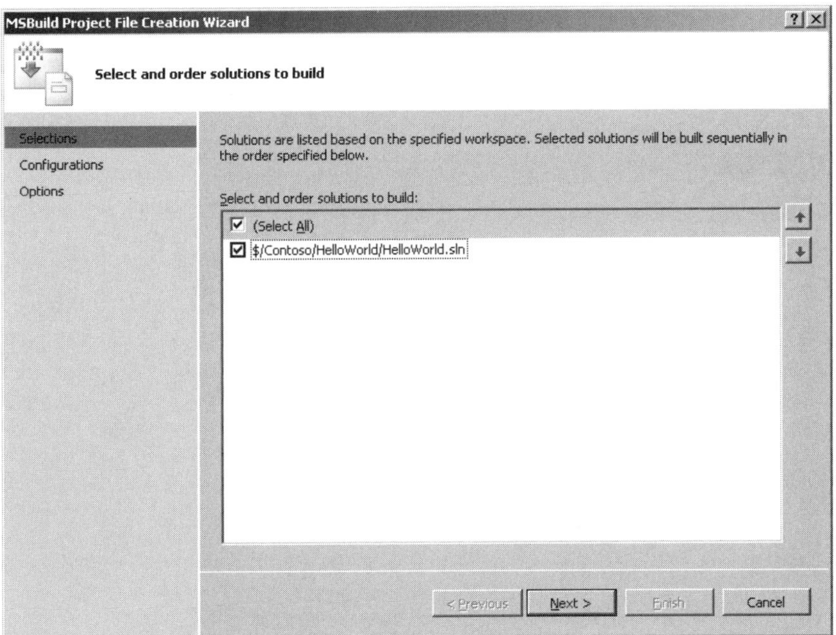

FIGURE 10-8 MSBuild Project File Creation Wizard: Selections

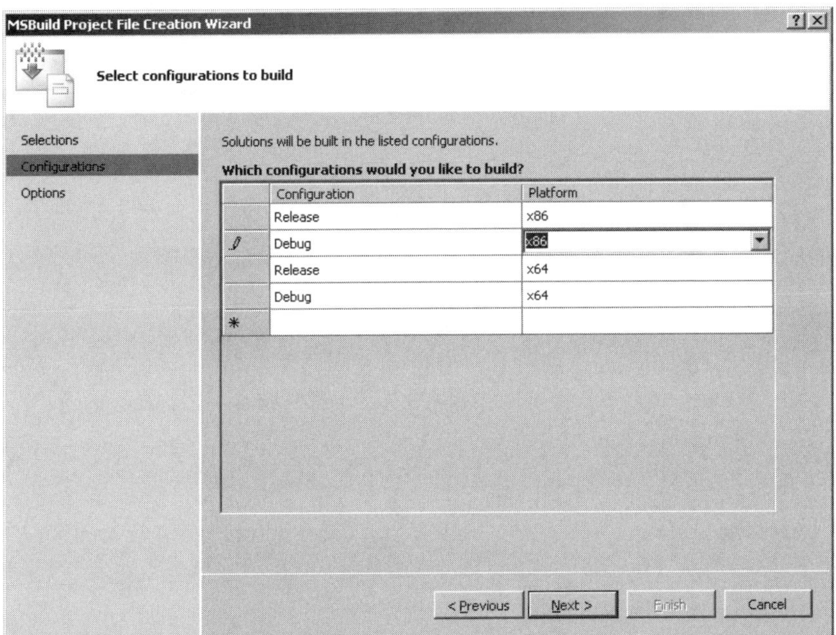

FIGURE 10-9 MSBuild Project File Creation Wizard: Configurations

Tip If the Configuration or Platform you would like to build isn't listed, you can type the name of the Configuration or Platform into the appropriate combo box.

The final (and optional) step of the MSBuild Project File Creation Wizard is the Options tab shown in Figure 10-10, which allows you to configure testing and code analysis.

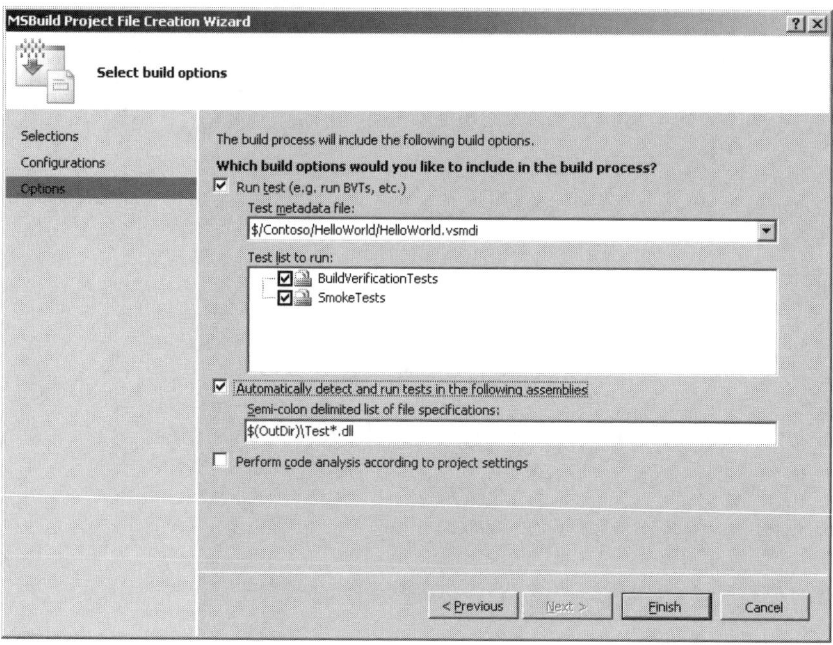

FIGURE 10-10 MSBuild Project File Creation Wizard: Options

From this tab you can enable unit testing using two methods:

- **Manually via test metadata file** If any test metadata files (*.vsmdi) are found in the workspace, these will be listed in the Test Metadata File dropdown list. Once you've selected a test metadata file, you can select one or more test lists that contain the tests you'd like to run as part of the build process.
- **Automatically via file specification** Rather than requiring developers to create and maintain test lists, you can alternatively provide a list of file specifications for the assemblies you'd like Team Build to run the tests from. Team Build will automatically detect the tests in the assembly and run them as part of the build process.

You can also enable code analysis from this tab, but whether or not code analysis is actually performed is determined by the Enable Code Analysis On Build option in each project's Code Analysis project property page as shown in Figure 10-11.

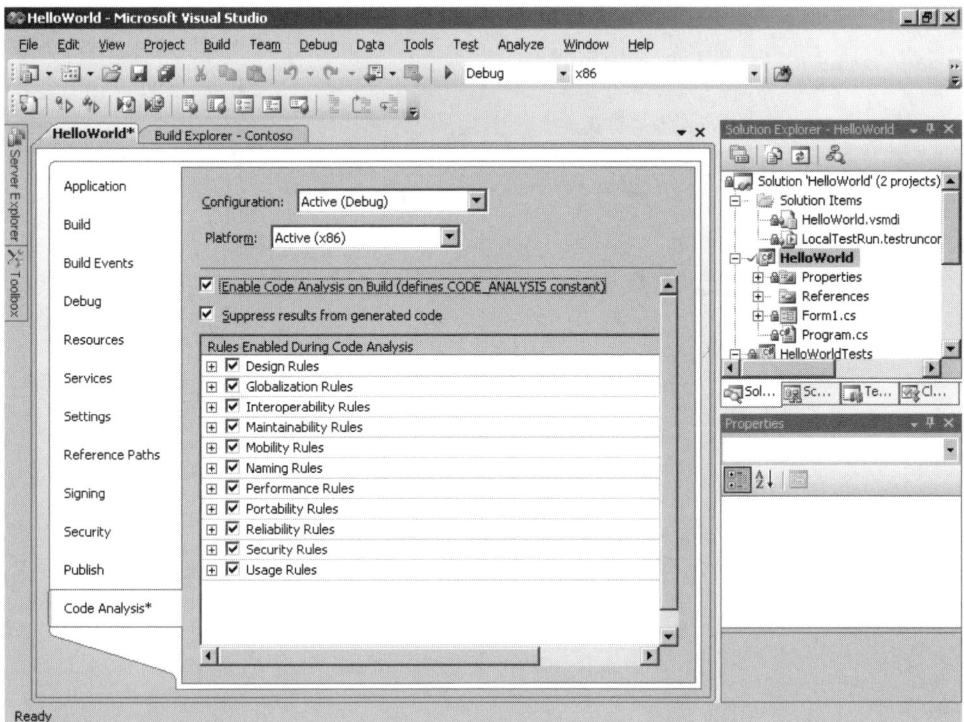

FIGURE 10-11 Code Analysis project property page

This completes the MSBuild Project File Creation Wizard and returns you to the Build Definition dialog.

Retention Policy

In Team Build 2005, build administrators often ran into an issue where they would run out of disk space in their drop folder. The reason for this is that Team Build 2005 did not provide an out-of-the-box solution to automatically remove builds that were no longer required.

Enterprising build administrators worked around this by either scripting the `TfsBuild.exe delete` command or by using third-party solutions (such as the Build Clean-up Service written by Mitch Denny).

Team Build 2008 solves this problem by introducing retention policies that allow you to specify which builds should be retained based on criteria in the build definition. The current version of this functionality is limited to retaining builds based on the outcome of the build (that is, successful, partially succeeded, stopped, and failed) and the number of builds (for example, retain the last two successful builds). If your requirements are more complex, such as wanting to retain builds based on number of days or on build quality, then you will still need to implement your own solution.

The Retention Policy tab shown in Figure 10-12 allows you to configure how many builds will be retained for each build outcome.

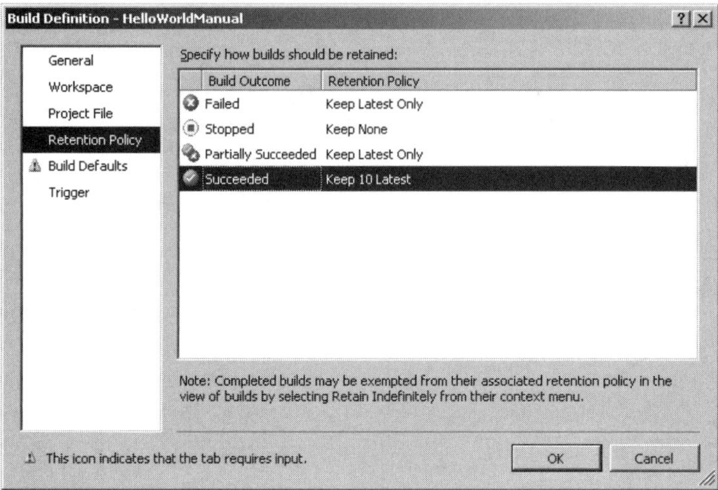

FIGURE 10-12 Build Definition: Retention Policy

Tip It's easy to think that you wouldn't want to retain any failed builds, but when builds are removed by the retention policy, everything associated with them, including the build log, is removed. If you don't retain at least one failed build, it might be very difficult to determine the cause of a build failure so that it can be resolved.

When a build is removed by the retention policy the following items are removed:

- Build history entry
- Drop folder, including the build log, test results, and binaries
- Version control label

Note Although the build history entry is removed, the build's details are still available for reporting in the TFSWarehouse database and OLAP cube if the warehouse was updated between the build completing and it being purged.

Because the build's label is removed when the build is removed, if you use these for tasks such as generating release notes or information for testing you will need to either exclude those builds from the retention policy, which is discussed in "Working with Build Queues and History" later in this chapter, or explicitly add an additional label that represents the version that was built.

Even if retention policies are enabled for a build definition, individual builds can still be explicitly deleted as discussed in "Working with Build Queues and History."

Build Defaults

The Build Defaults tab shown in Figure 10-13 allows you to specify the default build agent that the build will be queued on and where the build outputs will be dropped when the build completes. These are defaults and can be overridden by the developer when they queue the build.

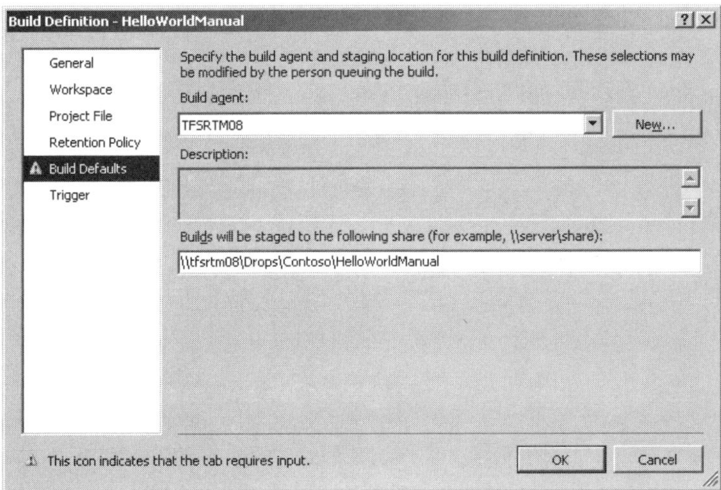

FIGURE 10-13 Build Definition: Build Defaults

Trigger

Team Build 2005 provided the ability for builds to be triggered manually either from within Team Explorer, using the `TfsBuild.exe start` command, from Team System Web Access, or using the Team Build API. These methods of starting builds provided build administrators and developers with a large amount of flexibility in how they started builds, but common requirements such as scheduled builds and continuous integration required additional programming, scripting, or third-party solutions to implement.

These are now implemented out of the box in Team Build 2008 by allowing build administrators to specify what triggers a build in the build definition. The triggers implemented in Team Build 2008 are:

- Manual
- Continuous integration
- Scheduled

These triggers are configured in the Trigger tab of the Build Definition Wizard shown in Figure 10-14.

Build Definition - HelloWorldManual

General
Workspace
Project File
Retention Policy
Build Defaults
Trigger

Team Foundation Build supports continuous integration by letting you trigger a build after a check-in.

Check-ins do not trigger a new build
Build each check-in (more builds)
Accumulate check-ins until the prior build finishes (fewer builds)
Build no more often than every [ ] minutes.
Build every week on the following days:
Monday Tuesday Wednesday Thursday
Friday Saturday Sunday

Queue the build on the default build agent at:
3:00 AM Pacific Daylight Time (GMT -07:00)
Build even if nothing has changed since the previous build

OK Cancel

FIGURE 10-14 Build Definition: Trigger

Manual

The simplest (and default) trigger is that builds need to be started manually. This trigger provides exactly the same experience that was available in Team Build 2005, with the exception that in Team Build 2008, builds can be queued rather than failing if a build is already in progress on the build agent.

This trigger is enabled by selecting the check-ins Do Not Trigger a New Build radio button.

Continuous Integration

Continuous integration (CI) is a set of practices from the agile community that provides early warning of bugs and broken code. By building and testing each changeset that has been checked-in, any issues can be identified and resolved quickly, minimizing the disruption caused to other developers.

When Team Build 2005 was released, many saw the lack of an out-of-the-box CI capability as a huge oversight, especially given its popularity at the time. Microsoft rectified this oversight in Team Build 2008 by adding two CI triggers that remove the need to rely on third-party CI solutions.

The first is the Build Each Check-in (More Builds) trigger, which causes each check-in to the build definition's workspace to queue a new build.

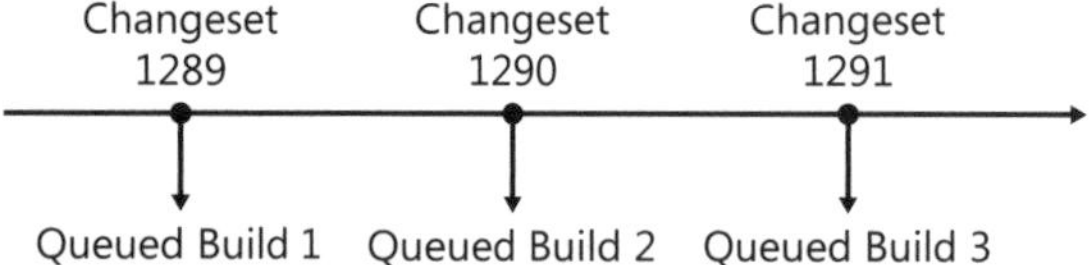

For long-running builds or workspaces that have a large number of check-ins, this option may result in unacceptably long build queues. The Accumulate Check-ins Until The Prior Build Finishes (Fewer Builds) trigger minimizes this issue by accumulating any check-ins to the build definition's workspace until the currently running build completes; once the build completes, a single build will be queued to build the changesets.

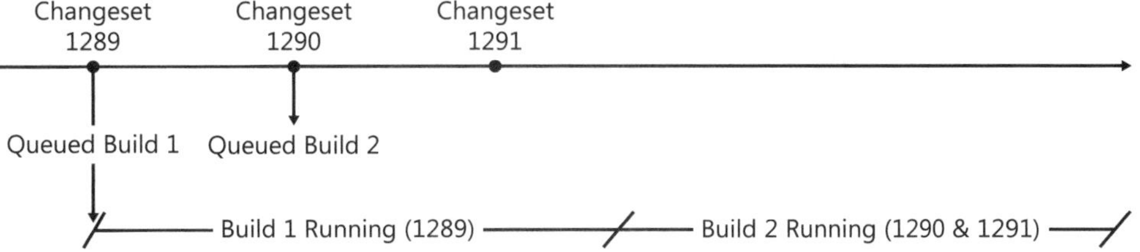

Even this trigger may result in build queues being dominated by a few build definitions. To add a lag between the builds to allow builds from other build definitions to be executed, you can enable the Build No More Than Every X Minutes option of this trigger, shown in Figure 10-15, to ensure that the builds are not executed back to back.

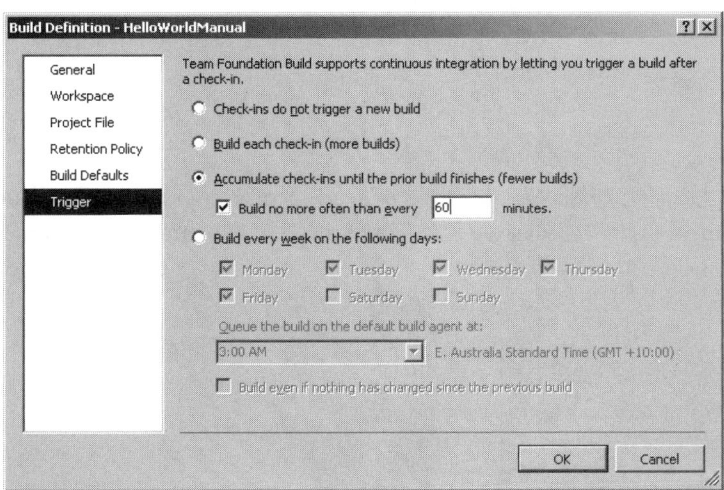

FIGURE 10-15 Build Definition: Trigger (with lag)

Scheduled

The Build Every Week On The Following Days trigger allows builds to be scheduled to run on specific days at a certain time rather than having to use third-party scheduling applications. By default, scheduled builds will be skipped if no changes have been checked-in since the previous build, this behavior can be overridden by clicking the Build Even If Nothing Has Changed Since The Previous Build checkbox.

Note One limitation of the scheduling functionality is that you can't schedule a build to be run multiple times a day. If you need this capability, you can either create a new build definition for each time you'd like the build to be run or use a scheduler (such as the built-in Windows Scheduler) to call the TfsBuild.exe command-line client to queue builds.

Working with Build Queues and History

Congratulations, you've now created your first build definition. Once you have a build definition you can use Team Build clients such as Visual Studio Team System or the TfsBuild.exe command line to queue builds and work with the build queues and history.

Visual Studio Team System

Developers spend the majority of their time in Visual Studio so it is logical to be able to work with builds from there. Team Explorer is the entry point to Team System functionality within Visual Studio Team System, and Team Build is no exception to this. The Builds node within a Team Project allows build administrators and developers to queue builds, and view and manage build queues and individual builds.

Queuing a Build

To queue a build, you right-click the Builds node in Team Explorer and choose Queue New Build to open the Queue Build dialog shown in Figure 10-16. Alternatively, you can right-click a specific build definition and choose Queue New Build, which opens the same dialog box but will automatically select that build definition.

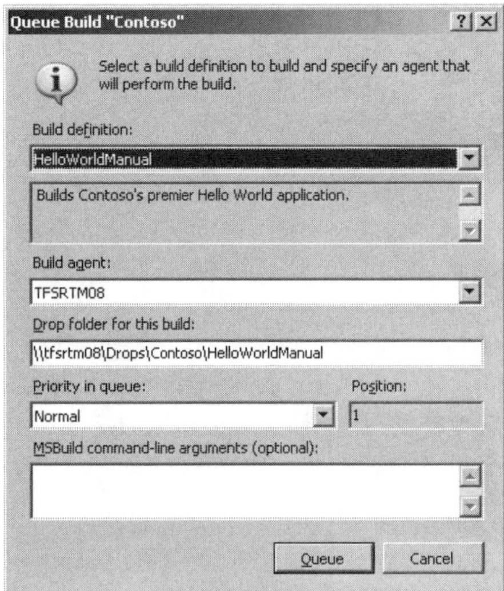

FIGURE 10-16 Queue Build dialog box

The Build Agent and Drop Folder For This Build will default to the values selected when you created the new build definition, but the developer can override these if desired.

The Position indicates where this build will be in the queue if queued on the selected build agent. This is refreshed whenever a different build agent is selected, but there can be a small delay while the position is calculated. You can also change the Priority that the build is queued with and, as expected, the higher the priority the higher in the queue it will be placed.

Developers can pass additional command-line arguments to the MSBuild process that runs the build by entering them in the MSBuild Command-Line Arguments fields. The most common use for this is to set the value of MSBuild properties when queuing the build to change how the build behaves. To be able to specify MSBuild Command-Line Arguments, the developer must have the Administer a Build permission on the Team Project.

For example, the default build process defines a property called RunTest that defines whether unit tests should be executed. When queuing a build, the developer could enter the following in the MSBuild Command-Line Arguments field to stop the unit tests from being executed and increase the logging verbosity to diagnostic:

```
/p:RunTest=false /v:diag
```

Clicking Queue will then queue the build on the selected build agent and open the Build Explorer window so you can monitor the progress of your build.

To always pass the same arguments when queuing a build, there are two options:

1. To pass properties, you can define the property in TFSBuild.proj as discussed in Chapter 12.
2. To pass any parameters, including properties if you'd like, you can add the parameters to TFSBuild.rsp (which is located in the same folder as TFSBuild.proj). The arguments listed in TFSBuild.rsp are appended to the MSBuild command line invoked by Team Build.

Build Explorer

The Build Explorer window shown in Figure 10-17 is the main way to manage build queues and view build history. The Build Explorer can be opened by right-clicking the Builds node in Team Explorer and choosing View Builds. You can also double-click a build definition, which will open the Build Explorer and automatically filter it to builds of that build definition.

When first opened, the Build Explorer window will show only queued builds, which can be confusing if you expect to see the completed builds as well (as was the case in Team Build 2005). To see completed builds, you need to click the Completed tab at the bottom of the window.

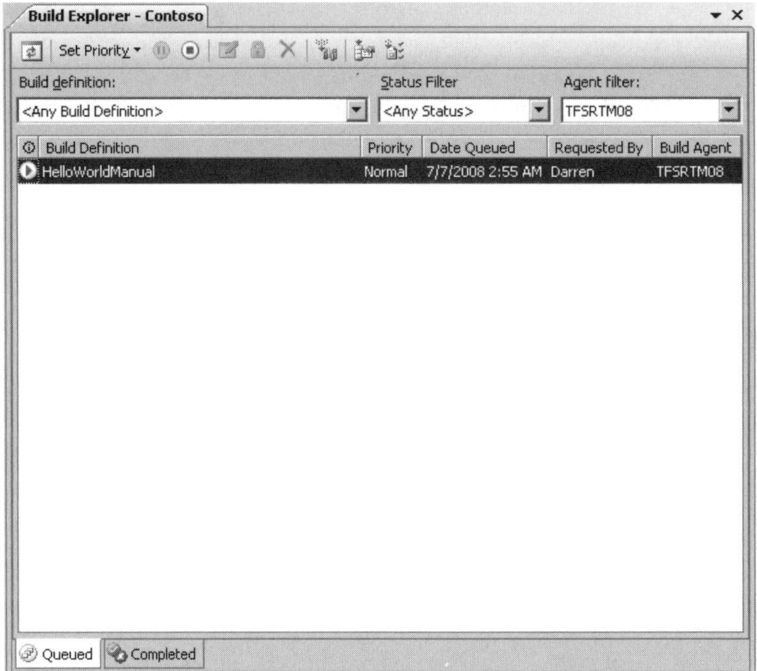

FIGURE 10-17 Build Explorer dialog box

Note Queued builds will remain on the Queued tab for up to 5 minutes after they complete.

The Queued build list can be filtered by selecting the filter criteria from the Build Definition, Status Filter, and Agent Filter lists at the top of the window. The Completed build list can be filtered as well, but by Build Definition, Quality, and Date.

Cancelling, Stopping, Postponing, and Reprioritizing Builds

If a build is queued but isn't running yet, you can right-click it and choose Cancel to remove it from the queue. Similarly, if a build is currently running on a build agent, you can stop it by right-clicking the build in the Queued tab of the Build Explorer and choosing Stop. This is significantly easier than it was in Team Build 2005, which required builds to be stopped using the TfsBuild.exe command-line client.

Rather than cancelling a queued build, you can postpone it by right-clicking it and choosing Postpone. This places the build on hold and it won't be built by the build agent until you right-click the build again and uncheck the Postpone option.

Builds can be reprioritized to change their position in the queue by right-clicking the build, choosing Change Priority, and then choosing the new priority for the build; the queue will then be refreshed to display the new queue order.

Viewing Build Details

Double-clicking a build in the Build Explorer will open the Build Details window shown in Figure 10-18, which shows detailed information about the progress of the build.

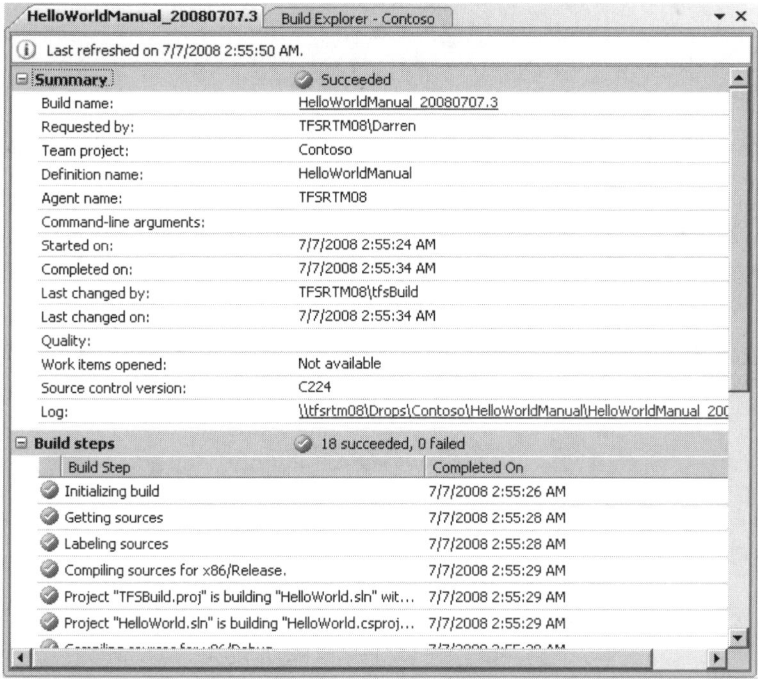

FIGURE 10-18 Build Details dialog box

The Build Details window shows details about the build, requestor (who queued or caused the build to be queued), build definition, and a progress summary. The Build Steps section shows a running log of the steps being executed and when they complete, which provides an easy way of monitoring the progress of the build as well as allowing you to quickly see what build step caused the build to fail. In Figure 10-19 you can see that the get and label steps succeeded but the compilation failed, and you can see exactly what project or configuration caused the build failure.

The Build Details window will automatically refresh until the build completes but by right-clicking the window you can explicitly refresh it at any time.

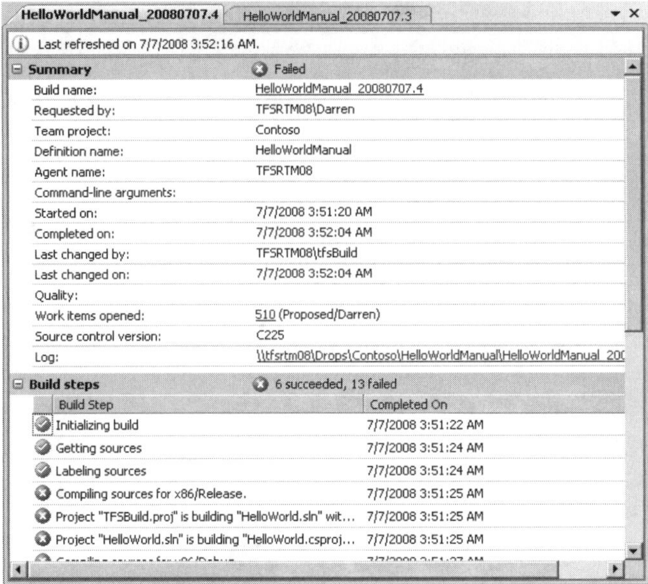

FIGURE 10-19 Build Details for a failed build

When the build completes, the Build Name will be hyperlinked to the drop folder where the build logs and build outputs have been dropped, and the log will be linked directly to the build log. If the build fails, the Work Items Opened will link to the build failure work item that is created automatically. Chapter 11 discusses how to configure build failure work item creation.

At the bottom of the Build Details window are a few more sections of interest. The Result Details section shown in Figure 10-20 (which shows a different build) shows the number of

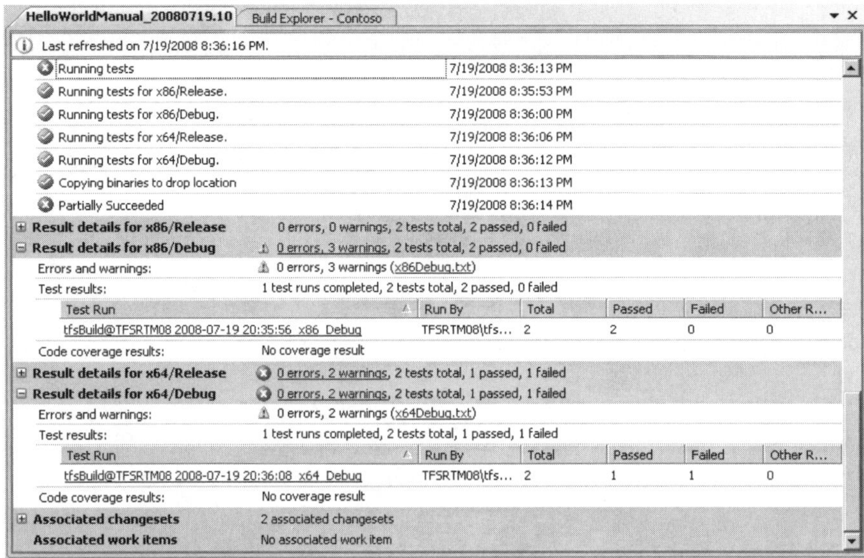

FIGURE 10-20 Build Details: Result details

errors, warnings, test passes and failures, and code coverage results for each configuration as well as a hyperlink to the test result details (*.trx).

The Associated Changesets and Associated Work Items sections shown in Figure 10-21 list the changesets and work items that are associated with this build but not earlier builds of the same build definition. This information is extremely useful for providing traceability and in identifying what change caused a build failure or to guide testing of specific builds. Clicking the changeset number opens changeset in the standard changeset dialog box, and clicking the work item number opens the work item in the standard work item form.

Associated changesets — 3 associated changesets

ID	Checked In By	Comments
234	TFSRTM08\Darren	
235	TFSRTM08\Darren	
236	TFSRTM08\Darren	Modified form to prompt for name of person to greet.

Associated work items — 1 associated work item

ID	Title	State	Assigned To
521	Enhance HelloWorld to prompt for name to greet.	Proposed	Darren

FIGURE 10-21 Build Details: Associated changesets and work items

Note One limitation of the Build Details window is that once the Build Steps section reaches a certain length (around 65,000 pixels) the rest of the window is truncated. Although it is not possible to view the truncated build steps, you can still minimize the Build Steps section to access the Associated Changesets and Associated Work Items sections.

Changing Build Qualities

Once a build has completed, it often goes through a number of other processes before it is released. For example, a build might be installed in a testing environment, pass testing, and then be released.

To provide the ability to track the status of a build, Team Build allows you to flag builds with a build quality. The first step is to define the list of build qualities you'd like to be able to flag builds with. You can open the Edit Build Qualities dialog shown in Figure 10-22 by right-clicking the Builds node of Team Explorer and choosing Manage Build Qualities. Figure 10-22 shows the default list of build qualities provided with Team Build, but these can be customized to meet your requirements.

Once the list of build qualities has been defined, you can assign a build quality to a build by right-clicking the build in the Completed tab of the Build Explorer and choosing Edit Build Quality as shown in Figure 10-23. Assigning or changing a build's build quality requires the user to be assigned the Edit Build Quality permission.

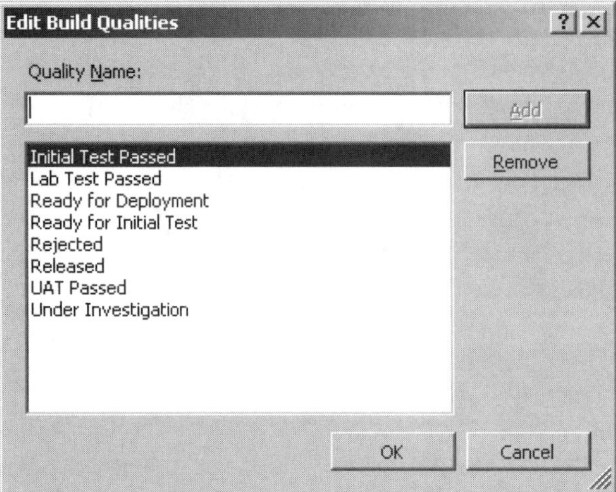

FIGURE 10-22 Edit Build Qualities dialog box

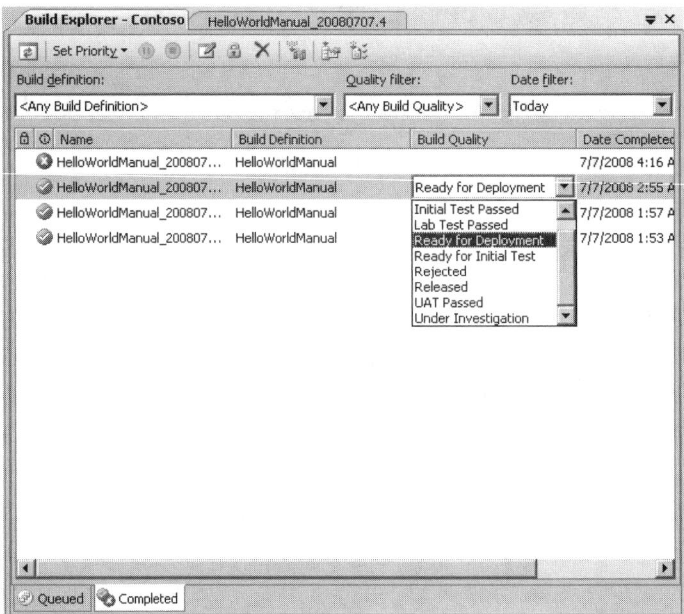

FIGURE 10-23 Changing a build's quality

Retaining Builds

There are situations where you may want to retain builds that otherwise would be removed by the build definition's retention policy, such as builds you are in the process of testing or have released to customers.

You can flag a build to be retained indefinitely by right-clicking the build in the Completed tab of the Build Explorer window and choosing Retain Indefinitely. If in the future you decide that you no longer want to retain the build, you can repeat this process to turn off the Retain Indefinitely flag.

Deleting Builds

Sometimes you might want to explicitly remove a build even though retention policies haven't been enabled for the build definition or before the retention policy would have removed the build automatically—this could be to recover disk space or to remove extraneous builds from the build history.

You can explicitly remove a build by right-clicking the build in the Completed tab of the Build Explorer window and choosing Delete. This will permanently remove the build from the build history, its associated drop folder, any test results associated with the build, and the build's version-control label.

From the Command Line

Build administrators (and most developers) are command-line junkies at heart and Team Build provides a command-line client for queuing, stopping, and deleting builds, and even if you're not a command-line junkie, it also provides a simple way to script Team Build commands as part of a larger process.

The command-line client is called TfsBuild.exe and is installed in the %ProgramFiles%\Microsoft Visual Studio 9.0\Common7\IDE directory as part of the Team Foundation Client. The easiest way to run it is from the Visual Studio 2008 command prompt, which includes this directory in its default path.

The first parameter to TfsBuild.exe is the command to execute. The available commands are listed in Table 10-3.

TABLE 10-3 TfsBuild.exe Commands

Command	Description
Help	Prints general help for the TfsBuild.exe command-line client as well as command-specific help.
Start	Starts a new build either synchronously or asynchronously.
Stop	Stops one or more running builds.
Delete	Deletes one or more builds from the build history.

To print general help and a list of available commands, run `TfsBuild.exe help`.

To print help for a specific command, run `TfsBuild.exe help` <command> (for example, `TfsBuild.exe help start`).

Note Any arguments containing a space should be enclosed in double-quotation marks.

Queuing a Build

The TfsBuild.exe command line provides two variations of the `start` command. The first has this syntax, and its parameters are described in Table 10-4:

```
TfsBuild start /server:<teamFoundationServer> /buildDefinition:<definitionSpec>
          [/dropLocation:dl] [/getOption:go] [/priority:p]
          [/customGetVersion:versionSpec] [/requestedFor:userName]
          [/msBuildArguments:args] [/silent] [/queue]
```

TABLE 10-4 TfsBuild.exe Start Parameters

Parameter	Description
/server:<teamFoundationServer>	Either the full URL of the Team Foundation Server (e.g., http://TFSRTM08:8080/) or, if the server has been registered in Visual Studio Team System, you can use just the host name (e.g., TFSRTM08).
/buildDefinition:<definitionSpec>	The full path of the build definition in the format \<TeamProject>\<BuildDefinitionName> (e.g., \Contoso\HelloWorldManual).
/dropLocation:<dl>	If specified, overrides the drop location in the build definition.
/getOption:<go>	If specified, specifies what version of the source code Team Build will get. Table 10-5 lists the available get options.
/priority:<p>	Either Low, BelowNormal, Normal, AboveNormal, and High. This parameter is optional and will default to Normal if not provided.
/customGetVersion:<versionSpec>	If /getOption:Custom is specified, this parameter must be supplied and specifies the version of the source code that Team Build should get. The available versionspec options are listed in Table 10-6.
/requestedFor:<userName>	By default, the build will be requested for the user that runs the TfsBuild.exe command line, or you can optionally pass this parameter to request a build on behalf of another user.
/msBuildArguments:<args>	Quoted arguments to be passed to MSBuild when executing TFSBuild.proj. For example, to disable running unit tests and increase the logging verbosity to diagnostic, you would specify /msBuildArguments:"/p:RunTest=false /v:diag".
/silent	If specified, suppresses any output from the TfsBuild.exe command line other than the logo information.
/queue	By default, the TfsBuild.exe command line will return an error immediately if the build won't be processed immediately by a build agent (i.e., needs to be queued). If the build is processed immediately by a build agent, TfsBuild.exe won't return until the build has completed. If this parameter is used, TfsBuild.exe will return as soon as the build has been queued.

TABLE 10-5 Get Options

Option	Description
GetLatestOnQueue	Builds the latest version of the source code at the time the build is queued.
GetLatestOnBuild	Builds the latest version of the source code at the time the build starts (default).
Custom	Builds the version specified by the /customGetVersion parameter.

TABLE 10-6 Versionspec Options

Name	Prefix	Example	Description
Date/time	D	D07/22/2008	Builds the source code at a specific date/time.
Changeset version	C	C1133	Builds the source code as at a specific changeset number.
Label	L	Lcheckpoint2label	Builds the source code at the version specified by the label.
Latest version	T	T	Builds the latest version of the source code.
Workspace version	W	Wmyworkspace; myusername	Builds the version of the source code currently in the specified workspace.

The second variation of the `start` command provides the same functionality as the first but mimics the syntax of the start command in Team Build 2005:

```
TfsBuild start <teamFoundationServer> <teamProject> <definitionName>
               [/dropLocation:dl] [/getOption:go] [/priority:p]
               [/customGetVersion:versionSpec] [/requestedFor:userName]
               [/msBuildArguments:args] [/silent] [/queue]
```

Stopping a Build

You can also stop a running build from the TfsBuild.exe command line by using the `stop` command.

There are three variations of the `stop` command, and their parameters are described in Table 10-7:

```
TfsBuild stop [/noPrompt] [/silent] /server:<teamFoundationServer>
              /buildDefinition:<definitionSpec> <buildNumbers> ...

TfsBuild stop [/noPrompt] [/silent] /server:<teamFoundationServer>
              <buildUris> ...

TfsBuild stop [/noPrompt] [/silent] <teamFoundationServer> <teamProject>
              <buildNumbers> ...
```

TABLE 10-7 TfsBuild.exe Stop Parameters

Parameter	Description
/noPrompt	If specified, suppresses TfsBuild.exe confirming you want to stop the build.
/silent	If specified, suppresses any output from the TfsBuild.exe command line other than the logo information.
/server:<teamFoundationServer>	Either the full URL of the Team Foundation Server (e.g., http://TFSRTM08:8080/) or, if the server has been registered in Visual Studio Team System, you can use just the host name (e.g., TFSRTM08).
/buildDefinition:<definitionSpec>	The full path of the build definition in the format \<TeamProject>\<BuildDefinitionName> (e.g., \Contoso\HelloWorldManual).
buildNumbers	Space-separated list of build numbers to be stopped.
buildUris	Space-separated list of build URIs to be stopped.

Deleting a Build

You can also delete a build from the TfsBuild.exe command line by using the `delete` command.

There are three variations of the `delete` command, and their parameters are described in Table 10-8:

```
TfsBuild delete [/noPrompt] [/silent] /server:<teamFoundationServer>
              /buildDefinition:<definitionSpec> <buildNumbers> ...

TfsBuild delete [/noPrompt] [/silent] /server:<teamFoundationServer>
              <buildUris> ...

TfsBuild delete [/noPrompt] [/silent] <teamFoundationServer> <teamProject>
              <buildNumbers> ...
```

TABLE 10-8 TfsBuild.exe Delete Parameters

Parameter	Description
/noPrompt	If specified, suppresses TfsBuild.exe, confirming you want to delete the build.
/silent	If specified, suppresses any output from the TfsBuild.exe command line other than the logo information.
/server:<teamFoundationServer>	Either the full URL of the Team Foundation Server (e.g., http://TFSRTM08:8080/) or, if the server has been registered in Visual Studio Team System, you can use just the host name (e.g., TFSRTM08).
/buildDefinition:<definitionSpec>	The full path of the build definition in the format \<TeamProject>\<BuildDefinitionName> (e.g., \Contoso\HelloWorldManual).
buildNumbers	Space-separated list of build numbers to be deleted.
buildUris	Space-separated list of build URIs to be deleted.

Performing Desktop Builds

Desktop builds allow developers to run a build on their workstation using the source code in their workspace. This can be used to resolve compilation errors and perform local testing before changes are checked-in.

The differences between the desktop build process and the end-to-end build process used when executing builds on the build agent are discussed in Chapter 11, but the key differences are that the build process includes only the compilation, testing, documentation generation, and binary packaging phases. The build and test results are not published into the operational or warehouse databases.

In addition to having the source code locally, the developer must also have a local copy of the build's configuration folder (which contains TFSBuild.proj). The developer can then start the desktop build process by:

1. Opening a Visual Studio 2008 command-prompt.
2. Changing directory to the directory containing TFSBuild.proj.
3. Running the TFSBuild.proj using MSBuild.exe. For example, MSBuild.exe TFSBuild.proj.

The desktop build process defaults the SolutionRoot property (which defines the root directory containing the source code and solutions) to ..\.., that is, up two levels from the directory containing TFSBuild.proj. If this default is incorrect, you can override it as shown here:

```
MSBuild.exe TFSBuild.proj /p:SolutionRoot=..\..\src
```

This syntax can also be used to set the values for other properties as shown in this example, which disables running unit tests:

```
MSBuild.exe TFSBuild.proj /p:RunTests=false
```

Chapter 12 discusses the different properties that can be set to modify the default build process provided by Team Build.

Team Build Security

Securing Team Build is a critical part of configuring Team Foundation Server and installing new build agents. Even if your Team System environment is safely contained within your corporate firewall, this is still important to prevent inadvertent changes to your build agents and the builds they produce.

Service Accounts

The first consideration when installing Team Build is to decide what account to run the Team Build service under. There are two options:

- **NT AUTHORITY\NETWORK SERVICE** This built-in Windows account is a limited privilege account that can access network resources using the computer account's credentials.[1] The account does not have a password and cannot be used to log in interactively or remotely to the computer.
- **Domain Account** Team Build can also run as an arbitrary domain account. Using a domain account allows you to log onto the build machine using this account to install or configure applications that use per-user settings (which you can't do with the NETWORK SERVICE account because you can't log in interactively with it). This can also be useful to debug build problems related to permissions on the build machine or other network resources.

The account you use needs to be granted the Log On A Service permission to the build machine. This will be granted automatically by the Team Build installer or if the account the Team Build service runs as is changed using the Services control panel as shown in Figure 10-24; otherwise, you will need to grant this permission using the Local Security Policy control panel.

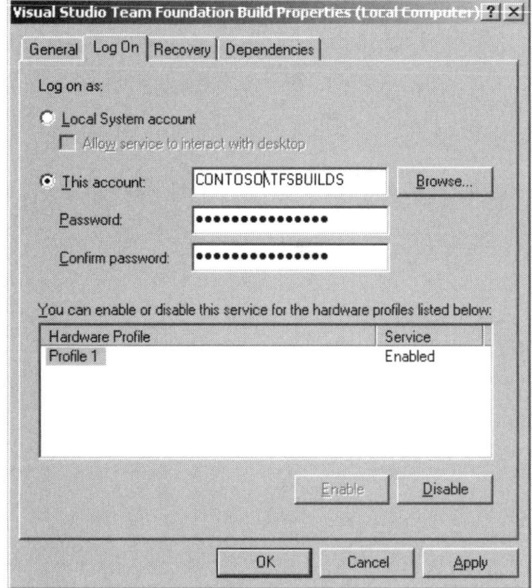

FIGURE 10-24 Configure Team Build service account

1 *http://www.microsoft.com/technet/security/guidance/serversecurity/serviceaccount/sspgch02.mspx#EBH*

Note The Team Build service account should not need to be a member of the build machine's Administrators security group. The account should be granted the specific permissions needed by your build processes rather than granting it administrator access to the build machine. This is to minimize the damage of malicious or badly written build scripts.

The account also needs to be added to the Build Services group for each Team Project that it will execute builds for as shown in Figure 10-25. This group grants Team Build access to the source as well as the required project and server permissions required to execute builds. To do this:

1. Open Microsoft Visual Studio 2008.
2. Open Team Explorer.
3. Right-click the Team Project.
4. Click Team Project Settings.
5. Click Group Membership.
6. Select the [Team Project]\Build Services security group.
7. Click Properties.
8. Click Windows User or Group.
9. Click Add.
10. Select the domain account that the Team Build service is running as or the build machine's computer account if it is running as NT AUTHORITY\NETWORK SERVICE.

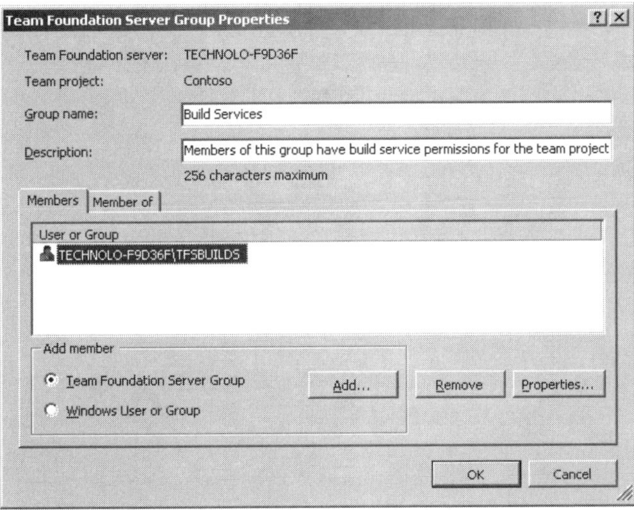

FIGURE 10-25 Build Services Security Group Properties dialog box

11. Click OK.
12. Click OK.
13. Click Close.

Note The Team Build service account should not be the Team Foundation Server service account or a member of the [SERVER]\Service Accounts security group. If the Team Build service account is a member of the [SERVER]\Service Accounts group, then malicious or badly written build scripts could cause irreparable damage to the Team Foundation Server.

The Team Build service account also requires Full Control file system permission to the drop location. This permission will also need to be granted to the Team Foundation Server service account if the build process, developers, testers, etc. will publish test results against builds. This is necessary because the test results are published by the Team Foundation Server rather than the Team Build service.

If changing the Team Build service account after Team Build has been installed (or changing Team Build's communication port, which is discussed in the "Configuring the Team Build Service" section of Chapter 11), you will need to associate Team Build's communication port (by default 9191) with the Team Build service account. To do this:

1. Log on to the build agent machine.
2. Open a command prompt.
3. Change directory to %ProgramFiles%\Microsoft Visual Studio 9.0\Common7\IDE\PrivateAssemblies.
4. Run `wcfhttpconfig.exe reserve DOMAIN\User PortNumber`. For example, `wcfhttpconfig.exe reserve CONTOSO\TFSBUILD 9191`.
5. Restart the Visual Studio Team Foundation Build service.

Permissions

Team Build provides a number of project level permissions for controlling access to Team Build functionality. These permissions are detailed in Table 10-9.

TABLE 10-9 Team Build Permissions

Permission	Description	Default Granted To
Administer a build	Permits the user to edit build agents and definitions, submit builds with MSBuild Command-line Arguments, and to cancel, postpone, or stop anyone's builds.	Project Administrators Team Foundation Administrators
Edit build quality	Permits the user to maintain the list of build qualities and to set or change the build quality for an individual build.	Project Administrators Team Foundation Administrators

TABLE 10-9 Team Build Permissions

Permission	Description	Default Granted To
Publish test results	Permits the user to publish test results against any build. Also permits the user to remove test results from any build.	Build Services Contributors Project Administrators Team Foundation Administrators
Start a build	Permits the user to queue builds and cancel, postpone, or stop their own builds.	Build Services Contributors Project Administrators Team Foundation Administrators
Write to build operational store	Permits the user to update details about builds.	Build Services Project Administrators Team Foundation Administrators

Permissions can be allowed or denied (or left unset) to both Team Foundation Server or Windows users and groups. When there is a conflict between allow and deny for a user, deny will take precedence. For more information about how permissions are granted and evaluated in Team Foundation Server refer to *http://msdn.microsoft.com/en-us/library/ms252587.aspx*.

Chapter 11

Team Build Deep Dive

Team Build ships with a default build process that is suitable for building most .NET 2.0 and higher-based applications, but to get the most value out of Team Build you can customize this default process to your needs and even to build non-.NET-based applications.

Default Build Processes

Before starting to customize or extend the default build process, it is important to understand the steps that make up the default process and the order in which they occur.

The default build process is implemented as a number of properties, targets, and items in an MSBuild project that is imported into the TFSBuild.proj project in each build definition. This imported project is %ProgramFiles%\MSBuild\Microsoft\VisualStudio\TeamBuild\Microsoft.TeamFoundation.Build.targets and is well commented and an invaluable reference when customizing the build process.

There are two variations of the default build process:

- **End-to-end** Used by Team Build when executing a build definition on a build agent.
- **Desktop** Used by MSBuild when executing a build definition on a developer's workstation as described in Chapter 10, "Team Build Quick Start."

You can detect which build process is being used using the IsDesktopBuild property as shown in this example:

```
<Target Name="BeforeCompile">
    <Message Text="Running a desktop build."
        Condition="'$(IsDesktopBuild)'=='true'" />
    <Message Text="Running an end-to-end build."
        Condition="'$(IsDesktopBuild)'!='true'" />
</Target>
```

End-to-End Build Process

When a build definition is executed on a build agent it is executed using the end-to-end build process, which is the more complete of the two. The end-to-end build process consists of this series of MSBuild targets:

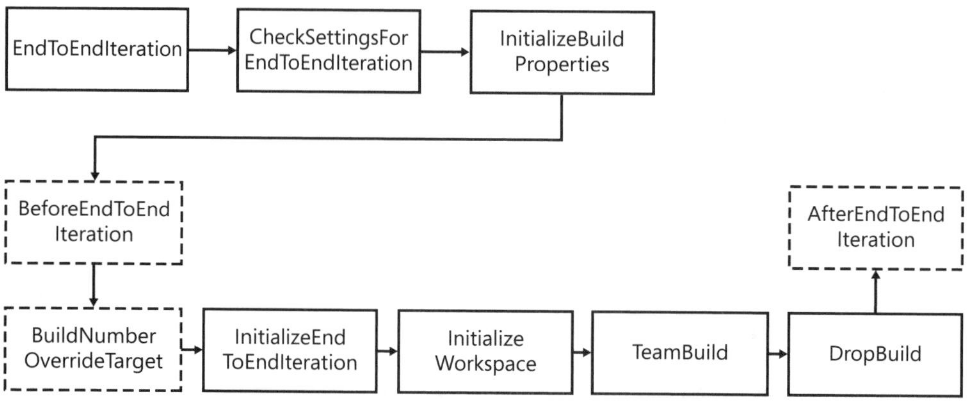

The entry-point is the EndToEndIteration target, which executes a number of initialization targets, the TeamBuild target, which is discussed next, and the DropBuild target, which deploys the build outputs to the drop location. The targets shown with a dashed outline are extensibility targets and the purpose of these is explained in the section "Overriding Extensibility Targets."

The TeamBuild target encompasses the targets that people normally think of when they think of a build process, such as cleaning build outputs, getting source code, compilation, testing, and packaging. The targets executed by the TeamBuild target are:

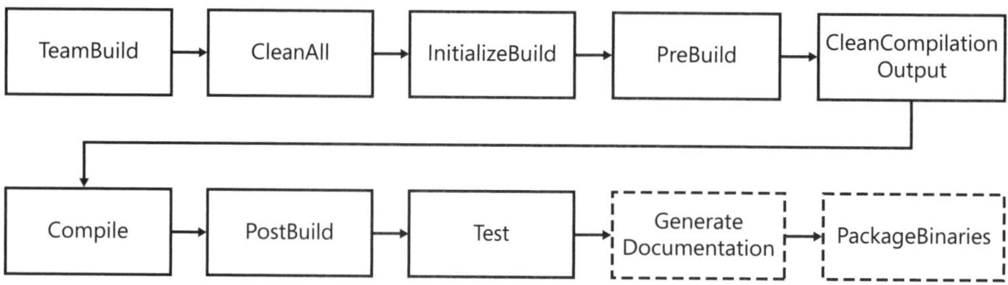

The PreBuild target is responsible for getting and labeling the source code using these targets:

The PostBuild target executes only a single target, which determines the changesets and work items associated with the build and updates the work items with the build's details:

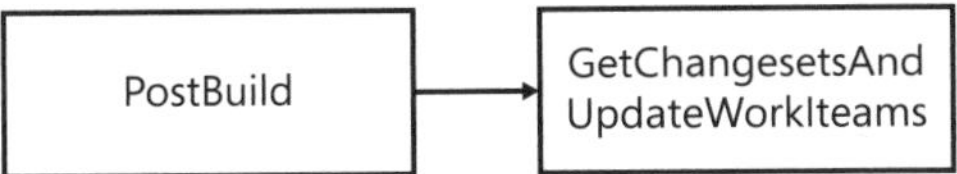

In the following "Customizing the Build Process" section, we'll elaborate on each of these targets, what they do, and how they can be customized.

Desktop Build Process

The desktop build process is a cut-down version of the end-to-end build process that can be used by developers to perform builds on their workstation before checking in their changes. Chapter 10 described how to run a desktop build, but in this section we describe the targets that are included in the desktop build process as well as how it can be customized.

The targets included in the desktop build process are:

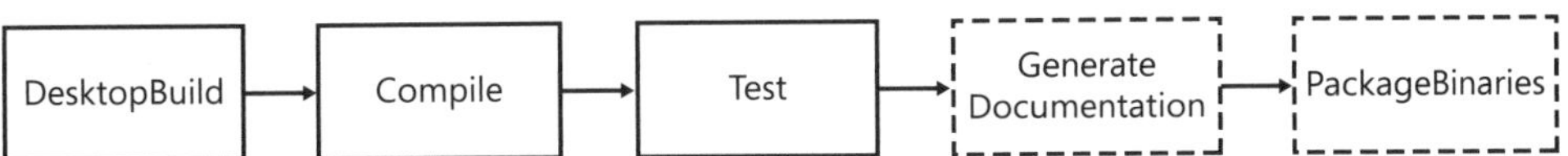

The desktop rebuild process executes the clean target before the desktop build process as shown here:

To execute a desktop rebuild instead, we pass this target name to the MSBuild command line as shown here:

```
MSBuild.exe TFSBuild.proj /p:SolutionRoot=..\..\src /t:DesktopRebuild
```

The main difference between the desktop and end-to-end build processes is that the desktop build process uses the source in the developer's local workspace rather than downloading the source from the Team Foundation Server and the resulting compilation outputs are not dropped to the drop folder.

Canonicalize Paths

The InitialTargets for the Microsoft.TeamFoundation.Build.targets project causes the CanonicalizePaths target to be invoked before the entry-point target for either end-to-end or desktop builds.

This target expands and normalizes the three key paths listed in Table 11-1.

TABLE 11-1 Key Path Properties

Property	Description
SolutionRoot	Path to the source code. This source code is either downloaded by the get phase (for an end-to-end build) or already exists in the developer's workspace (for a desktop build).
BinariesRoot	Path to the binaries generated during the compilation phase.
TestResultsRoot	Path to the test result files generated during the test phase.

Customizing the Build Process

In this section, we'll look at each of these phases, the targets they include, and how they can be customized by setting MSBuild properties, adding items to item groups, and overriding targets. The majority of these customizations apply equally to the end-to-end and desktop build processes but where there is a difference it will be highlighted.

The correct way to customize the build is by adding the customizations to the TFSBuild.proj project in the build definition's configuration folder in version control. These customizations can also be refactored into their own project file as discussed in Sharing Customizations between Build Definitions in Chapter 12, "Team Build Cookbook."

Note You should never edit the Microsoft.TeamFoundation.Build.targets project to customize the build process because:

- It is stored on each build agent and your customizations would have to be duplicated on each build agent.
- It is common to all build definitions and all team projects that are built using that build machine.
- Your customizations can be lost when applying service packs or hotfixes to Team Build.

You will generally make two types of customizations:

- Setting properties and adding items to item groups.
- Overriding extensibility targets.

Setting Properties and Populating Item Groups

In Team Build 2008, almost all of the targets provided in the default build process can be configured by setting MSBuild properties and/or populating item groups. The remainder of this chapter discusses most of the available properties and item groups and how they affect the build process, but in this section we'll look at how you set a property and how you populate an item group. To refresh your memory about MSBuild properties and item groups refer back to Chapter 2, "Deep Dive, Part 1."

Because TFSBuild.proj is a standard MSBuild project file, setting a property in Team Build is the same as for any other MSBuild project: Edit the project file and within an existing PropertyGroup (or in a new PropertyGroup if preferred) specify the property name and value. For example, to set the RunTest property to true you would add the following to TFSBuild.proj:

```
<PropertyGroup>
    <RunTest>true</RunTest>
</PropertyGroup>
```

Likewise, adding items to item groups and their metadata is the same as for other MSBuild projects. In this example, we're populating the ConfigurationToBuild item group with two entries (Debug|Any CPU and Release|Any CPU) and providing two metadata elements (FlavorToBuild and PlatformToBuild) for each of those entries:

```
<ItemGroup>
    <ConfigurationToBuild Include="Debug|Any CPU">
        <FlavorToBuild>Debug</FlavorToBuild>
        <PlatformToBuild>Any CPU</PlatformToBuild>
    </ConfigurationToBuild>
    <ConfigurationToBuild Include="Release|Any CPU">
        <FlavorToBuild>Release</FlavorToBuild>
        <PlatformToBuild>Any CPU</PlatformToBuild>
    </ConfigurationToBuild>
</ItemGroup>
```

Overriding Extensibility Targets

Although setting properties and adding items to item groups gives you some control over the default build process they are limited to the functionality and options provided out of the box. For this reason, Team Build provides a number of extensibility targets where you can implement your own custom logic using MSBuild and custom tasks, which provides almost limitless flexibility.

Most phases have an extensibility target that is invoked at the beginning of the phase and another that is invoked at the end, and some provide additional ones for specifically-defined purposes.

Note Although it is technically possible to override any target defined by Team Build you should override only the extensibility targets. The behavior and execution order of the non-extensibility targets (called core targets) is not guaranteed to remain the same across Team Build versions, potentially breaking your customizations.

To override an extensibility target you define a target in the build definition's TFSBuild.proj with the same name as the extensibility target. For example, to override the BeforeGet extensibility target you would add the following:

```
<Target Name="BeforeGet">
    <Message Text="Executing custom BeforeGet logic." />
</Target>
```

Most phases provide a property to skip the execution of that phase; for example, the get phase provides the property SkipGet and if this is set to true the get phase will be skipped. However, it is important to realize that the extensibility targets, in this example BeforeGet and AfterGet, for that phase will still be executed.

Customizing End-to-End Build Initialization

The initialization phase is responsible for initializing, normalizing, and validating the properties used in subsequent phases.

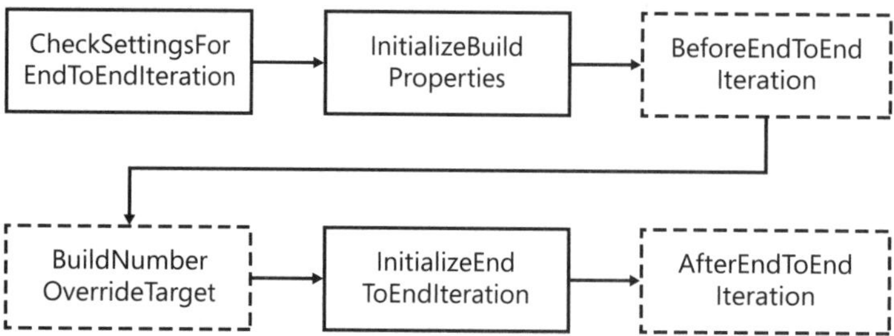

CheckSettingsForEndToEndIteration

The CheckSettingsForEndToEndIteration target then does basic validation of the BuildDefinition, BuildDefinitionId, BuildUri, ComputerName, TeamFoundationServerUrl, and TeamProject properties. Because these are provided by Team Build when it executes an end-to-end build, this validation is unlikely to fail unless you have inadvertently overwritten the value of these properties when customizing the build.

InitializeBuildProperties

The InitializeBuildProperties target is invoked next and calls the GetBuildProperties task to retrieve the build properties from the Team Foundation Server. These properties, which are listed in Table 11-2, provide a wealth of information about the build, build definition, build agent, and more.

TABLE 11-2 Properties Defined During InitializeBuildProperties

Property	Description
BuildAgentName	The name of the build agent running the build as shown in the Build Agent Properties dialog.
BuildAgentUri	The internal URI that represents the build agent running the build.
BuildDefinitionName	The name of the build definition as shown in the Edit Build Definition dialog.
BuildDefinitionUri	The internal URI that represents the build definition.
BuildDirectory	The working directory specified in the Build Agent Properties dialog.
BuildNumber	The build number allocated to the build by Team Build. This can be changed in the OverrideBuildNumberTarget target.

TABLE 11-2 Properties Defined During InitializeBuildProperties

Property	Description
CompilationStatus	The status of the compilation phase. Either Unknown, Failed, or Succeeded. This property will have the value Unknown until the compilation phase has completed.
CompilationSuccess	The Boolean status of compilation. Either False if compilation has not started or has failed, or True if compilation succeeded.
ConfigurationFolderUri	The internal URI for the folder containing TFSBuild.proj.
DropLocation	The drop location specified in the Edit Build Definition dialog.
LabelName	The name of the label to be applied to the version control files. Unless this has been set in TFSBuild.proj this property will be blank until the InitializeEndToEndIteration target has executed.
LastChangedBy	The username that last changed the build. This will typically be the build service account.
LastChangedOn	The date/time the build was last changed.
MachineName	The machine name of the build agent running the build.
MaxProcesses	The maximum number of processes MSBuild will use.
Port	The communications port of the build agent that is specified in the Build Agent Properties dialog.
Quality	The build quality assigned to the build. At this point in the build process this will typically be an empty string.
Reason	■ Manual – The build was manually queued. ■ IndividualCI – The build was queued by the Build Each Check-in trigger. ■ BatchedCI – The build was queued by the Accumulate Check-ins Until The Prior Build Finishes trigger. ■ Schedule – The build was queued by the Build Every Week On The Following Days trigger. ■ ScheduleForced – The build was queued by the Build Every Week On The Following Days trigger with the Build Even If Nothing Has Changed Since The Previous Build option enabled.
RequestedBy	The username that requested the build.
RequestedFor	The username that the build was requested for.
SourceGetVersion	The version specification of the source to get from version control.
StartTime	The date/time that the build started.
Status	The status of the build. At the point at which this property is populated it will always have the value InProgress.
TeamProject	The Team Project that contains the build definition.
TestStatus	The status of the test phase. Either Unknown, Failed, or Succeeded. This property will have the value Unknown until the test phase has completed.
TestSuccess	The Boolean status of compilation. Either False if compilation has not started or has failed, or True if compilation succeeded.

BeforeEndToEndIteration and AfterEndToEndIteration

After the InitializeBuildProperties target has completed the first extensibility target in the build process, BeforeEndToEndIteration, is invoked. This target provides an ideal place for any additional initialization that you need to perform for end-to-end builds.

For example, we can use this extensibility target to validate properties passed to the build as shown here:

```
<Target Name="BeforeEndToEndIteration">
    <Error Text="BuildStyle must be set to either 'quick' or 'complete'."
        Condition="'$(BuildStyle)'!='quick' AND '$(BuildStyle)'!='complete'" />
</Target>
```

The AfterEndToEndIteration target isn't part of the initialization phase but it is paired with the BeforeEndToEndIteration target so we'll discuss it here. This target executes at the very end of the build process and could be used to clean up after the build has completed.

BuildNumberOverrideTarget

The BuildNumberOverrideTarget is invoked next. Be careful: Unlike all the other targets this one's name actually ends in Target. It also differs from the other extensibility targets in that it has a defined purpose and a requirement that must be met when it is overridden. While other extensibility targets are designed for you to put any logic you want, this one is for you to provide custom logic for assigning the current build a build number.

If you choose to override the BuildNumberOverrideTarget you are required to populate the BuildNumber property with a unique build number that you want to assign to the current build; if you don't, it will remain as the number automatically assigned by Team Build (which is in the format BuildDefinitionName_YYYYMMDD.X where X is an auto-incrementing number that is reset each day).

Note Not returning a unique (within the Team Project) BuildNumber from the BuildNumberOverrideTarget will result in the build failing.

In this example, we override the BuildNumberOverrideTarget to set the build number to a standard four-part version number using the Version task from the MSBuild Community Tasks (*http://msbuildtasks.tigris.org*); a full version of this example is available in the Assembly Versioning recipe in Chapter 12.

```
<Target Name="BuildNumberOverrideTarget">
    <Version VersionFile="$(DropLocation)\version.txt" BuildType="Increment">
        <Output TaskParameter="Major" PropertyName="Major" />
        <Output TaskParameter="Minor" PropertyName="Minor" />
        <Output TaskParameter="Build" PropertyName="Build" />
        <Output TaskParameter="Revision" PropertyName="Revision" />
    </Version>
    <PropertyGroup>
        <BuildNumber>$(Major).$(Minor).$(Build).$(Revision)</BuildNumber>
    </PropertyGroup>
</Target>
```

InitializeEndToEndIteration

Finally, the InitializeEndToEndIteration target will be invoked. This target:

1. Updates properties that are dependent on other properties. For example, if IncrementalGet is set to true then this target will set CleanCompilationOutputOnly to true, SkipInitializeWorkspace to true, and ForceGet to false.
2. Updates the build number and drop location (which is dependent on the build number) in the Team Build operational database. This also creates the drop location and grants the build agent's service account Full Control permission to it.
3. If a custom label hasn't been specified in the LabelName property then the LabelName property is set to be the same as the BuildNumber.

InitializeWorkspace

The InitializeWorkspace target is responsible for removing workspaces from previous builds (where required) and creating the workspace for the current build.

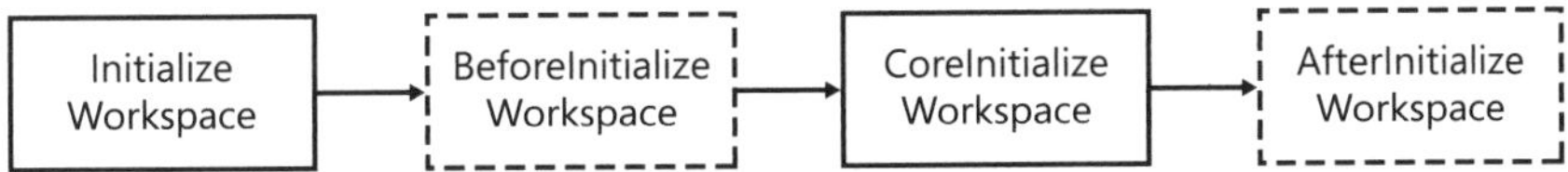

After the BeforeInitializeWorkspace extensibility target has been invoked the CoreInitializeWorkspace target will either:

- Leave the workspace from the previous build (if SkipInitializeWorkspace is true).
- Delete the workspace from the previous build (if CleanCompilationOutputOnly is true or SkipClean is true).
- Delete the workspace and the local files in that workspace (the source-code) from the previous build (in all other cases).

The CoreInitializeWorkspace target then creates a new workspace by calling the CreateWorkspaceTask task. This task will create a workspace with the name defined by the WorkspaceName property, comment defined by the CreateWorkspaceTaskComment property, and mappings defined by the build definition. This task then returns WorkspaceName and WorkspaceOwner properties that are used later in the build process.

For example, to set the workspace's comment you would add the following to TFSBuild.proj:

```
<PropertyGroup>
    <CreateWorkspaceTaskComment>
        This workspace was created by my custom build.
    </CreateWorkspaceTaskComment>
</PropertyGroup>
```

Lastly, the AfterInitializeWorkspace extensibility target is invoked, concluding the initialization phase.

Customizing Clean

The clean phase is responsible for removing build and test outputs from previous builds and under some circumstances the source code. There are two variations of the clean phase:

- **Clean All** In this variation the BinariesRoot, SolutionRoot, and TestResultsRoot directories are deleted from the build definition's workspace.
- **Clean Compilation Outputs Only** In this variation the BinariesRoot and TestResultsRoot directories are deleted from the build definition's workspace and the Clean target is then invoked for each solution/configuration combination.

For a desktop rebuild, the clean phase is performed by invoking the Clean target as shown in the following diagram. The CoreClean target then decides whether to call the CallClean or CoreCleanAll target based on whether the CleanCompilationOutputOnly property is set to true (the default for a desktop build or rebuild) or false.

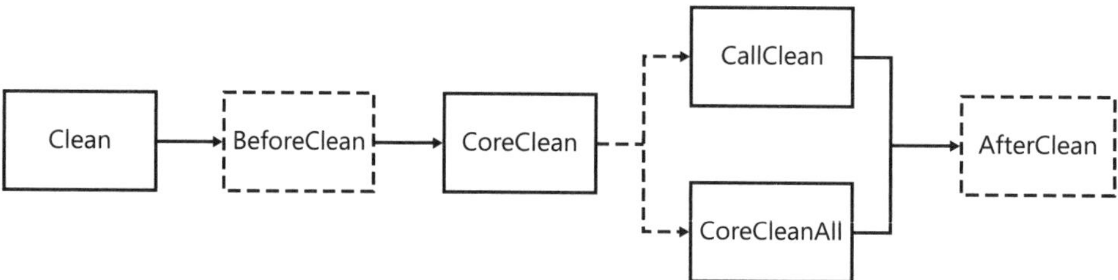

For an end-to-end build, either the CleanAll target or CleanCompilationOutput target will be executed as shown in the following diagram. As with the desktop rebuild, which is executed depends on the value of the CleanCompilationOutputOnly property with the CleanCompilationOutput target being executed if it's true; otherwise the CleanAll target is executed.

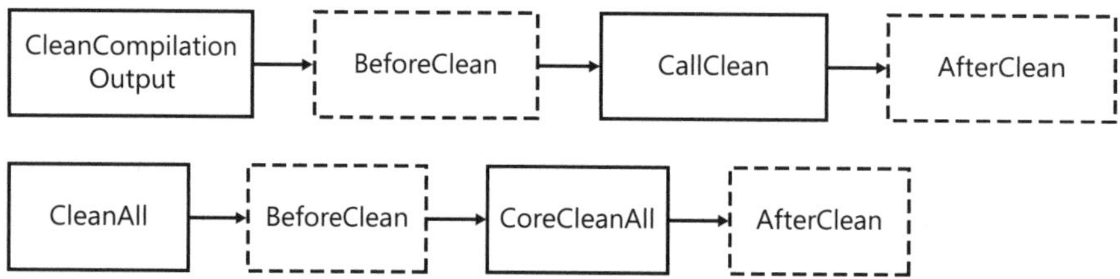

The reason this has been split into two separate targets in the end-to-end build process is because the CleanAll target must be executed before the Get target, and the CleanCompilationOutput target must be executed after it.

One important thing to be aware of about the CallClean target is that rather than invoking the CoreCleanCompilationOutput target directly it uses the MSBuild task to call back into the TFSBuild.proj to execute it. This is done primarily to take advantage of the multiple processor support introduced in MSBuild 3.5. The main impact of this is that dynamically-generated properties won't be passed through; to work around this the call also passes the property CustomPropertiesForClean, which can be used to pass dynamically-generated properties.

In this example, we use the Version task from MSBuild Community Tasks to generate a build number and we pass through the individual version number components to the CoreCleanCompilationOutput target by defining them in the CustomPropertiesForClean property:

```
<Target Name="BuildNumberOverrideTarget">
    <Version VersionFile="$(DropLocation)\version.txt" BuildType="Increment">
        <Output TaskParameter="Major" PropertyName="Major" />
        <Output TaskParameter="Minor" PropertyName="Minor" />
        <Output TaskParameter="Build" PropertyName="Build" />
        <Output TaskParameter="Revision" PropertyName="Revision" />
    </Version>
    <PropertyGroup>
        <BuildNumber>$(Major).$(Minor).$(Build).$(Revision)</BuildNumber>
        <CustomPropertiesForClean>
            $(CustomPropertiesForClean);
            Major=$(Major);
            Minor=$(Minor);
            Build=$(Build);
            Revision =$(Revision);
        </CustomPropertiesForClean>
    </PropertyGroup>
</Target>
```

The clean phase defines two empty extensibility targets, which can be overridden to implement custom clean logic. These targets are called BeforeClean and AfterClean and, as expected, they are invoked before the clean begins and after the clean completes respectively. To override one of these targets you define a target of the same name in TFSBuild.proj; for example:

```
<Target Name="BeforeClean">
    <Message Text="Starting the clean phase of my custom build." />
</Target>
```

You can skip the clean phase entirely by setting the SkipClean property to true and even if the clean phase is skipped the BeforeClean and AfterClean extensibility targets will still be invoked. Because incremental gets and incremental builds (discussed later in this chapter) give finer-grained control than skipping the clean phase it would be unusual to set the SkipClean property.

Customizing Get

The get phase is responsible for downloading the source code into the directory specified in the SolutionRoot property.

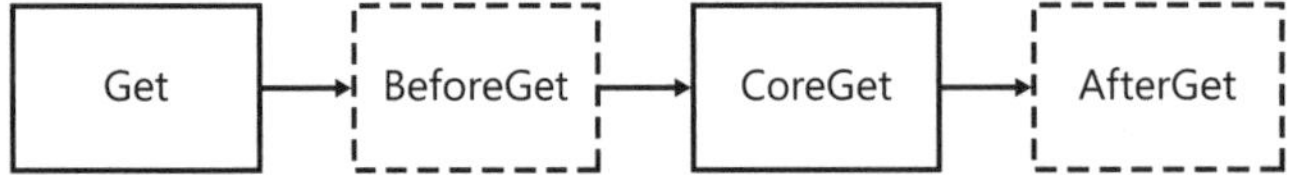

The default get is performed by the Get task in the CoreGet target, which does a get of the workspace named by the WorkspaceName property. This workspace is usually created automatically in the CoreInitializeWorkspace target based on the build definition's workspace.

The Get task can be configured to download only the top-level items in the workspace by setting the RecursiveGet property to false. Alternatively, the GetFileSpec property can be set to a file specification to get only a subset of the workspace.

You can skip the get phase completely; to do this set the SkipGet property to true. You might want to do this if you are retrieving the source code from somewhere other than Team Foundation Server's version control. Even if the SkipGet property is set to true, the BeforeGet and AfterGet targets will still be invoked making either of these an ideal place to implement your custom get logic.

For example, to skip the built-in get from version control and copy the source from a fileserver instead you would add the following to TFSBuild.proj:

```
<PropertyGroup>
    <SkipGet>true</SkipGet>
</PropertyGroup>

<ItemGroup>
    <SourceFile Include="\\CONTOSO\Projects\HelloWorld\src\**" />
</ItemGroup>

<Target Name="BeforeGet">
    <Copy SourceFiles="@(SourceFile)" DestinationFiles=
        "@(SourceFile->'$(SolutionRoot)\%(RecursiveDir)%(Filename)%(Extension)')"
    />
</Target>
```

Modifying Source-Code Destination

The SolutionRoot property for end-to-end builds defaults to $(MSBuildProjectDirectory)\..\$(SourcesSubDirectory) where the MSBuildProjectDirectory is the directory where Team Build downloads the TFSBuild.proj to (which is dictated by the working directory specified on the build agent) and SourcesSubDirectory defaults to Sources.

You can customize where the source code is downloaded to by editing TFSBuild.proj and either setting SolutionRoot to an absolute path or, if you just want to customize the directory name, setting SourcesSubDirectory to the new directory name. If overriding SolutionRoot, it is recommended that you set it to a value that is relative to MSBuildProjectDirectory; otherwise changing the build agent's working directory won't affect where the source code is downloaded to.

Tip Certain project types, including database projects, produce directories with very deep structures or files with very long names. In this scenario it is easy to exceed the operating system's maximum path length, which results in the build failing. Modifying the SolutionRoot or SourcesSubDirectory to use shorter names in addition to shortening the build agent's working directory, as discussed in the "Adding the Build Agent to Team Projects" section of Chapter 10, can minimize the chance of this occurring.

For example, to rename the SourcesSubDirectory from Sources to ProjectSources you would add the following to TFSBuild.proj:

```
<PropertyGroup>
    <SourcesSubDirectory>ProjectSources</SourcesSubDirectory>
</PropertyGroup>
```

Alternatively, you could use an absolute path by adding the following to TFSBuild.proj:

```
<PropertyGroup>
    <SolutionRoot>$(MSBuildProjectDirectory)\..\ProjectSources</SolutionRoot>
</PropertyGroup>
```

Building Specific Versions

When a build is queued it is queued for a specific version of the source; this could be a specific changeset (usually when triggered via continuous integration), the latest version (usually when triggered manually), or an arbitrary version. The version is defined using the same version specification format used by the TfsBuild command-line utility described in Chapter 10; for example, C125 for changeset 125.

The version that a build is queued for is specified in the SourceGetVersion property but to queue a build for an arbitrary version you set the GetVersion property, which overrides the SourceGetVersion property. This property can be set in TFSBuild.proj or TFSBuild.rsp to force a build definition to always build a specific version (for example, to "hard code" historical builds such as Version 1.0, Beta 2.0, etc.). It can also be specified in the MSBuild Command-line Arguments field when queuing a build as shown here:

```
/p:GetVersion=C125
```

If an arbitrary version has been specified then the CoreGet target will call the SetBuildProperties task to update the version in the Team Build operational database.

Performing Incremental Gets

For large workspaces one of the biggest performance improvements (beyond reducing the size of the workspace as discussed in the "Workspace" section of Chapter 10) that can be made is to enable incremental get. When incremental get is enabled there are four major differences to the build process:

1. Instead of the clean phase removing the BinariesRoot, SolutionRoot, and TestResultsRoot directories it invokes the Clean target on each solution/configuration combination. This removes any build outputs from previous builds without removing the source files; the exception to this is when incremental builds are also enabled in which case the clean phase skipped entirely.
2. The initialization phase does not remove the workspace created by earlier builds. Since the workspace is where the list of local files and versions is kept it must be kept between builds to allow the Get task to retrieve only the changed files.
3. Force get is disabled because it results in all files being downloaded regardless of the local version, which contradicts doing an incremental get.
4. Lastly, the Get task is instructed to do an incremental get and to download only files that have changed since the last get was performed.

To enable incremental get you can set the IncrementalGet property to true in TFSBuild.proj as shown here:

```
<PropertyGroup>
    <IncrementalGet>true</IncrementalGet>
</PropertyGroup>
```

This is actually a shortcut to setting the CleanCompilationOutputOnly and SkipInitializeWorkspace properties to true and the ForceGet property to false, but it is recommended that you use the IncrementalGet property over setting these properties individually.

Note A side effect of ForceGet being set to false is that if any of the downloaded files are made writable as part of the build process, the get will fail. Typically this isn't an issue because the default build process does not make any of the downloaded files writable but if you customize the process and manipulate any of the downloaded files then you may need to allow the Get task to overwrite these by setting the GetOverwrite property to true as shown in this example:

```
<PropertyGroup>
    <IncrementalGet>true</IncrementalGet>
    <GetOverwrite>true</GetOverwrite>
</PropertyGroup>
```

Populating Get Output Item Groups

One feature of the Get task is that it can populate item groups with the result of the get; this is disabled by default but can be enabled by setting GetPopulateOutput to true, which will populate the item groups Gets, Replaces, Deletes, and GetWarnings.

In this example, we enable the Get task populating the item groups and then output the contents of the item groups in the AfterGet target:

```
<PropertyGroup>
    <GetPopulateOutput>true</GetPopulateOutput>
</PropertyGroup>

<Target Name="AfterGet">
    <Message Text="Gets: @(Gets)" />
    <Message Text="Replaces: @(Replaces)" />
    <Message Text="Deletes: @(Deletes)" />
    <Message Text="GetWarnings: @(GetWarnings)" />
</Target>
```

Customizing Label

During the label phase, Team Build will apply a label to the source-code files.

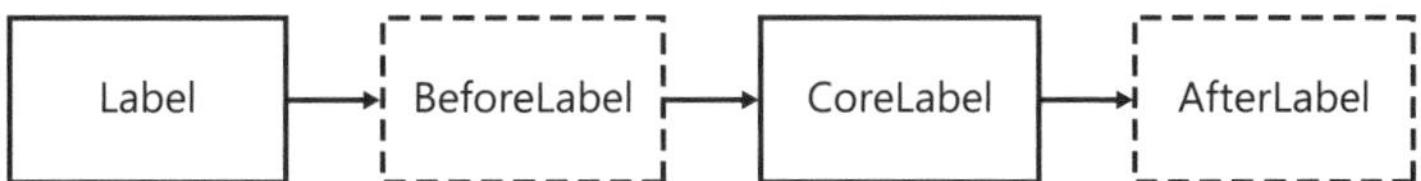

This is a quite important step because it allows you to do two things:

1. View which source-code files and the versions of those files that were included in each build.
2. Re-create a build by queuing a new build and setting the GetVersion property to the label associated with the build you want to re-create.

For example, to re-create build HelloWorldManual_20080823.1 we could submit a build using the MSBuild Command-Line Arguments:

```
/p:GetVersion=LHelloWorldManual_20080823.1
```

It is also possible to skip the label phase completely by setting the SkipLabel property to true and, as with the other skip properties, the BeforeLabel and AfterLabel extensibility targets will still be invoked; of course, by doing this you sacrifice the benefits listed previously.

Customizing Label Details

The name of the label created by Team Build is specified using the LabelName property and if one hasn't been specified it will default to the BuildNumber property. For example, we might want to label the source code based on the software version number rather than the build number as shown in this example:

```
<Target Name="BuildNumberOverrideTarget">
    <Version VersionFile="$(DropLocation)\version.txt" BuildType="Increment">
        <Output TaskParameter="Major" PropertyName="Major" />
        <Output TaskParameter="Minor" PropertyName="Minor" />
```

```
        <Output TaskParameter="Build" PropertyName="Build" />
        <Output TaskParameter="Revision" PropertyName="Revision" />
    </Version>
    <PropertyGroup>
        <LabelName>$(Major).$(Minor).$(Build).$(Revision)</LabelName>
    </PropertyGroup>
</Target>
```

Labels must have a unique name within the scope in which they're defined. The default scope for labels added by Team Build is $/$(TeamProject) (that is, at the Team Project level). This does not affect which files are included in the label, which is discussed in the next section, "Customizing What Is Labeled."

This default scope can be overridden by setting the LabelScope property to the desired scope. This may be necessary if you have overridden the LabelName property in such a way that it would not be unique if applied at the default Team Project level.

The label's comment (which can be seen in the Source Control Explorer) defaults to "Label created by Team Build." To override this with something more useful you can set the LabelComment property to the comment you would like to use; this could be used to store the build number if you set the LabelName property to something other than the build number.

In this example, we override the BeforeLabel extensibility target and define the name, comment, and scope of the label:

```
<Target Name="BeforeLabel">
    <PropertyGroup>
        <LabelName>LatestBuild</LabelName>
        <LabelComment>Label created by Team Build for build $(BuildNumber)</LabelComment>
        <LabelScope>$/$(TeamProject)/Main</LabelScope>
    </PropertyGroup>
</Target>
```

Customizing What Is Labeled

The CoreLabel target uses a number of properties to define what is labeled, what version is labeled, and what to do if the label already exists.

The LabelFiles property specifies the files to be labeled by the CoreLabel target; this property defaults to $/, which may lead you to believe that all the files in version control will be labeled, but this is not the case, and it will label only those files that are in the workspace. You can change the value for the LabelFiles property if you'd like to label only a subset of the files in the workspace. To label just the top-level items rather than applying the label recursively (which is the default) the LabelRecursive property can be set to false.

When labeling files Team Build defaults to labeling the version of the files that have been downloaded into the workspace (which is called the workspace version). This is generally the desired behavior but if you would like to label a different version of the files you can specify the version specification to use in the LabelVersion property. In this example, we label the files based on the GetVersion rather than the workspace version:

```
<Target Name="BeforeLabel">
    <PropertyGroup>
        <LabelVersion>$(GetVersion)</LabelVersion>
    </PropertyGroup>
</Target>
```

The LabelChild property defines what should happen if the label already exists and can be either:

- **Replace** The contents of the existing label should be replaced with the label contents defined in the build.
- **Merge** The contents of the existing label should be merged with the label contents defined in the build.

Customizing Compilation

Compiling the source code is arguably one of the most important phases of the build process and as you would expect is done in the compilation phase, which is, as you can see, one of the more complicated ones in Team Build.

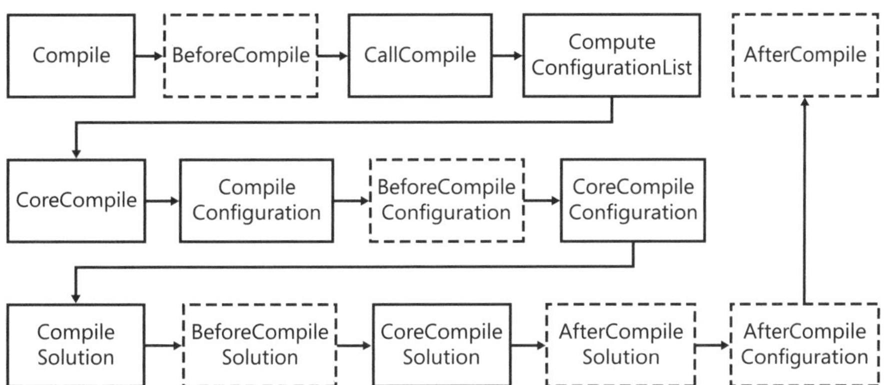

The CallCompile target starts the compilation process by calling back into the TFSBuild.proj project and invoking the CoreCompile target using the MSBuild task. As with the CallClean target this results in the values of dynamically-defined properties being lost, but also like the CallClean target the CallCompile target provides a property called CustomPropertiesForBuild that allows you to pass dynamically-generated properties into the CoreCompile target.

Defining Solutions to Build

The SolutionToBuild item group (which is normally populated by the MSBuild Project File Creation Wizard) defines the list of solutions (or individual projects) to be built, and the

Include attribute is the path to the solution. The item group also defines two important metadata items, as listed in Table 11-3.

TABLE 11-3 SolutionToBuild Item Metadata

Metadata Name	Description
Targets	Semicolon delimited list of the targets to be built.
Properties	Semicolon delimited list of name/value property pairs to pass to the solution when building it.

In this example, we add two solutions to the SolutionToBuild item group, and for the first solution (FrontEnd.sln) we list two targets (Build and MyCustomTarget) to be executed during the compilation phase and also pass two properties (SignAssembly and AssemblyOriginatorKeyFile):

```
<ItemGroup>
    <SolutionToBuild Include="$(SolutionRoot)\src\FrontEnd.sln">
        <Targets>Build;MyCustomTarget</Targets>
        <Properties>
            SignAssembly=true;
            AssemblyOriginatorKeyFile=$(SolutionRoot)\keypair.snk
        </Properties>
    </SolutionToBuild>
    <SolutionToBuild Include="$(SolutionRoot)\src\Server.sln" />
</ItemGroup>
```

Tip Despite its name, the SolutionToBuild item group can also build individual projects as well as solutions. Simply specify the path to a project rather than a solution in the Include attribute.

The CoreClean and CoreCompile targets both depend on the ComputeSolutionList target, which builds a list of the solutions to be built or cleaned and a list of solutions to be published either directly from the SolutionToBuild and SolutionToPublish item groups (in the case of desktop builds) or via the WorkspaceItemConverter task (in the case of end-to-end builds).

Defining Solutions to Publish

Team Build 2008 includes the ability to publish ClickOnce projects out-of-the-box but there are a few manual steps required to configure and enable this functionality.

The first step is to open the project you want to publish using ClickOnce and configure the ClickOnce settings in the Publish tab of the project's properties. Next you need to manually publish the project once by clicking the Publish Now (or Publish Wizard) button on the Publish tab. During the first publish of a project the ClickOnce settings are added to the project file. The updated project file then needs to be checked-in to version control to make it available to the build process.

In TFSBuild.proj the SolutionToPublish item group defines the list of solutions to invoke the Publish target on (which is used for ClickOnce as well as other deployment functionality). In this example, we populate the SolutionToPublish item group to publish the FrontEndApp.csproj project:

```
<ItemGroup>
    <SolutionToPublish Include="$(SolutionRoot)\src\FrontEnd\FrontEndApp.csproj" />
</ItemGroup>
```

The SolutionToPublish item group behaves similarly to the SolutionToBuild item group but forces the Targets metadata to be Publish. It still provides the CustomProperties metadata if you'd like to pass additional properties when invoking the Publish target.

Defining Configurations to Build

The CoreClean, CoreCompile, and CoreTest targets also depend on the ComputeConfigurationList target, which builds a list of configurations based on the ConfigurationToBuild item group.

The ConfigurationToBuild item group is initially populated by the configurations and platforms selected in the Configurations tab of the MSBuild Project File Creation Wizard discussed in Chapter 10. The Include attribute must be unique for each configuration to be built and defaults to FlavorToBuild|PlatformToBuild. Each ConfigurationToBuild item also includes metadata specifying the FlavorToBuild (Debug, Release, etc.) and the PlatformToBuild (Any CPU, x86, x64, etc.).

This example will build the solutions four times for each combination of the Debug and Release configurations and the x86 and x64 platforms:

```
<ItemGroup>
    <ConfigurationToBuild Include="Debug|x86">
        <FlavorToBuild>Debug</FlavorToBuild>
        <PlatformToBuild>x86</PlatformToBuild>
    </ConfigurationToBuild>
    <ConfigurationToBuild Include="Release|x86">
        <FlavorToBuild>Release</FlavorToBuild>
        <PlatformToBuild>x86</PlatformToBuild>
    </ConfigurationToBuild>
    <ConfigurationToBuild Include="Debug|x64">
        <FlavorToBuild>Debug</FlavorToBuild>
        <PlatformToBuild>x64</PlatformToBuild>
    </ConfigurationToBuild>
    <ConfigurationToBuild Include="Release|x64">
        <FlavorToBuild>Release</FlavorToBuild>
        <PlatformToBuild>x64</PlatformToBuild>
    </ConfigurationToBuild>
</ItemGroup>
```

The CoreCompile target calls back into the TFSBuild.proj project invoking the CompileConfiguration target for each configuration to be built using the MSBuild task. If you're building multiple configurations, then setting the BuildConfigurationsInParallel property to true will set the BuildInParallel property on the MSBuild task to true allowing MSBuild to build the configurations in parallel.

In this example, the Debug and Release configurations will be built in parallel:

```
<PropertyGroup>
    <BuildConfigurationsInParallel>true</BuildConfigurationsInParallel>
</PropertyGroup>
<ItemGroup>
    <ConfigurationToBuild Include="Debug|Any CPU">
        <FlavorToBuild>Debug</FlavorToBuild>
        <PlatformToBuild>Any CPU</PlatformToBuild>
    </ConfigurationToBuild>
    <ConfigurationToBuild Include="Release|Any CPU">
        <FlavorToBuild>Release</FlavorToBuild>
        <PlatformToBuild>Any CPU</PlatformToBuild>
    </ConfigurationToBuild>
</ItemGroup>
```

Note Configurations or solutions will be built in parallel only if the MaxProcesses setting in TFSBuildService.exe.config has been increased above 1. This is discussed in "Configuring the Team Build Service" later in this chapter.

If a specified configuration doesn't exist for one of the solutions the default behavior is to continue processing other configurations; to instead generate an error you can set the SkipInvalidConfigurations property to false.

The BeforeCompileConfiguration and AfterCompileConfiguration targets are invoked before and after each configuration is compiled respectively, and from within these (or any target that executes per configuration) you can access the Configuration and Platform properties to determine the current configuration being built. This example outputs the configuration and platform for each configuration as it builds:

```
<Target Name="BeforeCompileConfiguration">
    <Message Text="About to build configuration $(Configuration)
        for platform $(Platform)." />
</Target>
```

Compiling Solutions

The CoreCompileConfiguration target calls back into the TFSBuild.proj project invoking the CompileSolution target for each solution to be built using the MSBuild task.

As with configurations, if you're building multiple solutions then setting the BuildSolutionsInParallel property to true will allow MSBuild to build the solutions in parallel. Building solutions in parallel may not be appropriate if you have dependencies between solutions because there is no dependency analysis or synchronization between the solutions done by MSBuild. This example builds the HelloWorldDesktop.sln and HelloWorldWeb.sln solutions in parallel:

```
<PropertyGroup>
    <BuildSolutionsInParallel>true</BuildSolutionsInParallel>
</PropertyGroup>
```

```
<ItemGroup>
    <SolutionToBuild Include="$(SolutionRoot)\HelloWorldDesktop.sln" />
    <SolutionToBuild Include="$(SolutionRoot)\HelloWorldWeb.sln" />
</ItemGroup>
```

The CoreCompileSolution target is then invoked, which initializes compilation specific MSBuild and Visual C++ properties before executing the MSBuild task against the solution using the targets defined in the SolutionToBuild Targets metadata. The list of compilation outputs is returned from the MSBuild task and metadata is added to these items to identify the solution and configuration that produced each of the build outputs which can be used for post-compilation processing of the build outputs. In this example, we override the AfterCompile extensibility target and output a list of the compilation outputs, what solution they came from, and what configuration they're built with:

```
<Target Name="AfterCompile">
    <Message Text="CompilationOutputs: %(CompilationOutputs.Identity)
        %(CompilationOutputs.Solution)
        %(CompilationOutputs.Platform)
        %(CompilationOutputs.Flavor)"
    />
</Target>
```

The BeforeCompileSolution and AfterCompileSolution targets are invoked before and after each solution is compiled respectively and the Solution property allows you to determine the current solution being built. In this example, we override the BeforeCompileSolution target and output the name of the solution, configuration, and platform being built:

```
<Target Name="BeforeCompileSolution">
    <Message Text="About to build solution $(Solution)
        for configuration $(Configuration)
        for platform $(Platform)." />
</Target>
```

Controlling Build Output and Publish Directories

By default the build outputs are placed in the directory defined by the BinariesRoot and BinariesSubDirectory properties, which default to $(SolutionRoot)\..\$(BinariesSubDirectory) and Binaries respectively.

The output and publish directories for individual solutions can be overridden by defining the OutDir or PublishDir property as part of the SolutionToBuild's Properties metadata as shown here:

```
<ItemGroup>
    <SolutionToBuild Include="$(SolutionRoot)\HelloWorldDesktop.sln">
        <Properties>OutDir=$(OutDir)\Desktop\</Properties>
    </SolutionToBuild>
    <SolutionToBuild Include="$(SolutionRoot)\HelloWorldWeb.sln" />
        <Properties>OutDir=$(OutDir)\Web\</Properties>
    </SolutionToBuild>
```

```
    <SolutionToPublish Include="$(SolutionRoot)\HelloWorldDesktop\HelloWorldDesktop.csproj">
        <Properties>PublishDir=$(PublishDir)\DesktopPublish\</Properties>
    </SolutionToPublish>
</ItemGroup>
```

Note The OutDir and PublishDir properties must have a trailing backslash.

Team Build can also be instructed to honor the output or publish directory defined in each project file, which results in an output structure similar to that produced on a developer's workstation by setting the CustomizableOutDir and/or CustomizablePublishDir properties to true.

Note While this may seem desirable, you need to be aware that this path is entirely controlled by the developer and may result in build outputs being placed in incorrect directories that won't be picked up correctly by the drop or test targets.

Performing Incremental Builds

When IncrementalGet is set to true Team Build gets only files that have changed from version control but will still build all projects. Setting IncrementalBuild to true takes this to the next level by not cleaning build outputs from previous builds and re-building only projects that have changed.

Setting IncrementalBuild to true results in SkipInitializeWorkspace being set to true and ForceGet set to false as when doing an incremental get. The key difference is that when IncrementalBuild is set to true it also sets SkipClean to true, which will stop build outputs from previous builds from being removed.

This example shows how to enable incremental builds:

```
<PropertyGroup>
    <IncrementalBuild>true</IncrementalBuild>
</PropertyGroup>
```

Customizing Getting Changesets and Updating Work Items

Once the compilation phase has completed successfully the CoreGetChangesetsAndUpdate-WorkItems target will retrieve the list of changesets and work items that are associated with this build and set the Integration Build or Fixed In Build fields in the work items to the BuildNumber property. You can optionally have this process take place even if the compilation fails, which is discussed in the "Customizing Build Failures" section.

This process can be skipped by setting SkipGetChangesetsAndUpdateWorkItems to true. As with other targets the BeforeGetChangesetsAndUpdateWorkItems and AfterGetChangesets-AndUpdateWorkItems extensibility targets will still be executed if this is set to true; however, if the SkipPostBuild property is set to true then both the GetChangesetsAndUpdateWorkItems target as well as its extensibility targets will be skipped.

Customizing Testing

The testing phase is responsible for running tests against each configuration that is built.

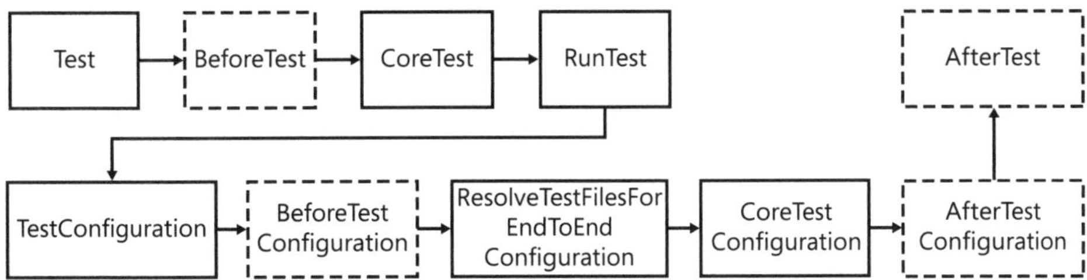

Unlike other phases where you need to opt-out by setting the Skip* property to true you need to opt-in to the testing phase by setting RunTest to true. However, as with the other extensibility targets, the BeforeTest and AfterTest targets will still be invoked even if testing hasn't been enabled.

The CoreTest target calls back into TFSBuild.proj and executes the RunTest target. As with CallClean and CallCompile this results in any dynamically generated properties being lost, but CoreTest does not provide a way to pass custom properties because there is nowhere that they could be referenced in the testing process.

The RunTest target creates the TestResultsRoot directory to store the test result files generated by the testing process and then calls back into TFSBuild.proj and executes the TestConfiguration target for each configuration in the ConfigurationToBuild item group. The tests to be executed can be defined using test metadata files (*.vsmdi), test containers (assemblies), or a combination of both using the MetaDataFile and TestContainer item groups.

The list of test metadata files is specified using MetaDataFile items that provide either a local or server path to the test metadata file as the Include attribute and the names of the test lists in the TestList metadata:

```
<ItemGroup>
    <MetaDataFile Include="$(BuildProjectFolderPath)/HelloWorld/HelloWorldDesktop.vsmdi">
        <TestList>SmokeTests;GeneralTests</TestList>
    </MetaDataFile>
    <MetaDataFile Include="$(BuildProjectFolderPath)/HelloWorld/HelloWorldWeb.vsmdi">
        <TestList>SmokeTests;GeneralTests</TestList>
    </MetaDataFile>
<ItemGroup>
```

The list of test containers is specified using TestContainer items that specify the local path to the test container as the Include attribute. Because the items Include attributes are resolved before the test containers have been compiled you should use %2a instead of *, and %3f instead of ? to prevent the wildcards from being expanded until after the compilation has completed. In this example we add a TestContainer that includes *.Tests.dll:

```
<ItemGroup>
    <TestContainer Include="$(OutDir)%2a.Tests.dll" />
</ItemGroup>
```

The TestConfiguration target invokes the CoreTestConfiguration target, which invokes the ResolveTestFilesForEndToEndConfiguration, which resolves the locations of the test containers and test metadata files in end-to-end builds.

The TestResultsRoot and TestResultsSubdirectory properties define the destination for the test result (*.trx) files produced by the testing process. These default to $(SolutionRoot)\..\$(TestResultsSubdirectory) and TestResults respectively.

In Team Build 2008 Service Pack 1 two properties determine what happens on test failure. The first is StopOnTestFailure (which defaults to false); if this is set to true then the build process won't continue if the tests fail. The second is TreatTestFailureAsBuildFailure (which also defaults to false), by default if compilation succeeds and testing fails the resulting build status will be Partially Succeeded; if this property is set to true then if the testing fails the resulting build status will instead be Failed.

Customizing Generating Documentation and Packaging Binaries

Team Build doesn't provide any out-of-the-box support for generating documentation or packaging binaries, but it does provide two extensibility targets in the build process for you to add this logic to your build process. These targets are:

1. GenerateDocumentation
2. PackageBinaries

This example overrides the PackageBinaries and uses a custom Zip task to compress the Debug and Release directories. This example is elaborated on in "Zipping the Binaries and Source-Code" in Chapter 12:

```
<Target Name="PackageBinaries">
    <CreateItem Include="$(BinariesRoot)\Debug\**">
        <Output TaskParameter="Include" ItemName="DebugFiles" />
    </CreateItem>
    <Zip Files="@(DebugFiles)" OutputFile="$(BinariesRoot)\Debug.zip" />
    <CreateItem Include="$(BinariesRoot)\Release\**">
        <Output TaskParameter="Include" ItemName="ReleaseFiles" />
    </CreateItem>
    <Zip Files="@(ReleaseFiles)" OutputFile="$(BinariesRoot)\Release.zip" />
</Target>
```

The "Generating API Documentation Using Sandcastle" example in Chapter 12 demonstrates how to use the GenerateDocumentation extensibility target to generate API documentation.

Customizing Drop

The drop phase is the last in the end-to-end build process (for a successful build) and is responsible for dropping the contents of the BinariesRoot directory to the drop location.

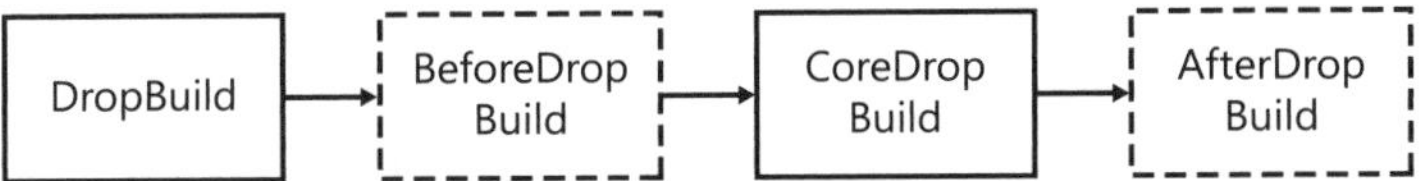

Dropping builds to the drop location occurs only for end-to-end builds and the CoreDropBuild target recursively copies all of the files in the BinariesRoot directory to the build's drop location, which is $(DropLocation)\$(BuildNumber).

As with other phases the drop phase can be disabled by setting the SkipDropBuild property to true, and again the BeforeDropBuild and AfterDropBuild targets will still be invoked.

Customizing Build Failures

The OnBuildBreak target and its dependencies define what occurs when an end-to-end build fails. The default process gets a list of changesets and work items included in the build, updates the work items, and creates a build failure work item.

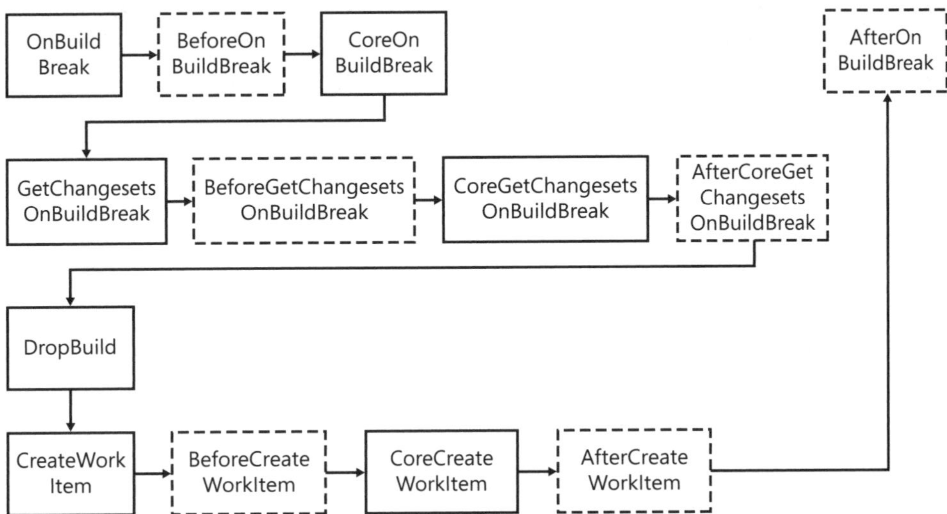

Updating Work Items on Build Failure

As mentioned earlier, part of the default end-to-end build process is to update the Integration Build or Fixed In Build field in work items that are associated with the current build. If the build fails the default behavior is not to update the work items; if you would like the work items updated regardless of the build's status you can set the UpdateAssociatedWorkItemsOnBuildBreak property to true.

Creating Build Failure Work Item

Finally, the build failure work item is created unless the SkipWorkItemCreation has been set to true. The type of the work item is defined in the WorkItemType property and an array of field/value pairs can be defined in the WorkItemFieldValues as shown:

```
<WorkItemFieldValues>
    System.AssignedTo=Build Administrator;
    System.Priority=High;
</WorkItemFieldValues>
```

The field is referred to using the field's reference name, which can be found in the work item type definition or by running the witfields.exe command-line utility.

Note The specified work item type must define the Microsoft.VSTS.Build.FoundIn field to store the build number of the failed build.

The title of the work item can be set using the WorkItemTitle property and Team Build automatically appends the BuildNumber to this. Also, the description of the work item can be set using the DescriptionText property and Team Build will automatically append a link to the build log prefixed with the value of the BuildlogText property and a link to the error/warning log prefixed with the value of the ErrorWarningLogText property.

This example demonstrates how to configure the build failure work item:

```
<PropertyGroup>
    <WorkItemType>Bug</WorkItemType>
    <WorkItemTitle>Build failure in build:</WorkItemTitle>
    <WorkItemFieldValues>
        System.Discipline=Release Management;
        System.Description=Start the $(BuildDefinitionName) build using Team Build.
    </WorkItemFieldValues>
    <DescriptionText>Build failure.</DescriptionText>
    <BuildlogText>Build Log:</BuildlogText>
    <ErrorWarningLogText>Errors/Warnings Log:</ErrorWarningLogText>
</PropertyGroup>
```

Stopping Build on First Failure

By default the build process will continue after the first failure. This is usually desirable because it can allow you to identify and fix multiple problems before re-running the build. However, it will take longer for the build to fail and there can be extraneous information in the logs that makes it harder to identify the root cause of the build failure. Team Build can be configured to stop cleaning, compiling, or testing on the first failure by setting the StopOnFirstFailure property to true.

Configuring the Team Build Service

While most settings can be configured through Visual Studio or the TFSBuild.proj MSBuild project file, some are service-level settings and are set in the TFSBuildService.exe.config file in %ProgramFiles%\Microsoft Visual Studio 9.0\Common7\IDE\PrivateAssemblies. This is a standard .NET application configuration file and should be edited in an XML editor such as Microsoft Visual Studio.

Once you've saved your changes, the Visual Studio Team Foundation Build service needs to be restarted before they'll take effect. This can be done using the Services control panel or by running the following commands at a command prompt:

```
net stop vstfbuild
net start vstfbuild
```

Changing Communications Ports

By default Team Build listens on port 9191 when run as a service and port 9192 when run interactively (later in this section we'll look at how to do this). Both of these ports can be changed in TFSBuildService.exe.config using the Port and InteractivePort settings respectively. Once they have been changed you will need to associate the port with the user that the service runs as, which is discussed in the "Team Build Security" section of Chapter 10.

You will also need to update the Communications Port in the build agent's properties as shown in Figure 11-1.

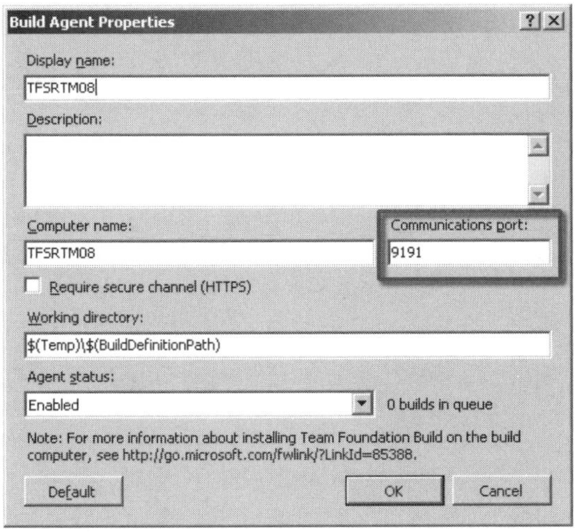

FIGURE 11-1 Build Agent Properties – Communications Port

Requiring SSL

Team Build can also require clients to use SSL to encrypt the requests to and responses from the communications ports. This is recommended when the network between the Team Foundation Server application tier and the build agent is untrusted.

The first step is to issue and install an X.509 certificate in the build service account's certificate store. To be used for securing Team Build the issued certificate must have an intended purpose of client authentication and be issued by a certificate authority trusted by the Team Foundation Server application tier. For information on how to issue and install an X.509 certificate refer to *http://msdn.microsoft.com/en-us/library/aa833873.aspx*.

You should note the certificate's thumbprint because it is needed later to bind the certificate to the build agent.

Once the certificate has been issued and installed edit TFSBuildService.exe.config and set the RequireSecureChannel setting to true. Before the service is restarted you must bind the certificate to the build agent's communication port by:

1. Install the Windows Support Tools from *http://technet.microsoft.com/en-us/library/cc758202.aspx*. This isn't necessary on Windows Vista or Windows Server 2008 where netsh.exe can be used instead.
2. Open the Windows Support Tools command prompt (or a standard command prompt on Windows Vista or Windows Server 2008).
3. On Windows XP or Windows Server 2003 bind the certificate to the build agent's communication port by running `httpcfg set ssl /i 0.0.0.0:9191 /h thumbprint`. Where 9191 is the communication port and thumbprint is the thumbprint of the certificate to be used.
4. On Windows Vista or Windows Server 2008 run `netsh http add sslcert ipport=0.0.0.0:9191 certhash=thumbprint appid=arbitrary_guid`. Where arbitrary_guid is a GUID you've generated to represent the binding.
5. Remove the HTTP binding by running `wcfhttpconfig free 9191`. Where 9191 is the communication port.
6. Add the HTTP binding by running `wcfhttpconfig reserve DOMAIN\Account` *`https://+:9191/Build/v2.0/AgentService.asmx`*. Where DOMAIN\Account is the Team Build service account and 9191 is the communication port.
7. Restart the Team Build service.

Finally, as when changing the communications port the build agent's properties need to be updated to reflect this change as shown in Figure 11-2.

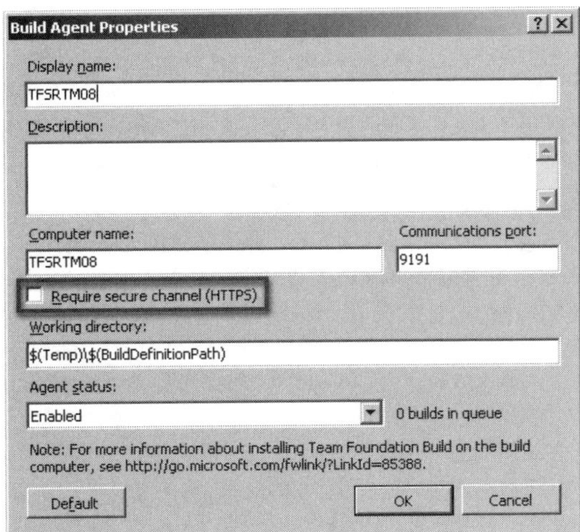

FIGURE 11-2 Build Agent Properties – Require Secure Channel

Configuring Communications from Build Agent to Application Tier

The previous settings define how the application tier communicates with the build agent but there are two additional settings that specify how the build agent communicates back to the application tier.

Each build agent is bound to a single application tier, and the URL for this application tier is stored in the Team Build service account's registry HKEY_CURRENT_USER\Software\Microsoft\VisualStudio\9.0\TeamFoundation\Build\Service\AllowedTeamServer. The value in the registry can be overridden by specifying a value for the AllowedTeamServer setting in the TFSBuildService.exe.config configuration file.

In scenarios where the build agent is on a different network than the application tier, it is sometimes necessary for the build agent to use a different URL to access the application tier. For example, the application tier's URL may be *http://TFSRTM08:8080* but from the build agent's network it needs to use the fully qualified domain name which results in the URL *http://TFSRTM08.contoso.com:8080*. To specify that the build agent should use an alternate URL to communicate with the application tier you can specify the alternate URL in the ServerAccessUrl setting in the TFSBuildService.exe.config configuration file.

Configuring Client Authentication

The Team Build service will authenticate its clients (which is nearly always the Team Foundation Server application tier) using NTLM authentication by default. The AuthenticationScheme setting in TFSBuildService.exe.config can be changed to one of the authentication schemes in Table 11-4.

TABLE 11-4 Authentication Schemes

Authentication Scheme	Description
Anonymous	The client will not be authenticated by the Team Build service.
Digest	The client will be authenticated using HTTP digest credentials.
Negotiate	The client will be authenticated using Kerberos. In workgroup scenarios Team Build must be running as NT AUTHORITY\Local Service for this to work. For this to work in domain scenarios Team Build must be running as NT AUTHORITY\Network Service or the account it is running as must have a valid SPN. To assign an SPN to the Team Build service account you need to run setspn –a ComputerName:CommunicationsPort DOMAIN\TeamBuildServiceAccount, for example, setspn –a TFSRTM08:9191 CONTOSO\TFSBUILDS.
Ntlm	The client will be authenticated using NTLM (the default).

Note For security reasons the Basic authentication scheme is not supported.

The Team Build service can be configured to restrict access to a single client account (usually the user that the Team Foundation Server application tier is running as) by setting the AuthorizedUser setting to that user's username.

Tip To ensure only the Team Foundation Server can submit builds to the build agent, you should set the AuthorizedUser setting to the Team Foundation Server's service account.

Running Interactively

By default Team Build runs as a service, which is typically desirable because it doesn't require the build agent to be logged in. However, because services can't access the desktop if your build process runs unit tests that display a user interface, then they will fail. This feature can also be used to run multiple instances of Team Build on a build machine.

To work around this Team Build can be run as an interactive process by running %ProgramFiles%\Microsoft Visual Studio 9.0\Common7\IDE\PrivateAssemblies\TFSBuildService.exe directly. When running interactively Team Build listens on the InteractivePort defined in TFSBuildService.exe.config, so when adding the build agent in the Manage Build Agents dialog you should ensure that you use this value.

The port used by the service as well as the port used interactively can both be changed by editing TFSBuildService.exe.config, but you need to ensure that the values in the Build

Agent Properties dialog match those in the TFSBuildService.exe.config; otherwise, the connection will fail.

Enabling Parallel Builds

So that Team Build 2008's behavior is as consistent as possible with Team Build 2005, it defaults to using only a single process, but to enable building configurations or solutions in parallel you must allow Team Build 2008 to use multiple processes. To do this:

1. Edit the TFSBuildService.exe.config file.
2. Change the MaxProcesses from 1 to 2 or more. You may need to experiment to find the best value for your environment but allowing for one process per processor is a good starting point.
3. Save the TFSBuildService.exe.config file.
4. Restart the Team Build service.
5. Set BuildConfigurationsInParallel and/or BuildSolutionsInParallel to true in the build definition's TFSBuild.proj as discussed earlier in this chapter.

Configuring Build Definition Download

One of the first steps of the build process is the Team Build service downloading the build definition's configuration folder (containing TFSBuild.proj, TFSBuild.rsp, etc.). Table 11-5 details the two settings in TFSBuildService.exe.config that control how this happens.

TABLE 11-5 Build Definition Download Settings

Setting Name	Default	Description
DoNotDownloadBuildType	False	Downloading of the build definition's configuration folder can be suppressed entirely by setting this to true. If this is suppressed then Team Build will use the copy that is on the build agent in the location that it would have downloaded the folder to.
ConfigurationFolderRecursionType	OneLevel	In Team Build 2008 the default is to download only immediate children of the build definition's configuration folder. In Team Build 2005 the folder was downloaded recursively. If you have sub-folders then you will need to change this setting to Full to revert to the Team Build 2005 behavior.

Enabling Building on FAT Partitions

Team Build will by default fail any builds that use a FAT partition on the build agent. Because FAT does not support access control, auditing, and other security features, Team Build does this to protect your source code from unauthorized access. While the ideal solution to this is converting the partition to NTFS, if you do need to allow building on FAT partitions you can enable this by setting the BuildOnFatPartitions setting to true in TFSBuildService.exe.config.

Enabling Per Project Log Files

Team Build by default logs any errors into a single ErrorsWarningsLog.txt as well as a per configuration log file (called <ConfigurationName>.txt) in the root of the drop location. If you set the LogFilePerProject setting in TFSBuildService.exe.config to true then Team Build will additionally create per project log files (called <ProjectName>_ErrorsWarnings.txt) in the configuration subdirectory of the drop location. This can be a huge timesaver for developers if you have large solutions or developers with responsibilities for different parts of a large system.

Enabling Tracing

The Team Build service utilizes the .NET Framework diagnostic tracing functionality internally but by default tracing is disabled. If you are unable to start the Team Build service or need more information to debug an issue you can enable tracing by:

1. Edit the TFSBuildService.exe.config file.
2. Uncomment the <system.diagnostics> element.
3. Optionally: Change the log path in the initializeData attribute of the myListener listener.
4. Save the TFSBuildService.exe.config file.
5. Create the directory that will contain the log if it doesn't already exist.
6. Restart the Team Build service.

When you have finished debugging the issue you should disable the logging by commenting out the <system.diagnostics> element and then restarting the Team Build service. The resulting log file looks like this:

```
TFSBuild.proj

[Verbose, PID 1236, TID 4000, 09:46:37.110] StartBuild: Added Build Process to a job
```

```
[Info, PID 2196, TID 2312, 10:22:49.288] Params: TeamBuildInstallPath - C:\Program Files\
Microsoft Visual Studio 9.0\Common7\IDE\PrivateAssemblies

[Info, PID 2196, TID 2312, 10:22:49.304] Params: TeamBuildInstallPath - C:\Program Files\
Microsoft Visual Studio 9.0\Common7\IDE\PrivateAssemblies

[Info, PID 2196, TID 2312, 10:22:49.319] Params: TeamBuildInstallPath - C:\Program Files\
Microsoft Visual Studio 9.0\Common7\IDE\PrivateAssemblies

[Info, PID 2196, TID 2312, 10:22:49.319] Build arguments: /nodeReuse:false
/m:1
/nologo
/noconsolelogger
/dl:BuildLogger,"C:\Program Files\Microsoft Visual Studio 9.0\Common7\IDE\
PrivateAssemblies\Microsoft.TeamFoundation.Build.Server.Logger.dll";"BuildUri=vstfs:///
Build/Build/41;TFSUrl=http://technolo-f9d36f:8080/;TFSProjectFile=C:\Documents and
Settings\TFSBUILDS\Local Settings\Temp\Contoso\HelloWorldManual\BuildType\TFSBuild.proj
;ServerUICulture=1033;LogFilePerProject=True;"*BuildForwardingLogger,"C:\Program Files\
Microsoft Visual Studio 9.0\Common7\IDE\PrivateAssemblies\Microsoft.TeamFoundation.
Build.Server.Logger.dll";"BuildUri=vstfs:///Build/Build/41;TFSUrl=http://technolo-
f9d36f:8080/;TFSProjectFile=C:\Documents and Settings\TFSBUILDS\Local Settings\Temp\Contoso\
HelloWorldManual\BuildType\TFSBuild.proj;ServerUICulture=1033;"
/fl /flp:logfile=BuildLog.txt;encoding=Unicode;
/p:BuildDefinition="HelloWorldManual"
/p:BuildDefinitionId="3"
/p:DropLocation="\\TECHNOLO-F9D36F\Drops"
/p:BuildProjectFolderPath="$/Contoso/TeamBuildTypes/HelloWorldManual"
/p:BuildUri="vstfs:///Build/Build/41"
/p:TeamFoundationServerUrl="http://technolo-f9d36f:8080/"
/p:TeamProject="Contoso"
/p:SourcesSubdirectory="Sources"
/p:BinariesSubdirectory="Binaries"
/p:TestResultsSubdirectory="TestResults"
/p:SourceGetVersion="C33"
/p:LastGoodBuildLabel=""
/p:LastBuildNumber=""
/p:LastGoodBuildNumber=""
/p:NoCICheckInComment="***NO_CI***"
/p:IsDesktopBuild="false"
/p:TeamBuildRefPath="C:\Program Files\Microsoft Visual Studio 9.0\Common7\IDE\
PrivateAssemblies" /t:EndToEndIteration
```

Team Build API

Team Build provides a rich application programming interface (API) that allows you to query and manage the build server, build agents, build definitions, and individual builds. There are a number of scenarios where the API is useful:

- Automating administration tasks
- Integrating Team Build into other processes
- Extending the build process beyond MSBuild

Creating a Project

The first step is to create a project that references the required assemblies. In this example, we'll create a new Console Application called TeamBuildAPI as shown in Figure 11-3:

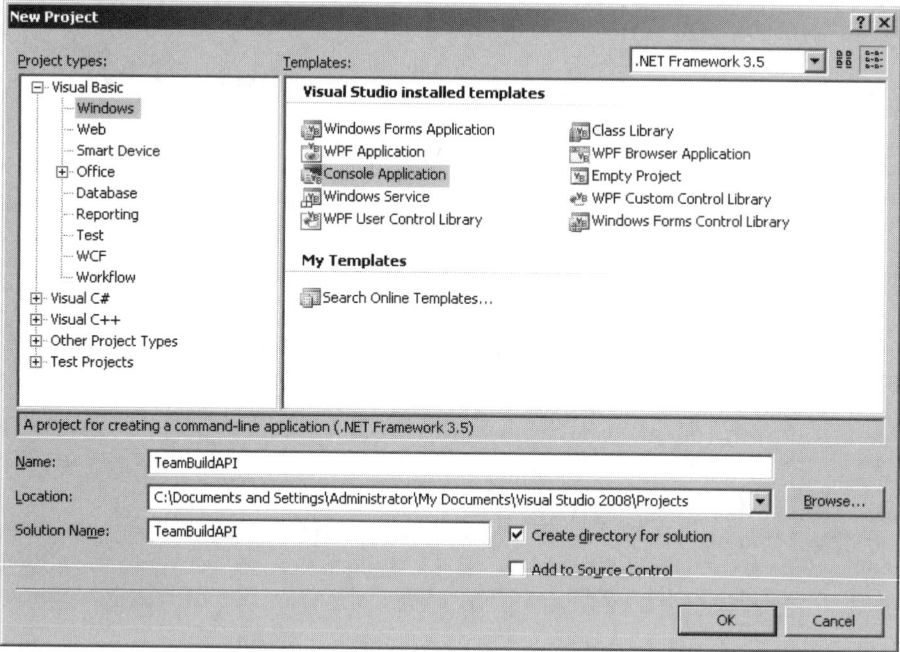

FIGURE 11-3 New Project dialog box

Using the Team Build API requires at least three references:

- **Microsoft.TeamFoundation.Client.dll** Provides the necessary classes to connect to Team Foundation Server.
- **Microsoft.TeamFoundation.Common.dll** Contains common classes such as exception classes.
- **Microsoft.TeamFoundation.Build.Client.dll** Contains the classes and interfaces relating to Team Build.

These references can be added from the .NET tab of the Add References dialog if the Visual Studio 2008 SDK has been installed, but ensure you select the 9.0.0.0 assemblies, which are for Team Build 2008. If this isn't installed you can reference these assemblies directly from the %Program Files%\Microsoft Visual Studio 9.0\Common7\IDE\PrivateAssemblies directory as shown in Figure 11-4.

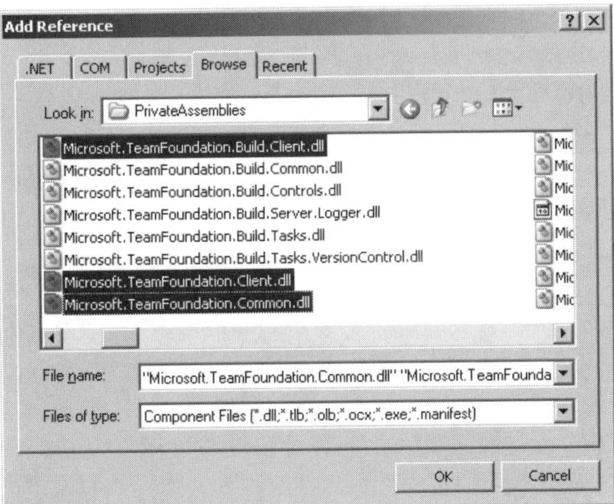

FIGURE 11-4 PrivateAssemblies directory

Connecting to Team Foundation Server

Once you've referenced these assemblies you need to obtain a TeamFoundationServer object, which represents a connection to a Team Foundation Server. This object provides access to all of the services offered by the Team Foundation Server such as build, version control, and work-item tracking.

The recommended way to create a `TeamFoundationServer` object is to pass the URL or Registered Server Name to the *GetServer* method of the `TeamFoundationServerFactory` class.

```
TeamFoundationServer server = TeamFoundationServerFactory.GetServer("http://TFSRTM08:8080");
```

The advantage of using the factory over creating an instance of the *TeamFoundationServer* class directly is that the factory will cache connections based on the URL or Registered Server Name and will return these cached connections, which can increase the performance of the application.

The API will attempt to authenticate the user automatically using integrated authentication but if this fails the API will throw a TeamFoundationServerUnauthorized exception. This behavior is inconsistent with Visual Studio Team System, which instead prompts users for their credentials if they can't be authenticated automatically. You can achieve this same behavior by passing an instance of the UICredentialsProvider to the *GetServer* method.

```
TeamFoundationServer server = TeamFoundationServerFactory.GetServer(
    "http://TFSRTM08:8080",
    new UICredentialsProvider()
);
```

When this overload is used then the API will try to authenticate the user automatically and if that fails will display the credentials prompt shown in Figure 11-5 and then use those credentials to authenticate the user to the Team Foundation Server.

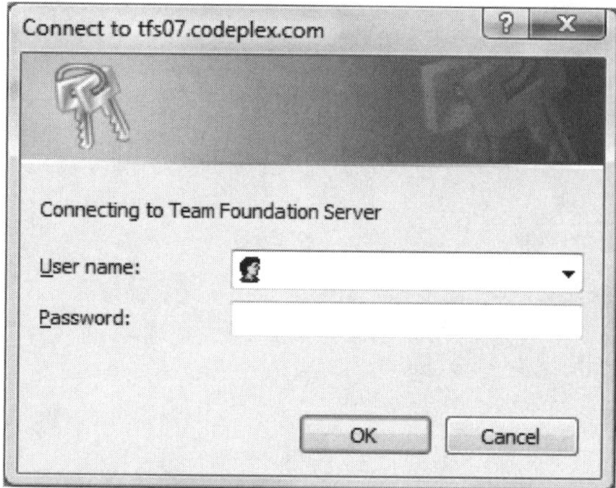

FIGURE 11-5 Credentials prompt

More Info The Registered Server Name can be used as a shortcut for the full Team Foundation Server URL in most command-line tools and APIs. When you add a Team Foundation Server in Visual Studio Team System the Registered Server Name is the host name from the URL.

Connecting to Team Build

In Team Foundation Server 2008, the Team Build functionality is exposed via the IBuildServer interface. You can't directly create an instance of IBuildServer (because it is an interface) but the *TeamFoundationServer* class has a *GetService* method that returns a concrete implementation that you can use:

```
IBuildServer buildServer = (IBuildServer)server.GetService(typeof(IBuildServer));
```

Working with Build Agents

Querying Build Agents

To list the build agents that have been defined for a specific Team Project you call IBuildServer.QueryBuildAgents and pass the Team Project name as shown here:

```
IBuildAgent[] buildAgents = buildServer.QueryBuildAgents("Contoso");
```

The *QueryBuildAgents* method returns an array of objects that implement the IBuildAgent interface shown in Figure 11-6.

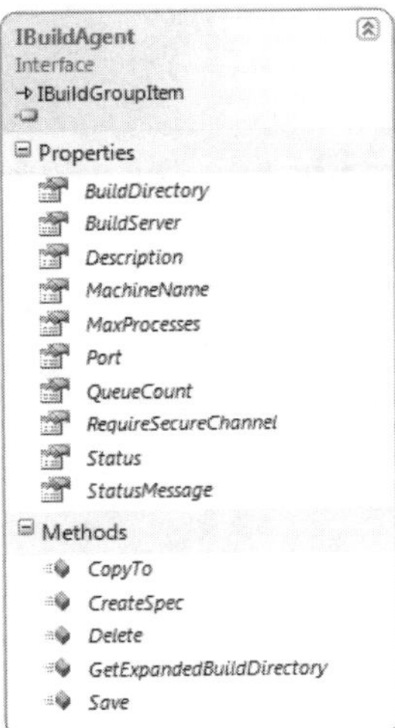

FIGURE 11-6 IBuildAgent interface

We can operate on each IBuildAgent instance by reading and writing properties and then calling Save to persist those properties back to the TfsBuild database as shown in this example, which disables all build agents that don't have any queued builds:

```
foreach (IBuildAgent buildAgent in buildAgents) {
    if (buildAgent.QueueCount == 0) {
        buildAgent.Status = AgentStatus.Disabled;
        buildAgent.Save();
    }
}
```

Adding a Build Agent

Build agents can also be created using the *CreateBuildAgent* method on the IBuildServer interface. In this example, we add the current machine as a build agent for the specified Team Foundation Server and project:

```
public static void Main(string[] args) {
    string serverUrl = args[0];
    string teamProject = args[1];

    TeamFoundationServer server = TeamFoundationServerFactory.GetServer(
        serverUrl,
        new UICredentialsProvider()
    );

    IBuildServer buildServer = (IBuildServer)server.GetService(typeof(IBuildServer));
    IBuildAgent buildAgent = buildServer.CreateBuildAgent(teamProject);
    buildAgent.MachineName = Environment.MachineName;
    buildAgent.Name = buildAgent.MachineName;
    buildAgent.Save();
}
```

Working with Build Definitions

Querying Build Definitions

The list of build definitions can be retrieved in a similar manner using the *QueryBuildDefinitions* method of the IBuildServer interface as shown here:

```
IBuildDefinition[] buildDefinitions = buildServer.QueryBuildDefinitions("Contoso");
```

This method returns an array of objects that implement IBuildDefinition, which is shown in Figure 11-7.

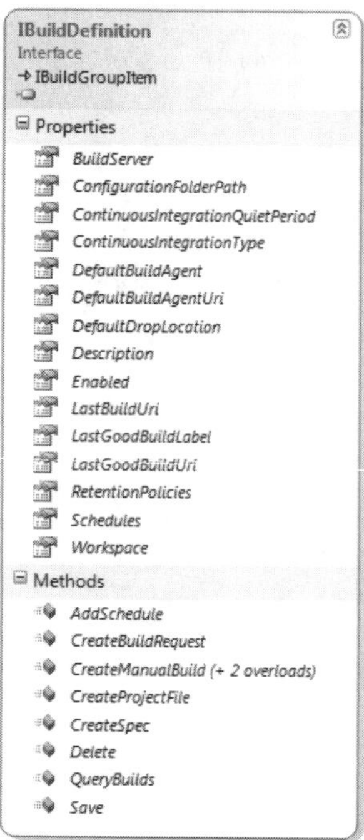

FIGURE 11-7 IBuildDefinition interface

In this example, we use the array of build definitions to change each of their default build agents to the first build agent in the Team Project:

```
IBuildAgent defaultBuildAgent = buildServer.QueryBuildAgents("Contoso")[0];

foreach (IBuildDefinition buildDefinition in buildDefinitions) {
        buildDefinition.DefaultBuildAgent = defaultBuildAgent;
        buildDefinition.Save();
}
```

Creating a Build Definition

Build definitions can be created using the *CreateBuildDefinition* method on the IBuildServer interface. This method returns an IBuildDefinition, which can be populated with the required values before calling Save to persist the build definition to the TfsBuild database.

This example creates a new build definition, which is configured to build on each check-in, defaults to the first build agent, and retains only two successful builds:

```
IBuildDefinition buildDefinition = buildServer.CreateBuildDefinition("Contoso");
buildDefinition.Name = "HelloWorld";
buildDefinition.ConfigurationFolderPath = "$/Contoso/TeamBuildTypes/HelloWorld";
buildDefinition.ContinuousIntegrationType = ContinuousIntegrationType.Individual;
buildDefinition.DefaultBuildAgent = buildServer.QueryBuildAgents("Contoso")[0];
buildDefinition.DefaultDropLocation = @"\\CONTOSO\Projects\HelloWorld\drops";
buildDefinition.RetentionPolicies[BuildStatus.Succeeded].NumberToKeep = 2;
buildDefinition.Save();
```

Note The ConfigurationFolderPath must be a version control path containing a valid TFSBuild.proj file.

Working with Builds

Queuing a Build

Queuing builds using the API can be useful for integrating builds into other processes and can give more control than what is available via the command-line interface or Visual Studio Team System.

The most flexible way to queue a build is by creating an IBuildRequest by calling the *CreateBuildRequest* method on the IBuildDefinition interface and then passing this to the *QueueBuild* method on the IBuildServer interface.

As you can see in Figure 11-8 the IBuildRequest interface allows you to specify all of the options available in the Queue Build dialog in Visual Studio Team System.

In this example, we queue a build for each build definition that has been defined in the Contoso Team Project:

```
foreach (IBuildDefinition buildDefinition in buildServer.QueryBuildDefinitions("Contoso")) {
    IBuildRequest request;
    request = buildDefinition.CreateBuildRequest();

    buildServer.QueueBuild(request);
}
```

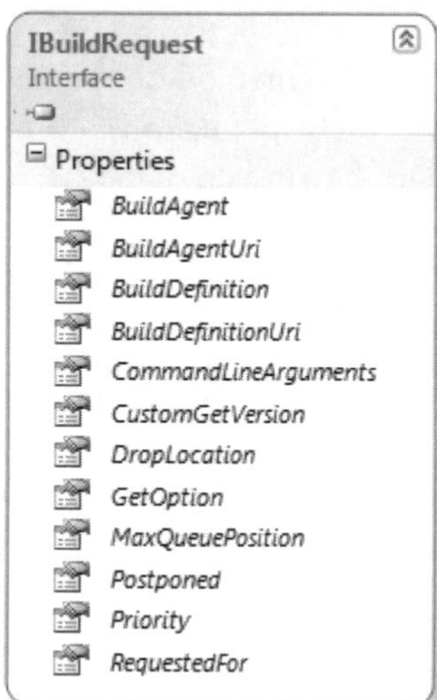

FIGURE 11-8 IBuildRequest interface

Querying Build Queues

Accessing the queued builds is slightly more complicated than querying build agents and build definitions. Firstly, you need to create an *IQueuedBuildsView* object using the *CreateQueuedBuildsView* method on the *IBuildServerInterface*.

```
IQueuedBuildsView queuedBuildsView = buildServer.CreateQueuedBuildsView("Contoso");
```

You then need to define the filters for the view. You can filter based on the build agent, build definition, or build status using the `AgentFilter`, `DefinitionFilter` and `StatusFilter` properties respectively. You can also determine for how long a completed build should remain in the build queue using the `CompletedWindow` property. We'll include just builds that have a status of Queued:

```
queuedBuildsView.StatusFilter = QueueStatus.Queued;
```

We then define how much information about each build should be returned using the QueryOptions property. This enumeration allows you to specify whether the build agent, build definition, or workspace details should be returned; as well, you can request multiple to be returned by OR-ing the values. We'll return the details about the build definitions and the build agents:

```
queuedBuildsView.QueryOptions = QueryOptions.Definitions | QueryOptions.Agents;
```

Finally, we call the *Refresh* method to retrieve the list of queued builds. The Boolean parameter indicates whether recently completed builds should also be returned, in this case because we only want queued builds. The list of queued builds can then be accessed from the QueuedBuilds property which returns an array of objects implementing the IQueuedBuild interface as shown in Figure 11-9. Finally, we cancel all of the queued builds returned by the view:

```
queuedBuildsView.Refresh(false);
foreach (IQueuedBuild queuedBuild in queuedBuildsView.QueuedBuilds) {
    queuedBuild.Cancel();
}
```

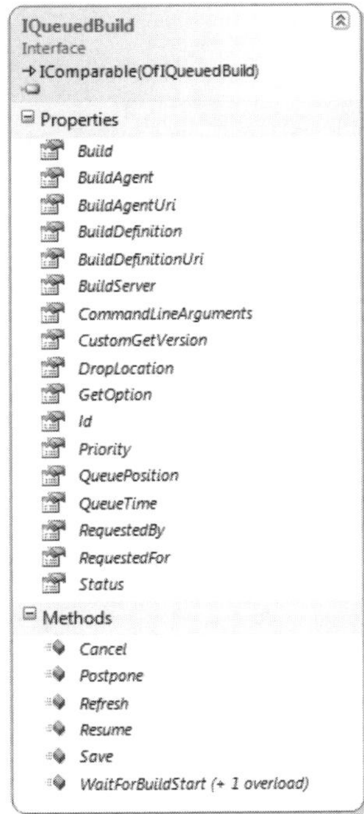

FIGURE 11-9 IQueuedBuild interface

Querying Build History

Completed builds can be queried using the *QueryBuilds* method on the IBuildServer or IBuildDefinition interfaces. If you call the *QueryBuilds* method on an object implementing IBuildDefinition it will return all builds for that build definition, whereas calling it on an object implementing IBuildServer allows you to filter the builds based on different criteria. All of these variants of *QueryBuilds* return an array of objects implementing the IBuildDetail interface shown in Figure 11-10.

In this example, we use a build detail specification to filter the list of all builds in the Contoso Team Project to those finished in the last five days:

```
IBuildDetailSpec spec = buildServer.CreateBuildDetailSpec("Contoso");
spec.MinFinishTime = DateTime.Now.AddDays(-5);
```

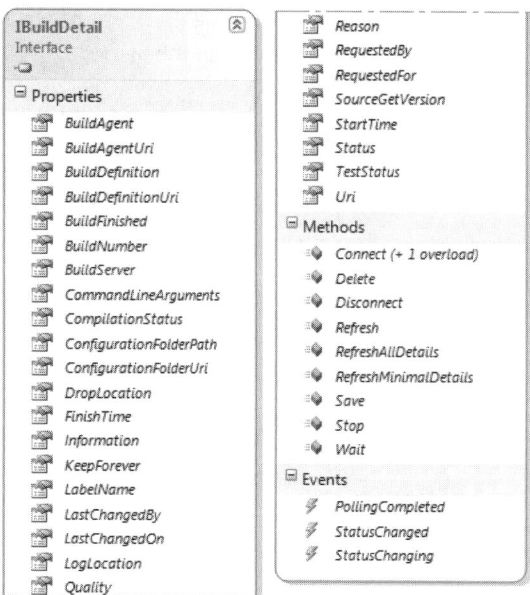

FIGURE 11-10 IBuildDetail interface

```
IBuildDetail[] builds = buildServer.QueryBuilds(spec).Builds;

foreach (IBuildDetail build in builds) {
    Console.WriteLine(build.BuildNumber);
}
```

Upgrading from Team Build 2005

Part of the upgrade process from Team Foundation Server 2005 to Team Foundation Server 2008 is the upgrade of the Team Build component. Team Build was one of the most improved components of Team Foundation Server 2008 and as a result has a quite rich upgrade process.

This upgrade process performs a number of actions:

1. Upgrades the schema of the TfsBuild and TfsWarehouse databases.
2. Upgrades the data in the TfsBuild and TfsWarehouse databases.
3. Imports the existing build types as new build definitions.
4. Imports WorkspaceMapping.xml files into the new build definitions.
5. Imports any build machines referenced in the build types as build agents.

Reviewing Applied Defaults

While the upgrade process is seamless and your project should continue to build as per usual after the upgrade, a number of assumptions are made and defaults applied that you may want to review when the upgrade process has completed.

Build agents weren't a separately defined entity in Team Build 2005 and there was simply a BuildMachine and BuildDirectoryPath property in TFSBuild.proj. Each unique BuildMachine will be added as a new build agent but the BuildDirectoryPath will be ignored (because there could be conflicting values in different build definitions). Additionally, in Team Build 2008 additional details can be recorded against each build agent. You should review the settings for each build agent defined in the Manage Build Agents dialog.

Retention Policies are a new feature in Team Build 2008 and each imported build definition is set to retain all builds for all statuses. You should review each build definition and determine how many builds for each status you would like to retain.

Triggers are also a new feature so each imported build definition is created with a default trigger of Check-Ins Do Not Trigger A New Build. You should review each build definition and determine whether you should use one of the continuous integration or schedule triggers.

You may have third-party products installed that implemented either retention policies or triggers for Team Build 2005. If you decide to use the built-in functionality in Team Build 2008 you should disable these, or if you decide to keep using them test that they work correctly in a Team Build 2008 environment.

Reviewing Customizations and Extensions

Any customizations or extensions you make to your build process add a certain level of risk to the upgrade. Once the upgrade is completed you should review and test any customizations and extensions you've made to the build process including overriding extensibility targets as well as any applications that use the Team Build API.

The API underwent a large number of changes between Team Build 2005 and Team Build 2008 and as a result you should expect to have to make a large number of modifications to code that used the Team Build 2005 API.

Supporting 2005 and 2008 Clients

When upgrading from Team Build 2005 to Team Build 2008 the BuildMachine, BuildDirectoryPath, and DropLocation properties are extracted from the TFSBuild.proj and the workspace mappings are extracted from the WorkspaceMapping.xml file in each build type in the TeamBuildTypes directory and stored in the TfsBuild database as part of the build definition.

Despite these being imported into the database, they are left in their respective files to support Team Build 2005 clients (such as Visual Studio Team System 2005 or utilities that use the Team Build 2005 API). These clients don't know that the database exists and as such still download and parse the TFSBuild.proj and WorkspaceMapping.xml files from version control to obtain the necessary values.

To continue supporting these clients you need to keep these settings in the TFSBuild.proj and WorkspaceMapping.xml files and almost certainly keep them in sync with the values in the database, which is something you need to do manually. If you don't need to support Team Build 2005 clients, then you can simply remove the WorkspaceMapping.xml file and set the properties listed in Table 11-6 to the defaults used in new build definitions.

TABLE 11-6 Team Build 2005 Compatibility Settings

Property	Default Value
BuildMachine	UNKNOWN
BuildDirectoryPath	UNKNOWN
DropLocation	\\UNKNOWN\drops

Running 2005 (8.0) Tests in Team Build 2008

Team Build 2008 will automatically determine if a test was built against the 8.0 or 9.0 version of the testing assemblies and will execute them using the appropriate version of MTest. However, if you find that the 9.0 version is being used instead of the 8.0 version you can force the 8.0 version to be used by setting the V8TestToolsTask property to true and setting the MSTestRefPath property to the path to the directory containing the 8.0 version of Microsoft.VisualStudio.QualityTools.MSBuildTasks.dll as shown in this example:

```
<PropertyGroup>
    <V8TestToolsTask>true</V8TestToolsTask>
    <MSTestRefPath>
        $(ProgramFiles)\Microsoft Visual Studio 8\Common7\IDE\PrivateAssemblies
    </MSTestRefPath>
</PropertyGroup>
```

Detecting If Running in Team Build 2008

The TeamBuildVersion property will be set to 2.0 if your build script is running in Team Build 2008, so you can use this to alter your build process depending on whether it is running in Team Build 2005 or Team Build 2008 as shown here:

```
<Target Name="BeforeGet">
    <Message Text="Running in Team Build 2008" Condition="'$(TeamBuildVersion)'=='2.0'" />
</Target>
```

Upgrade Checklist

In summary, you should consider the following items when upgrading from Team Build 2005 to Team Build 2008:

- Review settings for each build agent and build definition.
- Review and test customizations and extensions to the build process. This includes any applications that use the Team Build API.
- Ensure the Team Build 2005 compatibility settings are kept synchronized with the build definition.
- Check that unit tests are executing using the correct version of MSTest.
- Optionally, modify customizations to work under Team Build 2005 and Team Build 2008.

Chapter 12

Team Build Cookbook

In this chapter, we're going to explore solutions to some of the most common build requirements. Rather than focusing on compilation this chapter focuses on the noncompilation activities such as generating documentation, optimizing build infrastructure, packaging and deployment, and versioning. Please note that any line breaks in attributes within the XML are for printing only and should not be included when using these samples.

Documentation

Generating API Documentation Using Sandcastle

Developers creating class libraries or frameworks typically want to produce API documentation for the consumers of their assemblies. Even normal applications can benefit from producing API documentation because it allows other developers to understand the purpose and usage of the different classes the application is comprised of.

The standard method of documenting classes is by using the XML documentation syntax supported by both C# and Visual Basic .NET. This example shows the XML documentation on a simple *Person* class:

```
/// <summary>
/// Represents an individual person.
/// </summary>
public class Person {
    /// <summary>
    /// Gets or sets the person's first name.
    /// </summary>
    public string FirstName { get; set; }

    /// <summary>
    /// Gets or sets the person's last name.
    /// </summary>
    public string LastName { get; set; }

    /// <summary>
    /// Gets or sets the date the person was born.
    /// </summary>
    public DateTime DateOfBirth { get; set; }

    /// <summary>
    /// Calculates the age of the person.
    /// </summary>
```

```
    /// <returns>A <see cref="System.TimeSpan" /> representing the age
    /// of the person.</returns>
    public TimeSpan CalculateAge() {
        return DateTime.Now.Subtract(DateOfBirth);
    }
}
```

If the project's XML Documentation File option has been enabled (as shown in Figure 12-1) then when the project is compiled an XML file containing the XML documentation will be produced. By default, this file will have the same name as the assembly but with an XML extension; however in C# projects this filename can be customized.

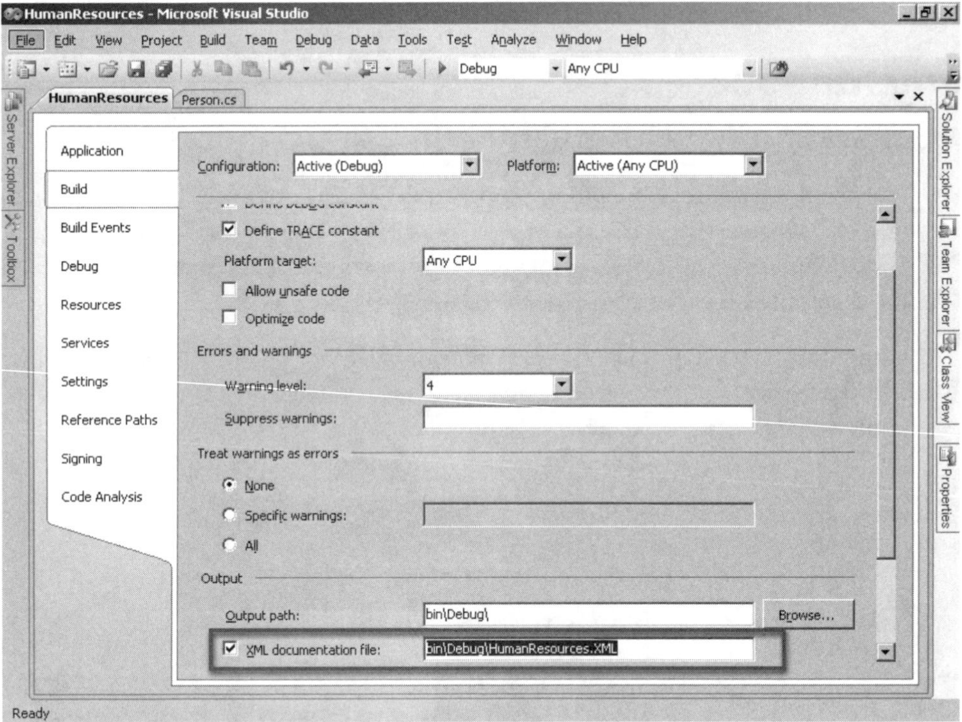

FIGURE 12-1 XML documentation file Project Property

Microsoft has released a tool called Sandcastle on CodePlex for converting these XML documentation files into HTML, Compiled Help (CHM), or Microsoft Help 2.0 format, and it is available from *http://www.codeplex.com/sandcastle* and includes a number of command-line utilities and templates for producing these different formats. Because Sandcastle requires a number of steps to generate documentation a number of tools have been released to help simplify and automate this process. The one we'll use in this example is the Sandcastle Help File Builder (SHFB) from *http://www.codeplex.com/SHFB*.

The first step is to install the prerequisite software on each build agent (the order of installation doesn't matter):

- Sandcastle
- Sandcastle Help File Builder
- Microsoft HTML Workshop (if generating Compiled Help files)
  http://www.microsoft.com/downloads/details.aspx?FamilyID=00535334-c8a6-452f-9aa0-d597d16580cc
- Visual Studio 2008 SDK (if generating Microsoft Help 2.0 files)
  http://www.microsoft.com/downloads/details.aspx?FamilyID=59ec6ec3-4273-48a3-ba25-dc925a45584d

The Sandcastle Help File Builder provides a user interface (Figure 12-2) similar to that of NDoc for defining the help file generation settings. These settings can then be stored in a .shfb file, which can be built using either the user interface or command line. Alternatively, all of the generation settings can be passed via the command line.

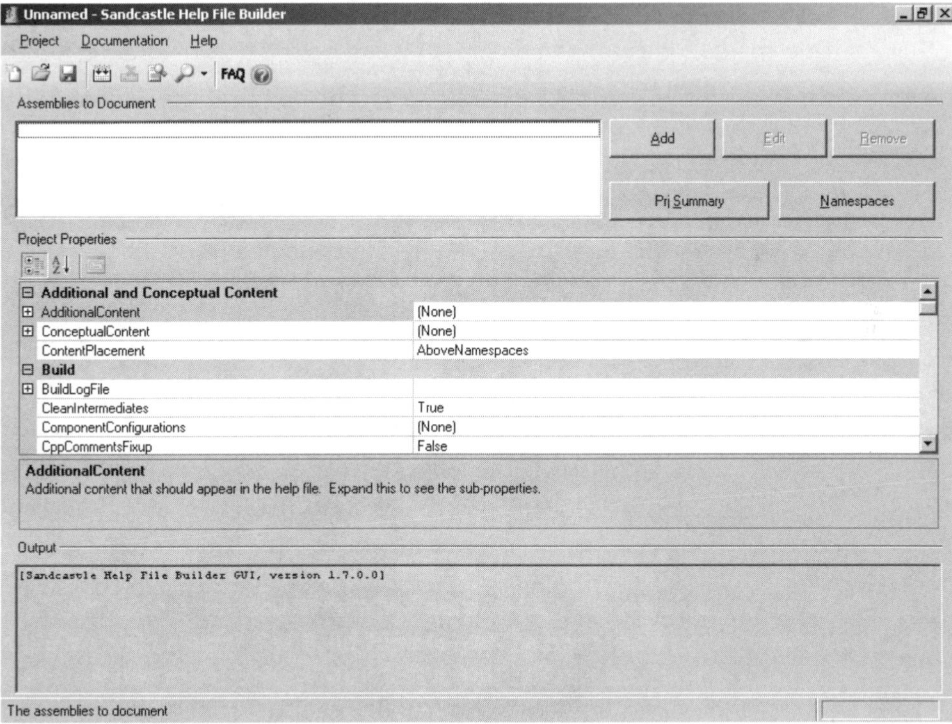

FIGURE 12-2 Sandcastle Help File Builder user interface

Although you can specify the list of assemblies to generate API documentation for in the user interface, we're going to generate this list dynamically and pass it to Sandcastle Help File Builder during the build process; all other settings will, however, come from the .shfb file. So the first step is to create a .shfb file that specifies the help file generation settings you want to use. For this example, we'll just set the Help File settings shown in Figure 12-3.

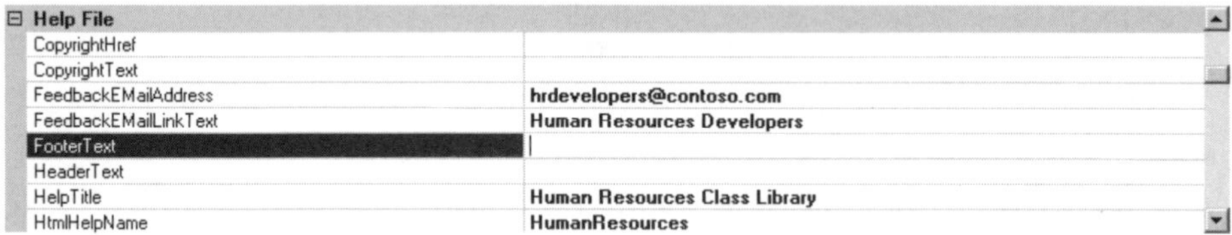

FIGURE 12-3 Help File settings

Next we'll add this file to source control so that it is available to the build process. We'll add it to the same folder as the solution (*.sln) file but it could be stored in any folder that is included in the build definition's workspace.

We then need to modify the build definition's TFSBuild.proj to call the Sandcastle Help File Builder command-line tool to generate the API documentation. Override the GenerateDocumentation extensibility target by adding the following to the bottom of the TFSBuild.proj within the Project element:

```
<PropertyGroup>
    <SandcastleHelpFileBuilderPath>
        $(ProgramFiles)\EWSoftware\Sandcastle Help File Builder\SandcastleBuilderConsole.exe
    </SandcastleHelpFileBuilderPath>
    <DocProjectFile>$(SolutionRoot)\HumanResources.shfb</DocProjectFile>
    <DocOutputDirectory>$(BinariesRoot)\Help\</DocOutputDirectory>
</PropertyGroup>

<Target Name="GenerateDocumentation">
    <ItemGroup>
        <AssemblyToDocument Include="$(BinariesRoot)\Release\*.dll" />
    </ItemGroup>

    <ItemGroup>
        <CommandLineParameter Include="$(DocProjectFile)" />
        <CommandLineParameter Include="-outputpath=&quot;$(DocOutputDirectory)&quot;" />
        <CommandLineParameter Include="
            @(AssemblyToDocument->'-assembly=&quot;%(FullPath)&quot;')
        " />
    </ItemGroup>

    <WriteLinesToFile Lines="@(CommandLineParameter)"
        File="$(MSBuildProjectDirectory)\$(MSBuildProjectFile).shfbrsp" />

    <Exec Command="&quot;$(SandcastleHelpFileBuilderPath)&quot;
        &quot;@$(MSBuildProjectDirectory)\$(MSBuildProjectFile).shfbrsp&quot;" />
</Target>
```

In this example, we create a property containing the path to the command-line tool that ships with the Sandcastle Help File Builder, another with the path to the .shfb file that we checked into source control, and another with the output directory for the generated documentation. By having the output directory under BinariesRoot the API documentation will be automatically copied to the DropLocation during the drop phase.

We then add the list of assemblies to be documented to the AssemblyToDocument item group. We create the item group inside the GenerateDocumentation target rather than within the project (at the same level as the property group) to defer the population of the item group so that we pick up any assemblies created up until the GenerateDocumentation target is executed.

Because the length of command lines is limited, we create a response file containing the command-line parameters including the list of assemblies to be documented. This is done by transforming the AssemblyToDocument item group into an item group in the format -assembly="<*Path to assembly*>". This item group is then written to a file using MSBuild's WriteLinesToFile task.

Finally, we call the Sandcastle Help File Builder command-line tool using MSBuild's Exec task passing the path to the response file, and the result is the help file shown in Figure 12-4 in the Help subdirectory of the build's drop location.

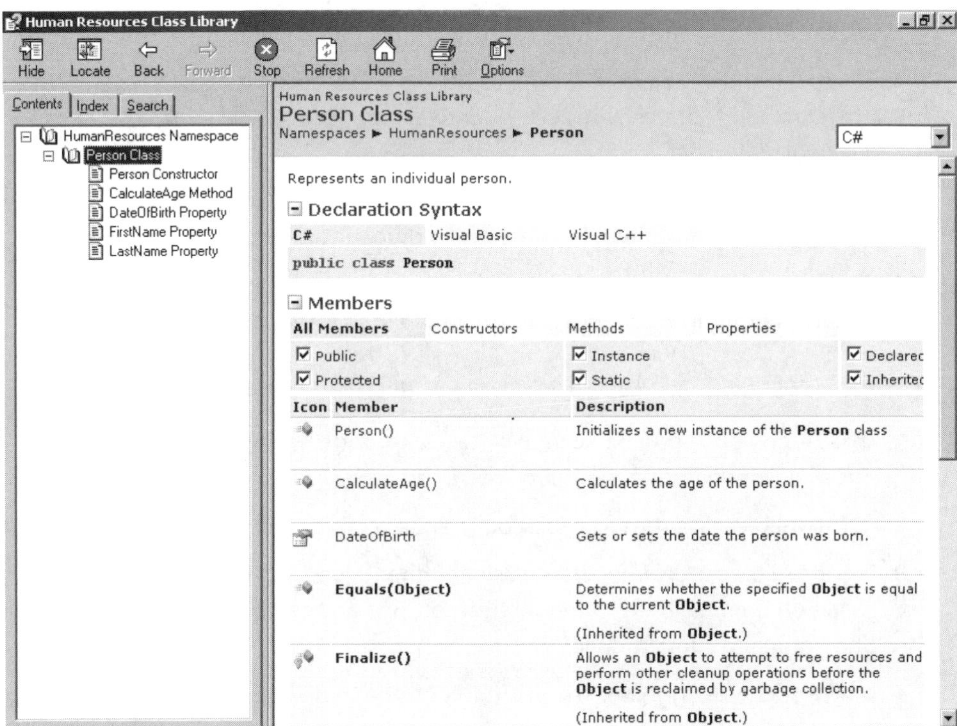

FIGURE 12-4 Generated Help file

Infrastructure

Load Balancing Builds between Build Agents

When builds are queued they are queued on a specific build agent selected by the person queuing the build. They can scroll through each build agent to find the one with the shortest queue, but with a large number of build agents this can take time.

A project has been published on CodePlex that can move builds from one build agent to an idle build agent to make the best use of the available build agents. This project consists of a very simple command-line utility built using the Team Build API discussed in Chapter 11, "Team Build Deep Dive," called TeamBuildLoadBalancer.exe, which takes the Team Foundation Server URL and an optional list of Team Projects as command-line arguments.

To set up the Team Foundation Build Load Balancer, do this:

1. Download the latest release from the CodePlex site *http://www.codeplex.com/teambuildloadbalance*.
2. Follow the installation instructions provided in the release.
3. Create a scheduled task to run TeamBuildLoadBalancer.exe passing the Team Foundation Server URL; for example, TeamBuildLoadBalancer.exe *http://TFSRTM08:8080/*.
4. If you'd like only selected Team Projects to be balanced, you can append these to the command-line, for example, TeamBuildLoadBalancer.exe *http://TFSRTM08:8080/* HelloWorldProject.
5. You can schedule the load balancing to occur as frequently as you like; the more often it runs, the shorter the delay until queued builds are moved to idle build agents.
6. The account that the scheduled task runs as must be a member of the Build Services security group in each Team Project that it load balances builds for.

When the scheduled task executes, the following process will occur:

1. The Team Build Load Balancer will iterate through each of the specified Team Projects (or all of them if none has been specified).
2. It will then iterate through each build agent configured for the Team Project.
3. If the build agent is idle, then it will find the earliest queued build on any build agent; it will then queue a build with identical settings on the idle build agent, and then cancel the originally queued build.
4. Any errors are logged to the event log on the machine running the scheduled task.

Configuring Team Build to Use TFS Proxy Server

If you have build agents that don't have the benefit of a fast network connection to the Team Foundation Server application tier, this can adversely affect the performance of your builds. While enabling incremental gets (as discussed in Chapter 10, "Team Build Quick Start") can reduce this performance impact, it can be reduced even further by configuring the build agent to use a TFS proxy server.

Using a TFS proxy requires the Team Foundation Client to be installed on the build agent and once this has been installed you can enable using the proxy by doing this:

1. Log into the build machine as the Team Build service account. If you have configured Team Build to run as NT AUTHORITY\NETWORK SERVICE, or the Team Build service account has not been granted the Allow Log On Locally right then you will need to use the alternate method outlined below.
2. Open Visual Studio 2008.
3. Open the Options dialog by clicking Tools and then Options.
4. Select Source Control and then Visual Studio Team Foundation Server from the Options Category tree on the left-hand side.
5. Click the Use Proxy Server check box and enter the Proxy Server Name, Port and select the appropriate Protocol as shown in Figure 12-5.
6. Click OK and close Visual Studio 2008.

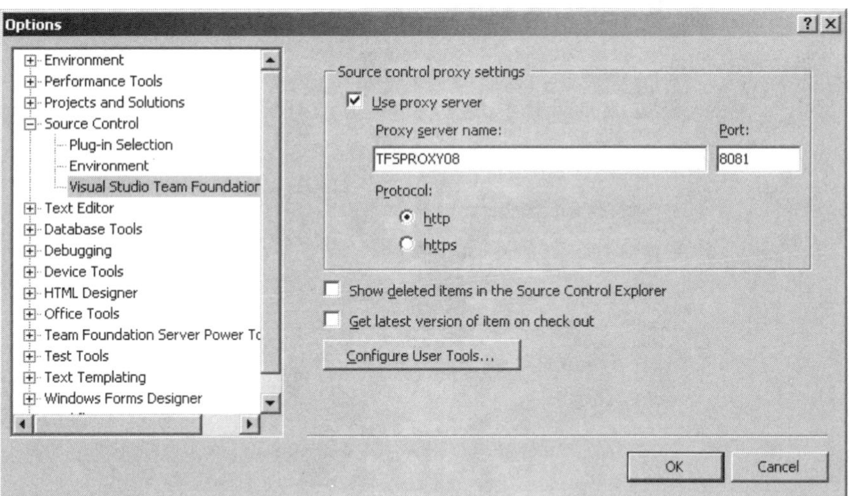

FIGURE 12-5 Source Control proxy settings

If you cannot log into the build agent as the Team Build service account then you can set the proxy details directly in the registry by doing this:

1. Log into the build machine as a user with local administrator privileges.
2. Determine the SID for the Team Build service account. The easiest way to do this is by running the psgetsid command-line utility (*http://technet.microsoft.com/en-us/sysinternals/bb897417.aspx*); for example, psgetsid CONTOSO\TFSBUILDS.
3. Open the Windows Registry Editor by running regedt32.exe from a command prompt.
4. Navigate to the registry key HKEY_USERS\<Team Build Service Account SID>\Software\Microsoft\VisualStudio\9.0\TeamFoundation\SourceControl\Proxy (where <Team Build Service Account SID> is the SID identified using psgetsid) creating any keys that don't exist.
5. Create a String value in the Proxy key with the name Enabled and the value true.
6. Create a String value in the Proxy key with the name Url and the full URL of the proxy as the value.

The Proxy registry key should look like Figure 12-6 when you're finished:

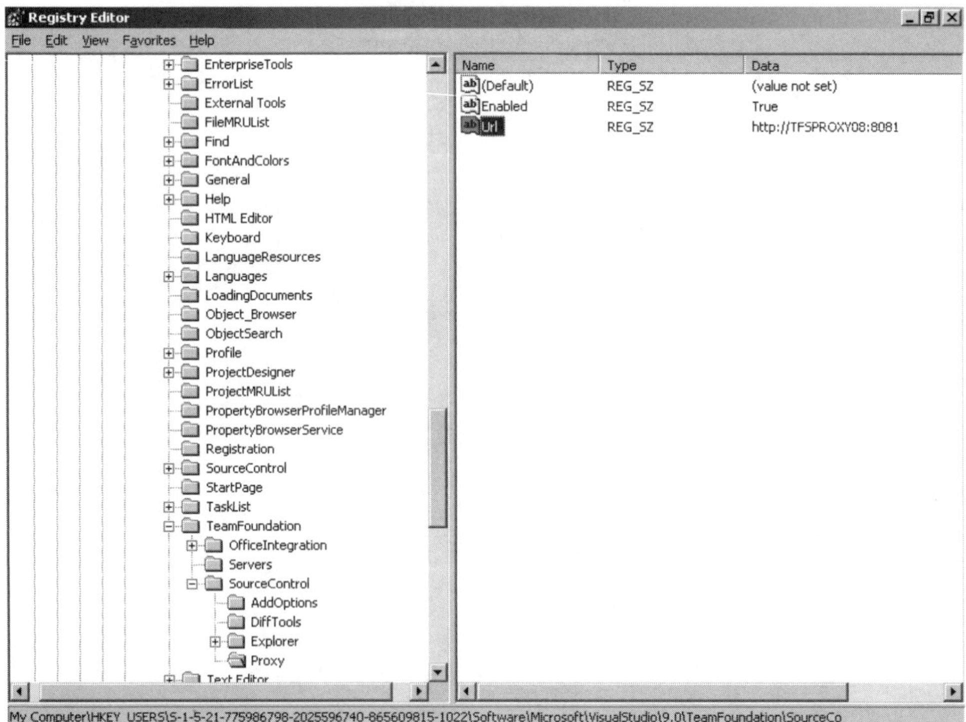

FIGURE 12-6 Proxy registry settings

Once you've made these changes, restart the Visual Studio Team Foundation Build service to ensure the changes are picked up. The proxy performance counters described in *http://msdn.microsoft.com/en-us/library/ms252455.aspx* should give you an indication if the build agent is using the proxy or not.

Running Processes on Remote Machines

The Exec task provides a large amount of flexibility by allowing build processes to run arbitrary executables as part of the build process. It is sometimes necessary to run executables on remote machines rather than the build agent but the Exec task does not support this out of the box.

The easiest solution to this problem is to use the psexec command-line utility (*http://technet.microsoft.com/en-us/sysinternals/bb897553.aspx*). This utility allows you to run processes on one or more remote machines. For example, to run the command `iisreset /restart` on the machine CONTOSOWEB01 we would run:

```
psexec \\CONTOSOWEB01 iisreset /restart
```

By default, the process will run in the context of the current user but without access to network resources; you can run as a specific user by passing the username and password as shown next but be aware that these are passed in clear text to the remote system and stored in clear text in TFSBuild.proj:

```
psexec \\CONTOSOWEB01 -u CONTOSO\WebAdministrator -p P2ssw0rd iisreset /restart
```

Because the Exec task allows us to run processes on the local machine we can use it to run psexec, which will then run the process on the remote machine as shown here:

```
<Target Name="AfterDropBuild">
    <Exec Command="psexec \\CONTOSOWEB01 iisreset /restart" />
</Target>
```

Calls to psexec wrapped in calls to the Exec task can become quite difficult to read and maintain, especially when there are a large number of quoted arguments. To make life simpler, the SDC Tasks (*http://www.codeplex.com/sdctasks*) provide a custom task that wraps PsExec, allowing you to call it like this:

```
<Target Name="AfterDropBuild">
    <Tools.PsExec ToolPath="C:\PsTools\"
        Command="iisreset /restart"
        Server="CONTOSOWEB01"
        User="CONTOSO\WebAdministrator"
        Password="P2ssw0rd" />
</Target>
```

Sharing Customizations between Build Definitions

There is often a requirement to reuse build customizations across build definitions. You may have separate build definitions for different versions of your product and want to use the same customizations in each of these build definitions.

Refactoring Your Customizations

The first step is to refactor the build definition containing the customizations you want to share by extracting the shared customizations out of TFSBuild.proj into a separate MSBuild project file.

For example, if you have the following customization in TFSBuild.proj:

```
<Target Name="PackageBinaries">
    <ItemGroup>
        <DebugBinaries Include="$(BinariesRoot)\Debug\**" />
    </ItemGroup>
    <Zip Files="@(DebugBinaries)"
        WorkingDirectory="$(BinariesRoot)\Debug\"
        ZipFileName="$(BinariesRoot)\Debug.zip" />
</Target>
```

You would extract it into its own MSBuild project file, which we'll call TFSBuildCustomizations.proj:

```
<Project xmlns="http://schemas.microsoft.com/developer/MSBuild/2003">
    <Target Name="PackageBinaries">
        <ItemGroup>
            <DebugBinaries Include="$(BinariesRoot)\Debug\**"/>
        </ItemGroup>
        <Zip Files="@(DebugBinaries)"
            WorkingDirectory="$(BinariesRoot)\Debug\"
            ZipFileName="$(BinariesRoot)\Debug.zip" />
    </Target>
</Project>
```

This project file is then imported into TFSBuild.proj using the *Import* element as shown here:

```
<Import Project="TFSBuildCustomizations.proj" />
```

Configuring Your Customizations

It is common to need to change the behavior of the shared customizations between different build definitions. To allow this, replace any parameters with properties that can then be specified in TFSBuild.proj. Extending the previous example we can make the name of the zip file customizable by replacing Debug with $(ZipFilename) as shown here:

```
<Project xmlns="http://schemas.microsoft.com/developer/MSBuild/2003">
    <Target Name="PackageBinaries">
        <ItemGroup>
            <DebugBinaries Include="$(BinariesRoot)\Debug\**" />
        </ItemGroup>
```

```
        <Zip Files="@(DebugBinaries)"
            WorkingDirectory="$(BinariesRoot)\Debug\"
            ZipFileName="$(BinariesRoot)\$(ZipFilename).zip" />
    </Target>
</Project>
```

If the TFSBuild.proj project doesn't define the ZipFilename property the build will fail because the resulting filename will be invalid. To avoid this we can provide a default value in case one hasn't been specified as shown here:

```
<Project xmlns="http://schemas.microsoft.com/developer/MSBuild/2003">
    <PropertyGroup>
        <ZipFilename Condition="'$(ZipFilename)'==''">Debug</ZipFilename>
    </PropertyGroup>
    <Target Name="PackageBinaries">
        <ItemGroup>
            <DebugBinaries Include="$(BinariesRoot)\Debug\**" />
        </ItemGroup>
        <Zip Files="@(DebugBinaries)"
            WorkingDirectory="$(BinariesRoot)\Debug\"
            ZipFileName="$(BinariesRoot)\$(ZipFilename).zip" />
    </Target>
</Project>
```

Alternatively, we can add validation to our customization so that it fails with a more meaningful message as shown here:

```
<Project xmlns="http://schemas.microsoft.com/developer/MSBuild/2003">
    <Target Name="PackageBinaries">
        <Error Text="You must specify a value for ZipFilename."
            Condition="'$(ZipFilename)'==''" />
        <ItemGroup>
            <DebugBinaries Include="$(BinariesRoot)\Debug\**" />
        </ItemGroup>
        <Zip Files="@(DebugBinaries)"
            WorkingDirectory="$(BinariesRoot)\Debug\"
            ZipFileName="$(BinariesRoot)\$(ZipFilename).zip" />
    </Target>
</Project>
```

You could also allow configuration using items instead of properties. In this example, the list of directories to be zipped is stored in an item called DirectoryToZip:

```
<Project xmlns="http://schemas.microsoft.com/developer/MSBuild/2003">
    <Target Name="PackageBinaries" Condition="'@(DirectoryToZip)'!=''">
        <ItemGroup>
            <FileToZip Include="$(BinariesRoot)\%(DirectoryToZip.Identity)\**">
                <DirectoryToZip>%(DirectoryToZip.Identity)</DirectoryToZip>
            </FileToZip>
        </ItemGroup>
        <Zip Files="@(FileToZip)"
            WorkingDirectory="$(BinariesRoot)\%(DirectoryToZip)\"
            ZipFileName="$(BinariesRoot)\%(DirectoryToZip).zip" />
    </Target>
</Project>
```

There are a few things of interest in this example:

- We use the condition `'@(DirectoryToZip)!=''` to prevent the PackageBinaries target from executing if the DirectoryToZip item group is empty.
- The new ItemGroup syntax in MSBuild 3.5 is used to create a FileToZip item group with each file assigned DirectoryToZip metadata identifying which zip file it should be included in.
- The Zip task is batched using the FileToZip item group (created by the ItemGroup) and uses the DirectoryToZip metadata (created by the *AdditionalMetadata* attribute) to create one zip file per directory.

Supporting TFSBuild.proj and Imported Customizations

One issue with the solution so far is that if both TFSBuild.proj and the imported project define a target with the same name, then whichever is declared last will take precedence and the other will be ignored. This would mean that each Team Build extensibility target could be declared only once in TFSBuild.proj or each imported project.

While in most scenarios this may not matter, if you want build administrators that use your imported project to still be able to override all of the extensibility targets then you will need to find an alternate way to include your custom targets in the build process.

The first step is to give your target a unique name; in this example we rename it to TFSBuildCustomizationsZip:

```
<Project xmlns="http://schemas.microsoft.com/developer/MSBuild/2003">
    <Target Name="TFSBuildCustomizationsZip">
        <Error Text="You must specify a value for ZipFilename."
            Condition="'$(ZipFilename)'==''" />
        <ItemGroup>
            <DebugBinaries Include="$(BinariesRoot)\Debug\**" />
        </ItemGroup>
        <Zip Files="@(DebugBinaries)"
            WorkingDirectory="$(BinariesRoot)\Debug\"
            ZipFileName="$(BinariesRoot)\$(ZipFilename).zip" />
    </Target>
</Project>
```

Tip If you prefix your target names with the filename (without the extension) then this gives you a certain level of uniqueness; you then just need to ensure that your target names are unique within each file.

We now need to inject the target into the build process without overriding one of the extensibility targets. If you examine Microsoft.TeamFoundation.Build.targets you'll find that the dependencies for each target are defined in a property; for example:

```
<PropertyGroup>
    <TeamBuildDependsOn>
        CleanAll;
        InitializeBuild;
        PreBuild;
        CleanCompilationOutput;
        Compile;
        PostBuild;
        Test;
        GenerateDocumentation;
        PackageBinaries;
    </TeamBuildDependsOn>
</PropertyGroup>
```

The names of these properties always end with DependsOn and you need to find the one that executes the extensibility target that you want to use. In this case, we find that the TeamBuildDependsOn property executes the PackageBinaries target. What we do now is modify the project containing our customization to add our custom target to the end of the list of targets as shown here:

```
<Project xmlns="http://schemas.microsoft.com/developer/MSBuild/2003">
    <PropertyGroup>
        <TeamBuildDependsOn>
            $(TeamBuildDependsOn);
            TFSBuildCustomizationsZip;
        </TeamBuildDependsOn>
    </PropertyGroup>
    <Target Name="TFSBuildCustomizationsZip">
        <Error Text="You must specify a value for ZipFilename."
            Condition="'$(ZipFilename)'==''" />
        <ItemGroup>
            <DebugBinaries Include="$(BinariesRoot)\Debug\**" />
        </ItemGroup>
        <Zip Files="@(DebugBinaries)"
            WorkingDirectory="$(BinariesRoot)\Debug\"
            ZipFileName="$(BinariesRoot)\$(ZipFilename).zip" />
    </Target>
</Project>
```

We could alternatively add our target to the beginning of the list if we wanted our target executed before the others as shown here:

```
<PropertyGroup>
    <TeamBuildDependsOn>
        TFSBuildCustomizationsZip;
        $(TeamBuildDependsOn);
    </TeamBuildDependsOn>
</PropertyGroup>
```

Choosing a Location for Your Customizations

Once you've refactored your customizations you now need to store them somewhere that TFSBuild.proj can access them. There are two ways to do this:

1. Branch and merge.
2. Build agent installation.

With the branch and merge method you add the project file containing the customizations to source control and then branch it into the directory containing TFSBuild.proj for each of the build definitions that uses the customizations. Because the project is located in the same directory as TFSBuild.proj it can simply import it without specifying a path as shown here:

```
<Import Project="TFSBuildCustomizations.proj" />
```

To modify the customizations you would edit the master copy (the one you branched from) and then merge those changes into each of the build definitions it was branched to. This method is quite simple and guarantees that the changes are in version control; however, if you have a large number of build definitions then it can become quite time consuming to manage and can be easy to forget to merge the changes into some of the build definitions.

The alternate method is to install the customizations on each build agent. In this method, you would store the project file containing the customizations on each build agent (usually under the %ProgramFiles%\MSBuild directory) and then TFSBuild.proj would import them from there as shown in this example:

```
<Import Project="$(MSBuildExtensionsPath)\Contoso\TFSBuildCustomizations.proj" />
```

Tip The MSBuildExtensionsPath property resolves to %ProgramFiles%\MSBuild, which makes this an ideal directory to use for build agent installation of customizations. This directory is used by Team Build, Visual Studio, and third-party MSBuild extensions.

To modify the customizations you would deploy your changes to each build agent. This method works well if you have a small number of build agents and a large number of build definitions. It doesn't enforce the same rigor as the branch and merge method as it doesn't force the use of version control. You should still keep the master copy in version control and deploy changes from there to the build agents.

Note Not keeping your customizations in version control can be highly detrimental to your ability to reproduce old builds because you may not be able to recreate the customizations as they existed at a certain point of time. Branching and merging the build customizations also suffers from this problem unless the build definition's configuration folder is included in the build definition's workspace (which will result in the customizations being labeled as part of the build process).

Executing Multiple Targets from an Extensibility Target

There is often a requirement to perform multiple tasks in a single extensibility target, such as zipping binaries and then deploying them to an FTP server. You could place both of these tasks in a single target as shown here:

```
<Target Name="PackageBinaries">
    <ItemGroup>
        <DebugBinaries Include="$(BinariesRoot)\Debug\**" />
    </ItemGroup>

    <Zip Files="@(DebugBinaries)"
        WorkingDirectory="$(BinariesRoot)\Debug\"
        ZipFileName="$(BinariesRoot)\Debug.zip" />

    <FtpPut Server="$(FtpServer)"
        Username="$(FtpUsername)"
        Password="$(FtpPassword)"
        ServerPath="$(FtpServerPath)"
        LocalPath="$(BinariesRoot)\Debug.zip" />
</Target>
```

A better approach would be to refactor these tasks out into their own targets, which can then be called from the PackageBinaries target as shown in this example:

```
<Target Name="ZipBinaries">
    <ItemGroup>
        <DebugBinaries Include="$(BinariesRoot)\Debug\**" />
    </ItemGroup>

    <Zip Files="@(DebugBinaries)"
        WorkingDirectory="$(BinariesRoot)\Debug\"
        ZipFileName="$(BinariesRoot)\Debug.zip" />
</Target>

<Target Name="FtpBinaries">
    <FtpPut Server="$(FtpServer)"
        Username="$(FtpUsername)"
        Password="$(FtpPassword)"
        ServerPath="$(FtpServerPath)"
        LocalPath="$(BinariesRoot)\Debug.zip" />
</Target>

<Target Name="PackageBinaries" DependsOnTargets="ZipBinaries;FtpBinaries" />
```

We can take this a step further and move the list of targets to be executed into a property like this:

```
<PropertyGroup>
    <PackageBinariesDependsOn>
        ZipBinaries;
        FtpBinaries;
    </PackageBinariesDependsOn>
</PropertyGroup>

<Target Name="PackageBinaries" DependsOnTargets="$(PackageBinariesDependsOn)" />
```

The advantage of this is that other customizations can add their targets to the list of targets defined in your property to add other steps to the extensibility targets, like this:

```
<PropertyGroup>
    <PackageBinariesDependsOn>
        $(PackageBinariesDependsOn);
        EmailBinaries;
    </PackageBinariesDependsOn>
</PropertyGroup>
```

Logging

Adding Build Steps to the Build Details Window

The Build Steps section of the Build Details window (shown in Figure 12-7) displays a line for each of the steps executed in the build process. Each build step consists of three parts:

1. Status Icon
2. Message
3. Completed On Date/Time

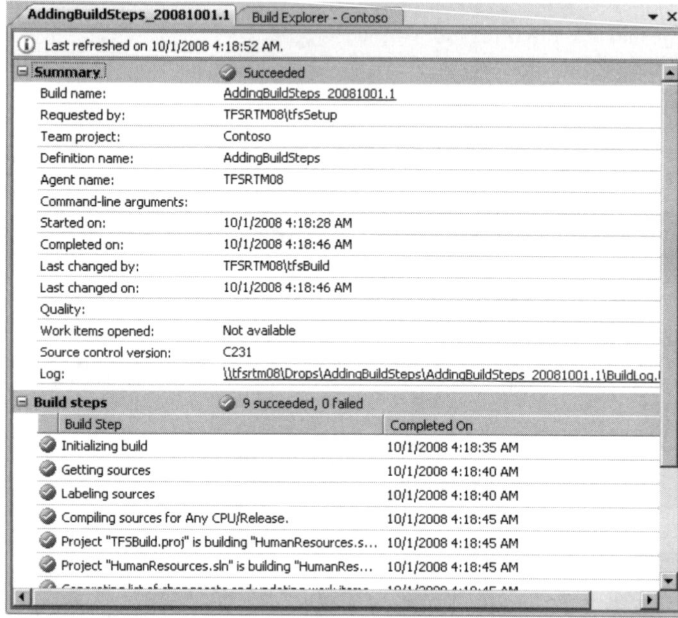

FIGURE 12-7 Build steps from the default build process

These build steps allow developers to track the progress of the build as well as easily determine which build step caused a build failure.

When customizing the build process it is recommended that you add your own build steps to the Build Details window. If you don't, then your custom targets will be included in the build step for the phase that they extend, which can make it harder to determine the step that failed.

The first step is to call the BuildStep task, passing a unique name for the build step (this isn't displayed in the user interface), the message to be displayed, and the Team Foundation Server URL and Build URL (which can be passed directly using Team Build properties). You should also add a Condition so the BuildStep task is executed only for end-to-end builds, because it will fail if called during a desktop build.

```
<BuildStep Name="CoreUnitTest" Message="Queuing unit test run"
    TeamFoundationServerUrl="$(TeamFoundationServerUrl)" BuildUri="$(BuildURI)"
    Condition="'$(IsDesktopBuild)'!='true'">
    <Output TaskParameter="Id" PropertyName="StepId" />
</BuildStep>
```

When you add a build step it is initially added as In Progress as shown in Figure 12-8, so that you can update the status. Once you've completed your custom logic, the BuildStep task has an output ID parameter that uniquely represents the build step.

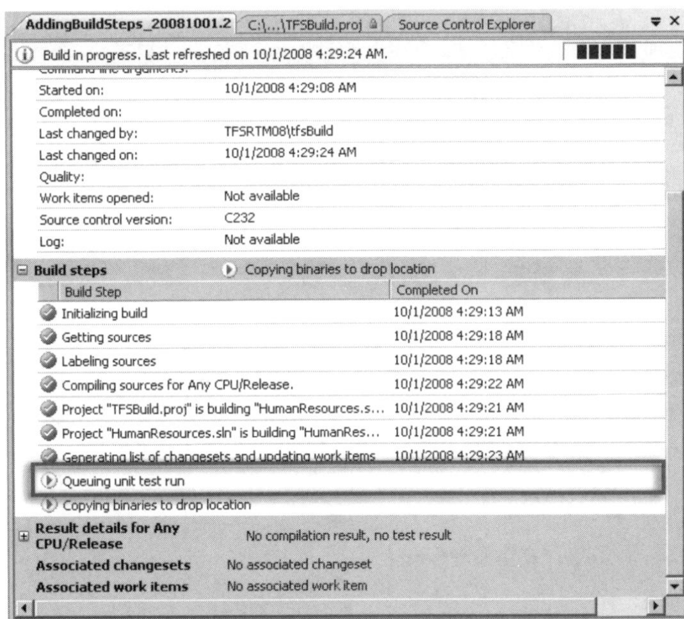

FIGURE 12-8 In-progress build steps

Once you've completed the custom logic you call the BuildStep task again, passing the ID stored earlier as well as the Name, TeamFoundationServerUrl, BuildUri, and Condition. You also need to pass the Status of the build step, which can be either:

- Succeeded
- Failed

This Status is used to update the Status Icon appropriately to indicate the status of the build step. The second call to the BuildStep task would look like this:

```
<BuildStep Id="$(StepId)" Name="CoreUnitTest" Status="Succeeded"
    TeamFoundationServerUrl="$(TeamFoundationServerUrl)" BuildUri="$(BuildURI)"
    Condition="'$(IsDesktopBuild)'!='true'" />
```

Packaging and Deployment

Deploying Source Code with the Binaries

There are two main ways to deploy additional files to the drop location with the build's other outputs (such as binaries, build logs, and test results). The first is to copy the files to the BinariesRoot directory at any point in the build process before the drop phase, and the other is to copy the files directly to the drop location once the build has been dropped.

The most important consideration when deploying the source code is the point in the process at which you copy the source code. The reasons for this are:

- If you copy the source code too early, then any modifications you make to the source code with the build process (such as updating AssemblyInfo files with version numbers) will not be included.
- If you copy the source code too late, then temporary files that are generated as part of the compilation process may be included.

The correct extensibility target to do this will depend on which extensibility targets you modify the source code in. However, in this example we assume that the modifications are done in the AfterGet target, so we perform the copy in the BeforeCompile target because this will include the modifications but not the temporary files generated by the compilation process.

```
<Target Name="BeforeCompile">
    <ItemGroup>
        <SolutionRootFiles Include="$(SolutionRoot)\**" />
    </ItemGroup>
    <Copy SourceFiles="@(SolutionRootFiles)"
        DestinationFiles="@(SolutionRootFiles->
            '$(BinariesRoot)\Source\%(RecursiveDir)%(Filename)%(Extension)'
        )"
    />
</Target>
```

In this example, we create an MSBuild item called SolutionRootFiles containing a list of all the files in the SolutionRoot directory and its subdirectories. We then copy those files to the Sources subdirectory (which will be created if it doesn't exist) of the BinariesRoot directory, and we maintain the directory structure of the copied files. Because the BeforeCompile target is executed before the drop phase, any directories and files we copy into the BinariesRoot directory will be dropped automatically as part of the drop phase.

Zipping the Binaries and Source Code

Zipping binaries and source code makes deployment via email, FTP, or the Web significantly easier. MSBuild and Team Build don't provide any out-of-the-box support for file compression but you can use the Zip task from the MSBuild Community Tasks (*http://msbuildtasks.tigris.org/*) to implement this.

The DropBuild target copies the entire contents of the BinariesRoot directory to the build's drop location and we can leverage this behavior to also copy the zipped binaries (and source if we wish) to simplify deployment.

The first step is to import the MSBuild Community Tasks using the following import statement:

```
<Import Project=
    "$(MSBuildExtensionsPath)\MSBuildCommunityTasks\MSBuild.Community.Tasks
        .Targets" />
```

We then create zip files for the debug and release binaries and the source code (zipping the source code assumes you also followed the Deploying Source Code with the Binaries recipe) by overriding the PackageBinaries extensibility target:

```
<Target Name="PackageBinaries">
    <ItemGroup>
        <DirectoryToZip Include="Debug;Release;Source" />
        <FileToZip Include="$(BinariesRoot)\%(DirectoryToZip.Identity)\**">
            <DirectoryToZip>%(DirectoryToZip.Identity)</DirectoryToZip>
        </FileToZip>
    </ItemGroup>
    <Zip Files="@(FileToZip)"
        WorkingDirectory="$(BinariesRoot)\%(DirectoryToZip)\"
        ZipFileName="$(BinariesRoot)\%(DirectoryToZip).zip" />
</Target>
```

Adding Symbols to Symbol Server

Symbol servers allow debuggers to automatically retrieve the correct symbols (PDBs) for the version of the assembly they are debugging. They do this by downloading the symbols from a symbol store (typically a network share or Web server) that indexes and stores the symbols in a structure that is understood by debuggers.

The first decision to be made is where the symbol store should be located. It should be easily accessible to the developers that will be using the symbols for debugging, but access to others should be restricted because symbols can simplify the process of reverse engineering or decompiling binaries. For this example we'll keep it simple and locate the symbol store in the drop location.

The Debugging Tools for Windows (*http://www.microsoft.com/whdc/devtools/debugging/*) includes symstore.exe, which is the tool used to add symbols to a symbol store. For the build process to be able to do this, you will need to install this on each of your build agents.

When adding symbols to a symbol store, you can either add the actual symbol file or a pointer to where the symbol file is located. Because Team Build is already going to copy our symbol files to the drop location we will simply add a pointer to the symbol store, which will save disk space because we're storing only one copy. The downside to this is if the build is removed by the retention policy, then the symbol store will no longer be able to access those symbol files.

To keep things simple we'll use the Exec task to execute symstore.exe but the most maintainable solution going forward would be to create a SymStore custom task that inherits from ToolTask. This would remove the complexity from the MSBuild project file into an easily testable and reusable assembly.

Because we want to work with the symbol files in the drop location we'll need to add them to the symbol store after they've been dropped, which implies that we should use the AfterDrop target. The resulting customization looks like this:

```
<PropertyGroup>
    <SymStoreToolPath>
        $(ProgramFiles)\Debugging Tools for Windows (x86)\symstore.exe
    </SymStoreToolPath>
    <SymServerPath>
        $(DropLocation)\..\symsrv
    </SymServerPath>
</PropertyGroup>
<Target Name="AfterDropBuild">
    <Exec Command="&quot;$(SymStoreToolPath)&quot;
        add
        /p
        /f &quot;$(DropLocation)\Release\*.pdb&quot;
        /s &quot;$(SymServerPath)&quot;
        /t &quot;$(BuildDefinitionName)&quot;
        /v &quot;$(BuildNumber)&quot;" />
</Target>
```

The first property we define is the path to symstore.exe. This keeps the Command parameter of the Exec task short and makes the path easy to change if necessary.

We then define a property for the path to the symbol server. The idea of a symbol server is that you have a single symbol server for all of your builds, since the DropLocation variable includes the build number. This isn't suitable as our symbol server, so we go up a directory from the DropLocation and use a single symsrv directory as our symbol server path.

Finally, we use the Exec task to call symstore.exe and pass it the following arguments (note that arguments that could contain spaces are quoted using "):

Argument	Description
add	Specifies the command to be executed against the symbol store. In this case we want to add symbols to the symbol store.
/p	Specifies that we want to add pointers to the symbol store rather than the actual symbol files.
/f "$(DropLocation)\Release*.pdb"	Specifies the symbols to be added. In this case all *.pdb files in the Release subdirectory of DropLocation.
/s "$(SymServerPath)"	Specifies the path to the symbol server. In this case we use the SymServerPath property we defined.
/t "$(BuildDefinitionName)"	Specifies the name of the product that the symbols are for. In this case we use the build definition's name.
/v "$(BuildNumber)"	Specifies the version of the product that the symbols are for. In this case we use the build number.

Note A full list of command-line options for symstore.exe is available in the Debugging Tools for Windows help file, which is included in the installer.

Versioning

Assembly Versioning

One of the most common customizations that people want to make to the default Team Build process is stamping each assembly with a unique version number each time they're built. Assemblies have two version numbers:

- **Assembly Version** Used by the .NET Framework for locating, loading, and referencing assemblies.
- **Assembly File Version** Visible in file's properties in Windows Explorer.

These version numbers are both stored as assembly-level attributes called *AssemblyVersion* and *AssemblyFileVersion* respectively and are typically set in a project's AssemblyInfo.cs/.vb file.

The Assembly Version typically stores only the major and minor version of the product being built with the build and revision fields left as zero. This is because assemblies that differ only by build and revision number are considered compatible with each other by the .NET Framework when locating, loading, and referencing strong-named assemblies.

From a configuration management perspective you still need to be able to differentiate between two different, although compatible, assemblies and this is where the Assembly File Version is used. Because this version isn't used by the .NET Framework for locating, loading, or referencing assemblies we can include the build number and possibly revision. The Assembly File Version will typically have the same major and minor version as the Assembly Version but this is not a requirement.

Because the build numbers allocated by default by Team Build are in the format BuildDefinitionName_YYYYMMDD.X and the fields in a version number are integers, we will need to allocate our own build numbers for versioning purposes. The easiest way to do that is using the Version task from the MSBuild Community Tasks (*http://msbuildtasks.tigris.org*). This task reads a version number in from a specified text file, increments using the algorithm you specify, and then writes the new version back to the text file.

In this example, we override the BuildNumberOverrideTarget and assign a new build number for the current build using the Version task:

```
<Target Name="BuildNumberOverrideTarget">
    <PropertyGroup>
        <VersionFilePath>$(DropLocation)\..\version.txt</VersionFilePath>
    </PropertyGroup>

    <WriteLinesToFile File="$(VersionFilePath)"
        Lines="1.0.0.0"
        Condition="!Exists('$(VersionFilePath)')" />

    <Version VersionFile="$(VersionFilePath)"
        BuildType="Increment"
        RevisionType="None">
        <Output TaskParameter="Major" PropertyName="Major" />
        <Output TaskParameter="Minor" PropertyName="Minor" />
        <Output TaskParameter="Build" PropertyName="Build" />
        <Output TaskParameter="Revision" PropertyName="Revision" />
    </Version>

    <PropertyGroup>
        <BuildNumber>
            $(BuildDefinitionName)_$(Major).$(Minor).$(Build).$(Revision)
        </BuildNumber>
        <AssemblyVersion>$(Major).$(Minor).0.0</AssemblyVersion>
        <FileVersion>$(Major).$(Minor).$(Build).$(Revision)</FileVersion>
    </PropertyGroup>
</Target>
```

To keep the example simple we are storing the version.txt file in the directory above the DropLocation (this is because the DropLocation is build-specific and we want to share the version.txt between builds). You could alternatively store the version.txt in source control and do a get before calling the Version task and a check-in after calling it. Because the Version task expects the file to already exist, we conditionally call the WriteLinesToFile task to create the file with a default version of 1.0.0.0 if it's missing.

We then call the Version task, passing in the path to the file and specifying what algorithms we want to use to increment the build and revision fields of the version number. In this case we're going to simply increment the build field and leave the revision field at zero. The documentation that comes with MSBuild Community Tasks details the other available algorithms. The Version task has an output parameter for each field of the version number so we store those outputs in appropriately named properties.

We then fulfill the contract for the BuildNumberOverrideTarget by creating a property called BuildNumber and set its value to the build definition's name, an underscore, and the version number. We prefix the version number with the build definition's name so that each build number is unique across the Team Project, not just the build definition, and since we may have two products in the Team Project with the same version number, the build definition name prefix ensures uniqueness. Team Build only requires the build number to be unique within a build definition, but it is recommended that build numbers are unique across the Team Project to make builds easier to identify.

We also create a property called AssemblyVersion and a property called AssemblyFileVersion, which we'll use to create the new AssemblyInfo files. We could either put this logic in AfterGet or BeforeCompile but I'm going to use AfterGet because it isn't executed for desktop builds, so we can avoid allocating build numbers unnecessarily. The resulting target would look like this:

```
<Target Name="AfterGet" >
    <Error Text="AssemblyVersion property has not been set."
        Condition="'$(AssemblyVersion)'==''" />
    <Error Text="FileVersion property has not been set."
        Condition="'$(FileVersion)'==''" />

    <ItemGroup>
        <AssemblyInfoFile Include="$(SolutionRoot)\**\AssemblyInfo.cs">
            <CodeLanguage>CS</CodeLanguage>
        </AssemblyInfoFile>
        <AssemblyInfoFile Include="$(SolutionRoot)\**\AssemblyInfo.vb">
            <CodeLanguage>VB</CodeLanguage>
        </AssemblyInfoFile>
    </ItemGroup>

    <Attrib Files="@(AssemblyInfoFile)" ReadOnly="false" />

    <AssemblyInfo OutputFile="@(AssemblyInfoFile)"
        CodeLanguage="%(AssemblyInfoFile.CodeLanguage)"
        AssemblyVersion="$(AssemblyVersion)"
        AssemblyFileVersion="$(AssemblyVersion)"
    />
</Target>
```

First we check that the AssemblyVersion and FileVersion properties have been specified and output an error message if they haven't. We then create a list of the AssemblyInfo files to be replaced and assign CodeLanguage metadata to each item so we know whether to generate a C# or Visual Basic .NET file.

Because these files have come from source control they will be read-only, so rather than relying on the AssemblyInfo task to overwrite them we remove the read-only attribute using the Attrib task (also from the MSBuild Community Tasks).

Note If you've enabled IncrementalGet you should set the GetOverwrite property to true if you are going to modify files locally. See the "Performing Incremental Gets" section of Chapter 11.

We then call the AssemblyInfo task, which will generate a new file over each of the existing AssemblyInfo files with the updated AssemblyVersion and AssemblyFileVersion.

Note It may not always be appropriate to simply overwrite the existing AssemblyInfo files with new ones. The AssemblyInfo files can contain a lot more than just the version attributes, and although the AssemblyInfo task does allow you to add other attributes to the generated AssemblyInfo (such as company name, copyright, and product name) you may need to preserve developer's changes to the AssemblyInfo files.

The easiest way to achieve this is to add an additional code file to each project (called, for example, VersionInfo.cs/vb) and move the AssemblyVersion and AssemblyFileVersion attributes from the AssemblyInfo file to the VersionInfo file. You would then modify this example to replace the VersionInfo files rather than the AssemblyInfo files, which will retain any changes developers have made.

Appendix A

New Features in MSBuild 3.5

MSBuild 3.5 shipped with a number of improvements from the previous version, MSBuild 2.0. Some of these changes improve performance and others will change how you create project files. We will discuss those changes in this appendix.

Properties and Items Declared Inside Targets

With MSBuild 2.0 you would declare static properties and items using the *PropertyGroup* and *ItemGroup* elements outside of tasks. When you needed to create dynamic properties or items, those defined inside targets, you could not use the same elements. Instead you had to use the CreateProperty and CreateItem tasks, which use a confusing syntax. Now you are able to create dynamic properties and items just as you would static ones. I recommend that you not use CreateItem and CreateProperty any longer. Throughout the book you have seen the usage of the *PropertyGroup* and *ItemGroup* inside of targets. To see the difference, take a look at the following two targets; the first uses 2.0 syntax and the second 3.5 syntax.

```
<Target Name="MSBuild20">
  <CreateProperty Value="value one">
    <Output PropertyName="myProp" TaskParameter="Value" />
  </CreateProperty>
  <CreateItem Include="item one">
    <Output ItemName="myItem" TaskParameter="Include" />
  </CreateItem>
  <CreateItem Include="item two">
    <Output ItemName="myItem" TaskParameter="Include" />
  </CreateItem>

  <Message Text="myProp: $(myProp)" />
  <Message Text="myItem: @(myItem)" />

</Target>
<Target Name="MSBuild35">
  <PropertyGroup>
    <myProp>value one</myProp>
  </PropertyGroup>
  <ItemGroup>
    <myItem Include="item one" />
    <myItem Include="item two" />
  </ItemGroup>

  <Message Text="myProp: $(myProp)" />
  <Message Text="myItem: @(myItem)" />
</Target>
```

The 3.5 syntax is much simpler and allows you to maintain a consistent approach to declaring properties and items.

Besides these benefits for items, the *ItemGroup* has some new functionality inside targets that CreateItem does not support. Using an *ItemGroup* inside of a target, you can remove items from an item list as well as modify, or add, metadata values to items. The following snippet contains most of the Items01.proj file. Some targets are missing, which we will discuss shortly.

```
<Project xmlns="http://schemas.microsoft.com/developer/msbuild/2003"
         DefaultTargets="PrintProperties"
         ToolsVersion="3.5">

  <ItemGroup>
    <Source Include="class1.cs">
      <Type>CS</Type>
      <Group>A1</Group>
    </Source>
    <Source Include="class2.vb">
      <Type>VB</Type>
      <Group>A2</Group>
    </Source>
    <Source Include="class3.vb">
      <Type>VB</Type>
      <Group>A2</Group>
    </Source>
    <Source Include="class4.cs">
      <Type>CS</Type>
      <Group>A2</Group>
    </Source>
    <Source Include="class5.vb">
      <Type>VB</Type>
      <Group>A1</Group>
    </Source>
  </ItemGroup>

  <Target Name="RemoveItemValue">
    <Message Text="Source: @(Source)" />
    <!-- Remove one value -->
    <ItemGroup>
      <Source Remove="class2.vb"/>
    </ItemGroup>
    <Message Text="Source: @(Source)" />
  </Target>

  <!--
   NOTE: Others targets defined here.
  -->
</Project>
```

Here the RemoveItemValue target is shown, which uses the *ItemGroup* element to remove a value from the Source item. If you execute the command `msbuild Items01.proj /t:RemoveItemValue` the result will be what is shown in Figure A-1.

```
C:\Data\MSBuildExamples\Misc>msbuild Items01.proj /t:RemoveItemValue /nologo
Build started 10/20/2008 11:43:07 PM.
Project "C:\Data\MSBuildExamples\Misc\Items01.proj" on node 0 (RemoveItemValue
target(s)).
  Source: class1.cs;class2.vb;class3.vb;class4.cs;class5.vb
  Source: class1.cs;class3.vb;class4.cs;class5.vb
Done Building Project "C:\Data\MSBuildExamples\Misc\Items01.proj" (RemoveItemVa
lue target(s)).

Build succeeded.
    0 Warning(s)
    0 Error(s)
```

FIGURE A-1 Removing a value from an item

From the result shown in Figure A-1, you can see that the class2.vb item value was successfully removed from the Source item. Changes to items are not localized to the target in which they are made; they are global, as other modifications to items are.

The target, UpdateMetadata, as shown in Figure A-2, is taken from the Items01.proj as well.

```
<Target Name="UpdateMetadata">
  <Message Text="Source: @(Source->'%(Identity):%(Group)')" />
  <ItemGroup>
    <Source Condition="%(Group) == 'A2'">
      <Group>A3</Group>
    </Source>
  </ItemGroup>
  <Message Text="Source: @(Source->'%(Identity):%(Group)')" />
</Target>
```

In this target, the *ItemGroup* element is used to modify the values for the Group metadata if it is currently set to A2. For those item values the Group is set to A3 instead.

```
C:\Data\MSBuildExamples\Misc>msbuild Items01.proj /t:UpdateMetadata /nologo
Build started 10/20/2008 11:57:26 PM.
Project "C:\Data\MSBuildExamples\Misc\Items01.proj" on node 0 (UpdateMetadata t
arget(s)).
  Source: class1.cs:A1;class2.vb:A2;class3.vb:A2;class4.cs:A2;class5.vb:A1
  Source: class1.cs:A1;class2.vb:A3;class3.vb:A3;class4.cs:A3;class5.vb:A1
Done Building Project "C:\Data\MSBuildExamples\Misc\Items01.proj" (UpdateMetada
ta target(s)).

Build succeeded.
    0 Warning(s)
    0 Error(s)
```

FIGURE A-2 Updating item metadata

From Figure A-2, you can see that the Group metadata was updated to A3 for those with the Group set to A2 previously. You can also use the *ItemGroup* element in order to add additional metadata to items. This is shown in the AddMetadata target, which is also taken from the Items01.proj file.

```
<Target Name="AddMetadata">
  <Message Text="Source: @(Source->'%(Identity):%(Level)')" />

  <ItemGroup>
    <Source Condition="%(Type)=='CS'">
      <Level>L1</Level>
    </Source>
```

```
    <Source Condition="%(Type) == 'VB'">
      <Level>L2</Level>
    </Source>
  </ItemGroup>

  <Message Text="Source: @(Source->'%(Identity):%(Level)')" />
</Target>
```

This usage of the *ItemGroup* element will add the Level to the Source item values. The value for the Level metadata will depend on the Type metadata value. If the Type is set to CS, then the Level is set to L1; if the Type is VB, then the Level will be set to L2. You can verify its behavior by using the command `msbuild Items01.proj /t:AddMetadata`.

Multiprocessor Support

MSBuild 3.5 now supports using multiple processors (cores) to execute the build process when available. This feature must explicitly be turned on in order to be used. You can turn it on by passing the /maxcpucount (/m) switch when invoking msbuild.exe. When you use this switch you can pass a specific number of concurrent processes that MSBuild can use by using the format /m:N where N is the number of processes to use. If N is not provided then it will default to the number of processors that are available on the machine. Typically using /m alone is ideal; however, if you want to try to optimize the build performance of a large solution, you could experiment with values of N that are a little different from the number of cores on the machine. Sometimes n-1 is faster because there is less disk contention.

If you are building a solution, then simply passing the /m switch will work great. MSBuild will organize the projects in the solution into the correct order, respecting project references and any manually specified build ordering in the solution file, and parallelize everything that can be parallelized. If you build a single VB.NET or C# project that has project references to other projects, they will be built in parallel as well. If you have constructed an MSBuild script that is used to build a set of projects then you should additionally set the *BuildInParallel* attribute to true on the MSBuild task. If this property is **not** set, then the projects will **not** build in parallel. Without this, when the MSBuild task is executed to build a set of projects, only one process will be used.

MSBuild parallelizes at the project level. Currently it doesn't parallelize individual targets or tasks within a single project. What this means is that the MSBuild task is executed in parallel when a set of projects is passed to it. An individual project is not built in parallel, but projects are built in parallel. This is how Visual Studio solutions are built using MSBuild. To clarify this, take a look at the following BuildProjects target.

```
<Target Name="BuildProjects">
  <!-- These will NOT be built in parallel -->
  <MSBuild Projects="project1.csproj" BuildInParallel="true" />
  <MSBuild Projects="project2.csproj" BuildInParallel="true" />
  <MSBuild Projects="project3.csproj" BuildInParallel="true" />

  <ItemGroup>
    <ProjectsToBuild Include="project1.csproj" />
    <ProjectsToBuild Include="project2.csproj" />
```

```
    <ProjectsToBuild Include="project3.csproj" />
  </ItemGroup>
  <!-- These will be built in parallel -->
  <MSBuild Projects="@(ProjectsToBuild)" BuildInParallel="true" />
</Target>
```

In this target, the MSBuild task is used three times to build three different project files. Because these projects are built individually by the MSBuild task, they will not be built in parallel. Each project will be built as if the /m switch was not specified. On the other hand, the next usage of the MSBuild task where the same project files are built will be parallelized. This is because the projects were sent simultaneously to the MSBuild task. In this example, I have placed the project files in the ProjectsToBuild item type, but this is not required. You could have invoked the MSBuild task with `<MSBuild Projects="project1.csproj;project2.csproj;project3.csproj" BuildInParallel="true"/>` instead.

One usage that may be confusing is when you are using the MSBuild task in a batched fashion. Consider the following target, BuildProjects2.

```
<Target Name="BuildProjects2">
  <ItemGroup>
    <ProjectsToBuild Include="project1.csproj" />
    <ProjectsToBuild Include="project2.csproj" />
    <ProjectsToBuild Include="project3.csproj" />
  </ItemGroup>

  <!-- These will NOT be built in parallel -->
  <MSBuild Projects="%(ProjectsToBuild.Identity)" BuildInParallel="true" />
</Target>
```

In this example, it may look as though the projects will be built in parallel because there is only one invocation of the MSBuild task, but because of batching with the expression %(ProjectsToBuild.Identity) they will be sent individually to the MSBuild task. If you need to brush up on batching, it is covered in detail in Chapter 6, "Batching and Incremental Builds." Many times batching is used in conjunction with the MSBuild task to specify different properties for each project. For example, you may use it in the following way:

```
<MSBuild Projects="%(ProjectsToBuild.Identity)"
         BuildInParallel="true"
         Properties="OutputPath=outputRoot\%(ProjectsToBuild.Filename)" />
```

In this case, we are batching the ProjectsToBuild in order to get the correct value for each project's OutputPath. You can use the Properties and AdditionalProperties metadata on the ProjectsToBuild item to circumvent the need for batching. Instead of the preceding statement, you could use the approach shown next instead.

```
<Target Name="BuildProjects3">
  <ItemGroup>
    <ProjectsToBuild Include="project1.csproj">
      <AdditionalProperties>
        OutputPath=outputRoot\%(ProjectsToBuild.Filename);
      </AdditionalProperties>
    </ProjectsToBuild>
```

```
    <ProjectsToBuild Include="project2.csproj">
      <AdditionalProperties>
        OutputPath=outputRoot\%(ProjectsToBuild.Filename);
      </AdditionalProperties>
    </ProjectsToBuild>
    <ProjectsToBuild Include="project3.csproj">
      <AdditionalProperties>
        OutputPath=outputRoot\%(ProjectsToBuild.Filename);
      </AdditionalProperties>
    </ProjectsToBuild>
  </ItemGroup>

    <!-- These will be built in parallel -->
    <MSBuild Projects="@(ProjectsToBuild)" BuildInParallel="true" />
</Target>
```

In this case, we are specifying the OutputPath value using the AdditionalProperties metadata, which will be used by the MSBuld task to build each project. For more information on this, see the section "MSBuild Task Changes."

Multitargeting

When .NET 2.0 was released, MSBuild was also introduced. MSBuild was first used as a Build Engine by Visual Studio 2005. One common question for those looking to adopt Visual Studio 2005 was, "Can it be used to build .NET 1.1 code?" At the time it wasn't possible, but a separate add-on was made available, called MSBee, that would assist users to target .NET 1.1. With Visual Studio 2008 it's a different story: Targeting .NET 2.0 is built into MSBuild as well as Visual Studio. MSBuild now has the concept known as Toolsets. A toolset consists of tasks, targets, properties, and items that are used to drive the build process. MSBuild 3.5 ships with two toolsets, 2.0 and 3.5. The 2.0 toolset is the exact same set of tasks and targets files that shipped with MSBuild 2.0. Since MSBuild 3.5 installs MSBuild 2.0 as well, they're always available. If you specify to use the 2.0 toolset then only .NET 2.0 assemblies will be created. The targets files delivered by Microsoft to build C# and VB.NET projects has an additional property, TargetFrameworkVersion, which enables you to build a project using MSBuild 3.5 toolset but .NET 2.0 assemblies. Toolsets and TargetFrameworkVersion are often confused. A Toolset is a concept built-in to the MSBuild platform. TargetFrameworkVersion is a property like any other that is consumed in the targets files that build VB.NET and C# projects. We will discuss that later in this section.

You can specify the toolsets to be used in one of the following ways:

- /toolsversion (/tv) command line switch for msbuild.exe
- ToolsVersion attribute on the MSBuild task
- Registry using the DefaultToolsVersion key on the `\HKEY_LOCAL_MACHINE\SOFTWARE\Microsoft\MSBuild\3.5\`
- msbuild.exe.config

The registry key referenced in the previous list is the DefaultToolsVersion key for HKEY_LOCAL_MACHINE\SOFTWARE\Microsoft\MSBuild\3.5\. Here is the order in which MSBuild will look for the tools version; the first one encountered will be used.

1. ToolsVersion on the MSBuild task
2. /tv command-line switch
3. ToolsVersion on the Project element
4. Default value from msbuild.exe.config file
5. Default Value from registry
6. Hard coded 2.0 default

If you would like to use MSBuild v3.5 for C# or VB.NET projects and create .NET 2.0 assemblies you can do so. These project types support a new property, TargetFrameworkVersion, which will determine which version of .NET will be used to build the project. When using this property you must use the MSBuild 3.5 toolset; MSBuild 2.0 is not aware of this property. This property has three valid values: v2.0, v3.0, and v3.5. If you are using Visual Studio you can set this property in the Application tab of the Projects properties. Figure A-3 shows this option.

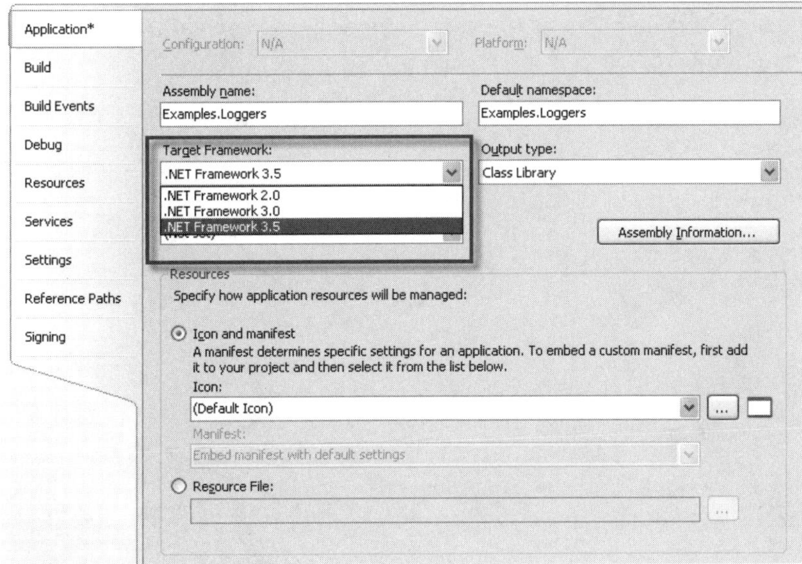

FIGURE A-3 Target Framework version setting

Visual Studio will default this value to v3.5 when creating new projects, but if no value is provided for the TargetFrameworkVersion then the targets files for C# and VB.NET projects will default this to v2.0. In future versions of MSBuild, Toolsets are likely to be more powerful and useful.

If you are targeting .NET 2.0, you have three options:

1. MSBuild 2.0
2. MSBuild 3.5 and Toolset=2.0
3. MSBuild 3.5, Toolset=v3.5, and TargetFrameworkVersion=v2.0

Here are the reasons why you might choose one of these options over the others. You will use MSBuild 2.0 when you are using Visual Studio 2005. The advantage of the second option versus the third is that you can be certain that you will get the **exact** same build results as you did with MSBuild 2.0. The advantage of the third option over the others is that you can build in parallel. The 3.5 targets have support for BuildInParallel.

Visual Studio 2008 will always create VB.NET/C# projects with ToolsVersion=3.5 in their root tag, and it will upgrade Visual Studio 2005 projects to 3.5 as well.

ItemDefinitionGroup

In MSBuild 3.5, you can use the *ItemDefinitionGroup* element if you need to specify a default value for an item's metadata. You can use this element to provide the default value for metadata and allow individual items to override the value as needed. You can see its usage in the following Items02.proj file.

```
<Project xmlns="http://schemas.microsoft.com/developer/msbuild/2003"
         ToolsVersion="3.5">

  <ItemDefinitionGroup>
    <MyItem>
      <!-- Default Group if not specified -->
      <Group>A1</Group>
    </MyItem>
  </ItemDefinitionGroup>

  <ItemGroup>
    <MyItem Include="Item01">
      <Group>A1</Group>
    </MyItem>
    <MyItem Include="Item02" />
    <MyItem Include="Item03">
      <Group>A2</Group>
    </MyItem>
    <MyItem Include="Item04">
      <Group>A2</Group>
    </MyItem>
    <MyItem Include="Item05">
      <Group></Group>
    </MyItem>
  </ItemGroup>
```

```
  <Target Name="PrintMetadata">
    <ItemGroup>
      <MyItem Include="Item06"/>
    </ItemGroup>

    <Message Text="@(MyItem->'%(Identity):%(Group)')" />
  </Target>
</Project>
```

This project file uses the *ItemDefinitionGroup* element to provide a default value for the Group metadata for the MyItem item type. Inside the PrintMetadata target a new value is added to the MyItem item type, and the values for the Group are printed. The results of executing this target are shown in Figure A-4.

```
C:\Data\MSBuildExamples\Misc>msbuild Items02.proj /t:PrintMetadata /nologo
Build started 10/22/2008 7:52:08 PM.
Project "C:\Data\MSBuildExamples\Misc\Items02.proj" on node 0 (PrintMetadata ta
rget(s)).
  Item01:A1;Item02:A1;Item03:A2;Item04:A2;Item05:;Item06:A1
Done Building Project "C:\Data\MSBuildExamples\Misc\Items02.proj" (PrintMetadat
a target(s)).

Build succeeded.
    0 Warning(s)
    0 Error(s)
```

FIGURE A-4 *ItemDefinitionGroup* usage

Because the *ItemDefinitionGroup* was used, the items Item02 and Item06 had a value for the Group metadata. Notice that the Item05 value did not use the default value for Group even though its value was empty. Another thing that is worth pointing out is that the dynamic item, Item06 also used the default value provided by the *ItemDefinitionGroup*. Once you create a default using the *ItemDefintionGroup*, that value will be used for all of its items, including previously declared ones and dynamically created ones.

Registry Syntax

Now, accessing registry values is **almost** as easy as getting the value of a property. Getting the value of a registry key uses a similar format to properties. To access a value from the registry the following syntax is used:

$(Registry:<*KeyName*>[@*ValueName*])

In this syntax, KeyName is the full name to the registry key and ValueName is an optional parameter specifying which value to extract. If ValueName is not provided then the default value, if it exists, for that key will be returned. To demonstrate this, take a look at the Reg01.proj file, which is shown next. The lines are wrapped here, but the text should be unbroken MSBuild files.

```
<Project xmlns="http://schemas.microsoft.com/developer/msbuild/2003"
         ToolsVersion="3.5">

  <Target Name="PrintRegValue">
    <Message
      Text="9.0: $(Registry:HKEY_LOCAL_MACHINE\SOFTWARE\Microsoft\
                   VisualStudio\9.0\Setup\VS@ProductDir)" />
```

```
    <Message
      Text="8.0: $(Registry:HKEY_LOCAL_MACHINE\SOFTWARE\Microsoft\
                      VisualStudio\8.0\Setup\VS@ProductDir)" />
  </Target>

</Project>
```

In this project file, the registry syntax is used to determine where Visual Studio 2008 (9.0) is installed as well as where Visual Studio 2005 (8.0) is installed.

```
C:\Data\MSBuildExamples\Misc>msbuild Reg01.proj /t:PrintRegValue /nologo
Build started 10/22/2008 11:22:12 PM.
Project "C:\Data\MSBuildExamples\Misc\Reg01.proj" on node 0 (PrintRegValue targ
et(s)).
  9.0: C:\Program Files\Microsoft Visual Studio 9.0\
  8.0: C:\Program Files\Microsoft Visual Studio 8\
Done Building Project "C:\Data\MSBuildExamples\Misc\Reg01.proj" (PrintRegValue
target(s)).


Build succeeded.
    0 Warning(s)
    0 Error(s)
```

FIGURE A-5 Registry Key retrieval

The result from executing the PrintRegValue target on my machine is shown in Figure A-5. Your results may vary depending on your configuration. In MSBuild 2.0, if you needed to get a value from the registry, you would have to use a custom task. Now you can use this new feature. This is only supports string values. If you need to set a registry value, you still have to use a custom task.

New Reserved Properties

MSBuild 3.5 introduces a few new reserved properties. These are summarized in Table A-1.

TABLE A-1 New Reserved Properties in MSBuild 3.5

Name	Description
MSBuildToolsPath	The full path to the location where the .tasks file containing the list of default tasks, and the default .targets files are found. Each toolset has a different value for this property. For MSBuild 2.0 this property is named MSBuildBinPath and is deprecated in MSBuild 3.5.
MSBuildExtensionsPath32	The full path to where MSBuild 32-bit extensions are located. This is typically under the Program Files folder. For 32-bit machines this value will be the same as MSBuildExtensionsPath. The motivation behind this is to avoid placing the targets files in both 64- and 32-bit program files folders when installing on a 64-bit machine.
MSBuildNodeCount	The number of nodes (processes) that are being used to build the project. If the /m switch is not used, then this value will be 1.
MSBuildStartupDirectory	The full path to folder where the MSBuild process is invoked.
MSBuildToolsVersion	The version of the tools being used to build the project. Possible values include 2.0 and 3.5.

MSBuild Task Changes

A number of changes to the MSBuild task have been made that might change the way you use the task. There are six new properties on the MSBuild task, which are outlined in Table A-2.

TABLE A-2 New MSBuild Task Properties

Name	Description
BuildInParallel	If true, the multiprocessor builds will be supported, otherwise not. The default value for this property is false.
SkipNonexistentProjects	If true, projects that don't exist on disk but are passed into the Projects property will be skipped. Otherwise the task will fail. The default value is false.
TargetAndPropertyListSeparators	An optional parameter that can be used to define the separator used for the targets and properties list. The default separator is a semicolon.
ToolsVersion	This determines what version of MSBuild tools will be used to execute the build. Valid values are 2.0 and 3.5. The default is 2.0. This value would override other values previously defined.
UnloadProjectsOnCompletion	If true, then once a project has been built it will be unloaded from memory. The default value for this is false. You should not modify this unless your builds are consuming too much memory. When this property is set to true, you should also set UseResultsCache to true.
UseResultsCache	When set to true, MSBuild will remember target outputs. This is necessary when projects are unloaded. The default value is false. You should not modify this value unless you have to set UnloadProjectsOnCompletion to true. Both this property, as well as UnloadProjectsOnCompletion, will be eliminated in MSBuild 4.0 (it will be handled automatically) so you should not use these unless you really need to. Better would be to split up your build into separate MSBuild projects and use the Exec task to invoke msbuild.exe.

In addtion to these new properties, there are some behavior changes as well. Two recognized pieces of metadata, Properties and AdditionalProperties, can be used for items passed into the Projects property. You can use these to specify properties that should be used to build the project when the project is passed into the MSBuild task. The MSBuild task is now able to process properties at the item level instead of just accepting values as the Properties input parameter. For a complete discussion of these metadata values take a look at the "Building Multiple Projects" section in Chapter 8, "Practical Applications."

If you are using the TargetOutputs output parameter, then the items that are output will have two new metadata values: MSBuildSourceTargetName and MSBuildSourceProjectFile. MSBuildSourceTargetName identifies the name of the target that places the item in the TargetOutputs, and the MSBuildSourceProjectFile contains the name of the file that contains the target.

Exec Task Changes

The Exec task has three new properties: CustomErrorRegularExpression, CustomWarningRegularExpression, and IgnoreStandardErrorWarningFormat. These three properties are related to a new ability of the Exec task. It can detect errors and warnings that are output from tools automatically if the messages adhere to a given format. For a full discussion about how this works see the "Exec Task" section in Chapter 7, "External Tools."

Appendix B

Common Properties and Items

There is a set of common properties and items that are used throughout the build process for VB.NET and C# projects. MSBuild itself is not aware of these; they are defined by the target files shipped by Microsoft, which VB.NET and C# project import. These values are declared in either the project file generated by Visual Studio or in the Microsoft.Common.targets file that is shipped by Microsoft along with MSBuild. Many of these values can be maintained by the Visual Studio UI. If you need to edit them yourself, you can do so by right-clicking on the project and selecting Unload Project, then right-clicking on the project again and selecting Edit Project File. When you are editing MSBuild files don't be surprised to see squiggly red lines under some elements, the schema used for MSBuild files is not complete. C# project files import the Microsoft.CSharp.targets file and VB.NET projects import the Microsoft .VisualBasic.targets file. Both of these files then import the Microsoft.Common.targets file. For more information regarding these topics see the MSDN references at: Common MSBuild Project Properties *(http://msdn.microsoft.com/en-us/library/bb629394.aspx)*, Common MSBuild Project Items *(http://msdn.microsoft.com/en-us/library/bb629388.aspx)*, and MSBuild Visual Studio Integration *(http://msdn.microsoft.com/en-us/library/ms171468.aspx)*.

Common Properties

In Table B-1 you will find a list of common properties that are used when building managed projects created by Visual Studio.

TABLE B-1 Common MSBuild Properties

Property or Parameter Name	Description
AssemblyName	The name of the final output assembly after the project is built.

AssemblySearchPaths	A list of locations to search during build-time reference assembly resolution. The order in which paths appear in this list is meaningful because paths listed earlier take precedence over later entries. This is a semicolon delimited list. You can modify this value by:
	
	`<PropertyGroup>`
	`  <AssemblySearchPaths>`
	`   FirstPath;`
	`   $(AssemblySearchPaths);`
	`   LastPath`
	`  </AssemblySearchPaths>`
	`</PropertyGroup>`

TABLE B-1 Common MSBuild Properties

Property or Parameter Name	Description
	Some reasons to modify this would be to disable searching the GAC, or to optimize the search path by placing the most common locations at the top. There are some special markers that can be used for this property. For a full list see the Microsoft.Common.targets file.
BaseOutputPath	Specifies the base path for the output file. If it is set, MSBuild will use `OutputPath = $(BaseOutputPath)\$(Configuration)\`. Example syntax: `<BaseOutputPath>c:\xyz\bin\ </BaseOutputPath>`
BaseIntermediateOutputPath	The top-level folder where all configuration-specific intermediate output folders are created. The default value is obj\. I would not recommend changing this value, certain tools may assume that this folder will be used. Specifies the base intermediate path for the output file. Example syntax: `<BaseIntermediateOutputPath>c:\xyz\obj\ </BaseIntermediateOutputPath>`
BuildInParallel	A Boolean value that indicates whether project references are built or cleaned in parallel when Multi-Proc MSBuild is used. The default value is true, which means that projects will be built in parallel if the system has multiple cores or processors. This will be enabled only if the /m switch is used on the command line for msbuild.exe. This is new with MSBuild 3.5.
CleanFile	The name of the file that will be used as the "clean cache." The clean cache is a list of generated files to be deleted during the cleaning operation. The file is put in the intermediate output path by the build process. This property specifies only file names that do not have path information.
Configuration	The configuration that you are building. This can be any defined configuration value, for example "Debug" or "Release." This is a property, and does not have any special behavior. The default value is "Debug."
DebugSymbols	A Boolean value that indicates whether symbols are generated by the build. Setting `/p:DebugSymbols=false` on the command line disables generation of program database (.pdb) symbol files.
DefineConstants	Defines conditional compiler constants. Symbol/value pairs are separated by semicolons and are specified by using the following syntax: symbol1 = value1 ; symbol2 = value2 The property is equivalent to the /define compiler switch.

TABLE B-1 Common MSBuild Properties

Property or Parameter Name	Description
IntermediateOutputPath	The full intermediate output path as derived from `BaseIntermediateOutputPath`, if no path is specified. For example, `\obj\Debug\.` If this property is overridden, then setting `BaseIntermediateOutputPath` has no effect.
OutputPath	This property is typically specified in the project file and resembles `OutDir`.
Platform	The operating system you are building for. Valid values are "AnyCPU," "x86," "x64," or "Itanium."
TargetFrameworkVersion	The version of the .NET Framework that is required to run the application that you are building. Specifying this lets you reference certain framework assemblies that you may not be able to reference otherwise. Valid values are "v2.0", "v3.0" or "v.5".
DebugType	Defines the level of debug information that you want generated. Valid values are "full," "pdbonly," and "none."
TreatWarningsAsErrors	A Boolean parameter that, if true, causes all warnings to be treated as errors. This parameter is equivalent to the /nowarn compiler switch.
CustomAfterMicrosoft CommonTargets	The name of a project file or targets file that is to be imported automatically after the common targets import. The default location for this file is `$(MSBuildExtensionsPath)\v3.5\Custom.After.Microsoft.Common.targets`. This is typically useful only for adhoc build process modifications.
CustomBeforeMicrosoft CommonTargets	The name of a project file or targets file that is to be imported automatically before the common targets import. The default location for this file is $(MSBuildExtensionsPath)\v3.5\Custom.Before.Microsoft.Common.targets. This is typically useful only for adhoc build process modifications.
AdditionalLibPaths	Specifies additional folders in which compilers should look for reference assemblies. This applies only to C# projects and is not normally used. It is better to use the Reference or ProjectReference item instead.
AddModules	Causes the compiler to make all type information from the specified files available to the project you are compiling. This property is equivalent to the /addModules compiler switch.
ALToolPath	The path where AL.exe can be found. This property overrides the current version of AL.exe to enable use of a different version. For example, you might want to use a checked-in version of AL.
ApplicationIcon	The .ico icon file to pass to the compiler for embedding as a Win32 icon. The property is equivalent to the /win32icon compiler switch.

TABLE B-1 Common MSBuild Properties

Property or Parameter Name	Description
ApplicationManifest	Specifies the path of the file that is used to generate external user account control (UAC) manifest information. Applies only to Visual Studio projects targeting Windows Vista. In most cases, the manifest is embedded. However, if you use Registration-Free COM or ClickOnce deployment, then the manifest can be an external file that is installed together with your application assemblies. For more information, see the NoWin32Manifest property in this topic.
BaseAddress	Specifies the base address of the main output assembly. This property is equivalent to the /baseaddress compiler switch.
BuildProjectReferences	A Boolean value that indicates whether project references are built by MSBuild. Set to false if you are building your project in the Visual Studio integrated development environment (IDE), true if otherwise.
CodePage	Specifies the code page to use for all source-code files in the compilation. This property is equivalent to the /codepage compiler switch.
CompilerResponseFile	An optional response file that can be passed to the compiler tasks.
CscToolPath	The path of csc.exe, the Visual C# compiler.
DefineDebug	A Boolean value that indicates whether you want the DEBUG constant defined.
DefineTrace	A Boolean value that indicates whether you want the TRACE constant defined.
DelaySign	A Boolean value that indicates whether you want to delay-sign the assembly rather than full-sign it.
DisabledWarnings	Suppresses the specified warnings. Only the numeric part of the warning identifier must be specified. Multiple warnings are separated by semicolons. This parameter corresponds to the /nowarn switch of the vbc.exe compiler.
DisableFastUpToDateCheck	A Boolean value that applies to Visual Studio only. The Visual Studio build manager uses a process called FastUpToDateCheck to determine whether a project must be rebuilt to be up to date. This process is faster than using MSBuild to determine this. Setting the DisableFastUpToDateCheck property to true lets you bypass the Visual Studio build manager and force it to use MSBuild to determine whether the project is up to date. You should set the property to true if you have customized the build process to have custom kinds of input files or output files. Visual Studio compares only the inputs and outputs that it is aware of. Fast up-to-date check is only used when debugging inside Visual Studio. When a full build is executed by Visual Studio, MSBuild will be called and the build is guaranteed to be correct.

TABLE B-1 Common MSBuild Properties

Property or Parameter Name	Description
DocumentationFile	The name of the file that is generated as the XML documentation file. This name includes only the file name and has no path information; it goes in the output directory. This is for C# projects; VB.NET projects use the GenerateDocumentation property instead.
ErrorReport	Specifies how the compiler task should report internal compiler errors. Valid values are "prompt," "send," or "none." This property is equivalent to the /errorreport compiler switch.
ExcludeDeploymentUrl	The GenerateDeploymentManifest Task *[http://msdn.microsoft.com/en-us/library/3k2t34e7.aspx]* adds a deploymentProvider tag to the deployment manifest if the project file includes any of the following elements: ❑ UpdateUrl ❑ InstallUrl ❑ PublishUrl Using ExcludeDeploymentUrl, however, you can prevent the deploymentProvider tag from being added to the deployment manifest even if any of the preceding URLs are specified. To do this, add the following property to your project file: `<ExcludeDeploymentUrl>true</ExcludeDeploymentUrl>` Note: ExcludeDeploymentUrl is not exposed in the Visual Studio IDE and can be set only by manually editing the project file. Setting this property does not affect publishing within Visual Studio; that is, the deploymentProvider tag will still be added to the URL specified by PublishUrl.
FileAlignment	Specifies, in bytes, where to align the sections of the output file. Valid values are 512, 1024, 2048, 4096, 8192. This property is equivalent to the /filealignment compiler switch.
FrameworkPathOverride	Specifies the location of mscorlib.dll and microsoft.visualbasic.dll. This parameter is equivalent to the /sdkpath switch of the vbc.exe compiler.
GenerateDocumentation	A Boolean parameter that indicates whether documentation is generated by the build. If true, the build generates documentation information and puts it in an .xml file together with the name of the executable file or library that the build task created. This is for VB.NET projects; C# projects use the DocumentationFile property instead.
KeyContainerName	The name of the strong-name key container.
KeyOriginatorFile	The name of the strong-name key file.
ModuleAssemblyName	The name of the assembly that the compiled module is to be incorporated into. The property is equivalent to the /moduleassemblyname compiler switch.

TABLE B-1 Common MSBuild Properties

Property or Parameter Name	Description
NoLogo	A Boolean value that indicates whether you want the compiler logo to be turned off. This property is equivalent to the /nologo compiler switch.
NoStdLib	A Boolean value that indicates whether to avoid referencing the standard library (mscorlib.dll). The default value is false.
NoVBRuntimeReference	A Boolean value that indicates whether the Visual Basic runtime (Microsoft.VisualBasic.dll) should be included as a reference in the project. This is an advanced setting, and you will most likely never have to set this.
NoWin32Manifest	Determines whether the compiler generates the default Win32 manifest into the output assembly. The default value of false means that the default Win32 manifest is generated for all applications. This property is equivalent to the /nowin32manifest compiler switch of vbc.exe. For applications which are targeting Windows Vista this is also a value that indicates whether user account control (UAC) manifest information will be embedded in the application's executable. In projects deployed using ClickOnce and Registration-Free COM, this element is ignored. False (the default value) specifies that user account control (UAC) manifest information be embedded in the application's executable. True specifies that UAC manifest information not be embedded. This property applies only to Visual Studio projects targeting Windows Vista. You should add NoWin32Manifest only if you do not want Visual Studio to embed any manifest information in the application's executable; this process is called virtualization. To use virtualization, set <ApplicationManifest> in conjunction with <NoWin32Manifest> as follows: For Visual Basic projects, remove the <ApplicationManifest> node. (In Visual Basic projects, <NoWin32Manifest> is ignored when an <ApplicationManifest> node exists.) For Visual C# projects, set <ApplicationManifest> to False and <NoWin32Manifest> to True. (In Visual C# projects, <ApplicationManifest> overrides <NoWin32Manifest>.)
Optimize	A Boolean value that when set to true, enables compiler optimizations. This property is equivalent to the /optimize compiler switch.
OptionCompare	Specifies how string comparisons are made. Valid values are "binary" or "text." This property is equivalent to the /optioncompare compiler switch of vbc.exe. This is a VB.NET only option.

TABLE B-1 Common MSBuild Properties

Property or Parameter Name	Description
OptionExplicit	A Boolean value that when set to true, requires explicit declaration of variables in the source code. This property is equivalent to the /optionexplicit compiler switch. This is a VB.NET-only option.
OptionInfer	A Boolean value that when set to true, enables type inference of variables. This property is equivalent to the /optioninfer compiler switch. This is a VB.NET-only option.
OptionStrict	A Boolean value that when set to true, causes the build task to enforce strict type semantics to restrict implicit type conversions. This property is equivalent to the /optionstrict switch of the vbc.exe compiler. This is a VB.NET-only option.
OutputType	Specifies the file format of the output file. This parameter can have one of the following values: ❑ Library. Creates a code library. (Default value.) ❑ Exe. Creates a console application. ❑ Module. Creates a module. ❑ Winexe. Creates a Windows-based program. This property is equivalent to the /target switch of the vbc.exe compiler. Visual Studio does not support setting this to Module; you have to modify the file yourself.
OverwriteReadOnlyFiles	A Boolean value that indicates whether you want to enable the build to overwrite read-only files or trigger an error. The default value is false.
PdbFile	The file name of the .pdb file that you are emitting. This property is equivalent to the /pdb switch of the csc.exe compiler. In most cases this will not have to be specified.
RemoveIntegerChecks	A Boolean value that indicates whether to disable integer overflow error checks. The default value is false. This property is equivalent to the /removeintchecks switch of the vbc.exe compiler.
SGenUseProxyTypes	A Boolean value that indicates whether proxy types should be generated by SGen.exe.
SGenToolPath	An optional tool path that indicates where to obtain SGen.exe when the current version of SGen.exe is overridden. This is useful if you wanted to use a checked-in version of this tool.
StartupObject	Specifies the class or module that contains the *Main* method or Sub Main procedure. This property is equivalent to the /main compiler switch.
ProcessorArchitecture	The processor architecture that is used when assembly references are resolved. Valid values are "msil," "x86," "amd64," or "ia64."
RootNamespace	The root namespace to use when you name an embedded resource. This namespace is part of the embedded resource manifest name.

TABLE B-1 Common MSBuild Properties

Property or Parameter Name	Description
Satellite_AlgorithmId	The ID of the AL.exe hashing algorithm to use when satellite assemblies are created.
Satellite_BaseAddress	The base address to use when culture-specific satellite assemblies are built by using the CreateSatelliteAssemblies target.
Satellite_CompanyName	The company name to pass into AL.exe during satellite assembly generation.
Satellite_Configuration	The configuration name to pass into AL.exe during satellite assembly generation.
Satellite_Description	The description text to pass into AL.exe during satellite assembly generation.
Satellite_EvidenceFile	Embeds the specified file in the satellite assembly that has the resource name "Security.Evidence."
Satellite_FileVersion	Specifies a string for the File Version field in the satellite assembly.
Satellite_Flags	Specifies a value for the Flags field in the satellite assembly.
Satellite_GenerateFullPaths	Causes the build task to use absolute paths for any files reported in an error message.
Satellite_LinkResource	Links the specified resource files to a satellite assembly.
Satellite_MainEntryPoint	Specifies the fully qualified name (that is, class.method) of the method to use as an entry point when a module is converted to an executable file during satellite assembly generation.
Satellite_ProductName	Specifies a string for the Product field in the satellite assembly.
Satellite_ProductVersion	Specifies a string for the ProductVersion field in the satellite assembly.
Satellite_TargetType	Specifies the file format of the satellite assembly output file as "library," "exe," or "win." The default value is "library."
Satellite_Title	Specifies a string for the Title field in the satellite assembly.
Satellite_Trademark	Specifies a string for the Trademark field in the satellite assembly.
Satellite_Version	Specifies the version information for the satellite assembly.
Satellite_Win32Icon	Inserts an .ico icon file in the satellite assembly.
Satellite_Win32Resource	Inserts a Win32 resource (.res file) into the satellite assembly.
TargetCompactFramework	The version of the .NET Compact Framework that is required to run the application that you are building. Specifying this lets you reference certain framework assemblies that you may not be able to reference otherwise.
UseHostCompilerIfAvailable	A Boolean parameter that, if true, causes the build task to use the in-process compiler object, if it is available. This parameter is used only by Visual Studio. There are rare circumstances where a build by Visual Studio differs from the build created by MSBuild. These are bugs in Visual Studio. If you encounter this you can set this property to false, but it will cause Visual Studio to run slower.

TABLE B-1 Common MSBuild Properties

Property or Parameter Name	Description
Utf8Output	A Boolean parameter that, if true, logs compiler output by using UTF-8 encoding. This parameter is equivalent to the /utf8Output compiler switch.
VbcToolPath	An optional path that indicates another location for vbc.exe when the current version of vbc.exe is overridden.
VbcVerbosity	Specifies the verbosity of the Visual Basic compiler's output. Valid values are "Quiet," "Normal" (the default value), or "Verbose."
WarningsAsErrors	Specifies a list of warnings to treat as errors. This parameter is equivalent to the /warnaserror compiler switch.
WarningsNotAsErrors	Specifies a list of warnings that are not treated as errors. This parameter is equivalent to the /warnaserror compiler switch.
Win32Manifest	The name of the manifest file that should be embedded in the final assembly. This parameter is equivalent to the /win32Manifest compiler switch.
Wint32Resource	The file name of the Win32 resource to be embedded in the final assembly. This parameter is equivalent to the /win32resource compiler switch.

Common Items

In this section you will find common items, and their known metadata, that are used when building Visual Studio project files.

Reference

Table B-2 contains managed references in the project.

TABLE B-2 Reference Item Metadata

Item Attribute Name	Description
HintPath	Optional string. Relative or absolute path of the assembly.
Name	Optional string. Specifies the simple or strong fusion name for the item. When this attribute is present, it can save time because the assembly file does not have to be opened to obtain the fusion name.
FusionName	Optional string. Specifies the simple or strong fusion name for the item. When this attribute is present, it can save time because the assembly file does not have to be opened to obtain the fusion name.

TABLE B-2 Reference Item Metadata

Item Attribute Name	Description
SpecificVersion	Optional Boolean. Specifies whether only the version in the fusion name should be referenced.
Aliases	Optional string. Any aliases for the reference. This can be used to reference two assemblies that have the same fully-qualified name; for instance, if you want to reference two different version of the same assembly.
Private	Optional Boolean. Specifies whether the reference should be copied to the output folder. If this metadata is set to false then the assembly will not be copied to the output folder, and if true then it will be copied to the output folder. If it is not specified then MSBuild will try to determine if it needs to be copied to the output path.

COMReference

Table B-3 contains COM references in the project.

TABLE B-3 COMReference Metadata

Item Attribute Name	Description
Name	Optional string. The display name of the component.
Guid	Optional string. A GUID for the component, in the form `{48D9951F-D25C-4b4b-AB1D-9C25E458FC8F}`.
VersionMajor	Optional string. The major part of the version number of the component. For example, "5" if the full version number is "5.46."
VersionMinor	Optional string. The minor part of the version number of the component. For example, "46" if the full version number is "5.46."
LCID	Optional string. The LocaleID for the component.
WrapperTool	Optional string. The name of the wrapper tool that is used on the component, for example, "tlbimp."
Isolated	Optional Boolean. Specifies whether the component is a reg-free component.

COMFileReference

Table B-4 contains a list of type libraries that are used by the ResolvedComreference target.

TABLE B-4 COMFileReference Metadata

Item Attribute Name	Description
WrapperTool	Optional string. The name of the wrapper tool that is used on the component, for example, "tlbimp."

NativeReference

Table B-5 contains items that represent a native manifest file or a reference to one.

TABLE B-5 NativeReference Metadata

Item Attribute Name	Description
Name	Required string. The base name of the manifest file.
HintPath	Required string. The relative path of the manifest file.

ProjectReference

Table B-6 lists items that contain references to other projects.

TABLE B-6 ProjectReference Metadata

Item Attribute Name	Description
Name	Optional string. The display name of the reference.
Project	Optional string. A GUID for the reference, in the form `{3C5454C6-6924-4182-B307-E9AF11DCBE5C}`. This GUID should match the ProjectGuid property, if it exists, on the target project file.
Package	Optional string. The path of the project file that is being referenced.

Compile

Table B-7 lists items that contains the source files that will be sent to the compiler.

TABLE B-7 Compile Metadata

Item Attribute Name	Description
DependentUpon	Optional Boolean. Indicates whether the file depends on another file to compile correctly.
AutoGen	Optional Boolean. Indicates whether the file was generated for the project by the Visual Studio integrated development environment (IDE).
Link	Optional string. The notational path to be displayed when the file is physically located outside the influence of the project file.
Visible	Optional Boolean. Indicates whether to display the file in Solution Explorer in Visual Studio. This defaults to true for items in the main project file, and false for imported items.
CopyToOutputDirectory	Optional Boolean. Default value = false. Specifies whether to copy the file to the output directory.

EmbeddedResource

Table B-8 lists items that contain resources that will be embedded into the generated assembly.

TABLE B-8 EmbeddedResource Metadata

Item Attribute Name	Description
DependentUpon	Optional Boolean. Indicates whether the file depends on another file to compile correctly.
Generator	Optional string. The name of any file generator that is run on this item. This is used only by Visual Studio.
LastGenOutput	Optional string. The name of the file that was created by any file generator that ran on this item. Used by Visual Studio only.
CustomToolNamespace	Optional string. The namespace in which any file generator that runs on this item should create code.
Link	Optional string. The notational path is displayed if the file is physically located outside the influence of the project.
Visible	Optional Boolean. Indicates whether to display the file in Solution Explorer in Visual Studio.
CopyToOutputDirectory	Optional Boolean. Default value is false. Specifies whether to copy the file to the output directory.
LogicalName	Required string. The logical name of the embedded resource. The default value of this is derived from the Project file, plus any RootNamespace. This is the name that must be passed to the ResourceManager to retrieve the resource. VB.NET and C# projects have slightly different rules for choosing the name. Occasionally the default name is not appropriate, or you wish to override it; if so, you set LogicalName, which overrides everything.

Content

Table B-9 lists item types that contain project files that are not sent to the compiler but those that may be embedded or published with the project.

TABLE B-9 Content Metadata

Item Attribute Name	Description
DependentUpon	Optional Boolean. Indicates whether, to be embedded or published correctly, the file depends on another file.
Generator	Optional string. The name of the file that was created by any file generator that was run on this item.
CustomToolNamespace	Optional string. The namespace in which any file generator that runs on this item should create code.

TABLE B-9 Content Metadata

Item Attribute Name	Description
Link	Optional string. The notational path is displayed if the file is physically located outside the influence of the project.
PublishState	Optional string. The publish state of the content, either: ❏ Default ❏ Included ❏ Excluded ❏ DataFile ❏ Prerequisite
IsAssembly	Optional Boolean. Specifies whether the file is an assembly.
Visible	Optional Boolean. Indicates whether to display the file in Solution Explorer in Visual Studio.
CopyToOutputDirectory	Optional Boolean. Default value is false. Specifies whether to copy the file to the output directory.

None

Table B-10 lists items used for Project files that do not fall into one of the previously defined item types. The ResolveAssemblyReference task will examine this item type, as well as Content, for candidate references.

TABLE B-10 None Metadata

Item Attribute Name	Description
DependentUpon	Optional Boolean. Indicates whether, to be embedded or published correctly, the file depends on another file.
Generator	Required string. The name of any file generator that is run on this item.
LastGenOutput	Required string. The name of the file that was created by any file generator that ran on this item.
CustomToolNamespace	Required string. The namespace in which any file generator that runs on this item should create code.
Link	Optional string. The notational path to be displayed if the file is physically located outside the influence of the project.
Visible	Optional Boolean. Indicates whether to display the file in Solution Explorer in Visual Studio.
CopyToOutputDirectory	Optional Boolean. Default value = false. Specifies whether to copy the file to the output directory.

The metadata covered here are values known to the item types listed. You are able to add any additional metadata to these items, and they will travel along with the item itself throughout the build process. Additional metadata can be used for custom build steps that have been inserted into the build process.

Appendix C

New Features in Visual Studio Team System 2010 Team Build

Visual Studio Team System 2010 (previously code name "Rosario") is the much anticipated third version of Visual Studio Team System. Just as with Visual Studio Team System 2008, this version promises to deliver a large number of new features for Team Foundation Build.

Windows Workflow Foundation

One of the biggest enhancements in Visual Studio Team System 2010 Team Build is the integration with Windows Workflow Foundation. While MSBuild is a fantastic language for expressing how to compile a solution or project or how to perform a task on a set of files (using batching), it has a number of limitations as you start to automate your entire end-to-end build process.

Build Process Designer

One of the biggest limitations is that as your build process grows and becomes more complicated it can be difficult to manage and visualize the dependencies between the various properties, item groups, tasks, and targets. It can also be quite daunting (even for experienced MSBuild developers) working with large XML files.

By integrating Team Build with Windows Workflow Foundation, we can take advantage of its built-in workflow designer to construct and visualize even the most complicated build processes as shown in Figure C-1.

This designer provides a number of features:

Workflow design surface Provides a graphical representation of the different tasks (called activities in Windows Workflow Foundation) that comprise the build process. Activities shown with a grey background have been disabled and won't be executed.

Property grid As with other designers in Microsoft Visual Studio, the property grid allows you to view and edit the properties of the selected item, in this case a workflow activity.

Activities toolbox Shows a list of the available activities that can be dragged and dropped onto the workflow design surface to construct the build process. Team Build ships with a number of build-focused activities that are discussed in the next section.

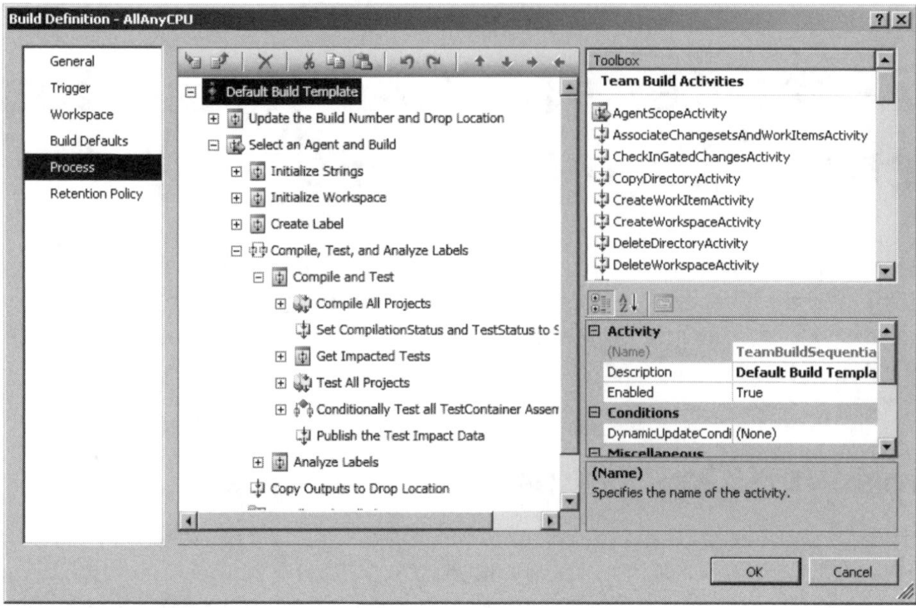

FIGURE C-1 Build Definition – Process dialog box

Build Activities

MSBuild is geared toward the requirements of compilation and the tasks provided with MSBuild (such as Vbc and Csc for compilation and AL for linking) reflect this. It is possible to add functionality to MSBuild using custom tasks, which can be implemented in any .NET language and provide almost any functionality, but this is an extension of MSBuild's primary purpose.

The various custom tasks called by Team Build 2008 have been migrated to the workflow activities listed in Table C-1.

TABLE C-1 Team Build 2010 Workflow Activities

Activity Name	Description
AgentScopeActivity	Groups activities and specifies the agents that the activities can be executed on. This is discussed in more detail in the section "Build Controllers."
AssociateChangesetsAndWorkItemsActivity	Links the build to the changesets and work items it includes.
CheckInGatedChangesActivity	Checks-in changes in the shelveset associated with the build. This is discussed in more detail in the section "Gated Check-in."

TABLE C-1 Team Build 2010 Workflow Activities

Activity Name	Description
CreateWorkItemActivity	Creates a work item with the fields set to the specified values.
DownloadFilesActivity	Downloads the specified files from version control to the specified location.
EvaluateCheckInPoliciesActivity	Evaluates whether the pending changes in the specified workspace meet the check-in policies defined on the Team Project.
ExecActivity	Executes the specified executable.
GetActivity	Performs a get of the specified workspace.
GetImpactedTestsActivity	Determines the test affected by the changes since the last partially successful or successful build.
LabelActivity	Labels the specified version control items.
LogErrorActivity	Adds an error message to the build log.
LogMessageActivity	Adds a message to the build log.
LogWarningActivity	Adds a warning to the build log.
MSBuildActivity	Executes an MSBuild project. This is discussed in more detail in the section "Where Does This Leave MSBuild?"
MSTestActivity	Executes tests using MSTest. This is discussed in more detail in the section "Integration with Symbol and Source Server, WiX, Visual Studio Team System for Database Professionals, and MSTest."
SetBuildPropertiesActivity	Updates the specified build properties.
TfsBuildActivity	Executes a Team Build 2008 build definition.

In addition to these build-specific activities, you can also use any of the activities that ship as part of Windows Workflow Foundation, including ParallelActivity, IfElseActivity, etc., which provides a level of control to the build process not possible in MSBuild. Additionally, you can create your own custom activities, which can provide a rich design-time experience.

Build Templates

To facilitate reusing build processes across build definitions Team Build 2010 introduces the concept of build templates. Once a build process has been defined you can click the Save Workflow As Template toolbar button as shown in Figure C-2 to save it to a build template file (*.btp). This template can then be distributed or stored in version control and then used to create new build definitions.

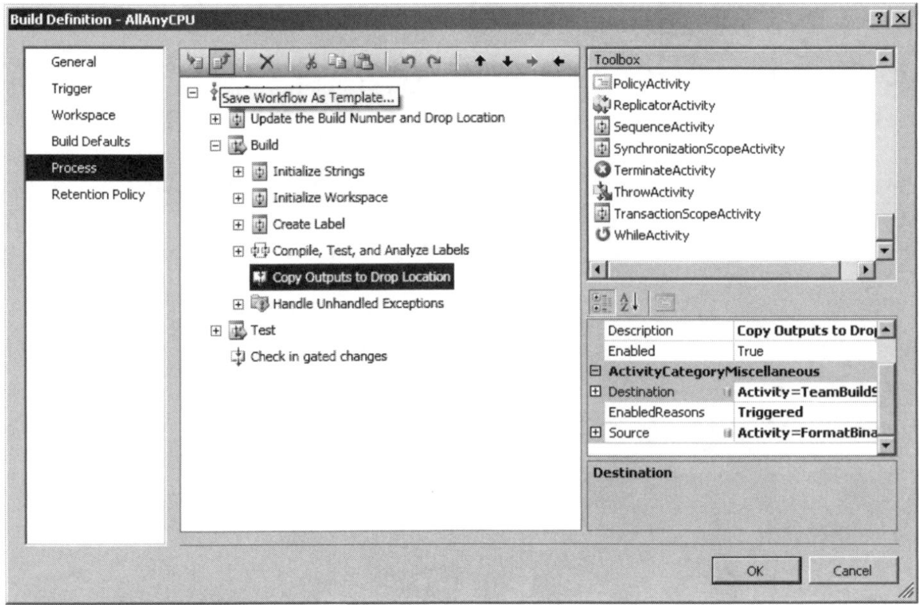

FIGURE C-2 Save Workflow As Template dialog box

Build Controllers

One limitation of Team Build 2008 is that when you queue a build you must select the particular build agent you want to queue it on, which means that developers need to browse through the available build agents to find the one with the shortest queue. This may not sound difficult or time consuming but if you have a lot of build agents or restrictions on which build definitions can be run on which build agents (for example, because certain software is installed only on some build agents) this can become more difficult.

Team Build 2010 solves this problem by introducing the concept of build controllers. When the developer queues a build they select a build controller rather than a specific build agent (as shown in Figure C-3) and the build controller is then responsible for locating the best build agent and queuing the build (or part of the build) on that build agent.

The Manage Build Agents dialog from Team Build 2008 has been replaced with the Manage Build Controllers dialog shown in Figure C-4. Each build agent is shown indented under the build controller it belongs to (a build agent is associated with a single build controller).

This solves half the problem: You can now queue a build against the build controller and have it processed by the first available build agent, but what about the requirement to be able to run certain builds (or parts of builds) on certain build agents? This is solved by

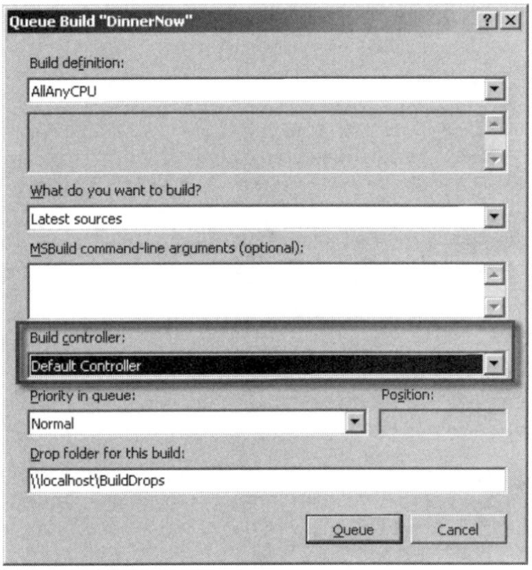

FIGURE C-3 Build controller selection when queuing a build

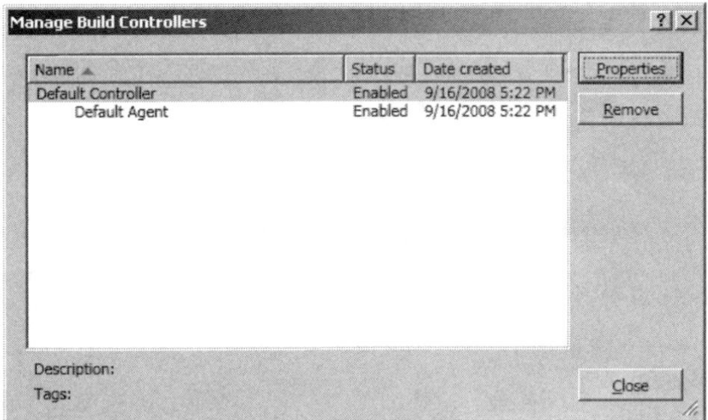

FIGURE C-4 Manage Build Controllers dialog box

applying tags (which are arbitrary strings) to build agents to advertise their capabilities as shown in Figure C-5. In this example, we've tagged the Default Agent with dbpro and test indicating that it has these editions of Visual Studio Team System installed, but the tags could be used to indicate the presence of any software package, the architecture of the build agent, the purpose of the build agent (private builds, mainline builds, or hotfix builds), or anything else you can imagine.

The next step is to modify the build definition's process to require the build agent to have certain tags. The Default Build Template shown in Figure C-6 includes an instance of the AgentScopeActivity (shown selected). This activity executes on the build controller and is responsible for selecting a build agent from the build agents associated with that build controller.

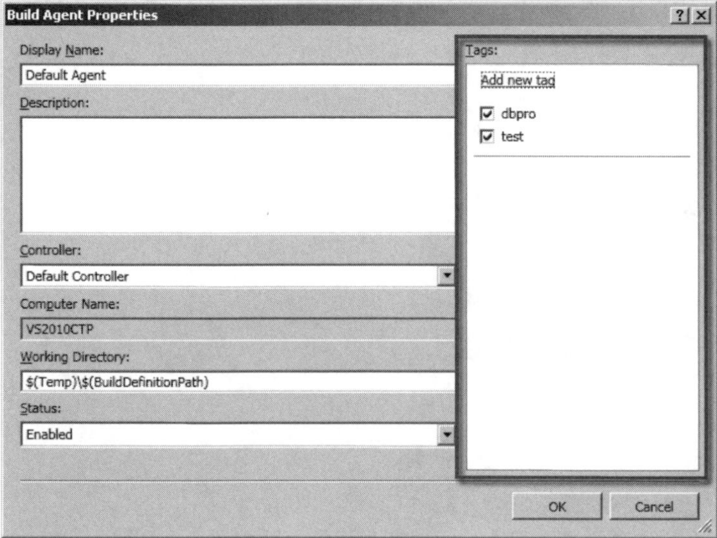

FIGURE C-5 Build Agent tagging dialog box

By default, this activity will select the first idle build agent it finds; however, in the Agent Selection category of the property grid we can modify the ReservationSpec to restrict the candidate build agents either by specifying the build agent's name or, as we've done here, specifying the tag(s) that the build agent must have.

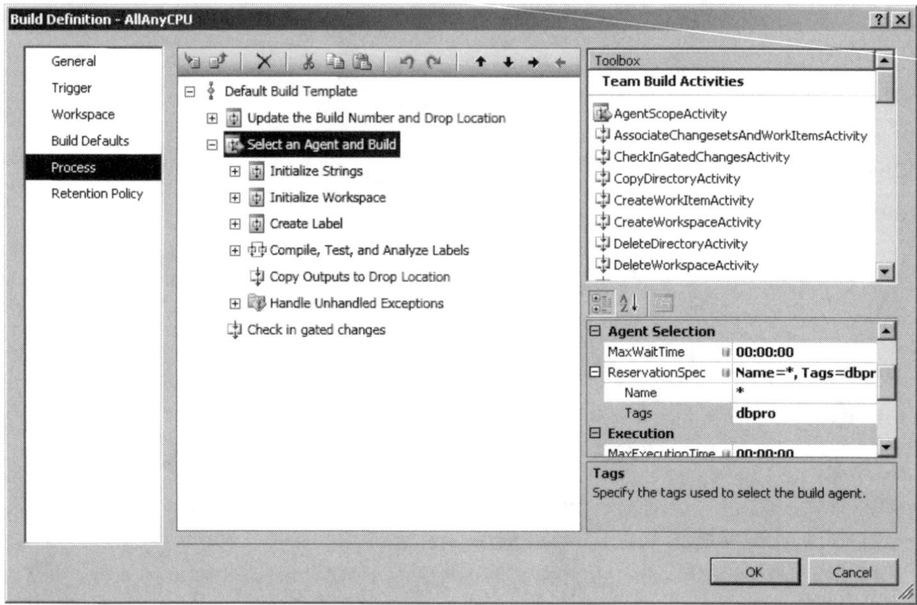

FIGURE C-6 Build Definition agent selection

While Team Build 2008 and MSBuild 3.5 allow you to build configurations and solutions in parallel, the build process is still limited to a single machine. As your build process becomes larger, more complicated, and runs for a longer period of time, it becomes desirable to scale your build across multiple machines and this functionality wasn't available out-of-the-box.

Team Build 2010 makes it effortless to run tasks on multiple build agents by allowing you to add multiple instances of the AgentScopeActivity to the build definition's process. Each of the activities can target the same or different build agents. For example, you could add two instances of the AgentScopeActivity, one to do a debug build and one to do a release build and configure these to execute on any available build agent. Alternatively, you could configure one to execute the debug and release builds on any build agent tagged with build and configure the other to execute the unit tests on any build agent tagged with test. Figure C-7 shows an example of what a build process like this could look like.

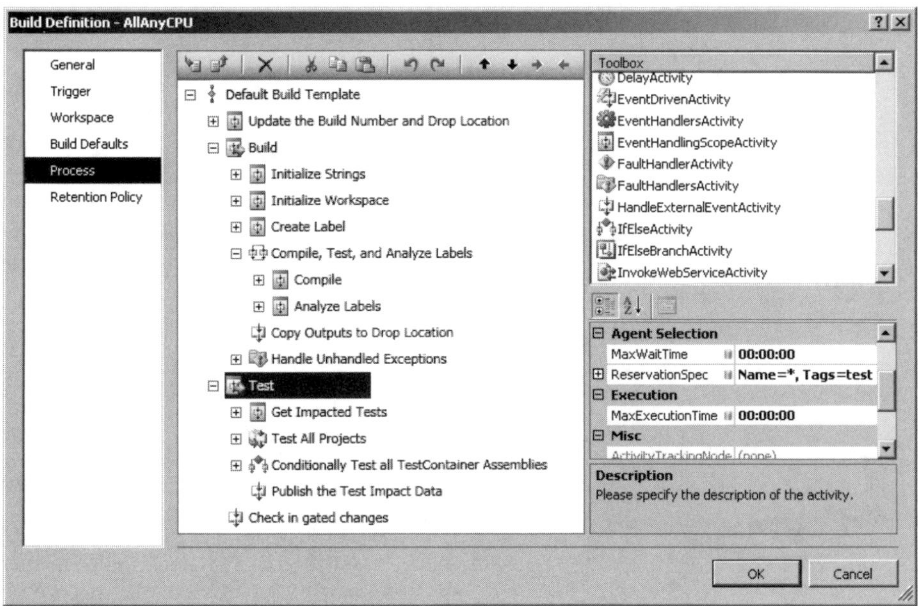

FIGURE C-7 Build process containing two instances of AgentScopeActivity

Gated Check-in

Continuous integration (CI) identifies integration issues early by compiling (and testing) every time a change is committed to the workspace. This improves productivity by integration issues being found and resolved early, before too many developers are affected.

There is one fundamental issue with CI, and that is that if the integration fails the change has already been committed and any developers working in that workspace are impacted until the integration issues are resolved. In smaller teams this can be desirable because it acts as an impetus to get the issues resolved as quickly as possible, but as the size of the development team increases, the interruption while the issues are resolved may be unacceptable.

Gated check-in takes CI to the next level by validating changes that are being committed before they're committed and can impact other developers. To enable gated check-in select the Gated Check-in trigger on the Trigger tab of the Build Definition dialog shown in Figure C-8.

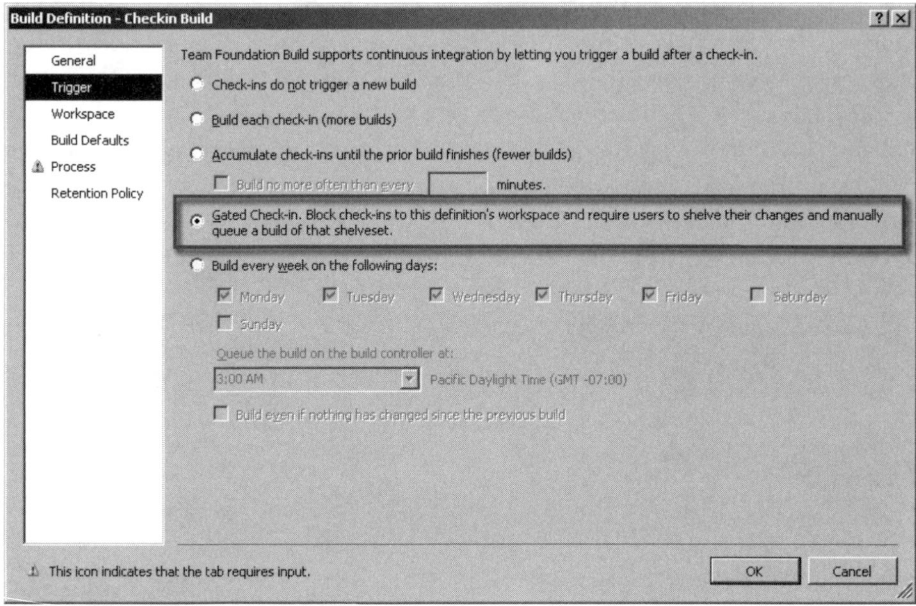

Gated Check-in. Block check-ins to this definition's workspace and require users to shelve their changes and manually queue a build of that shelveset.

FIGURE C-8 Gated check-in trigger

When a developer attempts to check a change into a folder in the workspace of a build definition with a gated check-in trigger, their changes will be shelved automatically and they will be informed that their changes need to be validated before they're committed as shown in Figure C-9.

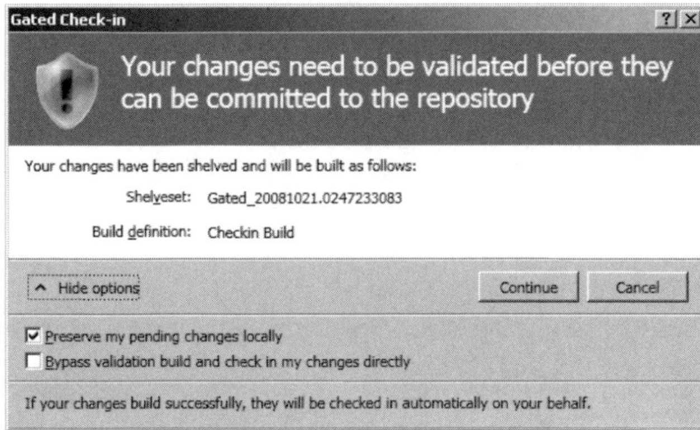

Gated Check-in
Your changes need to be validated before they can be committed to the repository
Your changes have been shelved and will be built as follows:
Shelveset: Gated_20081021.0247233083
Build definition: Checkin Build
Hide options
Continue
This icon indicates that the tab requires input.
Cancel
Preserve my pending changes locally
Bypass validation build and check in my changes directly
If your changes build successfully, they will be checked in automatically on your behalf.

FIGURE C-9 Gated check-in prompt

Developers can choose whether they want their changes preserved locally once they've been submitted to be validated (as you can when shelving manually) and, if they have the required permission (Override Check-in Validation By Build), they can choose to bypass the validation and check-in immediately.

When the developer clicks Continue a build is queued for the shelveset containing the check-in. The build process will get the source code per normal and then unshelve the developer's changes into the workspace before continuing the build process. If the build succeeds, the shelveset will be automatically checked-in on the developer's behalf.

Private Builds

Private builds (also called buddy builds) are similar to gated check-in builds because they involve submitting a shelveset to be built. The main difference is that once a private build has been completed the shelveset isn't committed to the repository.

This can be used as an alternate to desktop builds to build and test changes during the development process without having to do "progressive check-ins" or it could be used to create builds for testers, documenters, etc. without having to commit potentially incomplete changes to the repository.

Note The default build process copies binaries only to the drop location for triggered builds, which does not include private builds. To have the build outputs from private builds copied to the drop location you will need to modify the build process.

Developers can queue a private build the same way they queue a normal build, using the Queue New Build context menu on the build definition. Team Build 2010 adds a What Do You Want To Build drop-down to this dialog as shown in Figure C-10. The default is Latest Sources,

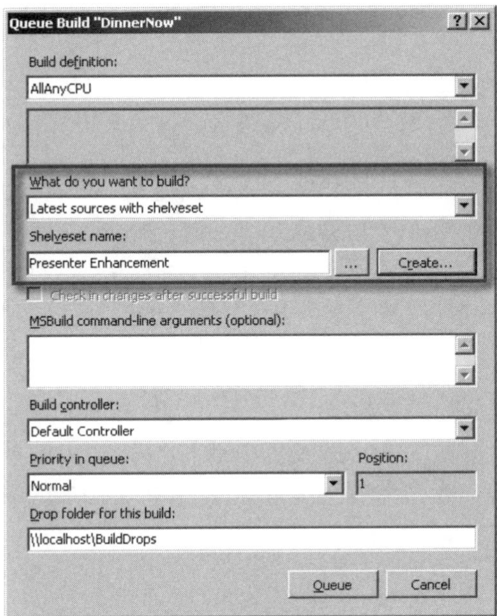

FIGURE C-10 Queuing a private build

which mimics the Team Build 2008 behavior, but to queue a private build you choose Latest Sources With Shelveset. When this option is selected you can select the shelveset to be built or click Create to create a new shelveset from the pending changes in the current workspace.

Because private builds are used for different purposes than triggered and manual builds they can be configured with different retention policies as shown in Figure C-11. Triggered and manual builds use one set of retention policies and private builds use a second set.

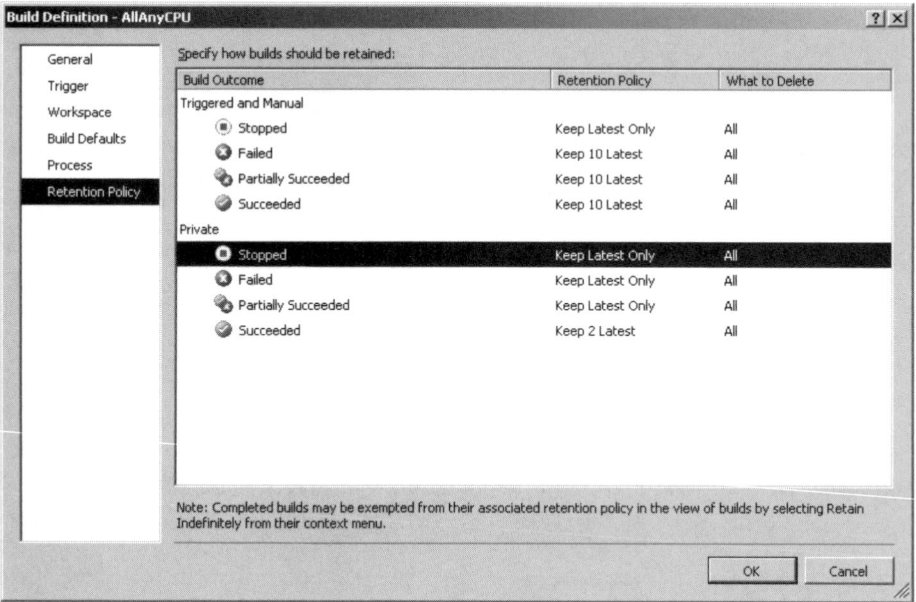

FIGURE C-11 Retention policy for private builds

Improved Control over Build Deletion

In Team Build 2008 when a build is deleted, everything relating to the build is deleted, leaving almost no trace that it ever existed. While this is thorough it is not always desirable and can severely hamper the ability to recreate builds that have been deleted.

Team Build 2010 improves this in a couple of ways. First, when manually deleting a build you are prompted to select what should be deleted as shown in Figure C-12.

Second, as shown in Figure C-13, you can specify what is to be deleted for each build outcome in the retention policy and these can differ between triggered and manual and private builds.

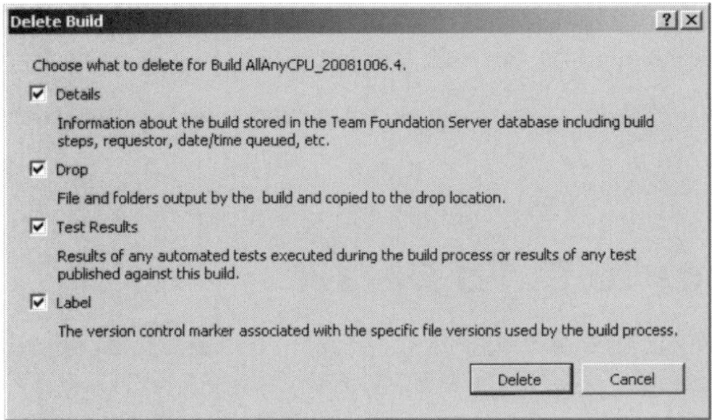

FIGURE C-12 Manually deleting a build

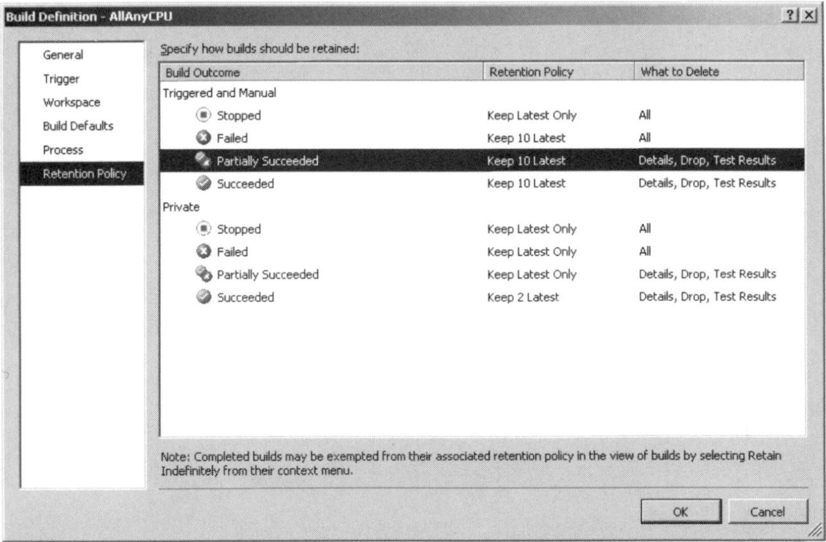

FIGURE C-13 Specify what to delete for retention policy

Integration with Symbol and Source Server, WiX, Visual Studio Team System for Database Professionals, and MSTest

Another area where significant investment is being made is to simplify integration with the products most commonly invoked as part of a build process. While the specifics aren't known at this stage, some of the planned enhancements include:

- Being able to easily index (for Source Server support) and publish symbols to a symbol server
- Easily build WiX-based installers

- Build and deploy Visual Studio Team System for Database Professionals projects without it needing to be installed on the build agent
- Execute tests without Visual Studio Team System for Testers needing to be installed on the build agent

Usability Improvements to Build Details

The Build Details screen is one of the most important in Team Build and it is important for developers, testers, and other users to easily find or link to the information they're looking for. Consequently a large amount of effort has been expended on making the Build Details screen easier to navigate, interpret, and work with.

Figure C-14 shows the Build Details screen for a successful build. If you compare this to the Build Details screen shown in Chapter 10 you'll see how dramatic the change is.

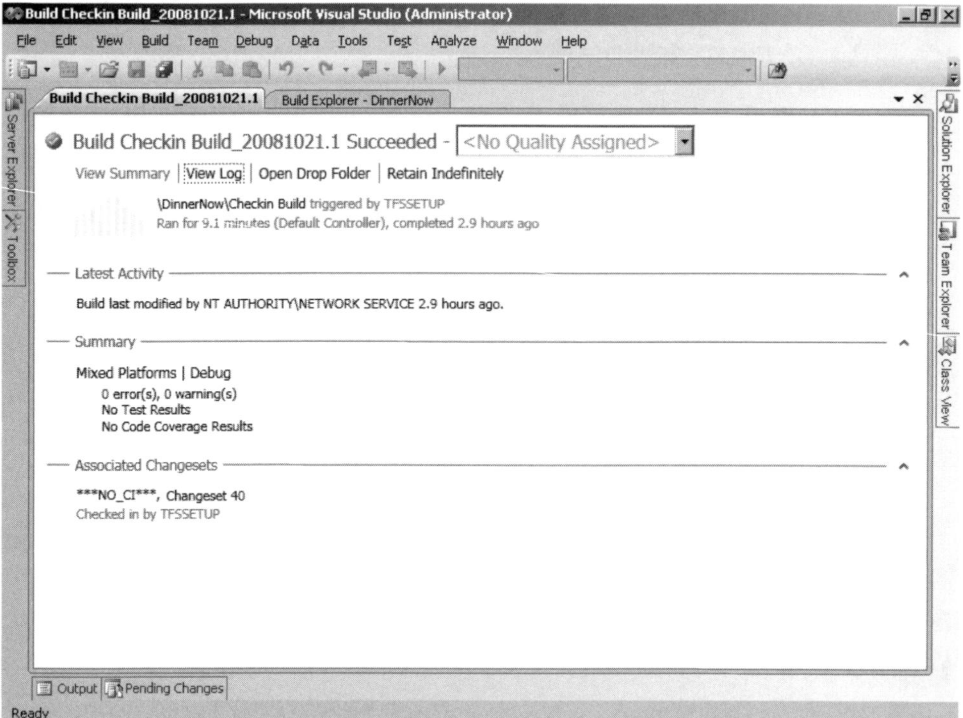

FIGURE C-14 Build details for a successful build

In the top section of the screen shown in Figure C-15 is the build name, build outcome, and build quality as well as a number of actions we can take with the build, such as changing the build quality, viewing the build log, opening the drop folder, and toggling whether or not the build is retained indefinitely.

FIGURE C-15 Build Details – Actions dialog box

Below this is a summary about the build shown in Figure C-16. The small graph on the left-hand side shows the past builds for this build definition with the height of the bar representing the amount of time the build ran for. Hovering over a bar will provide more details about the build and you can click to open that build's build details screen.

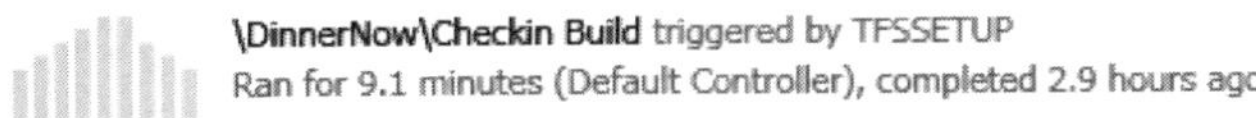

FIGURE C-16 Build Details – Summary dialog box

If we click the View Log link shown in Figure C-15 we are shown the hierarchy of build steps that were executed as shown in Figure C-17. This shows the hierarchy of build steps better than the flat list used in the build details screen in Team Build 2008.

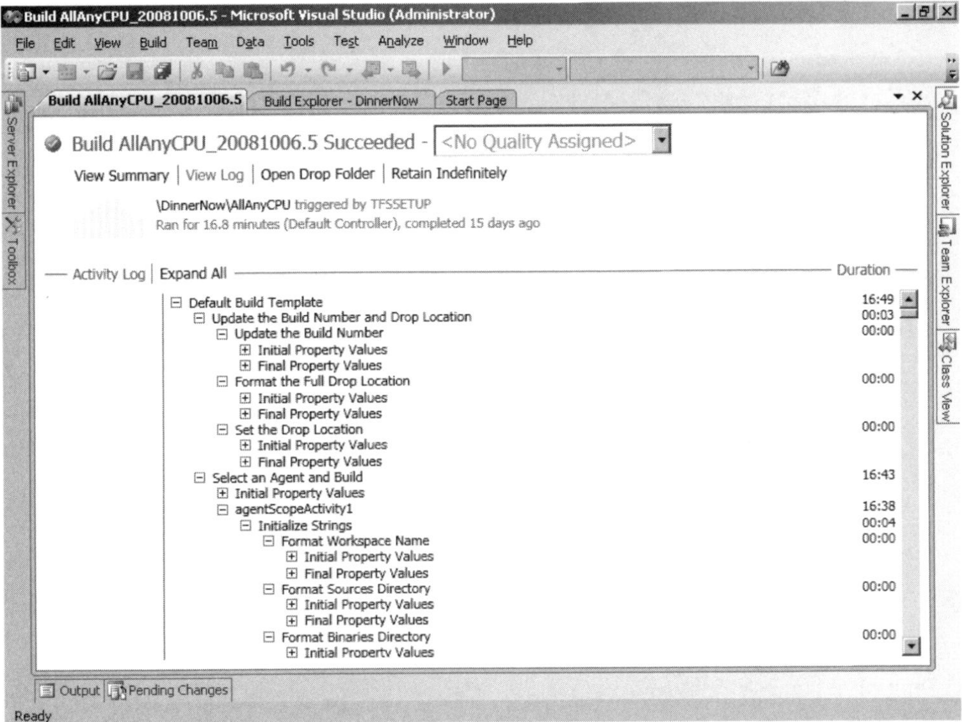

FIGURE C-17 Build log

For a failed build, any compilation errors are shown in the summary in Figure C-18 and one of the most useful features is that you can double-click on the compilation error to open the file, as at the version that was built, at the line where the error occurred.

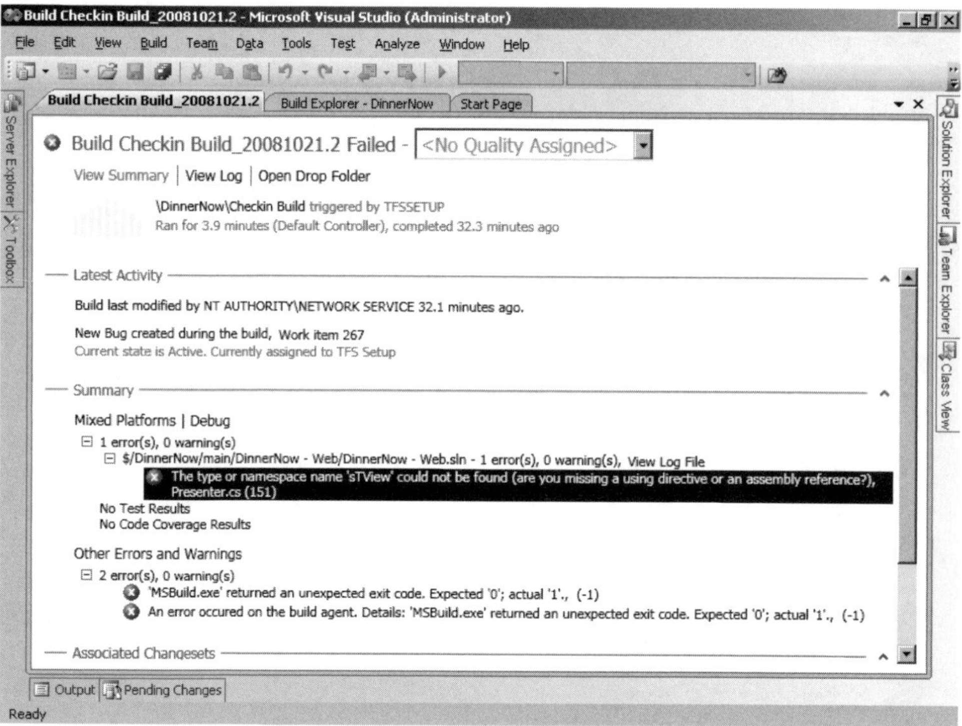

FIGURE C-18 Build details for failed build

Where Does This Leave MSBuild?

It seems fitting to conclude by answering the question, is MSBuild obsolete? Does moving to Windows Workflow Foundation make MSBuild redundant? The answer is an emphatic no for a few reasons:

- Visual Studio project files are (and will be for the foreseeable future) based on MSBuild.
- MSBuild is an ideal way to describe projects, how they should be compiled, and operations to be performed on sets of files.
- MSBuild is very flexible and an effective method for small teams to describe single machine build processes.

Team Build and Windows Workflow Foundation pick up where MSBuild leaves off, providing the ability to describe and manage complex, distributed, integrated, build processes. But when it comes to building individual solutions and projects, Team Build still calls MSBuild to perform the actual build (using the MSBuildActivity).

Index

Symbols and Numbers

A

B

C

D

E

F

G

H

I

J

K

L

M

N

O

P

U

V

W

X

Z

Sayed Ibrahim Hashimi

Sayed Ibrahim Hashimi has a computer engineering degree from the University of Florida. He has been working on MSBuild since early preview bits of Visual Studio 2005. He is the coauthor of *Deploying .NET Applications: Learning MSBuild* and *Click Once* (Apress, May 2006), and has written several publications for magazines such as the MSDN Magazine.

He works in Jacksonville, Florida, as a consultant and trainer.

He is an expert in the financial, education, and collection industries.

You can reach Sayed at his blog *sedodream.com*.

William Bartholomew

William Bartholomew is widely recognized as a leading Australian expert on the Visual Studio Team System (VSTS) suite and has been awarded as a Microsoft Most Valuable Professional (MVP).

Over the last two years he has worked closely with Microsoft's product team in the United States, providing user feedback on the latest release of VSTS and suggestions about future versions. William is the vice president of the Queensland VSTS User Group and has presented at numerous Microsoft events throughout Australia.

William works for an Australian-based business software solution company, TechnologyOne, where his primary focus is on improving developer productivity by implementing VSTS, focusing specifically on education, processes, and tools.

William can also be found occasionally blogging at *http://blogs.teamsystemnotes.com.*

For C# Developers

Microsoft® Visual C#® 2008 Express Edition: Build a Program Now!

Patrice Pelland

ISBN 9780735625426

Build your own Web browser or other cool application—no programming experience required! Featuring learn-by-doing projects and plenty of examples, this full-color guide is your quick start to creating your first applications for Windows®. DVD includes Express Edition software plus code samples.

Microsoft Visual C# 2008 Step by Step

John Sharp

ISBN 9780735624306

Teach yourself Visual C# 2008—one step at a time. Ideal for developers with fundamental programming skills, this practical tutorial delivers hands-on guidance for creating C# components and Windows–based applications. CD features practice exercises, code samples, and a fully searchable eBook.

Learn Programming Now! Microsoft XNA® Game Studio 2.0

Rob Miles

ISBN 9780735625228

Now you can create your own games for Xbox 360® and Windows—as you learn the underlying skills and concepts for computer programming. Dive right into your first project, adding new tools and tricks to your arsenal as you go. Master the fundamentals of XNA Game Studio and Visual C#—no experience required!

Programming Microsoft Visual C# 2008: The Language

Donis Marshall

ISBN 9780735625402

Get the in-depth reference, best practices, and code you need to master the core language capabilities in Visual C# 2008. Fully updated for Microsoft .NET Framework 3.5, including a detailed exploration of LINQ, this book examines language features in detail—and across the product life cycle.

Windows via C/C++, Fifth Edition

Jeffrey Richter, Christophe Nasarre

ISBN 9780735624245

Jeffrey Richter's classic guide to C++ programming—now fully revised for Windows XP, Windows Vista®, and Windows Server® 2008. Learn to develop more-robust applications with unmanaged C++ code—and apply advanced techniques—with comprehensive guidance and code samples from the experts.

CLR via C#, Second Edition

Jeffrey Richter

ISBN 9780735621633

Dig deep and master the intricacies of the common language runtime (CLR) and the .NET Framework. Written by programming expert Jeffrey Richter, this guide is ideal for developers building any kind of application—ASP.NET, Windows Forms, Microsoft SQL Server®, Web services, console apps—and features extensive C# code samples.

ALSO SEE

Microsoft Visual C# 2005 Step by Step
ISBN 9780735621299

Programming Microsoft Visual C# 2005: The Language
ISBN 9780735621817

Debugging Microsoft .NET 2.0 Applications
ISBN 9780735622029

microsoft.com/mspress